DATE DUE

Legal Conceptions

LEGAL CONCEPTIONS

*The Evolving Law and Policy of Assisted
Reproductive Technologies*

SUSAN L. CROCKIN, J.D., *and*
HOWARD W. JONES, JR., M.D.

The Johns Hopkins University Press

Baltimore

© 2010 The Johns Hopkins University Press
All rights reserved. Published 2010
Printed in the United States of America on acid-free paper
9 8 7 6 5 4 3 2 1

The Johns Hopkins University Press
2715 North Charles Street
Baltimore, Maryland 21218-4363
www.press.jhu.edu

Library of Congress Cataloging-in-Publication Data

Crockin, Susan L.
    Legal conceptions : the evolving law and policy of assisted reproductive technologies /
Susan L. Crockin and Howard W. Jones, Jr.
        p. ; cm.
    Includes index.
    ISBN-13: 978-0-8018-9388-9 (hardcover : alk. paper)
    ISBN-10: 0-8018-9388-7 (hardcover : alk. paper)
    1. Human reproductive technology—Law and legislation. 2. Human reproductive
technology—Law and legislation—United States. I. Jones, Howard Wilbur, 1910–
II. Title.
    [DNLM: 1. Reproductive Techniques, Assisted—legislation & jurisprudence—United
States. 2. Embryo Research—legislation & jurisprudence—United States. WQ 33 AA1
c938L 2009]
    K3611.A77C76 2009
    344.04'196—dc22   2009007056

A catalog record for this book is available from the British Library.

*Special discounts are available for bulk purchases of this book. For more information,
please contact Special Sales at 410-516-6936 or specialsales@press.jhu.edu.*

The Johns Hopkins University Press uses environmentally friendly book materials,
including recycled text paper that is composed of at least 30 percent post-consumer
waste, whenever possible. All of our book papers are acid-free, and our jackets and covers
are printed on paper with recycled content.

CONTENTS

~ BY Susan L. Crockin

By 1990 IT HAD become clear to the courts that "the in vitro fertiliza-tion genie is out of the bottle and you can't put it back."[1] The first divorce dispute over frozen embryos, *Davis v. Davis,* had erupted and captured the nation's attention as an intriguing "brave new world" fight over "preembryos" and all the competing views and values attendant to them. As *Nightline* and Ted Koppel aired the dispute night after night, highlighting the legal issues in this case, other fertility-related disputes were percolating up through the courts.

It seemed to this lawyer that the time had come to gather and share legal information and insights into how the courts were both viewing and responding to the issues surrounding these new families and the medical professionals whose talents and energies had made them possi-ble. The idea for "Legally Speaking" was born. In 1990, this author pro-posed, wrote, and submitted a pilot column to the American Fertility Society (now the American Society for Reproductive Medicine) entitled, "Legally Speaking: A Column Highlighting Recent Court Decisions Af-fecting the Assisted Reproductive Technologies (ART) and the Families They Create." It was accepted by the board of AFS on an experimental basis, to be published in *Fertility News,*[2] which was issued four or five times a year, with a distribution to all members of the Society. That experiment has now spanned twenty years, almost a hundred columns, with reports on close to a thousand legal cases, statutes, and develop-ments. All, except those noted as guest authored, were written by this

---

1. *Johnson v. Calvert,* 5 Cal. 4th 84 (Cal. 1993); *cert. denied,* 510 U.S. 874 (U.S. 1993). The quotation comes from the trial court's 1990 opinion. Cases are formally cited within each substantive chapter and in the table of cases and referenced by name and year within the commentaries.

2. Now *ASRM News.*

author. Guest authors appeared occasionally—columns by Terri Fine-smith Horwich, J.D.; Ami Jaeger, J.D.; Wendy Parmet, J.D.; and Kimberly Zieselman, J.D., are featured in this book—and brought particular expertise to a topic and column.

In December 1990, "Legally Speaking"™ debuted in *Fertility News*. It reported on six novel assisted reproductive technology–related court cases. Remarkably, each of those cases addressed issues that still vex courts today. In addition to the *Davis* dispute over frozen embryos, the column reported on the first parental claim by a gestational carrier (*Johnson v. Calvert*); a successful challenge to insurance coverage for infertility treatment (without a statutory mandate); a class action lawsuit by doctors asserting that Illinois's statute banning fetal experimentation was having a chilling effect on their research; a known sperm donor's assertion of paternity rights over a child he helped a lesbian couple to conceive; and a prisoner claiming an unconstitutional denial of access to artificial insemination services.

Unique among analyses of legal developments, "Legally Speaking" has reported in "real time" and in plain English on hundreds of court cases and legal developments as novel lawsuits were filed, appealed, settled, or decided and as legislation moved through the process from bills and revisions to laws or vetoes. By reporting on developing cases and legislation instead of merely the final decision or legal "bottom line," "Legally Speaking" has been able to illustrate, and thereby aid professionals in the field to understand, the changing legal landscape within which their actions and decisions are questioned and ultimately judged. To help contextualize the developing law and policy in the United States, selected international developments were also reported, as were selected non-ART cases that raised issues such as professional liability with respect to patients in other contexts, genetic testing claims, stem cell research, wrongful life and birth claims, and discrimination in health care, to name but a few.

Nearly twenty years after the first column appeared and thirty years after the birth of the world's first IVF baby, this book synthesizes and analyzes the still-evolving and conflicting legal developments for those interested in understanding both the distance we have come and the many legal and policy challenges we have yet to face and resolve. The case reports that have been published continuously since 1990 form the basis of this analysis and commentary, as we now pause to better understand the past and anticipate the future.

Our hope is that this work will help guide the myriad stakeholders to a better understanding of the evolving legal and policy issues as well as the inherent tensions and challenges in this multidisciplinary area and, by doing so, help shape the development of thoughtful policies that will influence and guide the future of reproductive medicine, law, and policy.

I would be remiss in ending this preface without thanking the many individuals who have supported this work and its underlying goals. First and foremost, I owe a very deep and personal thank you to Dr. Howard W. Jones, Jr., for twenty years ago believing in a young lawyer and her vision of the nascent legal field his pioneering medical work would spawn. Without his unwavering support, neither "Legally Speaking" nor *Legal Conceptions* would ever have been born. And without his vision, dedication, and willingness to reject a well-earned retirement and instead create the country's first IVF program together with the late Dr. Georgeanna Jones—his wife and life partner—this field of medicine and its prominence in the United States might have taken a very different course, and this lawyer would have missed the opportunity and career of a lifetime.

Thanks is also owed to the local business community in Norfolk, Virginia, including my father, who recognized the need for and helped establish Eastern Virginia Medical School, which would become the home of the Jones Institute.

I am grateful to Dr. Alan DeCherney and the 1989 board of what was then the American Fertility Society for taking the chance on an eager young lawyer and agreeing to publish "Legally Speaking" as an experiment. Twenty years later I believe we agree it was a successful one.

More recently and more hands-on, absolutely invaluable support for *Legal Conceptions* has come from Nancy Garcia, whose tireless efforts at inputting mountains of data for this book at lightning speed made me actually believe this day might come. This is the Nancy Garcia who for thirty years has been the administrative right arm of Dr. Howard Jones, who says that with Nancy's help anything is possible.

And to my research assistants, Melea Atkins, Lisa Berger, and Alexis Sherman, and editors at the Johns Hopkins University Press, thank you for everything each of you did to make this work a reality.

And a final and enduring thanks to my husband, for always believing in my work and in me.

Legal Conceptions

Introduction

THE BIRTHS OF the first English, Australian, and American IVF babies (Louise Brown in 1978, Candice Reed in 1980, and Elizabeth Carr in 1981) heralded a revolution in reproductive medicine and the modern family—creating previously and literally inconceivable babies and families. When news of Louise Brown's 1978 birth burst onto the public stage and caused a worldwide uproar, few immediately thought of the implications for the law. As medical advances brought more and more unique baby-making techniques into the public eye, including cryopreservation and the world's first frozen embryo babies, the public's attention remained firmly fixed on the medical breakthroughs. News reports and magazine covers touted or decried the "brave new world" of baby-making, but the challenges these new forms of baby-making would quickly force courts and legislatures to confront received little attention. If modern medicine could now make babies in totally new ways and combinations, it became the law's critical, if less publicly heralded, job to turn those babies, and those who would make them, into legally recognized and legally protected families.

For the first time in history, in vitro fertilization technology made it possible to separate embryos from the patients who created them. Until then, reproductive law was defined by constitutional decisions involving abortion, contraception, and sterilization, all inescapably intertwined with issues of bodily integrity. IVF created a new legal paradigm for reproductive rights outside a woman's body and inside an embryology lab. IVF with cryopreservation not only transformed patients' reproductive rights and timetables but also created new responsibilities and vulnerabilities for the professionals who maintained the cryopreserved tissue. IVF also made possible egg and, less frequently, embryo donation as well as gestational surrogacy. These procedures have exponentially expanded not only the pool of potential parents but also the number of individuals, both men and women, who could contribute genetically or gestationally to the creation of babies that they did not intend to raise. Access to reproductive services became fertile ground for constitutional arguments over discriminatory treatment, equal protection and due process rights, and legislative efforts to expand insurance coverage. Recent developments in preimplantation genetic diagnosis are currently transforming the field of genetic testing, creating yet another new arena where courts and legislatures are being called upon to address access and insurance coverage and to help shape additional new laws and policies around reproductive genetics.

By changing the ways families were created, IVF and the assisted reproductive and genetic technologies that followed have given birth to a host of novel legal issues, tensions, and challenges as well as an emerging body of sometimes inconsistent law and policy. Obstetrics, gynecology, genetic testing, and urology, all once seen as discrete specialties involving private medical decisions between patients and their doctors, instead increasingly became part of a complex set of interlocking medical, legal, and ethical issues and vulnerabilities.

In the process, providers, patients, third parties, and the children they all sought to create have become part of a grand social experiment, still unfolding today as courts and legislatures struggle to define and protect these newly possible families and those who help create them. One ongoing challenge for the professional communities is how to define the applicable rules to protect those involved in these new technologies. A second is to determine what values and societal frameworks we want to foster to protect participants and guide society at large, even as newer technologies and possibilities continue to emerge.

This book chronicles how the law has responded to these revolutionary medical advances and how courts have struggled to apply and expand legal principles and precedents to shape families and guide patients and providers in a terrain combining law and medicine that literally did not exist thirty years ago. Unlike medicine, the law is seldom accused of moving too quickly or revolutionizing a field with a singular, unanticipated development. By capturing the many disparate court decisions and arguments in real time and by examining the judicial perspectives that unfolded within individual cases as they moved through multiple appellate levels, this book provides a unique lens through which we can examine and, one hopes, learn from history.

If as a society we hope to create workable policies, laws, and guidelines for both existing and future reproductive technologies and those whose lives are touched by them, it is critical to understand the short, intense history of reproductive technology law. The still unfolding and often inconsistent rulings, what has gone right and what has gone, at times, terribly wrong with these families and providers is a story best understood by tracing the history of the controversies that have come before courts and legislatures.

Both the commentaries and the real-time case descriptions that make up this book give readers a rare glimpse into the evolution of the jurisprudence of reproductive technology law and provide an unparalleled opportunity to understand the thinking behind these decisions and the context within which they were reached. Most importantly, as the technologies and their applications continue to advance, they suggest paths to address and ways to meet future policy needs.

Making Reproductive History: One Doctor's Perspective on the Law
❖ BY Howard W. Jones, Jr.

When my wife, Georgeanna, and I came to Norfolk, Virginia, in 1979, it was not with the intention of making medical history. Recruited from the Johns Hopkins Medical School to start a division of reproductive medicine in the obstetrics and gynecology department at the fledgling Eastern Virginia Medical School, we arrived just as Louise Brown's momentous birth was announced from England. Halting our unpacking to take a call and questions from a local reporter, we gave an answer that launched an American odyssey. Asked if in vitro fertilization could be done here, we answered yes, and with that, opened the door on a revolutionary period of both medical and legal advances in the United States.

When the IVF project was initiated in Norfolk in 1979, it was not expected that a portion of the general public would regard IVF as contrary to good public policy. We thought that we were merely taking the next technical step to overcome infertility, our area of special interest for a number of years. However, the seemingly routine process of obtaining from the State of Virginia Health Department a Certificate of Need for the IVF project at Norfolk General Hospital triggered an unexpected series of public hearings, with witnesses from across the country testifying. Our initial application was denied as a result of protests, and it quickly became apparent that some vocal constituencies viewed our project not as a technical medical advancement but as a fundamental and unacceptable alteration to the concepts of life and family. After much, frequently contentious, debate, the Certificate of Need was eventually granted in February 1980, and what was to become the Jones Institute at Eastern Virginia Medical School opened its doors the following month.

Following the advice of IVF pioneers Drs. Robert Edwards and Patrick Steptoe of the United Kingdom, the Jones Clinic initially used the natural cycle—that is, retrieving only one egg by laparoscopy—after predicting with certain tests when the egg was ripe. During 1980, forty-one patients were processed without a single success. Beginning in 1981, the IVF technique was changed to use controlled ovarian stimulation through gonadotropins to stimulate in normally menstruating women more than the single egg that is characteristic of a typical menstrual cycle. With controlled ovarian stimulation, two, three, or four eggs could be obtained by laparoscopy after identifying the expected time of ovulation or the use of other drugs to induce ovulation. By using this new technique, success was achieved in Norfolk: Elizabeth Carr, the first IVF baby in the New World, was born in December 1981.

Throughout the early days of the Norfolk IVF Project, opposition continued, particularly from the right-to-life community. Many times, small picket lines were organized outside the hospital so that it was necessary for both patients and physicians to cross the picket line to carry out the medical procedures. Furthermore, the local newspaper editorially opposed the effort and occasionally printed both editorials and letters to the editor in opposition to the IVF.

In 1981, one particular editorial was published, claiming that the IVF program would not allow an abnormal child to be born because, by testing any pregnancy that occurred for abnormalities, the patient would be required to have a termination. This false but provocative claim led the IVF program to its next interaction between this new medical technology and the law, this time in the form of a lawsuit. A local attorney sought us out, urging us to sue the paper for libel in order to put a stop to the public opposition. This we did, and a settlement was finally reached that required the newspaper to recant its libelous statements, apologize for publishing the editorial, and provide financial support for research at the Foundation for Eastern Virginia Medical School and the IVF program. Unfortunately, this settlement did not end the legal and ethical battles that the Institute and we faced.

In 1984, we received an invitation to come to the Vatican for a conference about the "licitness"—that is, lawfulness according to Canon law —of IVF. During this five-day meeting, the technique of IVF was described in great detail, and moral theologians debated its merits. At the end of the conference, eight of the nine voting members indicated that they thought IVF would be licit; the sole dissenter was Monsignor Carlo Caffarra. In the end, that single dissenting vote became the Vatican's position. In 1987, the Vatican published the result of the group's deliberations under the title "Donum Vitae," in which the position of the Catholic Church was set forth: because IVF creates life outside the bonds of conjugal love, it is, indeed, illicit. To this day, this remains the official position of the Roman Catholic Church, as set forth in a new publication, *Dignitas Personae,* issued in December of 2008. That document goes into more detail in setting forth the church's opposition to IVF and related and newer techniques and practices. However, it should be noted that at the level of the parish, there is some liberality in the interpretation of the original document and the most recent document.

On the way home from the Vatican, we realized that in the United States IVF seemed to be carried out without any guidelines, regulations, or supervision. Our experience at the Vatican reinforced our view that there were (and remain today) segments of the population greatly concerned over the use of IVF to solve the problem of infertility. Therefore, it was suggested to the president of the American Fertility Society (AFS, now ASRM), Dr. Charles Hammond, that the AFS might wish to look into this matter and perhaps suggest guidelines for those practicing IVF. As a result, I was asked to form an AFS Ethics Committee. This committee of lawyers, ethicists, biologists, and physicians met a number of times, and in 1986, the AFS published "Ethical Considerations of the New Reproductive Technologies" as a supplement to *Fertility and Sterility* (1986; Supp 1, vol. 46, no. 3). Subsequent to this publication, the AFS appointed a permanent Ethics Committee, with the task of updating these guidelines at regular intervals and making them available on the ASRM website (www.asrm.org).

The challenges continue.

The Emotional Aspects of Infertility: One Physician's Perspective
❖ BY Howard W. Jones, Jr.

One item in the calculus of excellent patient care for infertility is attention to the emotional status of the couple confronting infertility. In practical terms, this means dealing with the frustrations over failure to achieve the innate drive for children and family. My experience leads me to believe that although this drive is usually more pronounced in the female, there is great individual variation; I have encountered some couples in which the husband's drive for a family seemed much higher than that of his wife.

There are several components to this drive, including ones with biological, sociological, and cultural roots. For example, in some African cultures, the infertile woman is ostracized. Not so long ago in some European cultures, it was a requirement that the bride be pregnant before marriage was considered. Indeed, in the early twentieth century, 80 percent of Dutch brides were pregnant at the time they were married.

There is an instinctive drive to reproduce common to all species that is readily observed in many mammals. It is an almost magical experience to observe the unattended birth of a barnyard mammal and the maternal protective action of the mother as the offspring wobbles to its feet and instinctively seeks the nipple for its first essential sustenance.

While the details of the experience are greatly modified in the human, the drive is nevertheless there. It needs to be added, however, that in American culture there are certainly exceptions, and many couples decide not to reproduce.

There are also those who delay having children for various reasons. All reproductive specialists are familiar with this situation of a female patient with fertility problems who has reached the age of forty or older and is frustrated because her reproductive system does not respond as it would have earlier in her reproductive years.

How does the physician deal with the patient's urge to have children? The simplest way, it seems to me, is to ask a question of the couple, to give them an opportunity to verbalize their emotional status. My favorite question (inserted only when appropriate) was, "Why do you wish to have a baby?" This brings forth a variety of replies, including blank stares. I try not to break the silence, hoping that this will elicit some response that will be helpful to the couple. Other questions to the couple can be more direct, such as, "Has your infertility affected your relationship?" Of course, there are many such questions. Ideally, the infertility specialist needs to ask some question of this sort in the presence of both members of the couple, but it is also helpful to have a meeting with each person separately, as this often brings forth some of the emotional problems that do not come out when they are both present.

How does one deal with this problem? Fortunately, in the twenty-first century there are very effective means of having a child. It is now possible to reassure almost every couple that if they are persistent and if they can afford, emotionally and financially, to utilize donor eggs and/or donor sperm in the still relatively rare situations where one or both will be necessary or use a gestational surrogate in the even rarer situation where that is necessary, we can now say to the couple that there is virtually a 100 percent chance of their having a child. Reaching these decisions, however, can be an emotionally laden experience, and the involvement of an experienced mental health professional in that process can be essential. Thus, while medicine today has more tools at its disposal than ever before to achieve pregnancy and parentage, the emotional issues that are attendant to that process cannot be overlooked or underestimated.

How This Book Is Organized

There were many ways this text could have been organized. We ultimately chose to group cases by medical procedure or practice rather than by the nature of the legal claim. The book has twelve chapters. The text begins with embryos (chapter 1) and then moves to access to care (chapter 2), followed by unique liability issues that did not fit into subsequent specific chapters (chapter 3). The second cluster of chapters addresses third party, or collaborative, reproduction. There are separate chapters on sperm, eggs, traditional and gestational surrogacy, same-sex parenting, and posthumous reproduction (chapters 4 through 8). The final chapters address developing technologies, such as preimplantation genetic diagnosis (PGD) and genetics (chapter 9), embryonic stem cell research–related ART cases (chapter 10), analogous legal developments in adoption (chapter 11), and abortion- and fetal-related litigation (chapter 12). Where doing so appeared useful to the reader, chapters are further separated into sections (such as the two sections in chapter 1: the first addressing embryo disputes against professionals and the second addressing embryo disputes between patients). Rather than separate chapters on legal issues such as jurisdiction, damages, or criminal liability, those issues are addressed within the chapter dealing with the specific practice claimed to have been legally actionable.

Each chapter begins with a medical and then a legal commentary, the purpose of which is to contextualize the legal developments in the area under discussion. Reflections on the evolving state of technology and the law from both a medical and legal perspective will give readers a lens through which to understand and follow this extraordinary transformation in reproductive medicine and law. Following the medical and legal commentary, the relevant cases are reviewed in chronological order. The date of the "Legally Speaking" column from which the narratives are drawn is shown under each title. If a case was either first reported from a media report, or appealed and heard by higher courts, there may be multiple narratives for that case, based on both court decisions and contemporaneous media reports. The references follow the last narrative and typically reference the final case citation if available or other published material as source documents. A table of cases with formal citations and page references appears at the back of the book. For example, for the first case in chapter 1, *Lifchez v. Hartigan*, 735 F. Supp. 1361 (D. Ill. 1990) references the title and published source for the court's full opinion of this case. Cases reported from the media were sometimes inaccurate or incomplete so it is necessary to read all the lettered subsections under a given case to see the evolving and ultimate unveiling of factual details as well as the resolution of a particular dispute.

Many of the reported cases went through multiple courts and appellate decisions, sometimes in both state and federal courts, as judges struggled to "get it right" in largely unfamiliar areas of both medicine and law. Courts heard scientific evidence, reviewed professional guidelines (from ASRM and its predecessor, AFS), and developed both the vocabulary and the law as they forged ahead into this brave new world.

Consistency across courts is often elusive, even in established areas of law, which this clearly is not. Within each chapter, each case is reviewed chronologically, starting with its first court filing, so that the reader can easily follow the developing law. Where appeals or related developments were reported in a particular case, they follow immediately after the initial entry, allowing readers to follow one case—and its evolving legal analyses—from beginning to end. "Legally Speaking" columns have been faithfully reproduced, but in many instances condensed to eliminate duplicative explanations.

Inevitably, cases may fit into more than one chapter. Wherever possible, cases are cross-referenced (the case numbers appearing in square brackets), and the legal commentary points out parallels between (as well as outside of) these categories. Readers will note the overlaps—for example, cases raising issues about both adoption and ART for same-sex couples, both embryonic stem cell techniques and embryo and fetal research, and both infertility insurance and PGD coverage. All point to the still-evolving nature of reproductive and reproductive technology law.

"Law 101: A Selective Primer for the Nonlawyer," which sets out a few general legal concepts, appears immediately following this introduction as an aid to nonlawyers. The medical and legal timelines, which appear after the legal primer, provide an overview of the most seminal developments discussed and described in the chapters that follow.

Looking Forward

Future medical advances will undoubtedly bring additional legal and policy challenges. For the foreseeable future, the medical development that is most likely to influence the legal aspects of reproductive medicine is the improvement of oocyte cryopreservation. It is now possible to cryopreserve oocytes, but the process is still very inefficient and not widely used. This is likely to change dramatically in the next decade, demanding legal guidance and necessitating policies for all the implications and potential consequences such advances will bring. Our experience with cryopreserved sperm should provide guidance as we face the inevitable issues involved with cryopreserved oocytes. On a nonmedical front, increasing legal recognition of same-sex and single-parent families will require consistent legal frameworks as these newly possible families emerge as a result of medical assistance. Advances in genetics and the science of embryos will bring new possibilities and challenges. In the distant future, stem cell research and regenerative medicine may make it possible to regenerate an injured organ, to reproduce without sperm and eggs, or to gestate a fetus outside the womb.

Without question, the assisted reproductive technologies will continue to be a dynamic, interdisciplinary field. Medically and legally speaking, advances will undoubtedly continue to challenge us in ways both conceivable and inconceivable. It is hoped that this opportunity to look back over the remarkable challenges the law has faced and the strides it has made in response to these advances will help guide and inform future practices and policies as we continue to remake the very concept of "family."

The book ends as it begins: the conclusion takes a hard look at the issues and challenges facing today's and tomorrow's stakeholders and policy makers. It then suggests concrete ways to frame, confront, and, we hope, resolve some of the most pressing challenges we will face as these remarkable technologies continue to propel society forward, whether we are ready or not. Our goal is for this work to make a contribution toward preparing ourselves for that future.

Law 101

A Selective Primer for the Nonlawyer

∽ BY Susan L. Crockin

THROUGHOUT THIS compendium, readers should be aware of the evolution of legal principles and language that the assisted reproductive technologies (ART) have given birth to. The recently coined term *retronym,* meaning the addition of an adjective to a previously understood term in order to differentiate its meaning in a new context, seems tailor-made for the ARTs. Rather than the previously clear, singular concept of "mother," we now refer to "gestational mother," "genetic mother," and "intended mother"; from "embryo" we now debate "preembryo," "zygote," and "blastocyst" (to name but a few); and the oddity of "gestational twins" has been added to our lexicon to explain an embryo mixup resulting in two children being born to one woman by mistake.

American jurisprudence is defined on both a state and a federal level. Most court cases that involve "family law" (including parentage status, rights, and obligations) raise issues of state law. No state need agree with, or follow, any other state's rulings on such issues. Within any given state, until the highest-level court decides a case, it is also of limited value as "precedent" (law which must be followed) in that state, and no court decision or legislation from one state is precedent for another state. At the same time, with a limited number of court decisions on these issues, many courts choose to look beyond their state borders for guidance (or nonbinding advice) to see how other courts have responded to similar disputes. On rare occasions (but increasingly common in multiparty ART cases) courts of one state may need to interpret another state's laws—for example, if parties from different states sign an agreement under one state law but sue in the other, or if a couple from one state receives medical or laboratory services in a second state. Federal courts generally must follow and interpret state law, unless the issue in dispute involves a uniquely federal law (such as discrimination under the Americans with Disabilities Act).

The "full faith and credit" clause of the U.S. Constitution requires courts in one state to recognize and uphold decisions made by courts from another state if brought before them to be enforced. For example, a same-sex adoption recognized in California must be recognized in Arizona if the family later moves there or if the child was born in Arizona and, following the adoption in California, a new birth certificate needs to be issued by that state. The federal Defense of Marriage Act (DOMA), 28 U.S.C.S. §1738C (2008), is a new, explicit, and significant exception to that principle; it allows any state to disregard a marriage from another state that violates its public policy and denies federal benefits based on such marriages. Thus, the legal rights flowing from a same-sex marriage from Massachusetts and a child born within that marriage can be entirely disregarded in Florida, for example, where same-sex adoptions are statutorily prohibited, and thus leave that family without legal protection there. One arena where patients, providers, and families have wandered into uncharted and problematic territory is when multiple states are involved in an ART matter and the applicable law issues have not been sorted out in advance. As of press time, a number of court cases were pending challenging the constitutionality of both DOMA and the Florida ban.

Finally, it is important to understand that new law emerges from older and established areas of the law. Family, health, contract, discrimination, tort (civil wrongs, such as negligence and malpractice), and constitutional law all come into play as courts sort out the legal issues raised by the ARTs. As the reported cases illustrate, the assisted reproductive technologies continue to both challenge and extend existing law and make new law.

Assisted Reproductive Technology Time Lines

Medical Time Line

1880   First attempt to fertilize a mammalian egg in vitro (rabbit and guinea pig). This effort failed.
S. L. Schenk, Vienna, Austria

1890   First transfer of early embryo from one animal to another animal of the same species (rabbit). This effort established an appreciation of the nonrejection, that is, immunological privilege, of a foreign developing embryo.
Walter Heape, Cambridge, U.K.

1954   First successful fertilization in vitro of a mammalian egg (rabbit), seventy-four years after Schenk's failure in Vienna.
Charles Thibault, Paris, France

1959   First birth after the use of an in vitro fertilized egg in a mammal (rabbit).
M. C. Chang, Worcester, Massachusetts, USA

1978   First live human birth from in vitro fertilization (IVF).
R. Edwards and P. Steptoe, Cambridge and Oldham, U.K.[1]

1. The work done in six countries is chronicled in this time line because twenty-five health care workers from the United Kingdom, Australia, the United States, France, Sweden, and Austria formed the nucleus of a group that convened at Bourn Hall, U.K., in September 1981 to exchange information about their experiences. This exchange of information facilitated some of the 1982 pregnancies. Members of this group formed strong friendships and worked together to make IVF successful. Subsequent meetings of these pioneers were held in various venues around the world—truly an international effort.

1980	First live birth in Australia from IVF (second country in the world).
	Alex Lopata and team, Melbourne, Australia

1981	First live birth in the United States from IVF (third country in the world).
	H. W. Jones, Jr., and team, Norfolk, Virginia, USA

1981	Introduction of the successful (live birth) use of ovarian stimulation to produce multiple eggs in a particular cycle, in contrast to the single egg available during a natural cycle. This strategy is still used worldwide.
	G. S. Jones and team, Norfolk, Virginia, USA

1982	First live births in France from IVF (fourth country in the world).
	René Frydman and team, Paris, France (February)
	and
	J. Cohen and team, Paris, France (June)

1982	First live birth in Sweden from IVF (fifth country in the world).
	Lars Hamberger and team, Gothenberg, Sweden

1982	First live birth in Austria from IVF (sixth country in the world).
	W. Feichtinger and P. Kemeter, Vienna, Austria

1983	First use of ultrastound-guided egg retrieval under local anesthesia.[2]
	J. H. Ravina and team, Paris, France

1983	First live birth from a cryopreserved early embryo.
	G. H. Zeilmaker and team, Rotterdam, The Netherlands

1984	First live births from a donated egg.
	P. Lutjen and team, Melbourne, Australia
	and
	M. Bustillo and team, Los Angeles, California, USA

2. With improved technology, ultrasound-guided egg retrieval is widely used, especially transvaginally. This procedure has transformed egg retrieval requiring a hospital setting into an office procedure, thus greatly simplifying IVF and making it widely available.

| 1985 | First successful use of gestational surrogacy, that is, with no genetic component from the carrier.[3] |
| | Wulf Utian, Cleveland, Ohio, USA |

| 1986 | First live birth from a cryopreserved egg.[4] |
| | Christopher Chen, Adelaide, Australia |

| 1990 | First birth of a specific disease–free child after screening by preimplantation genetic diagnosis (PGD). The disease was cystic fibrosis. |
| | Alan Handyside and team, London, U.K. |

| 1993 | First live birth after intracellular sperm injection (ICSI). |
| | Gianpiero Palermo and team, Brussels, Belgium |

| 1979–2005 | Gradual improvement of success rate due to many technical improvements. In 2005, according to the Centers for Disease Control (CDC), there were 134,260 IVF cycles in the United States. For fresh donor eggs, the pregnancy rate was 34 percent. This, of course, will be augmented by subsequent transfers from frozen material from the same aspiration cycle. There is wide variation in success rates due to age and the medical problem. |

Legal Time Line

| 1978 | First reported U.S. case involving patients' suit for destroyed (fresh) embryos and damages; court finds emotional distress damages appropriate, wife awarded $50,000, husband awarded $3 by jury. |
| | *Del Zio v. Presbyterian Hospital,* 1978 U.S. Dist. LEXIS 14450 (SDNY 1978) |

3. As the name implies, traditional surrogacy is an ancient practice. The book of Genesis (chapter 16) records that Abraham and Sarah were barren. Sarah gave her servant, Hegar, to Abraham to have his children. The traditional surrogate supplies not only the uterus but the egg. ART is not required but occasionally is necessary, as for example, if the surrogate's fallopian tubes are nonfunctional. There are no sophisticated data on the frequency of its use.

4. Cryopreserved sperm have been clinically used since 1953.

1985	Maryland becomes first state to statutorily require coverage for IVF.
1987	Massachusetts becomes first state to statutorily require comprehensive coverage for "diagnosis and treatment of infertility," including IVF, to the same extent as pregnancy benefits. Mass. Gen. Laws, ch. 176, 47H
1989	First reported U.S. case involving patient v. M.D. dispute over control of cryopreserved embryo; decided under property principles ("bailor and bailee"), with no need for court to consider nature of IVF embryo. *York v. Jones,* 717 F. Supp. 421 (D. Va. 1989)
1989	Filing of first reported U.S. case involving divorcing couple's control and disposition of their cryopreserved IVF embryos. *Davis v. Davis,* initial divorce action filed (Tenn. 1989)
1992	Final decision rendered in first divorce case involving embryos: (1) Tennessee court adopts AFS (now ASRM) characterization that "preembryos" are neither property nor persons but "occupy an interim category that entitles them to special respect because of their potential for human life"; and (2) court finds constitutional right not to procreate overrides right to procreate; embryos ultimately ordered discarded per ex-husband's wishes. *Davis v. Davis,* 842 S.W.2d 588 (Tenn. 1992)
1992	First U.S. case approving affirmative duty of care by legal, medical, and other professionals to third-party participant, traditional surrogate, based on having recruited her to participate (lower court finds them to be "brokers"). *Stiver v. Parker,* 975 F.2d 261 (6th Cir. 1992); *reh. en banc denied*
1993	First U.S. gestational surrogacy dispute involving carrier's ultimately unsuccessful claim to maternity; court rules intent to be mother is the "tie-breaker" when two women can each make claim to maternity via genetics or gestation (prior decisions found traditional surrogate to be a birth mother with adoption law protections).

Johnson v. Calvert, 5 Cal. 4th 84 (Cal. 1993); *cert. denied,* 510 U.S. 874 (1993)

1993   First two high state courts (Vermont and Massachusetts) allow same-sex co-parent adoptions, interpreting existing adoption laws to permit such adoptions.
In re B.L.V.B., 160 Vt. 368 (Vt. 1993): *Adoption of Tammy,* 416 Mass. 205 (Mass. 1993)

1996   First U.S. case (federal district) allowing Social Security benefits for posthumous born child.
Hart v. Chater, Comm'r Soc. Sec., U.S.D.C. #94-3944 (E. Dis. La 1996) (entry of Stip. of dismissal 3/18/96)

1998   U.S. Supreme Court rules reproduction is a "major life activity" under the Americans with Disabilities Act (illegal denial of dental care to HIV-positive patient with compromised reproductive capacity).
Bragdon v. Abbott, 524 U.S. 624 (U.S. 1998)

2000   First U.S. case involving a divorcing couple's dispute over enforceability of prior agreement that allowed procreation with frozen embryos after one spouse's change of mind. Court rules couple's prior agreement that wife can use embryos for procreation is unenforceable if husband has subsequent change of mind ("forced procreation is not amenable to judicial enforcement"). Court recognizes other, non-procreative, aspects of consent may be enforceable.
A.Z. v. B.Z., 725 N.E.2d 1051 (Mass. 2000)

2000   Massachusetts trial court allows two women to be placed on birth certificate as parents of child born with one woman contributing eggs and the other gestating the child, a practice that many courts today routinely allow.
Knoll v. BIDMC, No.00W-1343 (Suffolk Prob. & Fam. Ct. Mass. 2000)

2002   First reported U.S. case involving sperm bank liability for donor's genetic abnormality that was not communicated to recipients.

Johnson v. Superior Court, 124 Cal. Rptr. 2d 650 (Cal. Ct. App. 2002); *review denied*, 2002 Cal. LEXIS 8341 (Cal. 2002)

2003	First reported U.S. case finding negligence liability (by medical group) for egg donor's genetic abnormality tested for but accidentally not disclosed to recipients. *Paretta v. Med. Offices of Human Repro., et al.*, 195 Misc. 2d 568, 760 N.Y.s.2d 639 (2003); *App. withdrawn*, 6 A.D.3d 1249 (N.Y. App. Div. 2004)
2003	Massachusetts Supreme Judicial Court rules same-sex marriage is a constitutionally protected right. *Goodridge v. Dept. of Public Health*, 440 Mass. 309 (2003)
2008 (May)	California Supreme Court rules same-sex marriage is a constitutionally protected right and that availability of civil unions, despite conferring same benefits, does not merit different decision. *In re Marriage Cases*, 183 P.3d 384 (Cal. 2008)
2008 (Nov.)	California election referendum "Proposition 8" passes, amending California constitution to restrict marriage to "a union between a man and a woman," reversing court decision affirming constitutional right to same-sex marriage.
2008 (Nov.)	Multiple lawsuits filed in California challenging Proposition 8.
2008	Illinois appellate court rejects "wrongful death" lawsuit over destroyed embryo, reversing lower court ruling. *Miller v. Am. Infertility Group of Ill.*, 844 N.E.2d 424 (Ill. 2006), *rev'd*, 897 N.E.2d 837 (Ill. App. Ct. 2008)
2009 (Feb.)	California birth of octuplets to single mother through multiple-embryo IVF transfer (all eight babies brought home by April 2009).
2009 (April)	Vermont becomes first state to legislatively recognize same-sex marriage. VT. STAT. ANN. tit 15, § 1201 (2009)

2009 (April)   Iowa Supreme Court unanimously recognizes same-sex marriage.

Varnum v. Brien, 763 N.W.2d 862 (Iowa 2009)

2009 (April)   Washington, D.C., Council votes to recognize out-of-state same-sex marriages (mayoral approval, May).

D.C. Code § 46-401 (2009)

2009 (April)   Georgia legislature passes "Option of Adoption Act" authorizing transfer of all legal rights and responsibilities to embryo recipients by contract, as well as option of pre-birth "expedited order of adoption or parentage."

H. B. 388 (Ga. 2009) codified at Ga. Code Ann. §§ 19-8-40 to 19-8-43

CHAPTER ONE

Embryo Litigation

✦ MEDICAL COMMENTARY, BY Howard W. Jones, Jr.

A N EARLY CASE noted in this compendium (*York v. Jones*, 1989) raised the very important question of the moral status of the early fertilized egg. Is it a person? Is it a thing? Or is it something in between? The moral status was also a key point in *Davis v. Davis* (1990–92) and many other cases. When during development is personhood established? Personhood in this context can be defined as that state during development that deserves protection by society.

To this medical mind, the answer should be clear. The Supreme Court held in 1973 in *Roe v. Wade* that societal protection need not begin until viability, that is, late in pregnancy.

In the *Davis v. Davis* case, the lower court applied custody laws to the cryopreserved concepti, implying personhood at this early date. However, this view was reversed by the appellate court.

When moral theologians discus personhood, they inevitably ask the biologists to indicate some major biological shift during development that could be a sign of a change in status. Over the centuries, various set points have been selected. Examples include "quickening," or heart sounds by auscultation of the heart after the stethoscope was invented, and brain waves after it became possible to measure these.

Nevertheless, there are religious persuasions that hold that ensoulment, the ecclesiastical equivalent of personhood, occurs immediately after fertilization. Pope Pius IX in 1869 is usually credited with officially choosing this earliest juncture for ensoulment, as prior church fathers had placed it at a much later time in development.

The emergence of IVF as a clinical reality in the early 1980s made it necessary for the Catholic Church to issue instructions on whether or not

IVF and some of its offshoots represented a process suitable for the faithful to use to solve their problems with infertility.

In November 1984, the Pontifical Academy of Sciences organized a meeting at the Vatican to address this question. The Pontifical Academy of Sciences was founded in 1603; at that time it was called the Academy of Lynxes. In 1936 Pius XI re-founded the Academy and gave it its present name. Among its functions in the intervening years has been the convening of working parties to consider and recommend a stance to the Holy See on particular scientific matters of contemporary interest.

The working group was headed by President Carlos Chagas, a distinguished scientist in his own right. The eleven other members included three gynecologists—Dr. René Frydman of Paris, Georgeanna, and me—moral theologians and scientists, about half from within the Vatican. Our charge was to examine the question of whether or not in vitro fertilization was licit and consistent with Catholic doctrine and therefore to be used by the Roman Catholic community. The transcript of this discussion was to be published, as are all the deliberations of the Academy, and made available to the Holy See to consider in formulating instructions for the use of IVF by members of the church.

There was a very lively and extremely intellectual discussion for about five days. The role of the gynecologists was to describe exactly what the IVF process was, and the theologians asked many questions. On the last day of the discussion, President Chagas asked each moral theologian in turn to say whether they thought that IVF should be considered licit or illicit. All except Monsignor Carlo Caffarra thought the procedure was licit and, therefore, could be used. Monsignor Carlo Caffarra thought that it was illicit because it was outside the bonds of conjugal love.

We had another very lively discussion of what was meant by conjugal love. Caffarra's definition of conjugal love was sexual intercourse, and Chagas made a particular effort to persuade Monsignor Caffarra to change his position and then, after failing to do that, asked him if he would remain silent. Caffarra said that he could not. His position evidently held sway with the Pope, as the published document, titled "Instruction on Respect for Human Life in its Origin and on the Dignity of Procreation" (*Donum Vitae*), condemned IVF, cloning, cryopreservation, artificial insemination, and surrogacy. In the document *Donum Vitae*, not only was the principle of conjugal love emphasized but a second principle, "The Dignity of the Human Being from Its Inception," that is, from the moment of fertilization, was touted. It was on the basis of these two principles that the procedures mentioned above were condemned, as each procedure violated one or both. It is significant that *Donum Vitae* was issued by the Congregation for the Doctrine of the Faith, the prefect of which was none other than Cardinal Joseph Ratzinger, who now, of course, is Pope Benedict XVI. For unclear reasons, no transcript of our deliberations was ever published. Thus, the 1984 five-day meeting on the new reproductive technologies with its single dissenter was effectively obliterated from the records of the Pontifical Academy of Sciences. Monsignor Carlo Caffarra, the lone dissenter, was created Cardinal by Pope Benedict XVI in the consistory of the 24th of March, 2006.

Subsequent to the issue of *Donum Vitae*, several observers tried to make a case for ensoulment occurring with implantation, that is, five to seven days after fertilization. This would legalize oral contraceptives. However, Benedict XVI clarified this point in 2006 by affirming the Catholic teaching emphasized in *Donum Vitae*, that life begins at the moment of conception. He stated, "This moral judgment is valid for the status of the life of the embryo even before it is implanted in the maternal womb."

In December 2008 followed *Dignitas Personae* ("The dignity of a person") issued by the Congregation for the Doctrine of the Faith and, of course, approved by Pope Benedict XVI. In the first paragraph it reaffirms the instruction of *Donum Vitae* and states, "It is appropriate to bring it up to date."

Dignitas Personae states that evaluation of current reproductive practices is based on the two precepts of *Donum Vitae*, specifically (1) dignity of the human embryo from its beginning (that is, from fertilization); and (2) procreation must be within the bonds of conjugal love (that is, by sexual intercourse of married individuals).

Dignitas Personae discusses several components of assisted reproductive technology (ART), specifically IVF, including intentional destruction of embryos, intracellular sperm injection, cryopreservation of embryos, oocyte cryopreservation, selective reduction, preimplantation genetic diagnosis, contra-gestation (that is, contraception) and "pre-natal adoption" (embryo donation for procreation), all of which it finds illicit.

Dignitas Personae then discusses manipulation of the embryo, meaning by this certain procedures, including gene therapy. *Dignitas Personae* states that these procedures used on somatic cells are morally licit but that human germ cell therapy is morally illicit. In other words, there should be no designer babies. Human cloning of all types is illicit. And creating embryonic stem cells is illicit, but creating adult stem cells is licit, provided the latter are obtained with proper consent.

Donum Vitae and the updated *Dignitas Personae,* if observed strictly in their entirety, would revert reproductive medicine to its status prior to 1978. In other words, one half of infertile couples would not be able to realize their goal of having a family.

How do practitioners of twenty-first-century ART regard the instructions of *Donum Vitae* and *Dignitas Personae*? Furthermore, how do patients, and particularly Catholic patients, regard these teachings? I can give only one practitioner's view, but I should point out that ART is practiced throughout the world and is generally accepted worldwide.

The problem I find with the two Vatican documents is that the two principles on which ART is evaluated are faulty to a mind trained in science. What is the evidence to believe that personhood begins with fertilization, and what is the evidence that sexual intercourse is a necessary component for procreation, as in *Donum Vitae* and *Dignitas Personae*? Each of these principles is stated as a given. No evidence persuasive to the scientific mind is presented.

In the sweep of church history, the concept that personhood is acquired with fertilization is really a fairly recent notion. *Apostolicus sedis* (an apostolic proclamation) promulgated in 1869 by Pope Pius IX is generally cited as the source of the present concept that personhood is acquired with fertilization. This document imposed excommunication on those who were involved in or caused any abortion. The point is that in decreeing this excommunication, no time limit during pregnancy was stated. Therefore, it has been interpreted and often cited as meaning that personhood must begin from the very first, because otherwise the document could not be applied.

Prior to this teaching, the concept of the church was, generally speaking, Aristotelian; that is, it took the position that personhood was acquired at some time during development.

In more contemporary times, some have attempted to tie the acquisition of personhood with some major biological event, as already mentioned. Some who support the Vatican view hold that the major biological event is the union of the two gametes. Jérôme Lejeune, our translator while we were in the Vatican, held this view and testified as such before the U.S. Congress when during the mid-1980s a bill had been introduced to declare that personhood was acquired with fertilization. Fortunately, this bill failed.

There are serious biological flaws with the selection of the gamete-to-gamete union as the major biological event. By this event, a single human being does not necessarily result. The penetration of the sperm into the egg can result in twins, triplets, or even more—or it can result in a tumor, that is, a benign hydatiform mole or a malignant chorioepithelioma; more commonly, it can result in a genetic mismatch such that only about one in five fertilizations results in an embryo with the capacity to result in the creation of a normal person. It is not until about day fifteen that a single primitive streak (the antecedent of a single spinal column) guarantees biological individuation.

To this observer, the main physiological change during development is the ability of the conceptus to survive without dependence on its mother, that is to say, when it is viable without maternal support. If the contemporary notion holds that a major biological event marks the initiation of personhood, I believe that the Supreme Court got it right. Thus, in the United States, the civil law holds that personhood is acquired with viability.

The second basic point of evaluation in *Dignitas Personae* is that reproduction must be the result of sexual intercourse between married couples. As mentioned above, the problem with this criterion is that it is stated *ex cathedra*. No evidence is presented that this is the only way to reproduce. On the other hand, there is abundant evidence that ART has overcome problems that could not be solved otherwise. It has helped families achieve their reproductive goals and has provided, therefore, the means by which their family life can become whole. To this observer, that is what medicine is about, overcoming difficulties with therapeutic measures that will restore normalcy. In my view ART has accomplished that, further diminishing the persuasiveness of the Vatican conclusions. That ART is widely practiced and accepted the world over indicates that many others support this view or a similar one.

The advent of in vitro fertilization (IVF), followed shortly by embryo cryopreservation, transformed both the medical and legal landscape involving reproduction. Before the 1980s, reproductive law was defined by constitutional issues of reproductive choice, contraception, forced sterilization, and the lightning rod of all reproductive law issues: abortion. The United States Supreme Court made it clear in a series of landmark decisions (*Griswold v. Connecticut,* 1965; *Baird v. Eisenstadt,* 1972; and *Roe v. Wade,* 1973) that women had constitutional protections against sterilization, the constitutional right to obtain contraception, and the constitutional right to decide whether to continue or end a pregnancy prior to viability. As with other areas of the law (including family law, which the ARTs would also dramatically impact), states were free to enact their own laws so long as they did not curtail federally recognized constitutional principles. In the wake of *Roe v. Wade,* many states passed statutes designed to restrict abortion-related activities.

In the mid-1970s, before IVF made ex-utero embryos possible, state legislatures enacted statutory law that often defined a "fetus" to include an "embryo." Medical dictionaries of the times defined "embryo" in terms of an early conceptus in utero (*Stedman's Medical Dictionary,* 1976). Anti-abortion sentiment and reproductive laws that criminalized "fetal tampering" led to the prosecution of some obstetricians who performed late-term abortions. One highly publicized case involved Dr. Kenneth Edelin, then chief resident of Boston City Hospital, who was convicted of manslaughter for performing a late second-trimester abortion. The appellate court later reversed the conviction (*Commonwealth v. Edelin,* 359 N.E.2d 4 (Mass. 1976)).

When IVF first burst into the public eye with Louise Brown's birth in 1978, the fervor over this medical breakthrough and the promises of test-tube babies far overshadowed the legal changes and challenges they portended. Few noticed that three fundamental premises of constitutional and family law were quickly obliterated:

First, with fertilization or conception no longer occurring only inside a woman's body, and with the embryo or preembryo now able to exist physically separate from a woman, all of the established legal assumptions, constitutional protections, and applicability of legal principles established by prior court cases involving a woman's bodily integrity and right to reproductive privacy were strained. Within the medical and scientific communities, there was debate over the proper terms for ex-utero or IVF embryos, which were only permitted to develop for a limited number of days before being transferred to a woman's uterus (or later cryopreserved). The terms "preembryo" or "preimplantation embryo" were used to describe these early-stage embryos that were not permitted to develop beyond an eight-cell stage, long before the appearance of the primitive streak (implying the beginning of differentiation), which occurs on or about day fourteen. Many articles have discussed these issues, including ones by the authors of this book.[1] Although many within the medical and scientific communities do not find such distinctions critical, the distinctions have been repeatedly noted and accepted by courts in deciding, for example, divorce disputes involving such cryopreserved embryos. For purposes of simplicity, this text uses the word "embryo" or "IVF embryo" to refer to any ex-utero embryo, including those that may also be accurately described as "preembryos" or "preimplantation embryos." IVF thus created new and still unresolved legal questions and tensions, including revisiting definitions of "fertilization" and "conception" and identifying the nature of and attendant rights to the ex-utero embryo.

Second, with embryo cryopreservation extending the time from fertilization to birth indefinitely, not only were disputes over embryos—whether between the patients who created them or the patients and providers who were storing them—suddenly possible, but all of the legal assumptions based on a nine-month gestation immediately became antiquated. This technological development has had implications for contract, property, and family law, including parentage and custody as well as inheritance and trusts and estates law.

Finally, IVF opened up the possibility of female as well as male gamete donors, IVF embryo donors, and gestational carriers, creating a growing number of both potential patients and would-be parents, all with at

1. For readers interested in more detailed discussions of this issue, see, for example, H. Jones and M. Veeck, "What is an embryo?" 77 *Fertility and Sterility* 4, pp. 68–59 (April 2002); Susan L. Crockin, "What is an Embryo: A Legal Perspective," 36 *Conn. L. Rev,* 1177 (2004); H. Jones and S. Crockin, "On assisted reproduction, religion, and civil law," 73 *Fertility and Sterility* 3, pp. 447–52 (March 2000).

times conflicting legal rights, including those of a constitutional nature, and with little legal precedent to rely on to resolve them.

The first "Legally Speaking" column, published in December 1990, reviewed the country's first divorce dispute involving a couple's frozen embryos (*Davis v. Davis*). The column continued to report on that case as it wended its way through virtually every level of Tennessee's state court system until its final resolution three years later. Two earlier cases that predated "Legally Speaking" had involved disputes between patients and their physicians over the IVF embryos they had created (*York v. Jones*, 1989; and *Del Zio v. Presbyterian Hospital*, 1978). Each of these embryo disputes, dating back over twenty years, illustrate the courts' growing familiarity with the terrain and terminology involved in the assisted reproductive technologies and the recurring issues that still prove so difficult to resolve. Over the past two decades, two major categories of embryo disputes have emerged: patient v. patient (disputes arising most often in the context of divorce) and patient v. provider (disputes arising in a variety of contexts, often involving malpractice claims). Each presents unique issues and has called for the application of different legal theories and principles. Disputes between two patients or progenitors over their genetic material or over children born from it call into question difficult fundamental questions over the nature and limits of reproductive rights. Disputes between patients and providers meanwhile have stretched—and strained—established theories of contract, property, tort and malpractice law. Certain principles seem to have become widely accepted, but many others still reflect a lack of legal consensus.

Patient v. Patient Disputes

A trend, if not a consensus, appears to have emerged that rejects the concept of "forced procreation." No appellate court has permitted a man or woman to use frozen embryos to procreate over the objection of a former spouse. In 2000, after a number of courts had seemed consistently to confirm a couple's prior joint decision despite one party's change of mind, Massachusetts became the first court to confront and ultimately reject a couple's prior agreement that would have allowed procreation over a concurrent objection, basing its decision on public policy grounds. Shortly thereafter, New Jersey followed suit in a case equally notable because the couple's voided agreement would have authorized *donation* of the embryos for procreation in spite of the wife's later objection. That court declared forced procreation equally repugnant, significantly regardless of whether or not the ex-wife would be deemed the legal mother of any resulting child. The potential implication of these decisions for gamete donors has yet to be raised or explored, but the principle established here—that no one should be forced to be a *biological* parent prior to implantation—would seem to have potentially far-reaching future implications, especially if and as egg freezing becomes more widely accepted and used.

Courts have yet to reach a consensus over the nature of medical programs' cryopreservation forms or the significance of deeming them either legal agreements (contracts) or medical consent forms. While these documents are subject to a change of mind in the context of procreative choices, a number of courts have enforced them when the couple's prior recorded mutual choice was to discard or donate their embryos for research. The court decisions suggest some benefit to considering these documents legal agreements, which invites a contract analysis and contract law application, and thus results in some additional legal protections for assisted reproductive technology (ART) programs. Notwithstanding such a characterization, however, there is no consensus among the courts that such a self-declared "agreement" is in fact a contract, or whether any such contract is enforceable or subject to a change of mind, similar to a consent form under principles of health law. In endorsing a contract analysis outside the area of procreative choices, a number of courts have expressed concerns over, and sympathy for, the need for medical programs to have some degree of certainty in their practices.

In virtually all of these cases, the appellate courts demonstrated an admirable and sophisticated willingness to accept, consider, and embrace scientific evidence. Courts have taken great care to distinguish between in vitro–created "preembryos" (also referring to them as "prezygotes") and in utero embryos and fetuses. Only one court (Iowa, which noted that it did not receive scientific testimony) used the singular term "embryo." Ethics reports from the American Fertility Society (now the American Society of Reproductive Medicine) also figured prominently in the courts' analyses. In the seminal case of *Davis v. Davis*, the Tennessee Supreme Court quoted the ethics report's conclusion that preembryos were neither property nor persons but were entitled to "special respect" due to their capacity to become a person—a concept carried forward today. In a 2007 dispute, an ex-wife in Texas petitioned the U.S. Supreme Court to allow her to use cryopreserved embryos she claimed were the same to her as fetuses or babies. The somewhat unique aspect of that case was that the couple never used any of the embryos they had created, as the husband changed his mind between the retrieval and expected transfer of fresh embryos (the program consequently froze the embryos pending a resolution of the dispute). The ex-wife argued that any agreement was only intended to cover "left-over" embryos, not those intended for immediate transfer. The state court rejected her claims, and the U.S. Supreme Court refused to hear her petition. A number of commentators had wondered whether an increasingly conservative Supreme Court might agree to hear and then use such a case as a vehicle to reexamine reproductive law principles.

Patient v. Provider Disputes

As noted above, two seminal cases involving patients suing medical professionals predated "Legally Speaking": *Del Zio v. Presbyterian Hospital*, 1978 U.S. Dist. LEXIS 14450 (SDNY 1978), and *York v. Jones*, 717 F. Supp. 421 (D. Va. 1989). Without resolving the nature of an ex-utero embryo, both decisions suggested that patients had a greater claim to their embryos than did any medical professional.

The cases covered in "Legally Speaking" since 1990 support that view but show how defining the nature of the disputed claims and alleged harms was—and is—a complex endeavor. Courts have wrestled with defining the various interests in the embryo, assigning a value to whatever interest may be lost or damaged and identifying the nature of the alleged harm within the context of established law and precedent. For those disputes that resulted in born children, there were often multiple, overlapping lawsuits involving malpractice, negligence, breach of contract claims (by patients against providers), competing custody claims, and in rare instances, criminal prosecutions.

Taken together, these cases reflect both the courts' and litigants' necessarily creative approaches to crafting novel legal theories, causes of action, and a continuously evolving terminology. Medical professionals sued in civil courts have been found liable for money damages in cases involving frozen embryos that were lost, for malpractice in cases involving gamete or embryo mix-ups as well as lost embryos, and in at least one case, for the equivalent of child support for a child after an embryo transfer was done without her father's knowledge and against his wishes.

One final note for both the lawyer and nonlawyer to keep in mind: trial-level disputes, which often result in a settlement rather than an appeal to a higher court, are of little or no official legal significance as "precedent" within a given state. Settlements—likely within malpractice insurance coverage limits—often reflect a pragmatic decision that the extraordinary expenses of litigation far outweigh the potential benefits of attempting to clear one's name. While those outcomes, therefore, do not establish legal theories of liability and may not be widely reported, they can be invaluable tools in evaluating litigation outcomes for similar disputes.

Litigation

1.1 Physician's Class Action Strikes Down Fetal Experimentation Ban
December 1990

A Chicago reproductive endocrinologist has won his eight-year fight to declare Illinois's fetal experimentation ban unconstitutional. Dr. Aaron Lifchez, originally working with an IVF patient and with considerable backing from the ACLU, brought a successful federal class action on behalf of a group of infertility specialists, arguing that the law interfered with their practice as well as with the rights of their patients.

The defective portion of the Illinois abortion law made it illegal to perform "non-therapeutic, experimental" procedures on a fetus. "No person shall sell or experiment upon a fetus produced by the fertilization of a human ovum by a human sperm unless such experimentation is therapeutic to the fetus thereby produced . . . nothing in this subsection (7) is intended to prohibit the performance of in vitro fertilization."

Since there was no single medically accepted definition of "experimental," the court agreed that the law left physicians unable to determine which medical procedures they might legally perform without fear of prosecution—including amniocentesis, embryo transfer or donation or fetal tissue testing for genetic disease. The court also ruled the law restricts a woman's right to a medical procedure to "bring about pregnancy" and this violated her constitutional right to privacy.

Lifchez v. Hartigan, 735 F. Supp. 1361 (D. Ill. 1990)

1.2(a) Tennessee Frozen Embryos Decision Overturned
December 1990

The seven frozen embryos of the now-divorced Davis couple of Tennessee were once again the subject of national attention as the Tennessee Court of Appeals overturned the trial court's ruling.

Rejecting the lower court's unprecedented decision (granting sole "custody" of these "children in vitro" to Mary Sue), this court granted "joint control" to the former spouses, giving each of them "an equal voice in their disposition." Mary Sue's attorneys have now appealed this new decision to Tennessee's highest court. During the appeal process, both parties have remarried and neither wants to bear the child of the other. Mary Sue now wants the embryos donated to an infertile couple for implantation. Junior continues to want them destroyed. However, in yet another unusual twist, Junior is now married to another woman who is unable to have children. "If the court rules that these things must be implanted then I want to be their father," Junior recently told the court. His attorney, while denying a published report that Junior is prepared to hire a surrogate for that purpose, says his clients would seek legal and physical custody of any children produced following implantation. (In yet another development, a local lawyer asked to be appointed guardian of the embryos, a request which the trial court recently denied.)

In marked contrast to the trial court's view, the appellate court recognized that "there are significant scientific distinctions between fertilized ova that have not been implanted and an embryo in the mother's womb" and moreover, that even viable fetuses—entitled to more constitutional protection than four eight-cell embryos—are not entitled to all of the constitutional rights and privileges of persons already born. Using Nazi Germany's attempt to control reproduction through mandatory sterilization as an example of the "evils of uncontrolled state action," the appellate court condemned the lower court's attempt to insinuate itself and the state into the couple's private decision.

"... It would be repugnant and offensive to constitutional principles to order Mary Sue to implant these fertilized ova against her will [a logical extension of the lower court's decision that they deserved their best chance at life]. It would be equally repugnant to order Junior to bear the psychological, if not the legal, consequences of paternity against his will. ..."

The court did not address the subject of how the sparring custodians should resolve their "equal" but opposing views on the embryos' desirable fate or what the IVF clinic's role should be. In the meantime, the freezer bills keep mounting.

Davis v. Davis, Tenn. Ct. Apps. (9/13/90)

1.2(b) Status of Frozen Embryos Remains in Dispute Despite State Supreme Court Ruling

September 1992

A recent court ruling concerning seven frozen embryos of a divorced couple has failed to put their fate to rest. In a lengthy and thoughtfully analyzed decision, the Tennessee Supreme Court ruled that Junior Davis had a constitutionally protected right not to procreate, which overrode Mary Sue Davis's right to procreate. The decision, however, has not had its intended result of discarding the seven embryos. Instead, the parties are reportedly headed back to court after the doctor whose facility was storing the embryos stated he would neither discard nor continue to store them and asked for judicial guidance. As a result, the trial court issued a temporary restraining order preventing disposal of the embryos.

Meanwhile, an appeal has also been filed with the U.S. Supreme Court.

The state supreme court rejected the trial court's initial rulings, which gave "custody" to the mother and called the embryos "children in vitro" and deserving of life. It reviewed the few other court decisions involving embryos, the scientific testimony presented, the medical and legal literature available on the point, and "friends of court" briefs submitted by the AMA and AFS. The court also rejected suggestions that preembryos are either "persons" or "property." The court quoted the AFS Ethics Committee's conclusion that "special respect" is due preembryos because of their potential for human life, as well as its suggestion that "decision-making authority regarding preembryos should reside with the persons who have provided the gametes...."

The court ruled that an agreement regarding future disposition of preembryos should be "presumed valid" and "should be enforced." It noted that the case could have been avoided had the Davises signed such an agreement.

Noting that "human emotions run particularly high when a married couple is attempting to overcome infertility problems...." and that their initial informed consent might not be truly informed because of the future's uncertainty, the court endorsed the right to modify an initial agreement, but only by agreement of both parties.

Reviewing the constitutional law on privacy and procreational autonomy, including rulings on contraception and abortion, the court ruled that the right to procreational autonomy is composed of two rights of equal significance: the right to procreate and the right to avoid procreation.

Despite the woman's greater involvement in IVF, the court emphasized that the constitutional focus must be on the future. "As they stand on the brink of parenthood, Mary Sue Davis and Junior Davis must be seen as entirely equivalent gamete-providers."

Finally, without an initial agreement between the now-opposing gamete providers, the court concluded that the right not to procreate must win out over the right *to* procreate. That decision, the court admitted, was made easier by the fact that Mary Sue now wanted to donate the embryos rather than gestate and parent them herself. However, the court went on to say that it would have reached the same decision regardless. It pointed out that she had other means to achieve parenthood, including IVF or adoption.

The court concluded by saying that where the preferences of the progenitors are unclear or in dispute, their prior agreement should govern the decision. In the absence of a prior agreement, the balance should tip in favor of the party wishing to avoid procreation unless no other reasonable possibility of achieving parenthood by the other party exists.

As ethicist Arthur Caplan remarked, "A court has now said that a man cannot be forced to become a parent against his will. This raises the interesting questions of whether courts would be willing to compel a woman to do what this court is not willing to compel a man to do."

1.2(c) State Supreme Court Orders Tennessee Couple Back to Court
March 1993

The Tennessee Supreme Court has ordered Junior and Mary Sue Davis back to court in an effort to have them reach an agreement over their seven frozen embryos. . . . The court has also now ruled that if the estranged couple cannot agree, the only remaining choice will be to discard the embryos.

1.2(d) Tennessee Frozen Embryo Suit Continues
June 1993

The long-running divorce dispute over seven frozen embryos continues. The U.S. Supreme Court declined to review the case, leaving the Tennessee Supreme Court's ruling in place. Mary Sue Davis's attorney is now arguing that Junior Davis should be ordered to personally destroy the embryos that have been stored for over four years. Junior Davis has reportedly responded that he will destroy the embryos if necessary. The doctor whose fertility clinic is storing them has said he would prefer to donate them for scientific use rather than destroy them.

1.2(e) Frozen Embryos Destroyed
September 1993

The fate of seven embryos was finally resolved when the ex-husband destroyed them in June (1993). Neither Junior Davis nor his attorney have disclosed how he disposed of the embryos. There are currently no established standards for such destruction. Some observers have expressed disappointment that the case failed to answer the many novel and difficult questions it raised, including whether embryos are considered life or property.

Davis v. Davis, 1992 Tenn. LEXIS 622 (Tenn. 1992)

1.3 Rethinking Debate of When Life Begins
March 1991

Leading Catholic theologians have recently published two scholarly articles that question traditional Catholic thinking on the subject of "when life begins." This development may have significant implications in medical, legal, and ethical circles. According to a January

New York Times report, the authors conclude that while preembryos have "genetic individuality" they lack "determinant and irreversible" or "developmental" individuality. Thus, while life is deserving of protection, the authors suggest that preembryos do not require full or absolute protection as does individual human life. Widening the debate on this issue is likely to impact decisions and policies in the areas of testing, research, and freezing of preembryos.

New York Times, 1/13/91

1.4 England's First Donated Embryos Reported
June 1992

In what has been described as an "adoption before birth," a British couple has become the first to donate their frozen embryos to another infertile couple under that country's Human Fertilisation and Embryology Authority (HFEA) law. Enacted last year, the law requires that stored frozen embryos be donated for research, disposed of, or given to another couple within five years of freezing. The law also requires that limited genetic information be made available to the children resulting from this procedure when they are eighteen years old.

After seventeen years of infertility treatments, the couple, both thirty-nine, conceived twins as a result of an IVF transfer of three embryos. The remaining five embryos were frozen and, eighteen months later, donated to another infertile couple.

Times Newspapers Ltd., 2/9/92

1.5 Lawsuit Seeking to Stop NIH Human Embryo Research Panel Filed and Dismissed
December 1994

An effort to stop the work of the NIH Human Embryo Research Panel, and enjoin the release of its report, failed when a federal district judge dismissed a lawsuit purportedly brought by "Mary Doe," defined as a "pre-born child in being as a human embryo on behalf of 20,000 frozen embryos," the Michael Fund, and Michael Policastro, a young adult with Down Syndrome for whom the Fund is named. The Michael Fund is a nonprofit organization that sponsors research involving Down Syndrome and is opposed to fetal research in the belief it will diminish available research funds resulting in "making socially acceptable, and ultimately fully legal," the "destruction" of people affected with Down Syndrome. The defendants included the panel, Secretary Shalala, HHS, the NIH and its director, and the individual members of the panel. The lawsuit was filed July 18 and dismissed September 26, 1994. In dismissing the case, the court first concluded that any recognizable interest of an embryo would require the appointment of a "guardian ad litem." It then ruled that a human embryo, like a fetus in utero, was not a person with "legally protectable interests." The court concluded that the remaining plaintiffs also did not have standing and further determined that their claim was not a proper matter for judicial decision. In reaching these conclusions, the court noted that the plaintiffs had only shown a generalized grievance, which should not be resolved in a judicial forum. While recognizing that "the issue of fetal research is undoubtedly one of the broadest social importance," it concluded that "a federal court has no role to play in the resolution of the questions plaintiffs seek to have decided." The suit highlights the intense interest and reaction that the NIH panel and its conclusions have generated. Public hearings have reportedly been the focus of vocal opposition, with voluminous mail in response to letter-writing campaigns.

Doe v. Shalala, 862 F. Supp. 1421 (D. Md. 1994);
*vacated and dismissed: Int. Fdtn for Genetic Research
v. Shalala*, 1995 U.S. App. LEXIS 14790
(4th Cir. 1995)

1.6(a) Divorce Court Awards Woman Frozen Embryos
Summer 1995

A New York Supreme Court (a trial-level court) recently held that a woman had the right to control the future outcome of embryos she created with her husband despite the couple's prior agreement to donate for research. Maureen and Steven Kass underwent six unsuccessful IVF cycles before Maureen petitioned for divorce. The only contested issue was possession of their remaining frozen embryos. Maureen decided she wanted to implant the embryos in herself. Steven still wanted to donate them to research.

The Court gave possession of the embryos to the divorcing wife. In rejecting the rights of the divorcing husband the court noted that a man (whether or not married) cannot control the conception nor continuance of a pregnancy since a woman has the sole right to use contraceptives or terminate a pregnancy. "The fact is that an in vivo husband's rights and control over the procreative process ends with ejaculation." The court wrote that there is no legal, ethical, or logical difference between in vivo and in vitro fertilization: "It matters little whether the ovum/sperm union takes place in the private darkness of the fallopian tube or the public glare of a Petri dish."

In contrast to the *Davis* court, the court in *Kass* did not recognize the man's right not to procreate nor consider the man's support obligations or other legal claims he may have against his ex-wife. Those issues should be decided by a court if and when a pregnancy (and live birth) occurs.

1.6(b) New York Court Reverses Frozen Embryo Decision in Favor of Couple's Agreement
Winter 1997

A state appellate court has reversed the much-criticized *Kass* decision ruling that the couple's previously agreed upon disposition, as evidenced by their consent form document, should govern the disposition of the embryos. One judge dissented; another wrote a separate opinion agreeing with the result but finding the informed consent document too ambiguous to rely upon.

The Kasses had signed a multi-page document the court referred to as an "informed consent document." On page six, they had jointly recorded their intention to donate the embryos for research in the event they were unable to make a joint decision regarding another disposition. The court noted that throughout the document liberal references to "we," "us," and "our" made clear that the parties were participating in the IVF program as a married couple with joint decision-making. Their signed "uncontested divorce" document also expressed a mutual intent not to individually seek possession of the embryos but to dispose of them in accordance with the informed consent document.

In deferring to the clinic's document, the court ruled that decisions about family building through IVF and cryopreservation were "intensely personal and essentially private matters which are appropriately resolved by the prospective parents rather than the courts where the parties have indicated their mutual intent. That decision must be scrupulously honored and the courts must refrain from any interference with the parties' expressed interests."

Notable was the court's confusion over the nature of the document in issue. The majority opinion concluded that, "regardless of whether it is sufficient to constitute a binding contract, it provides irrefutable evidence" of the parties' intentions. In a separate opinion, one judge found that the document was not "sufficiently unambiguous to determine the disposition . . . based solely on the terms of the agreement." That judge ruled in favor of the husband on the grounds that without a reliable contract, the party opposing implantation should usually be able to veto a former spouse's proposed implantation. Another judge dissented, arguing that a balancing of the parties' rights and circumstances would be determinative.

The decision, with all of its separately reflected views, once again points toward the need for clear and unambiguous documentation for cryopreservation to create more predictable outcomes in the event of changed circumstances.

1.6(c) Kass Frozen Embryo Decision Affirmed on Appeal
Fall 1998

New York's highest court has now affirmed the decision upholding the Kasses' original agreement to donate their frozen embryos for research.

Finding that the parties' agreement governed as to dispositional authority over the remaining embryos, the high court acknowledged that it was able to skirt difficult issues such as whether embryos were entitled to "special respect" by the program. Employing a contract analysis, the court ruled the agreement was not so ambiguous that the couple's intentions were not clear. The court recognized that while the value of such agreements was apparent, so was the "extraordinary difficulty" in reaching such an agreement, especially in light of future uncertainties, which the court noted included death, divorce, incapacity, aging, and birth of other children. It was these very uncertain future factors that made it "particularly important that courts seek to honor the parties' expressions of choice made before disputes erupt. [K]nowing that advance agreements will be enforced underscores the seriousness and integrity of the consent process; advance agreements as to disposition would have little purpose if they were enforceable only in the event the parties continued to agree." The court was not concerned by the fact that the agreement was drafted by the IVF program, as neither party disputed that the agreement was an expression of their intent or that their choices were not freely and knowingly made.

The court also noted that, "[e]xplicit agreements avoid costly litigation in business transactions; they are all the more necessary and desirable in personal matters of reproductive choice, where the intangible costs of any litigation are simply incalculable. Advance directives, subject to mutual change of mind that must be jointly expressed, both minimize misunderstandings and maximize procreating liberty by reserving to the progenitors the authority to make what is in the first instance a quintessentially personal, private decision. Written agreements also provide the certainty needed for effective operation of IVF programs."

Kass v. Kass, 91 N.Y.2d 554 (N.Y. 1998)

1.7(a) Hospital Sued over Allegedly Missing Embryos
September 1995

Women and Infants Hospital in Providence, Rhode Island, has been sued by a couple who claim it lost their six frozen embryos. The couple filed a lawsuit in state court on July 24, 1995, seeking an explanation and damages. Their complaint alleges that they had an unsuccessful IVF attempt at the hospital in 1992, subsequently returned for another attempt with their frozen embryos, but that the hospital was unable to locate the embryos. The hospital reportedly said the embryos never made it to, or through, the freezing process. From initial news reports it is not clear whether the hospital claims the eggs did not fertilize or that despite fertilization, cryopreservation did not occur. The case is pending.

Associated Press, *Boston Globe*, 7/25/95

1.7(b) Women and Infants Hospital Faces Additional Suits over Frozen Embryos; Lab Passes State Scrutiny with Minor Recordkeeping Errors Noted
Spring 1996

Another Rhode Island couple has sued Women and Infants Hospital over their lost, and apparently destroyed, frozen embryos. George and Susan Doyle filed a complaint in state court through the same attorney, David Olivera, who filed the initial two suits. The complaint charges the hospital with negligence and breach of contract over the loss of five frozen embryos from a 1992 cycle in which the Doyles conceived and gave birth to a child from a fresh embryo. The lawsuit seeks an unspecified amount of money damages. The hospital reportedly has said that the embryos were destroyed during a move by the clinic from one building to another in February 1993.

The Doyles' lawsuit claims that after being notified in May 1995 that the hospital's three-year storage limit was about to be reached, they notified the hospital that they wanted to retrieve and have implanted the five embryos. They claim to have been assured three times by the hospital that the embryos were available and only told that they had been destroyed after beginning to prepare to have a transfer in July 1995.

A state health department investigation completed following the filing of the first two lawsuits reportedly concluded that there were only minor problems at the clinic, including record-keeping deficiencies in which twenty-one patient records did not agree with freezer logs due to a failure to consistently report when embryos did not survive the freezing process. The investigation reportedly found no evidence of misappropriated embryos. While the hospital says it would be "next to impossible" for there to have been any misplaced embryos, the couple's attorney argues that the record-keeping "gaps in the trail" may suggest otherwise and insists his clients need "an explanation that makes sense" and assurances that any needed changes will be made.

Immediately after the discovery, hospital officials notified the Doyles, met with them in person, sent a letter of apology, and offered them a free IVF cycle.

Frisina v. Women and Infants Hosp. of R.I.,
2002 R.I. Super. LEXIS 73 (R.I. Super. Ct. 2002)
(consolidated cases)

1.8(a) Court Voids Clinic's Cryopreservation Agreement, Denies Wife's Use of Frozen Embryos

Winter 1996

A Massachusetts trial court has permanently enjoined a wife from use of her four cryopreserved embryos over the objection of her estranged husband, despite the fact that the couple had signed seven cryopreservation agreements agreeing to her use of the embryos in the event of a separation. After a two-day evidentiary hearing, at which the program's mental health counselor and an embryologist testified, the court ruled that intervening circumstances over the four years since the last cryopreservation agreement was signed effectively nullified the agreements. Despite concluding that each of the couple's changes in circumstances was predictable, the judge concluded that the totality of the changed circumstances over several years was not, specifically a successful twin pregnancy, a restraining order filed by the wife against the husband for unstated reasons, and a decision to separate and divorce. Treating the situation as if no agreement existed, he then ruled against the wife's use of the embryos. She has appealed.

According to the ruling, the couple began infertility treatments shortly after their 1977 marriage, and in 1988 began treatment at the IVF clinic currently storing the embryos. They underwent numerous GIFT and IVF cycles between 1988 and 1991, with the final IVF cycle resulting in twins and seven frozen embryos. The clinic's practice was to require that separate consent forms be signed for each retrieval, and the couple had executed seven such forms, with the wife specifically stating (in an area reserved for individual choices to be written in) that the embryos should be returned to her for implantation in the event of a separation.

The judge found that the husband had signed all but the initial consent form before his wife had completed the area reserved for writing in individual choices and signed the majority of the consents at home, without legal or psychological counseling or discussion with a physician. In addition, some of the witnesses had signed days after the husband signed. The court also found that the clinic encouraged couples to take the forms home and bring them back signed to encourage their thoughtful review. In the spring of 1995, the wife underwent an unsuccessful transfer of three of the frozen embryos. Because the IVF clinic's protocol did not require a husband's consent to frozen embryo transfer, the husband was not consulted and he only learned of the attempt through correspondence from the couple's insurance company. The clinic had a protocol in place for changes of mind, which was not used. It required a written letter, signed and notarized by both husband and wife. The wife subsequently obtained a restraining order against the husband for unspecified reasons. Later that year the husband filed for divorce and moved to restrain the wife's use of the remaining four embryos.

The judge acknowledged that a "dispositional contract" should usually be enforced and acknowledged that such an agreement encourages thoughtful decisions, minimizes the expense and frequency of lawsuits, and balances the protection of procreational liberties while giving a couple and clinic guidance for an "efficient means to resolve such a dispute." "All parties involved, to wit, the gamete providers, the doctors, and the clinicians can rely on the agreement as a fundamental means for resolving disputes which may arrive." The judge also accepted the *Davis* [1.2] court's recognition of embryos as deserving of special respect, and the need to balance the rights of the two gamete providers. Acknowledging that the forty-year-old wife had lost both Fallopian tubes, undergone significant pain and suffering in attempting to have a child, and had limited options for another child, the judge nonetheless found that it would be unfair to the husband and to the child who would be unwanted by him (but to whom he would be obligated for child support under state law) to allow the wife use of the embryos.

The judge also pointed out that the clinic's current "GIFT and IVF handbook" stated that the cryopreservation consent form is "good for one year" and interpreted this as a "recognition that intervening events, often uncontemplated by the couple, will change their situation so dramatically that it would be unfair to restrict them to the choices they choose at a remote date." For long-term storage, he suggested periodic reviews.

The court's reasoning calls into question the enforceability of consents and agreements concerning cryopreservation and, if upheld by a higher court, may raise concerns for clinics attempting to establish reliable procedures and guidelines for their patients and themselves.

1.8(b) Court Decides Cryopreservation Agreements Allowing Former Wife's Use of Embryos Violate Public Policy

Summer 2000

BY T. HORWICH

The highest court in Massachusetts has affirmed a lower court ruling that a woman cannot override her ex-husband's objections in order to become pregnant using embryos created during their former marriage. In a one-page order that initially gave no indication of its rationale, the Massachusetts Supreme Judicial Court (SJC) upheld a lower court decision in *A.Z. v. B.Z.* that ruled in favor of the ex-husband, even though he had signed several cryopreservation agreements in which he specifically consented to her use of the embryos in the event of a separation. It followed that with a full written opinion detailing the basis of its decision.

The high court's affirmation was based on a different and potentially far-reaching basis: "As a matter of public policy, we conclude that forced procreation is not an area amenable to judicial enforcement." Although the court had specific criticisms of the cryopreservation agreement, it concluded that even without those, "we would not enforce an agreement that would compel one donor to become a parent against his or her will."

With that statement, Massachusetts has become the first state high court to unequivocally rule that a couple may not make a binding agreement as to the future use of their frozen embryos for one or the other to become a parent. The court took care to note that its ruling did not necessarily rule out enforceable, binding agreements between patients and clinics or between a couple as to nonprocreative choices, such as, "destruction or donation of the preembryos either for research or implantation in a surrogate." The latter is particularly curious, as it would still make one or both a parent of the resulting child, and may reflect the court's lack of complete understanding of the ARTs.

As to its specific criticisms, the court pointed out that the form was insufficient "in several important respects and does not approach the minimum level of completeness needed to denominate it as an enforceable contract in a dispute between the husband and wife." Amongst those deficiencies, the court noted that the form did not state that the husband and wife intended it to be a binding agreement between themselves in the event of their future disagreement, that it did not contain a "duration" clause, that its use of the undefined term "separated" did not necessarily cover divorce, and, finally, that the couple's conduct wherein the husband signed some of the forms in blank did not adequately demonstrate the husband's true intention as to disposition.

Several questions were left unanswered by the court, including when and under what specific circumstances cryopreservation agreements will be binding. If the court's concern is solely in preventing forced parenthood, it is unclear whether agreements to donate embryos to another infertile couple would be enforceable, or whether the analysis would change if the embryos had been created with one spouse's gametes and a donor. The current draft of model legislation being prepared by the American Bar Association's Reproductive Technology and Genetics Committee addresses this issue by converting a spouse who previously consented, but now objects, into a gamete donor, allowing a related child to be born against the former spouse's objection, but relieving him or her of all parental rights and obligations.

This case is only the third time that a high state court has ruled on disputes over the use of cryopreserved embryos (*Kass v. Kass*, [1.6]; *Davis v. Davis*, [1.2]). It is the first in which one party was seeking to enforce a prior agreement that the embryos could be used to create a child after the couple separated. Both previous cases generally supported the view that prior written agreements about embryo disposition should be enforced, lending some comfort to physicians and patients seeking a reliable means for anticipating future circumstances. Yet, as the Massachusetts court noted, neither involved an agreement in which the husband and wife consented to the use by one spouse to become pregnant in the event they separated in the future. The case is likely to have far-reaching implications in other states as to how such agreements should be drafted and executed and under what circumstances they will be deemed enforceable.

A.Z. v. B.Z., 431 Mass. 150 (Mass. 2000)

1.9 Israeli Court Grants Wife Right to Frozen Embryos over Husband's Objection

Spring 1997

Israel's highest court, sitting in an unprecedented eleven-justice panel, has overturned its own earlier five-justice panel to allow a wife access to frozen embryos over her husband's objections. The now-estranged couple, Ruth and Danny Nahmani, had initially undergone IVF and sought a surrogate as a result of the wife's hysterectomy. Their earlier efforts were largely responsible for Israel's recently enacted surrogacy laws. The couple later separated, the wife refused to divorce, and the husband has since had two children with a new partner he cannot marry.

Ruth Nahmani was initially granted access to the embryos over three years ago, but her husband successfully appealed to the full panel of the Israeli Supreme Court. The court's Chief Justice granted her request and ordered a unique eleven-judge panel to reconsider. The ultimate seven-four ruling in her favor held that having a child is a "basic and existential value both for the individual and society as a whole . . . there is no intrinsic value to the absence of parenthood." The decision is being both hailed and criticized within Israel, as feminists express concerns that while the decision gives women autonomy it also advances a conservative national agenda of population growth and forces fatherhood on men.

Nahmani v. Nahmani, Israeli S.Ct. (full bench),
DNC 240/95 (9/9/96)

1.10 Divorcing Michigan Woman Sues Clinic over Access to Frozen Embryos

Spring 1998

A divorced woman, Sara Bohn, has sued Ann Arbor Reproductive Medicine Associates to attempt to force them to release five frozen embryos to another clinic for implantation. Her ex-husband wants them destroyed. The clinic has refused to release the embryos, absent a court order or custody agreement. The couple, who successfully had one child from treatment at the clinic, subsequently divorced but the divorce settlement reportedly did not address the status or "custody" of the embryos.

Note: The trial court ruled neither ex-spouse could unilaterally dispose of the "zygotes," and granted summary disposition to all defendants, a ruling the appellate court affirmed.

Bohn v. Ann Arbor Reproductive Med. Assocs., P.C.,
1999 Mich. App. LEXIS 2210 (Mich. Ct. App. 1999)

1.11(a) Unwanted Fatherhood Gives Birth to Lawsuit against Program
Winter 1998

A now-divorced man has sued a Boston IVF program for allowing his estranged wife to have a frozen embryo transfer without his knowledge or contemporaneous consent. The couple had already successfully used the IVF Program, resulting in a son and excess frozen embryos. The wife gave birth to a healthy baby girl whom the husband did not want to parent. The man's lawsuit is in the nature of a "wrongful birth" action and includes a claim for the costs of child support for which he will be responsible as the child's father.

1.11(b) Massachusetts Jury Awards Child Support for Frozen Embryo Transfer Consent Case
Spring 2004

A Massachusetts jury has awarded $98,000 as the estimated cost of childrearing and $10,000 for emotional distress to a man whose estranged wife became pregnant with his now seven-year-old daughter using frozen embryos they had created with donor eggs during their marriage. The clinic argued the man knew his wife was trying to have another baby and was obligated to tell them he had changed his mind following the first consent. The jury cleared the two physicians of negligence and malpractice charges but held the clinic liable for breach of contract, characterizing the clinic's cryopreservation form as a binding contract, which the clinic had disputed at trial.

Most programs now require a contemporaneous re-consent at the time of any subsequent transfer, so this dispute and the issues it raises may be relatively unusual and time-limited. Unlike an appellate court's decision, a jury decision carries no weight as precedent even within the same state. The clinic reported it intended to appeal, but no subsequent appeal was filed.

Gladu v. Boston IVF, MA Lawyers Weekly,
32 M.L.W. 1195 (2/9/04) (Middlesex Probate & Fam. Ct. 1/30/04)

1.12(a) New Jersey Court Decides Fate of Frozen Embryos

Spring 1999

Yet another state court has had to wrestle with the legal uncertainties created when a divorcing couple disagrees about disposition of their cryopreserved embryos. In New Jersey, a trial judge recently decided in favor of an ex-wife over control of seven frozen embryos created during the marriage.

The facts stipulated by the parties indicate that the wife, M.B., and the husband, J.B., sought help from a fertility program due to difficulties conceiving and were advised that M.B. suffered from endometriosis resulting in blockage of one of her tubes. J.B. had a normal sperm count. M.B. became pregnant following IVF treatment and gave birth to a baby girl. Six months later, the couple separated, and shortly thereafter began divorce proceedings. From that time on, M.B. took the position that the couple's seven cryopreserved embryos should be discarded, as she no longer wanted to implant them or see them used in any other manner. J.B. claimed he should be able to use the embryos in the future or donate them to another couple. J.B. buttressed his position by arguing that the embryos are "living entities," endowed with a status greater than property. Because of his religious convictions, J.B. explained, he believes in the preservation of human life.

Prior to beginning the IVF treatment, the infertility program had both spouses sign a consent agreement that stated that control and disposition of any cryopreserved embryos belongs to the patient and her partner. A separate "legal statement regarding control and disposition of cryopreserved embryos" was also signed by both parties. The latter statement did not force a final resolution in the event of divorce, however, but instead deferred the problem by stating the embryos would be "relinquished to the IVF Program [in the event of] dissolution of our marriage by Court Order, unless the Court Order specified who takes control and direction of the tissues. . ." Although the program presumably drafted this language with an eye toward avoiding litigation, in fact it forced the judge to decide the case without benefit of a prior statement of intent by the parties.

The New Jersey judge first reviewed the leading case that governs embryo disposition in the absence of a written agreement between the parties, *Davis v. Davis*, 842 S.W. 2d 588 (Tenn. 1992), which established the principles that the mutual wishes of the parties, preferably expressed in a written agreement, control disposition; but that absent such agreement, a balancing test must be applied that weighs the relative interests of the parties in using or not using the embryos. In this case, the Court said, the couple's original reason to create the embryos was to create a child together whom they would raise together in the context of a happy marriage, a "raison d'etre" that no longer existed once they had a child and then divorced. Particularly since the husband had no fertility problems and could go on to have a child himself with another woman, there was no compelling reason why the embryos should continue to be cryopreserved. The court firmly rejected the husband's argument that any so-called "right to life" principle should change this analysis, stating that the embryos were not "living entities," and that the purpose of the IVF procedure was not to "create life" in some abstract sense or to create embryos for use by others, but only to create a particular child as part of a marriage that no longer existed. Therefore, the Court granted M.B.'s motion for summary judgment, allowing her to have the embryos destroyed.

1.12(b) New Jersey Court Orders Frozen Embryos Destroyed
Fall 2000

Affirming a lower court ruling, a New Jersey appellate court has ordered frozen embryos destroyed following a divorce and disposition dispute. The husband had argued that his wife had agreed to donate the embryos, and indeed had offered them to his childless sister. His mother, father, and sister (who did not want the embryos) corroborated his assertion.

Following the reasoning of a recent Massachusetts decision (*A.Z. v. B.Z.*, [1.8]), the New Jersey court ruled that "a contract to procreate is contrary to New Jersey public policy and is unenforceable." It distinguished earlier frozen embryo cases, specifically *Davis v. Davis* [1.2] and *Kass v. Kass* [1.6], on the grounds that despite their "expansive dicta" (language unnecessary to the actual issue and decision of the case) neither enforced an agreement to procreate. The court also made reference to its now-infamous *Baby M* decision (voiding

traditional surrogacy in New Jersey), noting that permitting donation and use of the embryos would, similar to the *Baby M* case, result
in "the impairment, and perhaps termination, of the parental rights
of the wife in the resulting offspring." That, the court noted, can only
be done with "clear and convincing evidence of just cause," which the
court implied was not present in the context of frozen embryos.

Although it ultimately did not decide the case on constitutional
grounds, the court also remarked that, "[e]ven if the wife were re-
lieved of the financial and custodial responsibility for her child, the
fact that her biological child would exist in an environment controlled by strangers is understandably unacceptable to the wife. Arguably, therefore, enforcement of the alleged contract to create a
child would impair the wife's constitutional right not to procreate,
whereas permitting the destruction of the embryos would not effectively impair the husband's reproductive rights."

The court concluded with an approving quote from the Massachusetts decision: "agreements to enter into familial relationships (marriage or parenthood) should not be enforced against individuals who
subsequently reconsider their decisions."

New Jersey is now the second appellate court to recently rule on
public policy grounds that a couple's prior decision to use embryos
for procreation is not enforceable in the event of either's change of
mind. Both courts also distinguished prior cases in a way that may
make it easier for future courts to follow this line of reasoning. Programs with cryopreservation forms may wish to consider adding language to the effect that it cannot predict whether any similar agreements will be held enforceable in the event of a future dispute.

1.12(c) New Jersey Supreme Court to Hear Frozen Embryo Appeal
Winter 2000

Opening the way for another high court pronouncement on the subject of disposition of frozen embryos by divorcing couples, the New
Jersey Supreme Court has now agreed to hear a further appeal of a
recent appellate court decision in that state.

The higher court has now "stayed" the lower court order and for-
bidden the destruction of the embryos pending the ex-husband's further appeal. The couple's divorce settlement had left open the embryo

custody question, and the storage facility has reported it would discard the embryos in the event of a divorce, unless a court orders otherwise.

1.12(d) Court Honors Wife's Current Objection to Donation and Orders Embryos Destroyed
Spring 2001

The New Jersey Supreme Court ruled that the embryos should be destroyed, unless the husband wished to pay for their continued storage (although he cannot use them). The court found that the clinic's consent agreement and its attachment further detailing "control and disposition" of the embryos did not constitute a separate binding contract because it was vague as to the couple's intentions. Instead, the court stated that by the language of the forms, the couple had agreed only that the control and disposition of their embryos would be determined by a court in the event of their divorce. Further, the Supreme Court agreed with the lower courts that the wife's ultimate decision not to procreate should be honored. Thus, an agreement entered into at the time of IVF treatment regarding control and disposition of embryos is enforceable, but subject to the right of the husband or wife to change his or her mind about the disposition of the embryos. The court however, limited its decision to the facts of this case, where the wife wished to avoid procreation and the husband had demonstrated fertility and was capable of fathering additional children. "We express no opinion in respect of a case in which a party who has become infertile seeks use of stored preembryos against the wishes of his or her partner, noting only that the possibility of adoption also may be a consideration, among others, in the court's assessment."

J.B. v. M.B., 170 N.J. 9 (N.J. 2001)

1.13(a) Ex-Husband Seeks Custody of Child Born from Frozen Embryos
Summer 1999

In a "first-of-its-kind" custody suit, an ex-husband in Texas is claiming paternity of a child born to his ex-wife with their frozen embryos, which she used after their divorce was final. The child's birth certificate reflects him as the father and has his last name. A trial judge agreed, naming Don McGill the father of the child and awarding him visitation rights. The child lives with her mother, Mildred Schmidt. That decision is now on appeal.

Several questions were raised by the trial judge, including the applicability of Texas's sperm donor statute. Texas, like Florida, is one of only a handful of states that has passed comprehensive ART legislation. Both states have now had a challenge to the applicability of their law in the context of defining paternity and sperm donors [discussed at 4.15].

At issue are the terms of the parties' agreement regarding Schmidt's use of the embryos to achieve a pregnancy and whether the Texas sperm donor law applies. The consent form the couple signed said only that in the event of divorce the embryos should be disposed of according to their "wishes." Schmidt now claims McGill conditioned his agreement on having no parental or financial responsibilities for any such resulting child. McGill claims they agreed he would be the father of any resulting child. Questioned whether any agreement needed to be in writing; both parties agreed it did not.

Schmidt also argued that, by the time of the embryo transfer, McGill was no longer a "consenting husband" but a "sperm donor" under the law, with no parental rights. McGill's attorney claims the sperm donor provisions do not apply to a man who provides sperm during a marriage to fertilize his wife's eggs. Although McGill's attorney argued that it was in the child's best interest to have a father, he conceded that had there been a written agreement that the embryos should be Schmidt's property, his client would be "out in the cold." Schmidt's attorney claimed a "best interest test was irrelevant to the question of whether McGill had paternity rights, and that, to protect mothers in assisted conception cases from interference from donors and donors from support obligations, public policy required recognizing sole parental rights in the mother absent a clear contrary agreement." Schmidt asked that the case be remanded to a jury to determine the terms of the oral agreement. McGill has asked the court to uphold the determination of his paternity in the absence of a clear, written agreement to the contrary.

National Post, 3/25/99; Associated Press, 3/27/99

1.13(b) Texas Appeals Court Upholds Divorced Father's Paternity Rights to Child Born from Frozen Embryo

Spring 2000

A Texas appellate court has upheld Donald McGill's legal paternity of a child born to his ex-wife after a frozen embryo transfer that occurred with his consent and after their divorce.

The court's detailed analysis of the applicable law is very instructive. First, the court rejected Schmidt's suggestions that the Texas artificial insemination law should apply, stating unequivocally that there was no authority to suggest artificial insemination is analogous to IVF. Next, it rejected both the application of Texas's laws on the parental rights of children born through egg or embryo donation and cases cited by Schmidt that relied upon the parties' expressed intentions in ART donation cases, concluding that those authorities did not address the narrow facts of a "biological father seeking paternal rights to a child born from his ex-wife through IVF from embryos conceived during marriage."

The court narrowed the issue to determining paternity under the specific facts presented: a consenting biological ex-husband who wished to retain his paternity rights. Because of the complex legal issues, the court said it wanted to defer to the legislature to enact laws deciding the rights of parties involved in IVF.

Whether the court would have permitted McGill to avoid paternity obligations if he so desired is unclear. The court's reluctance, however, to rely on related, but not precisely applicable, ART statutes should serve as a cautionary note to all involved in providing or utilizing ART services without the benefit of clear legal guidelines. The court also rejected Schmidt's request for over $300,000 in attorney's fees.

In the interest of O.G.M., 988 S.W.2d 473 (Tex. Ct. App. 1999)

(case dismissed 6/15/00)

1.14(a) "Twin" Embryo Mix-up Lawsuit Filed—Baby Returned

Summer 1999

A New Jersey couple has sued both an IVF clinic and a New York couple who were also patients of the clinic after their embryos were mistakenly transferred to the wife of the other couple along with that couple's own embryos. The transfer resulted in the birth of two children, one of whom is the genetic child of Deborah Perry-Rogers and Robert Rogers of New Jersey. The Rogers are black; the other couple, the Fasanos, are white. The Rogers only obtained custody of the four-month-old child after filing suit against the program, two physicians, an embryologist, and the other couple. In the lawsuit they sought custody of the child and claimed negligence, malpractice, and breach of contract by the physicians. After learning the New York couple was surrendering the child to them after confirmatory DNA testing, their lawyer has said they intend to drop the couple as defendants from their lawsuit. The Rogers have also requested the court declare them their son's parents.

The Fasanos' attorney says they will insist on a visitation agreement so the boys will know each other as brothers. Some commentators have referred to the boys as "twins." Ethicists have raised questions as to the likelihood of other such mix-ups occurring undetected, whether more regulation is needed or whether existing malpractice suits sufficiently deter such mix-ups.

1.14(b) Visitation Arrangements Lands "Twin" Embryo Mix-up Back in Court

Fall 1999

Custody of a six-month-old child is now back in court. Deborah Perry-Rogers and Robert Rogers refused to comply with a visitation agreement for their biological son, Joseph, which they had entered into with the couple who carried him to term, saying it is "unreasonable" and "one-sided." The agreement included a monthly overnight visit for the child, another eight-hour weekend visit per month, one week during the summer, and specified holidays. Reportedly it also contained a $200,000 damage provision for any failure to follow the terms of the agreement. The Rogers' attorney reports his clients became concerned the Fasanos would use the visits to assert "their authority as parents" over their son. Donna Fasano, the woman who carried both boys, has reportedly said, "God gave me Joe for a reason," that she considers the children brothers, herself one of Joseph's two mothers, and that they "want to be a part of his life forever."

The Fasanos' attorney has accused the Rogers and their attorney of fraud, but the Rogers' attorney suggested his clients had no choice but to enter into the initial agreement to get custody of their child. The judge, who is coincidentally a twin, has ordered psychiatric exams on the babies to help assess the impact of separation and also ordered interim visitation to continue, without overnights.

New York Post, 6/29/99; Daily News, 6/25/99

1.14(c) No Amicable Resolution Near in "Gestational Twin" Case
Summer 2000

A case that began when a fertility clinic mistakenly transferred embryos to the wrong woman has escalated into a protracted legal battle over the child born as a result, disappointing many who had hoped that the parties' competing claims of parenthood would be resolved amicably.

The relationship between the two couples has become increasingly strained, as reportedly Mrs. Fasano continues to refer to herself as the boy's mother and the Rogers feel the heavy visitation schedule is an inappropriate burden. In February, the Rogers asked the New York State Appellate Division to void the visitation agreement, arguing that once the court decided that they were the boy's legal parents, it did not have the authority to order visitation with people who were strangers under the law. According to their attorney, "the law does not recognize what the Fasanos have been claiming—that the children are gestational siblings." After expedited consideration, the appeals court stayed the lower court's order, thus stopping the visitation until a five-judge panel can hear the case in June.

Then, in March, the battle escalated sharply as the Fasanos decided to turn the case into a full-blown custody fight over the boy, rather than simply a dispute over visitation. Relying on a procedural technicality, the Fasanos asked that the original decision declaring the Rogers Joseph's legal parents and giving them custody be overturned. Legal experts watching the case agree that there is no clear precedent on which the case can be decided; cases and statutes involving adoption, surrogacy, and traditional family law all may come into play. Ultimately, the court's decision could have importance beyond cases involving mistakes by clinics in transferring embryos to the wrong patients and also help define which biological or social relationships are sufficient to establish parenthood of children created through ART. Multi-million dollar lawsuits against the physicians involved in the erroneous embryo transfer are still also pending.

Perry-Rogers v. Fasano, 276 A.D.2d 67

(N.Y. App. Div. 2000)

1.14(d) Appellate Decision Denies Visitation in Baby Mix-up Case
Winter 2000

A unanimous appellate court has now ruled that the embryo mix-up that resulted in Donna Fasano giving birth to both her own son and the biological son of Deborah and Robert Rogers did not entitle her to any rights to the second child.

Notwithstanding existing New York law, which presumes the woman who gives birth to the child is the mother, the court ruled that the case was similar to a mix-up of newborns at a hospital, which should, "simply be corrected at once." The Fasanos have reportedly appealed this latest decision.

1.14(e) "Embryo Twins" Legally Separated
Summer 2001

After three years, Deborah Perry-Rogers and Robert Rogers may call their son theirs and theirs alone. On May 8, the New York Court of Appeals, the state's highest court, affirmed the lower court's ruling that Donna Fasano, the woman who gave birth to him due to an embryo transfer mix-up, has no rights to the child.

Counsel for the Fasanos has said they will consider a federal case on constitutional grounds, and both couples have lawsuits pending against the clinic.

Perry-Rogers v. Fasano, 276 A.D.2d 67 (N.Y. App. Div.

2000); *Perry-Rogers v. Obasaju*, 282 A.D.2d 231 (N.Y.

App. Div. 2001); *Fasano v. Nash*, 282 A.D.2d 277 (N.Y.

App. Div. 2001)

1.14(f) Couples Settle Embryo Mix-up Lawsuits against New York Fertility Clinic
Winter 2005

The tort lawsuits against the medical providers arising out of the 1998 embryo mix-up that resulted in one patient carrying both her own IVF child and that of another couple has now been settled for undisclosed sums.

Kaisernetwork.org, *Daily Reproductive Health Report,*
9/15/04; *Newsday.com,* 9/13/04

1.15(a) Two New Frozen Embryo Disputes Erupt in Illinois
Winter 1999

Two frozen embryo divorce disputes have been coincidentally assigned to the same judge. In the first, Tiffany and John Morahan are attempting to resolve the disposition of their fourteen frozen embryos, among other issues, including issues involving the couple's toddler triplets conceived from the same batch of embryos.

Morahan v. Morahan; Cook Cty., Ill.; *Cook Cty. Reporter,*
10/13/99

1.15(b) Divorcing Illinois Couple Fights over Whether the Wife May Use Their Two Remaining Frozen Embryos
December 1999

The terms of a second Illinois couple's cryopreservation agreement, which may be determinative, have not been revealed to date. Todd Ginestra contends the couple agreed not to cryopreserve any unused embryos. The hospital's attorney reportedly contends the hospital would not have agreed to toss out excess embryos after only a single transfer without first cryopreserving, but would also not do a transfer procedure without contemporaneous and specific consent of both the wife and husband. The wife is a nurse and the husband a medical resident. The hospital attorney describes the center's role as limited to a holder of the two embryos and says that it is prepared to "abide by whatever the court tells us to do." The trial court has temporarily enjoined Margaret Hale from having the two embryos transferred and has scheduled further hearings.

Ginestra v. Hale; Cook Cty., Ill. (temp. ruling
9/29/99); *Chicago Tribune,* 9/30/99

1.15(c) Divorce Settlement Keeps Embryos in Limbo While Upholding Couple's Right to Decide Their Fate
Summer 2000

The Ginestra-Hale divorce settlement now includes an agreement to delay a decision about disposition of their two remaining frozen embryos. Todd Ginestra objected to his wife's intention to attempt a pregnancy with the two cryopreserved embryos and wanted them destroyed. The embryos were the remainder of five embryos created during the marriage in an IVF cycle that ultimately failed. Ginestra contended in the court proceedings that he had never consented to having the unused embryos frozen in the first place.

Under the settlement, the couple has agreed that the embryos will remain preserved for fifty years unless they can mutually agree about their disposition. The settlement stipulates that each of them must designate someone in their will to represent them in their decision in case one of them dies before the other. According to Hale, both parties were pleased with the settlement, since it took the decision out of the hands of the courts and put it back with the couple.

The hospital that performed the IVF and cryopreservation procedures was drawn into the lawsuit as a result of Ginestra's contention that he had not consented to the cryopreservation. The hospital has disputed that claim, but the details of any consent forms that may have been signed by the couple have not been released. It is not known, for example, whether the couple made a prior decision about disposition and whether their current positions are consistent with such prior choices. The hospital agreed to pay $25,000 to the parties for potential attorneys' fees and for releasing it from all liability.

Ginestra v. Hale, Cook Cty., Ill.; *Chicago Tribune*,
3/25/00

1.16 Debate Continues in Australia over New Frozen Embryo Legislation
Spring 2000

Despite a parliamentary committee's recommendations, the West Australia government remains stalled on the Human Reproductive Technology Act. Labor health spokeswoman Sheila McHale has urged the government to tighten storage regulations of IVF frozen embryos. Under the present act, frozen embryos may remain in storage for three years, with a possible extension to five years. The parliamentary committee recommends the storage time be increased to ten years, but that couples be contacted at five and nine and a half years to reaffirm their desire to retain the embryos. While Health Minister John Day expects the amended legislation to include a finite period, the length of that period is still at issue.

> *Note*: In 2003, the Human Reproductive Technology Amendment Bill of 2003 allowed for an increase in the storage period for embryos from three to ten years.

News Interactive, News Limited, 11/26/99

1.17 Canadian IVF Clinic Hit with Second Lawsuit over Embryo Mix-ups
Spring 2000

After settling a lawsuit in which it admitted transferring embryos into the wrong woman, the London Health Sciences Centre (LHSC) has now been sued by a second couple, Shanna and Peter Hoenig, who claim their three embryos were thawed without their consent. The clinic claims this second suit resulted from a misunderstanding when the couple failed to appear for their transfer. The couple, who say the clinic left them a voice mail message that they retrieved after the embryos had expired, called it "ludicrous" to suggest they would fail to show for something as important as an embryo transfer. The couple had already had two IVF cycles and a frozen embryo transfer when they say they told the clinic they needed a break before trying to use their only remaining embryos. The couple claims they brought their lawsuit only after being assured their mix-up was unprecedented and then reading about the first couple's out-of-court settlement with the same clinic.

London Free Press, 9/18/99

1.18(a) British Parents Win Lawsuit against Clinic after Triplet Birth
Winter 2000

A British couple who gave birth to IVF triplets has won a lawsuit against the Sheffield clinic that transferred three embryos to the mother. The court ruled for the couple on a breach of contract claim. The couple, Patricia and Peter Thompson, claimed they had agreed with the clinic to only transfer two embryos, not three, and are seeking damages for the costs associated with raising a third child. After learning of the multiple pregnancy, the couple declined a fetal reduction. They have described raising the triplets, born in 1997, as a "joy" but "absolutely exhausting." Peter Thompson, age fifty-seven and with three adult children from a prior marriage, had a heart attack and bypass surgery three months after the triplets' birth and has given up his work to help care for the children.

There was no written agreement on the number of embryos to be transferred, but the couple claimed that they and the doctor had earlier agreed on two. According to published reports of the case, the clinic argued that the patient was told on the day of the procedure that three embryos were to be transferred, was shown them on the screen, and consented. The doctor testified that she did not remember this specific discussion but that it was the clinic's standard practice to agree on such a number with patients beforehand. The clinic director denied the suggestion by the couple's attorney that the three-embryo transfer was because the clinic was under pressure to raise success rates. The court will rule on damages at a later date.

Thompson v. Sheffield Fertility Centre,
Associated Press, 11/18/00

1.18(b) British Case of Extra Embryo Implant Settles
Summer 2001

A sum of £20,000 has been accepted by Patricia Thompson, a British woman who gave birth to triplets after doctors implanted three embryos despite her alleged consent to transfer only two embryos. The mother and her husband claimed that the extra child forced them to abandon their business, causing loss of earnings. The clinic argued that it is against public policy to award damages for the cost of raising a healthy child. The settlement sum will go toward the woman's legal costs and will not result in any profit to her.

BBC News, 2/23/01

1.19 Federal Appellate Court Finds Fetal Tissue Research Ban Unconstitutional

Spring 2001

A federal appellate court has struck down Arizona's state laws that banned fetal tissue research as too vague and unclear to pass constitutional muster. The Ninth Circuit upheld a lower court's decision to permanently enjoin the statute. The law was originally enacted as part of Arizona's regulation of abortion, which, like many states, passed such laws in the wake of *Roe v. Wade*. Similar laws in many states have been cited as reasons why physicians have feared performing embryo research or even embryo donation. The decision brings to four the number of courts that have struck down such laws.

The lawsuit was brought by a group of doctors and patients, including Robert Tamis, M.D., who the court noted "specialized in fertility treatments" and had been the target of a potential criminal investigation years earlier for having "endeavored to study" whether drugs passed through the placental wall by studying the effects on the fetus of a drug ingested by a woman before an induced abortion. Dr. Tamis stated he was "still uncertain" about the proper interpretation of the law. The plaintiff patients suffered from Parkinson's disease and claimed the law prevented them from receiving fetal tissue transplants; the physicians claimed the law dissuaded them from providing various medical services for fear of prosecution. Violation of the law was a criminal felony and penalties included prison, fines, censure, and loss of license.

Unlike some such statutes, the law applied only to tissue obtained from aborted fetuses: "[a] person shall not knowingly use any human fetus or embryos, living or dead, or any parts, organs, or fluids of any such fetus or embryos resulting from an induced abortion in any manner for any medical experimentation or scientific or medical investigation purposes except as is strictly necessary to diagnose a disease or condition in the mother of the fetus or embryo and only if the abortion was performed because of such disease or condition. This section shall not prohibit any routine pathological examinations conducted by a medical examiner or hospital laboratory provided such pathological examination is not a part of or in any way related to any medical or scientific experimentation."

Criticizing the law's failure to define what it called its "key terms," including "experimentation," "investigation," and "routine," the court concluded that the challenged statutes failed to establish any "core" of unquestionably prohibited activities. Without a definition either within the law or within the medical community, the lower court suggested any examination of post-abortion fetal tissue "beyond simply mounting it on a slide would expose doctors to criminal liability." The physicians also pointed out that it was difficult to know at what stage or point in time "experiments" become "treatment." One expert testified, "virtually every procedure with a therapeutic objective is experimental to some extent."

The state's defenses of the statute were unpersuasive. It argued the statute only narrowly applied to aborted fetuses and that a physician could avoid any liability concerns "by performing no tests or other procedures on fetal tissue from induced abortions." The court found this ignored the statutory exceptions and asked whether or not a DNA test on fetal tissue would violate the law. The state also argued the law was not vague because the physicians all agreed as to what procedures would violate it. The court rejected that argument, finding the law no clearer than those struck by the Fifth, Seventh, and Tenth Circuits, only that at this time the plaintiff physicians agreed about the risks of prosecution they were not willing to endure.

One of the three judges on the panel wrote a separate concurring opinion outlining his concerns about the effects such a law could have on reproductive technologies and choices for patients. In it, he took note that the statute being struck was part of a broader statutory scheme enacted after *Roe* to "curb access to abortion" and should not be examined in isolation. He noted the law's prohibition on aborted fetal tissue research could "burden the rights of women and couples to make both present and future reproductive choices," and that such research and experiments "may foster the development of reproductive technology that is related to reproductive choices." He concluded by noting that none of the three state interests identified by the U.S. Supreme Court in regulating abortion—protecting the health of the woman, the potential life of the fetus, and regulating the medical profession—justified Arizona's prohibition on fetal experimentation.

The Ninth Circuit court concluded that a criminal statute that provides "no guidance as to where the state should draw the line between experiment and treatment gives doctors no constructive notice, and gives police, prosecutors, juries, and judges no standards to focus the statute's reach" could not stand. In doing so, it joins the other three federal circuits that have been called upon to interpret state fetal experimentation laws. All have struck such laws down as unconstitutional.

Forbes v. Napolitano, 2000 U.S. App. LEXIS
38596 (9th Cir.) (12/29/00)

1.20 Challenge to British Embryo Transfer Guidelines Heard in Court
Summer 2001

The head of Britain's most successful IVF clinic, Dr. Mohammed Taranissi, and his forty-six-year-old patient have now argued their case in a London courtroom, seeking a judicial review of the Human Fertilisation and Embryology Authority (HFEA) guidelines that limit embryo transfers to three embryos per transfer. While the HFEA deems the risk of triplet pregnancies and unhealthy babies unacceptable, Taranissi has argued that the rule is an unfair restriction on doctors' freedom to use their medical judgment in treating patients on a case-by-case basis.

> *Note*: Ultimately the British High Court dismissed Dr. Taranissi's petition, finding there was "no arguable case to go to a full hearing." HFEA subsequently announced a change in policy to reduce the number of embryos that may be transferred in a single IVF treatment cycle from three to two, to encourage best practice in clinics and reduce the number of multiple births resulting from in vitro fertilization.

Guardian, 4/23/01

1.21 Court Reverses, Upholds Cryopreservation Agreement in Frozen Embryo Dispute
Fall 2002

The Washington State Supreme Court has issued its long-awaited opinion in a case involving the disposition of two frozen embryos embroiled in a divorcing couple's lawsuit. In upholding the couple's prior agreement, the court gave neither party what it sought. The couple had one child born from the initial embryo creation, which involved both an egg donor and a gestational carrier. The husband wanted the remaining embryos donated to an out-of-state couple. The wife wanted them implanted in a gestational carrier to carry and birth a sibling for the couple's child born from the initial embryo transfer. Both the egg donor and previous gestational carrier had supported her in her claim. Neither of the parties sought to have the embryos destroyed.

Despite their competing claims to use the embryos, the court upheld the provision in the former couple's cryopreservation agreement with their IVF program to thaw and discard the embryos after five years under a strict contract analysis. The decision reversed the Court of Appeals decision, which had awarded the embryos to the ex-husband. In embracing a contract analysis, the court's decision lines up with an earlier previous frozen embryo decision from New York (*Kass v. Kass*, [1.6]) and opposes the first such decision from Tennessee (*Davis v. Davis*, [1.2] and more recent ones in Massachusetts (*A.Z. v .B.Z.*, [1.8]) and New Jersey (*J.B. v. M.B.*, [1.12]).

One consistent point, however, is that by upholding the prior agreement, neither party could use the embryos against the other's wishes. To date, no high state court has reached such a decision, by whatever analytical route.

Litowitz v. Litowitz, 146 Wash.2d 514
(Wash. 2002); *amended by*
In re Marriage of Litowitz, 53 P.3d 516 (Wash.
2002) (concurring opinion amended to partially
dissent and recommend remand on contract,
equity and public policy rationales)

1.22 White Couple Gives Birth to Black Twins after British Clinic Mix-up
Fall 2002

A white couple living in Britain has given birth to black twins, apparently the result of a mix-up by their infertility clinic. The exact nature of the clinic's mistake is unknown, whether the children resulted from a misimplanted fertilized embryo or from a mistake in fertilizing the woman's own eggs. Court injunctions prohibit the media from publishing details of the case, including the names of the parties, the clinic, or the hospital. Reportedly the white couple and a black couple who also underwent in vitro fertilization at the clinic each want custody of the children, and the case is expected to be heard in court in October. Similar cases have been reported in the United States and the Netherlands, involving both mistransferred embryos and misfertilized eggs.

The case has sparked much controversy, not only over how the error could have occurred and can be avoided in the future, but also suggestions that this case is just a more obvious example—due to the interracial nature of the error—of an error occurring more frequently than acknowledged within ART programs.

Globe and Mail, 7/9/02; *Guardian*, 7/9/02;
Scotsman.com, 7/10/02

1.23(a) California Custody Battle Ongoing over Child Born through Embryo Mix-up

Winter 2002

A California case is pending over the custody of a child born over a year and a half ago to a single woman who thought she had achieved her IVF pregnancy using both anonymous donor egg and donor sperm. The pregnancy was apparently the inadvertent result of an embryo transfer from the same group of embryos created by a married couple, who had used donor egg and husband sperm and who were cycling at the same time. That couple gave birth to a girl; the single woman to a boy. The patients became aware of the mix-up when the children were almost a year old, reportedly through an anonymous letter to the state and instigation of a state medical board investigation after which, with the doctor's encouragement, the three patients met in January in an unsuccessful attempt to work out an informal resolution. A month later, the married couple sued the single woman for custody. The lawsuit is currently pending.

The single woman has since sued the medical program for malpractice. Egg donation combined with an inadvertent embryo mix-up presents a unique challenge in defining maternity and paternity. By agreement, the parties are not making public comments. Attempts to mediate the case have been unsuccessful to date.

Mercury News, 8/2/02

1.23(b) California Court of Appeals Affirms "Split" Parentage in Embryo Mix-up Case

Fall 2003

Two mothers were one too many, and no father was one too few, for an appellate court asked to determine parentage of a child born through an embryo mix-up. The two-year-old child, known as "Daniel B.," has been declared the legal child of Susan, the single woman who birthed him, and Robert, the married genetic father whose embryo was inadvertently transferred to her. In affirming the lower court's ruling, the court rejected both the single mother's claim to sole parentage and the wife's claim of motherhood. The facts and the court's analysis raise significant issues about parentage in the face of such mix-ups.

The court ruled that Robert could not be characterized as a "donor" within the meaning of California's donor statute, because he did not intend to inseminate anyone other than his wife; that Susan's claim of a right to sole parentage was better suited to the legislature; and that any constitutional claims on behalf of Daniel to a "stable, permanent placement" was an argument for a future potential custody claim by the father and his wife.

The court also rejected the wife's arguments, ruling she lacked legal standing under California law because she has no biological relation to the child and rejected any application under these facts of that state's statute that allowed "any interested person" to bring an action to determine a mother-child relationship. The court quoted approvingly the lower court's finding that "there really is only one mother in this case at this point." Any contractual rights Denise had were to the embryos, "but now what we're talking about is a live person, not an embryo." The court also refused to extend either of the landmark California cases of *Johnson v. Calvert* [6.1] (intended genetic mother, not gestational carrier, found to be mother) or *Jaycee B. v. Superior Court et al.* [6.19] (husband liable for child support as father of child born via donated egg and sperm to gestational carrier with his consent). The court noted that, if it were to "invoke the concept of intended mother here, which party would qualify? Both and neither. Susan intended to be the mother of the child created from an embryo implanted in her uterus that day at the clinic—but not that embryo. . . . Denise intended to be the mother of the child created from this very embryo—but not at that time, and she did not intend for another woman to bear the child." An appeal and further hearings on custody and visitation are anticipated.

Robert B. v. Susan B., 109 Cal. App. 4th 1109
(Cal. Ct. App. 2003) *review denied* 2003 Cal.
LEXIS 6671 (Cal. 2003)

1.24 HFEA Announces Change to Code of Practice for Embryo Storage and Destruction
Fall 2003

Although not passed, a bill introduced in the United Kingdom's Parliament involving frozen embryos and aimed at protecting both partners involved in IVF treatments has resulted in a change of practice in that country regarding stored embryos. HFEA has announced recently it is changing what is known as a "code of practice" to require consent of both parties to continue storing embryos.

The bill and change stemmed from an earlier incident where embryos were destroyed at the request of an ex-husband without notice to the ex-wife because donated eggs had been used. The change of practice means women in similar positions will have to be given reasonable notice. HFEA has announced guidelines to clinics to take all reasonable steps to inform each of the parties in writing or by telephone before allowing any embryos to be destroyed. To prevent destructions, however, court intervention will still be necessary.

IVF.net, 5/24/03

1.25 Iowa Supreme Court Freezes Embryos Pending Mutual Consent
Spring 2004

The Iowa Supreme Court has become the latest high state court to rule on the disposition of a divorcing couple's frozen embryos. That court upheld a trial court's order that neither spouse of a divorcing couple may use or dispose of the couple's seventeen frozen embryos without the consent of the other party, or what it called "contemporaneous mutual consent." The couple had signed an "Embryo Storage Agreement," which explicitly acknowledged that their frozen embryos would be used for "transfer, release or disposition only with the signed approval of both Client Depositors," and the court rejected each of the ex-wife's arguments to use the embryos to have a child over her ex-husband's current objection.

The court disagreed with the wife's arguments that public policy should support her right to procreate and should also invalidate any agreement that would allow her husband to back out of his prior agreement to become a parent. Instead, the court ruled, ". . . [w]e think judicial enforcement of an agreement between a couple regarding their future family and reproductive choices would be against the public policy of this state." The court held that agreements entered into at the time of IVF are enforceable and binding on the parties, subject to the right of either party to change his or her mind about disposition up to the point of the use or destruction of any stored embryo. The court's decision is in line with recent rulings from Massachusetts, New Jersey, and Washington. The court took note of "surveys . . . that suggest [couples] may be prone to changing their minds while their embryos remain frozen." In the event that the parties reach a "stalemate" as to the use of the embryos, the court ruled the embryos should be stored indefinitely until both parties reach agreement, with the party opposing destruction bearing the storage costs. The court rejected the wife's argument to apply a "best interest" test as "simply not suited to the resolution of disputes over the control of frozen embryos." It also reviewed the varying arguments used by different courts and commentators to interpret and decide whether to enforce prior cyropreservation disposition documents and struck something of a middle ground by not employing a strict contract analysis but also not rejecting the enforceability of those agreements under some circumstances. The court also took note of the role and needs of the fertility clinic. It noted that "in fairness to the medical facility that is a party to the agreement, . . . any change of intention must be communicated in writing to all parties in order to reopen the disposition issues covered by the agreement. It also noted that agreements serve an important purpose in "defining and governing the relationship between the couple and the medical facility," and it is that relationship that these "dispositional contracts" are designed to address.

In re Marriage of Witten, 672 N.W.2d 768 (Iowa 2003)

1.26 Australia Grants Licenses for Human Embryo Research

Summer 2004

The Embryo Research Licensing Committee of the National Health and Medical Research Council in Australia has issued the country's first licenses allowing research on excess human embryos. The licenses provide strict regulations on the research, including that the embryos are no longer required for IVF procedures and the couple has given their informed consent.

> Media Release, National Health and Medical
> Research Council, 4/16/04

1.27(a) Trial Court's Controversial Frozen Embryo Ruling Sparks Reactions

Spring 2005

In a case generating national publicity, an Illinois trial judge has ruled that a frozen embryo is a human being and refused to dismiss a "wrongful death" suit filed on its behalf after an IVF program accidentally failed to freeze a couple's embryos.

1.27(b) Appellate Court Reverses "Wrongful Death" Ruling

Spring 2009

The Illinois Appeals Court has ruled that a couple whose embryo was inadvertently improperly frozen by an IVF program may not bring an action under that state's Wrongful Death Act, which permits suits for harm to an in utero fetus as part of an attack or accident against a pregnant woman. The court ruled that the Illinois law did not apply to IVF or IVF embryos that had not been implanted.

> *Miller v. Am. Infertility Group of Ill.*, 844 N.E.2d
> 424 (Ill. 2006), *rev'd*, 897 N.E.2d 837
> (Ill. App. Ct. 2008)

1.28 Pope Pronounces IVF Embryos Have Same Rights as "Every Human Life"

Spring 2006

Pope Benedict has repeated and extended the Vatican's position with a specific edict that preimplantation IVF embryos have the same rights as born children or later-stage fetuses. Opening a Vatican-sponsored conference on the ethics surrounding such embryos, he moved beyond the 1995 encyclical, which did not explicitly address preimplantation embryos. Referring to the "sacred and inviolable character of every human life," the Pope proclaimed "[t]his moral judgment is valid already at the beginnings of life of an embryo, before it is implanted in the womb of the mother. . . ."

Associated Press, 2/28/06

1.29(a) HFEA Rule Requiring Mutual Consent Upheld
Spring 2006

The European Court of Human Rights has ruled that Natalie Evans, a British woman left infertile following cancer treatment, cannot use the six frozen embryos she had created before treatment with her former fiancée in 2001 to now have a baby against his wishes. Evans had been advised to wait two years after treatment for ovarian cancer, during which time the couple separated. Under the Human Fertilisation and Embryology (HFEA) Act, consent from both partners is required at every stage of the IVF process, including implantation. Evans unsuccessfully argued in the British courts that her ex-partner should not be allowed to withdraw his earlier consent to the creation, storage, and use of the embryos. After exhausting all avenues of appeal in the United Kingdom, Evans turned to the European Court of Human Rights based in Strasbourg, France, which rules on violations of the European Convention on Human Rights, and unsuccessfully argued that ordering the destruction of her embryos would breach Article 8 of the Convention, which guarantees the "right to . . . family life" and is in violation of discrimination laws. The Court of Human Rights upheld HFEA. Evans has one final avenue of appeal to the Grand Chamber, a panel of seventeen European judges. Evans has reportedly garnered much sympathy, with some commentators using it as an example of the current inequity between the science of preserving male and female gametes. October 2006 marks the time after which the five-year maximum embryo storage period dictated by British law expires, thus the Court urged the British government to preserve the embryos while the appeal is considered.

www.theherald.co.uk, 3/8/06

1.29(b) Final Frozen Embryo Appeal Lost in Europe

Spring 2007

British cancer survivor Natalie Evans has lost her final appeal to use six frozen embryos over her former partner's objection. The seventeen-member Grand Chamber of the European Court of Human Rights affirmed the British courts that no violations of law had occurred. Evans tried, but failed, to demonstrate that there was both discrimination and human rights violations (for the embryos and herself under privacy and family life principles) under the European Convention of Human Rights. The Grand Chamber noted that the rules were clear, told to Evans, and fairly balanced her and her former partner's rights. No further avenues of appeal are available.

Press release issued by the Registrar of the
European Court of Human Rights, 4/10/07;
various sources, 4/11/07

1.30(a) Texas Court Upholds Couple's Disposition Agreement on Frozen Embryos

Spring 2006

In a case of first impression in Texas, a state appellate court has ruled that an ART program's written consent signed by a couple, Randy and Augusta Roman, and specifying that their frozen embryos be discarded in the event of divorce was valid. The ruling reversed a trial court's award of frozen embryos to the wife, who had wanted to use them for procreation. After determining the program's "Informed Consent for Cryopreservation of Embryos," which the court termed an "embryo agreement," was consistent with public policy, the court ruled solely as a matter of contract law. Although it reviewed most of the cases from other states, it was able to sidestep controversial constitutional issues such as the right not to have children against one's will or how to characterize embryos. That issue has been addressed in only a few of these cases, where the initial agreement was for one partner to use the embryos for procreation, and resulted in a refusal to enforce such a prior choice.

The opinion thus falls into line with other states that have ruled that a divorcing couple's prior embryo storage agreement, at least as to discarding unused embryos, is enforceable and a proper subject of a valid contract. Texas law expressly permits parties to withdraw their consent to any ART procedure prior to placement of genetic material, and the court noted that neither party had withdrawn their consent to the embryo disposition provisions. The court also rejected the ex-wife's suggestion that the medication she was taking might have affected her mental state. As the court concluded, "We believe that allowing the parties voluntarily to decide the disposition of frozen embryos in advance of cryopreservation, subject to mutual change of mind, jointly expressed, best serves the existing public policy of this State and the interests of the parties." The case suggests, once again, that carefully drafted cryopreservation disposition agreements as to nonprocreative choices will be enforced as consistent with public policy.

1.30(b) New Frozen Embryo Appeal Raises Constitutional Issues
Summer 2007

A wife's pending appeal of a decision that allowed her husband to stop her from using their frozen embryos is raising potentially significant constitutional issues with both sides threatening to go to the U.S. Supreme Court if they lose before the Texas Supreme Court. On the eve of returning to their IVF clinic for a fresh embryo transfer, Randy Roman informed his wife that he was dissatisfied with their marriage and unwilling to go forward with the scheduled transfer. The couple therefore told the clinic the next morning to freeze the embryos. They are now litigating whether or not the wife may force the husband to allow her to use them. Her somewhat novel argument is that the program consent forms they signed three weeks before the IVF cycle, and which recognized the right to a change of mind and destruction in the event of a divorce, was only intended to apply to leftover embryos, not all embryos. Her attorneys are also arguing that a woman should have the right to control embryos just as she would a pregnancy. Many commentators have suggested the case raises right-to-life issues that may take on more significance with a newly composed, more conservative Supreme Court that in the 2006–2007 term cut back on the protections of *Roe v. Wade* with its partial birth abortion ruling.

1.30(c) U.S. Supreme Court Refuses to Hear Texas Frozen Embryo Dispute

Spring 2008

Augusta Roman's final attempt to gain access to frozen embryos that her husband refused to allow her to implant when they were fresh or since appears to have met a final dead end. The U.S. Supreme Court has declined to hear the case, leaving the Texas state court ruling intact. Some observers had predicted that the high court might take the case as a vehicle to express more conservative "right to life" views of the status of IVF embryos.

Roman v. Roman, 193 S.W.3d 40 (Tex. App.
2006), *cert. denied*, 2008 U.S. LEXIS 2480

1.31 Couples Win Exception to HFEA Rule on Frozen Embryo Storage Limits

Fall 2006

Pointing up the unpredictability of individual situations and blanket rules, HFEA has backed away from its five-year limit for storing frozen embryos intended to be used by a gestational surrogate in an individual case. The current rules allow ten years' storage for a woman to use her own embryos, but only five if they were created with the intention of having another woman carry the pregnancy.

The couple gave birth to one child, now six years old, after which the mother, Michelle Hickman, age thirty-three, had an emergency hysterectomy. Wanting a large family, the couple created and stored embryos and has been searching for a gestational carrier. Friends who had volunteered were ruled out medically, and the five-year storage limit was reached in May 2006. The clinic had continued to store the embryos, in violation of their license, while the couple appealed to HFEA for permission to continue to store the embryos and export them to a clinic outside of Great Britain. Although refusing further comment, HFEA noted that storage time can extend beyond its stated limits in "extremely extenuating circumstances," and the couple's clinic has recently informed them the time line is now "open-ended" for them to locate a clinic abroad willing to accept the embryos.

Timesonline.co.uk, 8/3/06

1.32 Arizona Court Denies Wrongful Death Claim for Lost Embryos
Winter 2006

Frozen embryos that were either lost or destroyed by the Mayo Clinic may not form the basis for a "wrongful death" suit according to a ruling by the Arizona Court of Appeals. A couple's missing five of ten frozen embryos may give rise to legal claims for breach of contract, breach of fiduciary duty, or loss of irreplaceable property, but as days-old "preembryos," the court ruled that they cannot be defined as a human person or viable fetus capable of life outside a womb. The case arose after a couple had their frozen embryos moved from the Mayo Clinic to the Arizona Center for Fertility Studies after two unsuccessful transfer attempts at the first program. They achieved a pregnancy and birth, but on their second attempt reportedly discovered that five of their remaining ten frozen embryos were not in the straws that had been shipped between the two clinics. Their suit was initially denied by a lower court in its entirety but the appellate court reinstated all but the wrongful death claim. The court ruled that any redefinition of personhood or when life begins was a function for the legislature, and that it was speculative whether a child would have been born absent the loss. The court opinion echoed that of other appellate courts by defining "preembryos" as occupying an "interim category between mere human tissue and persons because of their potential to become persons."

Jeter v. Mayo Clinic Arizona,
121 P.3d 1256 (Ariz. Ct. App. 2005)

CHAPTER TWO

Access to ART Treatment

Insurance and Discrimination

✤ MEDICAL COMMENTARY, BY Howard W. Jones, Jr.

WHAT IS "INFERTILITY"? Is it a condition, a disability, a disease, or something else? Use of the word is often confused in the lay literature, the legal literature, and, indeed, the medical literature. From a medical point of view, infertility is a symptom of many diseases, in both the male and the female. Among couples with infertility, approximately 40 percent of cases are due to a disease of the male, 40 percent are due to a disease of the female, and 20 percent comes either from disease in both the male and the female or is of unknown origin. Since 1993 (updated in 2008), ASRM Practice Guidelines have formally defined infertility itself as a "disease": specifically, "the failure to achieve pregnancy after twelve months or more of regular unprotected intercourse," and cited prevailing medical dictionaries' definition of disease.[1]

Age is one contributing factor of infertility that is poorly understood in the legal world. In this section, there are cases that address, for example, the issue of whether refusing insurance coverage for patients of advanced reproductive age constitutes age discrimination. In one case, the argument was presented that denying insurance coverage to infertile women in their late forties would unfairly prevent their use of donor eggs. (*Pacourek v. Inland Steel Co.*, 1996). Donor eggs may help solve this

---

1. The guideline, "Definitions of Infertility and Recurrent Pregnancy Loss," refers to the current definition of *disease*: "any deviation from or interruption of the normal structure of function of any part, organ, or system of the body as manifested by characteristic symptoms and signs; the etiology, pathology, and prognosis may be known or unknown." *Dorland's Illustrated Medical Dictionary*, 31st ed., 2007:535. *Fertility and Sterility* (June 2008), vol. 89, no. 6.

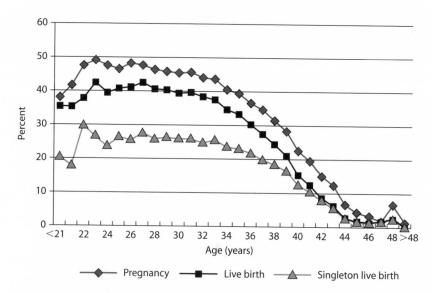

FIGURE 1. Percentages of ART cycles using fresh nondonor eggs or embryos that resulted in pregnancies, live births, and singleton live births, by age of woman, 2005. For consistency, all percentages are based on cycles started. *Source*: www.cdc.gov/ART/ART2005.

reproductive obstacle and enable older women to become pregnant. Extending insurance coverage to this age group, however, requires an insurer and, ultimately, its policyholders to generate sufficient funds to cover situations where the likelihood of pregnancy without donor eggs is very small. From a medical perspective, the issue, therefore, is what expectation of pregnancy is reasonable for insurance coverage.

It is useful to see the age/pregnancy data in figure 1, which indicate that the expectancy of pregnancy starts to diminish in the thirties. Some coverage cutoff points for women in their early forties would seem reasonable, at least from a medical perspective. In Belgium, where the country's national insurance covers IVF for all citizens, there is an age cutoff of forty-three years. And as one of the reported cases from Canada in this compendium noted, a cutoff may be discriminatory but justifiable under Canadian law.

To correlate age-related expectations for pregnancy from IVF or natural conception with age-related expectations for pregnancies with donor eggs is medically naive. A great deal of research shows that pregnancy expectation with donor eggs is closely related to the age of the eggs, that is, the age of the donor and not the age of the recipient. Again, from a medical perspective, it would make more sense to treat these two different medical situations as two separate legal situations.

Failure to provide comprehensive definitions of terms in some state insurance laws also demonstrates a certain amount of medical naiveté. Montana, for instance, requires HMOs to cover infertility services as part of basic preventive health care, but the law does not define infertility or the scope of services covered, nor did the state ever draft explanatory regulations. On the other hand, Massachusetts has a detailed explanation of what infertility is and what is covered, although in recent years there have been arguments over whether the definition needs to be clarified or amendments proposed to include, for example, multiple miscarriages.

Insurance that presumably covers infertility can nonetheless raise issues over the scope of such coverage. For example, there have been coverage denials for examinations and treatments relating to multiple miscarriages and for women in their mid- to late forties. This raises questions such as, "What exactly is infertility?" and "What reproductive medical conditions should be covered by insurance?" This practitioner has always considered it to mean "the inability to create a living child," while some insurers interpret infertility to mean "the inability to achieve a pregnancy." A narrow interpretation of infertility put forth by many in the insurance industry and a refusal to cover services that do not specifically address that narrow definition raise significant "scope of coverage" issues. A 2008 report from ASRM suggests that "repetitive pregnancy loss" (defined as two or more failed pregnancies) is a disease distinct from infertility. Clearly, in policy terms, "infertility" and "recurrent pregnancy loss," as well as the proper scope of reproductive services, need to be accurately and carefully defined from a medical perspective.

This section also addresses litigation concerning mandated state infertility insurance laws. Of the fourteen states that currently mandate some form of infertility coverage, there is tremendous variation as to exactly what conditions and procedures, and which insureds, are covered. The website of the American Society for Reproductive Medicine (www.asrm.org) provides detailed state-by-state information. Table 1 summarizes state coverage for infertility. Some of the listed states man-

TABLE I.   State Infertility Coverage at a Glance, October 2005

State	Date enacted	Mandate to cover	Mandate to offer	Includes IVF coverage	Excludes IVF coverage	IVF coverage only
Arkansas	1987	X(1)				X
California	1989		X		X(2)	
Connecticut	1989	X		X		
Hawaii	1987	X				X(3)
Illinois	1991	X		X(4)		
Maryland	1985	X(5)				X
Massachusetts	1987	X		X		
Montana	1987	X(6)				
New Jersey	2001	X		X		
New York	1990				X(7)	
Ohio	1991	X(8)				
Rhode Island	1989	X		X		
Texas	1987		X			X
West Virginia	1977	X(8)				

(1) Includes a lifetime maximum benefit of not less than $15,000.
(2) Excludes IVF but covers gamete intrafallopian transfer (GIFT).
(3) Provides a one-time-only benefit covering all outpatient expenses arising from IVF
(4) Limits first-time attempts to four oocyte retrievals. If a child is born, two complete oocyte retrievals for a second birth are covered. Businesses with 25 or fewer employees are exempt from having to provide the coverage specified by the law.
(5) Businesses with 50 or fewer employees do not have to provide coverage specified by law.
(6) Applies to HMOs only; other insurers specifically are exempt from having to provide the coverage.
(7) Provides coverage for the "diagnosis and treatment of correctable medical conditions." Does not consider IVF a corrective treatment.
(8) Applies to HMOs only.

If a state is not listed here, or if you have questions about insurance laws in your state, please call your state's Insurance Commissioner's office. To learn about pending legislation in your state, please contact your state representatives.

Source: www.asrm.org/Patients/insur.html

date coverage, while others, like California, require only a "mandate [for insurers] to offer" coverage for infertility services but do not require employers to purchase such insurance or cover all insureds. Sometimes IVF is included, sometimes it is excluded, and some mandates require IVF coverage only. Input from medical professionals may enable those drafting the laws to understand the benefits and limits of these procedures, so that legislators can more accurately determine which procedures should be covered for which populations.

If there were to be a state-by-state extension of mandated coverage for infertility or reproductive services, surely serious medical input would be helpful in providing coverage that is consistent with both social and medical reality.

∿ LEGAL COMMENTARY, BY Susan L. Crockin

Access to treatment for infertility (and genetic conditions that impair fertility) sparked considerable legal developments throughout the 1990s. State and federal courts and, ultimately, the United States Supreme Court were confronted with claims that infertility was a protected disability and that denials of treatment or termination of employment based on either fertility-related conditions or treatment for such conditions violated federal or constitutional law. Litigants brought claims under Title VII, the federal Pregnancy Discrimination Act (PDA) (with mixed results), as well as under the federal Americans with Disabilities Act (ADA), culminating in a major Supreme Court victory in 1998 in *Bragdon v. Abbott*, a successful discrimination claim brought by an HIV-positive patient against her dentist for refusing her treatment. Building on earlier legislative successes in states such as Massachusetts (1987), consumers and advocacy groups pressed to enact mandated insurance coverage for fertility-related treatment and succeeded in adding additional states, including Illinois in 2000 and New Jersey in 2001.

The court decisions throughout the 1990s illustrate a developing picture of evolving judicial perspectives on reproduction. In order for a disability to be protected under the ADA, it must be "a physical or mental impairment" that substantially limits "a major life activity." Until the Supreme Court took up the issue, the appellate courts were markedly split on whether reproduction was a "major life activity." One court contrasted reproduction to breathing and working, finding that reproduction was not required for daily living, and rejected the argument. Another court accepted the argument, finding reproduction was more important than work.

The Supreme Court resolved this issue in *Abbott* in 1998: "Reproduction and the sexual dynamics surrounding it are central to the life process itself." While this was a major legal milestone, the ADA has not proven to be the protection many had hoped. Subsequent Supreme Court cases narrowed the ADA's definition of disability and read its insurance provisions to offer broad exemptions for insurance companies and plans. 2008 amendments to the ADA have broadened its definition of disability. The extent to which the ADA may yet prove to be a legal protection for reproduction-related conditions and treatments remains to be seen. Claims under the PDA have also met with mixed results, with some courts accepting and rejecting infertility as a pregnancy- or childbirth-related disability and others finding that infertility is a gender-neutral condition.

As single patients and same-sex couples increasingly access the ARTs to create families, discrimination claims have also expanded to include treatment inequities based on sex, sexual orientation, and marital status. In 2006, one such case brought, and ultimately won, by a single lesbian patient denied treatment raises both constitutional issues and physician defenses based on religious freedom (*Benitez v. North Coast Women's Care Medical Group*, 2008). This line of cases will almost certainly evolve as states and practices continue to address such issues in disparate ways. A more thorough description of these cases is found in chapter 8.

Access to treatment in terms of insurance coverage has been, and will likely continue to be, a major issue in ART treatment. Efforts to pass state mandates for insurance coverage of infertility treatment, including assisted reproductive technologies, have spanned the past two decades with significant variation in outcome. Of the fourteen states that currently mandate some form of infertility treatment insurance coverage, ten were enacted prior to 1990, and only one since 2000. The earlier statutes may reflect less cost-sensitive times, greater grassroots involvement, or both. In Massachusetts, this writer was privileged to have been part of the small group of individuals who initially drafted and, as part of the state's local RESOLVE chapter, RESOLVE of the Bay State, lobbied for two years until that state's mandate was enacted. Cost analysis projections prepared as part of that effort proved accurate and prescient, as subsequent studies confirmed the relatively modest economic impact of infertility coverage on insurance costs. The legislature's efforts to pare back coverage and to impose numerical cutoffs or "caps" for both IVF cycles and patient age were successfully rejected. Coverage in that state remains one of the most comprehensive mandates enacted to date. In a few states, other legislative or regulatory measures were reported, such as Rhode Island's investigation into age discrimination in coverage (1998) and state laws that have made the status of families created through third-party or collaborative reproduction more secure (those developments are discussed in later chapters).

If infertility is recognized as a disease or a cluster of diseases, it is difficult to justify excluding diagnosis and treatment from comprehensive insurance coverage. Both court cases and legislative lobbying efforts have raised discrimination as a basis to overturn refusals to cover or limitations on coverage. Nonetheless, absent an explicit mandate to cover or proof of illegal discrimination based on a protected class status, discretionary coverage of medical conditions, including infertility, remains legally permissible.

As discussed more fully in chapter 9, genetic advances are also expanding and creating new disputed avenues over access and insurance coverage. Preimplantation genetic diagnosis (PGD) has made it possible to detect embryos that carry a lethal or major life-limiting genetic abnormality, such as cystic fibrosis and Huntington's disease, with IVF necessary to obtain the embryos to be tested. Regardless of whether a given insurer considers genetic carrier status a form of "infertility," patients seeking out these services are increasingly pressing for insurance coverage for both the IVF and PGD procedures. In a number of such cases, patients' attorneys (including this author) have successfully argued that insurance coverage that includes birth control, infertility, genetic counseling, prenatal testing, and maternity and family medical coverage cannot exclude a related advancing technology that is an extension of these forms of services and may, in many cases, eliminate the extraordinary expenses of insuring a severely affected child. As the technologies improve, both increased demand and expanded coverage for such services are likely inevitable.

Access to treatment, including insurance coverage for infertility, genetic diagnosis, and ART treatment continues to be an evolving area of both law and medical practice. As both older and nontraditional patients increasingly turn to ART treatments to create families, defining infertility and coverage limits will likely continue to vex policy makers. Same-sex couples who cannot reproduce without medical assistance but who may not be considered medically infertile, couples who can achieve pregnancies but carry lethal or significant genetic defects and seek preimplanta-tion genetic diagnosis to avoid carrying affected pregnancies, and single or older would-be parents who seek out ART treatments will all likely present future challenges to coverage for available treatments.

In many ways, the infertility insurance efforts of the 1980s and 1990s can now be viewed as leading the way into a continuing exploration of appropriate insurance coverage for family-building efforts. Current pa-tient advocacy efforts are finding some restrictive interpretations of those laws by insurers or courts hindering efforts for insurance coverage. As one example, the question of whether multiple miscarriages or genetically caused stillbirths or neonatal deaths constitute infertility and thus man-dated coverage has been the subject of several emotional debates between insureds and insurers, with inconsistent coverage outcomes. Efforts are also under way in some states to expand the definition of infertility under existing mandates to address some of these issues. Defining infertility and mandating some form of coverage for infertility was a hard-fought and dramatic advance in those decades. Part of meeting that challenge was proving that infertility was a medical condition or disease and that cover-age was both appropriate and could be cost-effective.

The current challenge must include moving beyond attempts to fit newer developments into those hard-fought, and now accepted, catego-ries to also focus on similarly thoughtful arguments and policy proposals to address these newer options to meet the medical challenges to family-building efforts today and into the future.

Litigation and Legislation

I. INSURANCE AND DISCRIMINATION LITIGATION

2.1 Illinois Couple's Insurer Ordered to Cover IVF Costs
December 1990

An Illinois couple's successful fight to get their insurer to cover IVF attempts even without a mandated infertility benefits law in place suggests there may be reimbursement refusals that are vulnerable to a challenge. Patients and office managers may want to read the fine print of their insurance policies carefully.

The insurer's policy or so-called "plan" covered "treatment" of "illnesses" without defining those terms. Internal company guidelines, however, distinguished between tubal repair and infertility counseling, which were reimbursed, and IVF, which was not.

Finding those distinctions "arbitrary and capricious," the court ordered the insurer to add IVF to its covered "treatments." The court showed little sympathy for the company's argument that tubal repair treats the illness whereas IVF circumvents it. This was an issue "better left to doctors than judges," the court wrote and noted in passing that counseling would certainly not cause the fallopian tubes to repair themselves.

Had the policy itself, and not merely the internal guidelines, eliminated IVF coverage the result might not have been as favorable.

Egert v. Connecticut General Life Ins. Co.,
900 F.2d 1032 (7th Cir. 1990)

2.2 Supreme Court Hands Women Victory on Reproductive Freedom
June 1991

In a victory for women in the workplace, the nation's highest court has ruled in a favor of employees who claimed that a company's "fetal protection" policy, which kept them out of lead-infested sites (and higher-paying positions), was a clear example of sex discrimination in violation of Title VII of the Civil Rights Act of 1964, the Pregnancy Discrimination Act.

In its decision, the Court stated that "Congress . . . prohibited discrimination on the basis of a woman's ability to become pregnant . . . the decision to become pregnant or to work while being either pregnant or capable of becoming pregnant was reserved for each individual woman to make for herself . . . decisions about the welfare of future children must be left to the parents who conceive, bear, support, and raise them rather than to the employers who hire those parents."

The Court did recognize that employers may be liable to children born with defects as a result of contaminated workplaces, but ruled that with federally mandated safety standards the chances of this were slim and were not a sufficient reason to preclude fertile women from the workplace. The federal law applies to almost all businesses with fifteen or more employees.

The implications of the decision are far-reaching; whether they can be extended to policies concerning infertility and reproductive technologies remains to be explored.

International Union, United Auto. Aerospace and Agr.
Implement Workers of America, UAW v. Johnson
Controls, Inc., 499 U.S. 187, 111 S.Ct. 1196 (1991)

2.3 Workmen's Compensation Covers Artificial Insemination
December 1991

A Pennsylvania couple's expenses for artificial insemination were held to be covered under the state's workmen's compensation law because the husband was infertile due to a work-related spinal injury. A Pennsylvania court reversed the Workmen's Compensation Appeal Board's dismissal of the claim. The court recognized that the procedure was necessary to replace a function that was lost because of an on-the-job injury. Since the wife's participation was essential, her expenses were also reimbursable.

Tobias v. Workmen's Compensation Appeal Bd.
(Nature's Way Nursery, Inc.), 141 Pa. Comm. 438
(Pa. Comm. Ct. 1991)

2.4(a) Fired Employee Sues over Alleged Infertility Discrimination
June 1994

In what has been described as a ground-breaking case, a fired worker is claiming that her employer of eighteen years discriminatorily discharged her because she had to miss work to receive fertility treatments.

Charlene Pacourek, an employee of Chicago-based Inland Steel Company, charges the company with violating federal anti-discrimination laws and is seeking both reinstatement and $25 million in damages. The claims are based on novel interpretations of infertility as protected under both the federal Pregnancy Discrimination Act (PDA—Title VII of the Civil Rights Act) and the recently enacted Americans with Disabilities Act (ADA). These interpretations had been previously analyzed and reported by [this author and others for] RESOLVE, Inc.

The Title VII claim is based on that law's language, which states that "women affected by pregnancy, childbirth, or related medical conditions shall be treated the same for all employment-related purposes." Similarly, Pacourek's ADA claim is that infertility falls within that law's definition of a "disability." No court has yet ruled that infertility falls within the legal protections of either statute.

Pacourek, now forty-five years old, alleges that her absences from work during seven years of infertility treatment were all approved and made up for by overtime. Her immediate supervisor has reportedly confirmed that her work did not suffer from her absenteeism, which in one year included twenty-six sick days for infertility treatments. Pacourek, who married at age thirty-eight and had been attempting to achieve a pregnancy since the beginning of her marriage, is now pregnant as the result of a successful egg donation transfer.

Pacourek was fired in June 1993 as she began preparing for the embryo transfer. She claims that she was warned by another supervisor who allegedly said, "If God had wanted you to have children, then he would have given them to you."

Inland Steel denies Pacourek's allegations and claims that she was laid off as part of a 3,500 workforce reduction over the past three years. Pacourek claims she was replaced by a man.

2.4(b) Fired Infertile Employee Wins First Round on Novel Discrimination Claims

December 1994

Charlene Pacourek has had an initial victory in her court case against her former employer, with the court refusing to grant Inland Steel's motion to dismiss her claims. This case appears to be the first of a number of such potential lawsuits which may provide more legal definition to infertility and have potentially far-reaching implications both in the workplace and for insurance coverage of this medical condition.

In its July 27 ruling, the federal district court rejected the company's claim that the PDA does not apply to women who are unable to become pregnant "naturally." Instead, the court ruled, "[a] common-sense reading of the PDA" supported its conclusion that the PDA more broadly applies to infertility. "Discrimination against an employee because she intends to, is trying to, or simply has the potential to become pregnant is therefore illegal discrimination."

The court also preliminarily ruled that the ADA applied because it found infertility was a disability as defined under that law's language: "a physical or mental impairment that substantially limits one or more of the major life activities." The parties had agreed that infertility was a covered impairment since the regulations under the ADA clearly stated that a disorder or condition of the reproductive system was a covered impairment. They disagreed over whether the impairment was of a major life activity. The court ruled that "the conclusion that infertility substantially limits the major life activity is a matter of common sense." A pretrial conference is scheduled in December.

The underlying theories of the case, which were initially put forth by RESOLVE advocates and still under consideration for future test case litigation, may have widespread implications regardless of the ultimate decision on the merits of Pacourek's claims. For example, if other courts similarly rule that infertility is a protected disability under the federal ADA law, arguments may be advanced that it would be illegal to discriminate against infertility treatment in the provision of insurance.

A recent federal appellate decision involving insurance coverage for AIDS suggests that insurance companies may be defined as "employers" to come within the mandates of the ADA (*Carparts v. Auto. Wholesalers Ass'n. of N.E.*, 37 F.3d 12 (1st Cir. 10/12/94)).

Court interpretations such as these could provide an alternate forum to state and federal legislatures to achieve insurance coverage for the treatment of infertility.

2.4(c) *Pacourek v. Inland Steel Co.* One of Three Inconsistent ADA Test Case Rulings
Summer 1996

Inconsistent litigation outcomes surrounding the application of the ADA to infertility continue. Most recently, the *Pacourek* court concluded, it defies common sense to say that infertility is not a psychological disorder or condition affecting the reproductive system. In fact, infertility is the ultimate impairment of the reproductive system . . . infertility, whether explained or not, is an impairment under the ADA."

In definitively ruling that reproduction was a "major life activity" under the ADA, the *Pacourek* court rejected two other courts' criticisms of its earlier decision and those courts' contrary rulings, concluding that they overly simplified and misunderstood its reasoning and trivialized reproduction. It criticized the *Zatarain* [2.5] court's finding that "major life activities" were only those a person was required to do day in and day out, such as walk, see, breathe, and work, as a definition far too narrowly focused on quantity rather than quality. In contrast it ruled, "none of us, nor any living thing, would exist without reproduction. Many, if not most, people would consider having a child to be one of life's most significant moments and greatest achievements, and the inability to do so, one of life's greatest disappointments . . . to call working a major life activity, but to deny the same status to reproduction, seems ludicrous. The court suspects that people have been producing offspring for far longer than they have been working. This holds all the more true for women, who, until relatively recently, had to choose between working and childbearing, and more frequently chose the latter."

The court concluded unequivocally that Pacourek had infertility, which was an impairment and limited the major life activity of reproduction as defined under the ADA. Following that ruling, the parties reportedly settled the case.

Pacourek v. Inland Steel Co., 858 F. Supp. 1393 (N.D. Ill. 1994) (denying Inland Steel's motion to dismiss plaintiff's amended complaint); 916 F. Supp. 797 (N.D. Ill. 1996) (denying Inland Steel partial summary judgment on ADA claim).

2.5(a) Appeal Filed after Federal Court Rejects TV Broadcaster's ADA Claim
September 1995

An appeal has been filed by a female newscaster whose contract was not renewed after she requested alterations and a temporary reduction in her work hours for "fertility treatments." A federal district court in New Orleans rejected the woman's legal claims that reproduction was a "major life activity" under the ADA, reaching the opposite conclusion from another federal district court in *Pacourek v. Inland Steel Co.* [2.4].

Lynn Gansar Zatarain was a popular reporter for a New Orleans

TV station for nine years. Her request to temporarily reduce her hours on the advice of her doctor resulted in the nonrenewal of her contract. She charges discrimination under two federal laws: the ADA and Title VII of the Civil Rights Act of 1964. The defendant TV station asked the court to dismiss on the grounds that infertility or a reproductive disorder was not a "disability" under the ADA, that Zatarain's infertility was the result of age and stress and not a physiological condition, and that it did not substantially limit her ability to engage in a "major life activity" as defined under the ADA.

The lower court ruled that although infertility was a physiological impairment or disability as defined by the ADA's definition it did not impair a "major life activity" and granted summary judgment for the defendant station. The court reviewed the ADA's regulations, which include working, walking, seeing, hearing, speaking, breathing, and learning. It rejected both the notion that Zatarain's work was significantly impaired and the conclusion reached by the Illinois court in *Pacourek* that reproduction is a major life activity. The court noted, "a person is required to walk, see, speak, breathe and work through the day, day in and day out. However, a person is not called upon to reproduce through the day, every day." To find that infertility impairs reproduction as a major life activity is circular reasoning, the court said.

Zatarain's attorneys hope that her appeal will draw supporting legal briefs from organizations such as RESOLVE, the ASRM, and the Equal Employment Opportunity Commission (EEOC) and succeed in reversing the unfavorable interpretation of the ADA as it relates to infertility and other disabilities.

2.5(b) Zatarain's ADA Rejection Affirmed on Appeal
Summer 1996

A federal appellate court has affirmed a lower court's dismissal of Lynne Zatarain's claim that she was discriminated against on technical grounds without reaching the merits of her ADA claim.

In contrast, two federal court decisions in Illinois (*Pacourek* [2.4] and *Erickson* [2.6]) have recently ruled that both the PDA and the ADA are applicable to infertility-based discrimination.

Zatarain v. WDSU-Television, 881 F. Supp. 240 (D.
La. 1995); *affirmed* by 79 F.3d 1143 (5th Cir. 1996)

2.6(a) Federal Court in Illinois Allows Woman to Pursue Infertility Discrimination Claims against Former Employer

December 1995

BY K. ZIESELMAN

Melinda Erickson, a former Northeastern Illinois University employee, sued the university for firing her because of her use of vacation time and sick days to undergo infertility treatment and claimed discrimination on the basis of her infertility, in violation of both the ADA and the PDA.

Citing the factually similar case of *Pacourek v. Inland Steel Co.* [2.4], the court denied the university's request to dismiss the case on the grounds that infertility is not a condition covered by the PDA, holding: "(1) The PDA applies to discrimination based upon intended or potential pregnancy in addition to actual pregnancy . . . and (2) infertility is a pregnancy-related condition for purposes of the PDA." The court also determined Ms. Erickson had a reasonable claim of sex discrimination due to her potential to become pregnant and specifically made a distinction between male and female infertility, reasoning that a male employee's infertility treatment does not seek to achieve his own pregnancy. This holding contradicts the decision in *Krauel* [2.7].

The court also agreed about the applicability of the ADA: "infertility is by definition a substantial limitation of reproduction in that it constitutes the inability to reproduce," and once again cited *Pacourek* [for that proposition]. Furthermore, the court disagreed with *Zatarain v. WDSU-Television* [2.5], which held that reproduction is not a major life activity, criticizing the ruling as appearing "to view reproduction as the act of conception only, thus ignoring the processes that occur continually in both male and female reproductive systems in order to achieve conception." The decision allows Ms. Erickson to continue to pursue her discrimination claims.

2.6(b) Third ADA Test Case, *Erickson v. Board of Governors*, Continues

Summer 1996

Melinda Erickson won a court ruling that both the ADA and PDA apply to her claims of discrimination based on infertility, and that she may therefore proceed with her lawsuit against her former employer whom she charges fired her for using vacation and sick leave for medical treatment.

> *Erickson v. Board of Governors*, 911 F. Supp. 316
> (N.D. Ill. 1995); subsequently *reversed* by 207 F.3d
> 945 (7th Cir. 2000) [Reversing denial of university's
> motion to dismiss; finding private federal litigation
> to enforce ADA claim cannot proceed but employee
> can bring ADA claim in state court]

2.7(a) Federal Court in Iowa Rejects Infertile Employee's Insurance Discrimination Claims

December 1995

BY K. ZIESELMAN

In the first court decision regarding application of the ADA to insurance coverage for infertility treatment, a federal court in Iowa rejected a woman's claim that excluding infertility from her health insurance policy was discriminatory.

Mary Jo Krauel, a nurse at Iowa Methodist Medical Center, was denied insurance coverage for infertility treatments (including a GIFT procedure that resulted in the birth of her daughter) under her employee health plan's exclusion for treatment of "fertility or infertility problems." Krauel sued her employer under two separate discrimination theories based on federal law: violations of both the ADA and the PDA.

The court agreed with the defendant medical center, dismissing Krauel's ADA claim on the grounds that infertility is not a disability protected under the provisions of the ADA and that the health plan's exclusion is not disability-based. Although agreeing that infertility constitutes a physical impairment, the court found that procreation is not a major life activity within the meaning of the statute. Relying heavily on the reasoning used by a federal district court in Louisiana to dismiss the case of *Zatarain v. WDSU-Television* [2.5], the court determined the act of reproduction to be a "lifestyle choice" and an activity which is not engaged in with the same degree of frequency as major life activities such as "walking, seeing, speaking, breathing, learning, and working." In doing so, the court also specifically rejected the reasoning that led to the opposite decision in *Pacourek v. Inland Steel Co.* [2.4].

The court also rejected Ms. Krauel's PDA claim, finding that, "the treatment of infertility is not the treatment of a medical condition related to pregnancy and childbirth." The court reasoned that pregnancy and childbirth both refer to conditions that occur after conception, whereas, "infertility, by definition, occurs prior to conception." In doing so, the court appeared unaware that infertility can include the inability to carry a pregnancy to term.

Again, the court specifically rejected the reasoning of *Pacourek*, which held that a medical condition preventing a woman from becoming pregnant naturally is a pregnancy-related medical condition for the purposes of the PDA. The court criticized the *Pacourek* decision for failing to recognize that although childbirth and pregnancy are conditions specific to a woman, infertility is gender-neutral, as it applies to both men and women. Ms. Krauel's attorney has filed an appeal.

2.7(b) ADA Decision Denying Discrimination Coverage for Infertility Upheld
Winter 1996

A federal appeals court has upheld the decision of the lower court, which had rejected Mary Jo Krauel's claim that excluding infertility coverage from her health plan was an illegal violation of two federal laws. The court affirmed the ruling that barriers to a woman's reproduction are not impairments that limit "major life activities" within the meaning of the federal law or supporting regulations and rejected the applicability of the PDA, concluding that infertility is not protected as a pregnancy-related condition but is a "strikingly different" condition, which is gender-neutral. Despite statements put into evidence that executives of the defendant employer made sexist remarks including there being "too many women of childbearing age," the court rejected the claim that the exclusion was sex discrimination. It also cited a lack of statistical evidence to support the woman's claim that denial of coverage disproportionately affects women.

Krauel v. Iowa Methodist Medical Ctr.,
95 F.3d 674 (8th Cir. 1996)

2.8(a) First Circuit Rules Reproduction Is a Major Life Activity
Fall 1997

BY W. PARMET

The legal rights of individuals who are infertile have increasingly become intertwined with the rights of individuals infected with HIV. Both groups experience discrimination in the workplace and in access to health insurance. In response, both groups are looking to the ADA for legal protection and finding that their right for protection under the ADA depends, at least in part, on whether courts find that reproduction is a "major life activity."

In an important case on the issue, the U.S. Court of Appeals for the First Circuit recently held that reproduction is a "major life activity" under the ADA. Sydney Abbott, an HIV-positive woman, was denied dental care because of her HIV status. To determine whether she was entitled to legal protection, the court first had to decide whether she had a disability. Under the ADA, an individual has a disability if he or she has a physical or mental impairment that substantially limits a major life activity. In Abbott's case, there was no doubt that her infection constituted a physical impairment. The question instead was whether that impairment substantially limited one of her major life activities. Because she was asymptomatic, she could not claim that the disease limited the major life activities, such as walking or working, that are listed in the ADA regulations. Instead, she claimed that the risk of perinatal transmission limited her ability to reproduce.

The court, therefore, had to consider whether reproduction is a major life activity. In analyzing that question, the court thoroughly reviewed earlier infertility cases, especially *Krauel v. Iowa Methodist Medical Center* [2.7] and *Zatarain v. WDSU-TV* [2.5], which had found that reproduction is not a major activity.

The First Circuit disagreed with those cases. The court noted that although reproduction is not listed in the regulations as a major life activity, the regulations were not meant to be exclusive. Moreover, the court found that the legislative history of the ADA supported the conclusion that reproduction is a major life history.

The Court of Appeals also disagreed firmly with the argument that individuals with infertility have frequently heard—that reproduction is not a major life activity because it is a lifestyle choice. The court termed that argument "emaciated" and noted that "most acts that human beings perform—or refrain from performing—have elements of volition." Instead, the court declared, because of reproduction's "singular importance," it is a major life activity and those who can show that their ability to reproduce is substantially limited due to a physical impairment are entitled to protections under the ADA.

The *Abbott* ruling, with its strong rejection of *Krauel* and *Zatarain* and its carefully reasoned conclusion that reproduction is a major life activity, is sure to be of major importance in future infertility cases. Also relevant to such cases will be a decision in another HIV case now pending before a full panel of the U.S. Court of Appeals for the Fourth Circuit. In that case, *Runnebaum v. NationsBank of Maryland* (123 F.3d 156 (4th Cir. 1997)), the court is once again considering whether an individual who is asymptomatic and HIV positive has a disability on the basis of HIV's impact on reproduction. A decision in that case is expected shortly.

2.8(b) ADA Applicability to Reproduction Headed to U.S. Supreme Court
Spring 1998

The United States Supreme Court has granted "certiorari" in the First Circuit case, *Abbott v. Bragdon,* to resolve the conflict amongst the federal appellate courts' interpretations of the ADA and its applicability to reproduction. The First Circuit ruled that the patient's condition was a recognized disability under the ADA and her dentist's refusal to treat her amounted to illegal discrimination in violation of the ADA. (Other circuits have reached opposite conclusions.)

Regulations promulgated by the EEOC clearly establish that both HIV and diseases of the reproductive system are qualifying impairments under the ADA. However, the law and regulations leave open the question of whether such an impairment limits or affects a protected "major life activity." Since Abbott was asymptomatic, she claimed that the risk of perinatal transmission limited her ability to reproduce. The First Circuit recognized this as a disability, comparing reproduction to the most basic and essential of life functions, whereas other courts have characterized it as a legally unprotected lifestyle choice.

The U.S. Supreme Court accepts certiorari in only a very small percentage of cases. With major implications for infertility status likely, legal scholars and practitioners in the field will follow this case closely. Abbott is being represented on appeal by the Gay and Lesbian Advocates and Defenders (GLAD) as well as by Professor Wendy E. Parmet, of Northeastern University School of Law, a past guest author of "Legally Speaking" [2.8a, 2.10, and others].

2.8(c) U.S. Supreme Court Rules Reproduction Is a Protected Major Life Activity

Winter 1998

In a long- and anxiously awaited decision, the country's highest court has ruled that reproduction *is* a major life activity and that "physical or mental impairments" such as HIV, which substantially limit that activity, are protected disabilities under the ADA. The Supreme Court's affirmation of the First Circuit's decision ends the simmering debate amongst the appellate courts as to whether reproduction is a protected major life activity or an unprotected lifestyle choice.

In strikingly brief and clear language, the court found that "[r]eproduction and the sexual dynamics surrounding it are central to the life process itself." It rejected arguments advanced by some lower courts that the ADA was intended to cover only those parts of a person's life that had a public, economic, or daily character. The ADA applies to places of public accommodation, defined under the law as a "professional office of a health care provider," and to private employers with over fifty employees. In a strongly worded dissent, Chief Justice Rehnquist remarked that, "[r]eproduction is not an activity at all, but a process . . . a human being (as opposed to a copier machine or a gremlin) would never be described as reproducing."

The implication of the decision is that reproductive impairments, including infertility, can be disabilities within the meaning of the ADA, and infertile individuals will be entitled to that federal law's protections in the workplace. How far those protections will extend is yet to be explored. Legal experts have long debated, for example, whether health insurance plans are employers subject to the ADA, whether issuance of insurance by those companies are "public accommodations" within the meaning of the law, and whether or not failure to provide particular health insurance benefits run afoul of the ADA.

According to Professor Wendy Parmet, appellate co-counsel for Sidney Abbott, "*Abbott* . . . absolutely clarifies that reproduction is a major life activity. It thereby opens up the possibility of using the ADA in the area of infertility. But many questions remain, most critically the ways in which the ADA regulates the issuance of health insurance. The next few years should see many more court cases grappling with this problem. Ultimately, the Supreme Court will need to look at the relationship between the ADA and health insurance."

Bragdon v. Abbott, 524 U.S. 624 (U.S. 1998)

2.9 Federal Court Finds Woman with Incompetent Cervix Has a Disability
Fall 1997

In recent months, the federal district courts have considered several ADA cases dealing directly with reproductive health issues. Soodman concerned a pregnant legal secretary who was discharged while on bed rest, made necessary because of an incompetent cervix. In reviewing her claim that her discharge violated the ADA, the court found that reproduction is a major activity and that any other conclusion would be inconsistent with the importance Congress affords pregnancy and childbearing.

The court also rejected the defendant's argument that Soodman was not disabled because she could indeed bear a child, holding the ADA does not require a total limitation of a major life activity, merely a substantial limitation. Because Soodman's reproductive troubles stemmed from a longstanding condition, and would likely reappear and limit her ability to bear children, the court found that she experienced a substantial limitation of the major life activity of reproduction and therefore had a disability.

Next, the court considered whether Soodman was a "qualified employee" as one must be to receive employment protection under the ADA. The answer to this question depended upon whether the unpaid leave she had received was a "reasonable accommodation." The court found that there was no evidence to show that the leave was not a reasonable accommodation, hence the employer's motion for summary judgment was denied.

The district court also considered claims under the Family and Medical Leave Act (FMLA) and the PDA. With respect to the FMLA claim, the court held that because Soodman had received twelve weeks of unpaid leave as required by the Act, and was not physically able to return to work at the end of it, she was not entitled to relief under the Act. Her PDA claim also failed because her employer had discharged other employees on leave, hence she could not show that she was fired due to her pregnancy rather than her leave status.

> *Soodman v. Wildman, Harrold, Allen & Dixon*, 1997 U.S.
> Dist. LEXIS 1495 (D. Ill. 1997) (on reconsideration
> Court granted employer's motion for summary judgment
> re: employee's claim for intentional infliction
> of emotional distress).

2.10 Denial of Sick Leave for Adoption Does Not Violate ADA When Employer Not Aware of Individual's Infertility
Fall 1997
BY W. PARMET

Cheryl Clapp, a nurse with endometriosis, filed an ADA claim when her employer denied her sick leave to adopt a child.

The federal district court in Maine, citing *Abbott,* assumed for purposes of analysis that Clapp's infertility was a protected disability. However, the court found no evidence that her employer was aware of her infertility. Because her employer did not know she was trying to adopt due to her infertility, the court found she could not show discrimination on the basis of her disability.

The court considered the fact that her employer may have known about a prior miscarriage that Clapp had experienced. Noting that miscarriages are common, the court found that knowledge of a miscarriage did not put the employer on notice of Clapp's infertility. Moreover, because Clapp had spoken about "the rights of adoptive parents," her employer could have believed she was adopting due to a preference for adoption rather than infertility. Infertility, the court noted, is an invisible disability. Unless the employee can present clear evidence that the employer knew of the condition, a finding of discrimination cannot be sustained.

> *Clapp v. Northern Cumberland Mem. Hosp.,*
> 964 F. Supp. 503 (D. Me. 1997)

2.11 Rhode Island Attorney General's Office Investigates Age Discrimination Infertility Coverage

Spring 1999

In an unusual action, a state attorney general's office has reportedly prodded insurance companies to drop age limits that previously restricted access to coverage for infertility treatment. Rhode Island's attorney general's office, which has an insurance advocacy unit, found evidence of illegal age discrimination in insurance practices that had the effect of barring middle-aged women from receiving infertility treatment.

Rhode Island is one of several states that by statute treats infertility as a medical condition and thus mandates coverage for treatment subject to various definitions and limitations. Until recently, many insurers assumed that one such permissible limitation was menopause, since postmenopausal women either would not meet the definition of infertility or would not meet the requirement of medical necessity. Rather than making individual determinations, some insurers refused to provide coverage based on the age of the female patient (usually about forty).

But doctors and patients challenged such practices, particularly in light of the availability of egg donation. With such treatment, an older woman's chances of success increase significantly, therefore undermining the view that a legitimate medical reason justifies denying coverage in such cases. Rhode Island's investigation into the issue apparently has prompted several insurers to drop their age limits or seriously consider doing so. In addition, officials in Massachusetts, another state with mandated infertility coverage, have cooperated with Rhode Island and begun their own inquiry in response to complaints.

Wall Street Journal, 11/4/98

2.12 Nova Scotia Court Rules Infertility Insurance Denial Discriminatory but Permissible

Winter 1999 and Spring 2000

The appellate court for the province of Nova Scotia has rejected a couple's appeal for coverage of their $40,000 IVF treatments despite concluding that they were discriminated against. In its opinion, the two member majority opinion noted that ". . . it can [not] be seriously disputed that a person unable to have a child has a physical disability," and went on to say that the government had let infertile patients down by denying a medically recommended and appropriate treatment. However, the court concluded that, in light of the limited financial resources of the government's health care system, the system was subject to "reasonable limits" and that the violation of rights was unfortunately justified. One judge dissented, saying there was no discrimination.

The Supreme Court of Canada declined to hear the couple's appeal.

Halifax National Post, 9/15/99; *CMAJ*, 10/3/00

2.13 Woman Files Federal Charges Alleging Discriminatory Health Coverage
Summer 2001

An American Airlines flight attendant has filed charges with the U.S. EEOC alleging that the airline's employee health plan policy constitutes sex, pregnancy, and disability discrimination. The health plan covers Viagra for men, but does not cover reproductive care for women, including infertility treatments, pap smears, or birth control pills. The employee's attorney expects the EEOC to give her approval to file a federal lawsuit against the airline in sixty to ninety days.

Alexander v. Am. Airlines, Inc., 2002 U.S. Dist. LEXIS 7089
(ultimately dismissing class action suit filed after EEOC approval)

2.14 Infertile Woman's Termination for Day Off to Undergo Egg Retrieval Presents an ADA, but Not a PDA, Claim
Fall 2001
BY N. ELSTER

Plaintiff Michelle Laporta was fired from her job as pharmacist at a Michigan Wal-Mart for failing to report for work on a day she requested to be off in order to undergo in vitro fertilization. Laporta advised her employer in the spring of 1997 that she was planning to undergo IVF necessitating her being absent from work periodically. Her supervisor informed her that he would work with her to provide her with the necessary time off. On a Friday, her physician informed her that she was ready to undergo egg retrieval, which was scheduled for that Monday. Laporta advised her employer of her need for the day off and was informed that no one was available to cover her shift. Laporta did not report to work on Monday but did work her full shift the following day. Two days later Laporta was terminated, her refusal to report for work that day cited as one of the reasons. She subsequently filed an action in the U.S. District Court for the Western District of Michigan.

Laporta filed an action under the ADA and PDA, asserting her infertility was a disability under those federal laws as well as under similar state statutes. Defendant Wal-Mart moved for summary judgment claiming Laporta did not show either that she suffered from a disability under the ADA or that infertility was covered by the PDA.

The court denied the defendant's motion for summary judgment on the ADA claim finding that Laporta did in fact suffer from a disability that substantially limited a major life activity and that "Wal-Mart's refusal to grant an arguably reasonable accommodation by granting plaintiff one day off, followed by its decision to terminate her for her failure to appear for work on that very day," presented an appropriate issue for a jury to consider. The court granted the defendant's motion for summary judgment on the PDA claim finding that infertility does not meet the statutory definition of discrimination "because of or on the basis of pregnancy, childbirth, or related medical conditions." The court reasoned that if Laporta's position was accepted, "the protected class must certainly include infertile people as well as pregnant women. If so, who would not be in the protected class? ... The court concludes that infertility is not a medical condition related to pregnancy or childbirth within the meaning of the PDA."

Laporta v. Wal-Mart, 163 F. Supp. 2d 758; 2001
U.S. Dist. LEXIS 7019

2.15 Personal Injury Insurance Policy Must Cover IVF Expenses
Fall 2001

A Delaware Superior Court recently addressed the issue of whether a no-fault automobile insurance policy's personal injury protection (PIP) provision covers IVF. Plaintiffs both suffered severe injuries in an automobile accident in February 1998. As a result of his injuries, the husband suffered from "obstructive azoospermia" rendering him unable to reproduce through sexual intercourse. The couple therefore underwent IVF using ICSI to conceive their child, paying more than $14,000.

The couple claimed that their PIP coverage provided by Liberty Mutual should cover their expenses for IVF not only for the two-year period of coverage, but also for any subsequent IVF attempts as well. Liberty Mutual, however, asserted that the claimants' IVF expenses were not "'reasonable and necessary expenses' resulting from prescribed medical treatment, but were merely for their comfort, convenience or other personal reasons." The court, finding in favor of the couple's claim for reimbursement of the initial IVF expenses, found that "the decision to undergo IVF may have been the husband's, but the need for it was precipitated by the accident. . . . But for the accident, [he] could have chosen to have children." The court went even further to hold that the wife's expenses associated with the procedure must also be covered because "[i]n order for [the husband's] IVF procedure to work, services must be provided to [the wife], too."

The court did, however, hold that the policy clearly stated a two-year limitation on personal injury protection coverage and thus Liberty Mutual was only bound to provide such protection for IVF occurring within that period. The court held that "Liberty Mutual must provide coverage under its policy for all of the couple's IVF expenses incurred within two years of the accident up to the Policy's PIP limit."

Liberty Mutual Fire Ins. Co. v. [name withheld],
2001 Del. Super. LEXIS 216 (6/27/01)

2.16(a) Physicians' Religious Objection to Treating Lesbian under Further Review
Winter 2006

A California appellate court has now ruled twice on two physicians' refusal to perform artificial insemination on an unmarried, lesbian patient, without resolving the legal issue.

The physicians claimed their refusal to treat was based on religious objections to treating unmarried women and does not violate California's antidiscrimination law, known as the Unruh Act. The patient, Guadalupe Benitez, had sought artificial insemination to have a child with her partner of fifteen years and, when the physicians refused to treat her, sued claiming a violation of her civil rights.

The trial court found no religious exemption under the state's anti-discrimination law. That decision was initially reversed on appeal, with the court ruling that the doctors presented a factual issue as to whether their refusal to treat was based on marital status or sexual orientation, with only the latter being clearly protected by the law. Benitez's attorneys, from Lambda Legal Defense, prevailed in having the appellate court vacate its opinion, grant a rehearing, and allow additional briefing, including amicus (friend-of-the-court) briefs on both sides by multiple professional and civil rights organizations.

2.16(b) California Court to Rule on M.D.'s Refusal of Services to Lesbian Mother
Fall 2007

In a case garnering national attention, including front-page coverage in *USA Today* and the involvement of more than forty interest groups, the California Supreme Court has agreed to consider a lesbian mother's claim that her former doctors violated California's antidiscrimination laws and whether the defendant doctors may raise as a defense that such treatment would violate their fundamentalist Christian views and thus their constitutionally protected principles of religious freedom.

The physicians referred Benitez to another, more expensive physician, where she ultimately underwent IVF and gave birth first to a son and then to twin daughters. Benitez claims that as an infertility patient of the defendant physicians for eleven months, she was repeatedly promised, but ultimately denied, donor insemination treatment. In 2000, California courts had interpreted its antidiscrimination law to apply to sexual orientation, but had not yet addressed marital status. Since that time, the law has been explicitly extended to both, with the legislative history to the amendment noting it was intended to clarify, not alter, the law. Despite such language, the lower intermediate court found the 2000 version of the law did not protect against marital status.

The case has had a long procedural history and multiple gay rights and civil rights groups, including the ACLU, have filed briefs in support of Benitez. More than a dozen conservative religious organizations and legal groups have filed briefs in support of the physicians.

The case is being watched closely, and its outcome will likely have a significant impact, if not a direct one, on patients and providers both within and beyond California.

2.16(c) California Supreme Court Weighs M.D.'s Refusal to Treat Lesbian in Wake of Gay Marriage Approval in that State

Summer 2008

Following on the heels of the California Marriage Cases, the California Supreme Court has now heard arguments in Guadalupe Benitez's appeal of a discriminatory access claim. The issue they will decide is whether any business, including physicians, which are subject to the state's antidiscrimination law can invoke religious beliefs to refuse services to a specific person or group.

Having less than two weeks earlier decided the Marriage Cases, which found that sexual orientation is a constitutionally suspect classification and that laws based on such classification must meet "strict scrutiny," the highest test of constitutionality, the justices reportedly peppered the attorneys with questions over how a religious belief could be used to justify denying treatment. One of the justices who had dissented in the Marriage Cases suggested from the bench that doctors have only two choices: provide services to anyone who needs them or chose another field of medicine. Benitez's lawyer argued that "doctors can choose their procedures, but they can't pick and choose among their patients."

The parties filed supplemental briefs with updated arguments following the decision in the Marriage Cases. Benitez's attorneys argued that the Court's gay marriage decision acknowledges that the state has a compelling interest in ending sexual-orientation discrimination, and that any such refusal of services must, and here has not and cannot, meet that test.

2.16(d) California Supreme Court Unanimously Confirms Right to Treatment

Spring 2009

The California Supreme Court has now affirmed that a lesbian patient cannot be refused fertility treatment under California's antidiscrimination statute based on sexual orientation.

The state Supreme Court found the Appeals Court erred, and that the defendants had not been precluded from arguing at a trial that their refusal was based solely on marital status. The court ruled it need not reach the question of whether such a refusal would be legally permissible since Benitez did not base her claim on marital status. The court did note that only the government, not a private citizen, can abridge First Amendment rights and that the physicians were still free to voice their views about, just not free to refuse to deliver, legally protected medical care.

The ruling is a major and long-awaited verdict that makes clear there is no religious exemption to California's Civil Rights Act based on sexual orientation, and that physicians may not deny medical services based on their patients' sexual orientation

North Coast Women's Care Medical Group, Inc. et al. v.
S.C. (Benitez), 2008 Cal. LEXIS 10756

II. MANDATING ACCESS TO TREATMENT: LEGISLATIVE DEVELOPMENTS

2.17 Consumers and Physicians Promote Mandated Infertility Legislation
September 1991

Both Illinois and Massachusetts experienced frenetic legislative activity this past session on the subject of mandated infertility insurance. The successful efforts of RESOLVE of Illinois, aided by the AFS Washington office, resulted in passage of favorable legislation in Illinois. RESOLVE of the Bay State, the Massachusetts RESOLVE chapter, with support from local physicians and IVF centers, as well as Serono Symposia, USA, saved their mandated coverage from elimination.

In Illinois, a bill mandating insurance coverage for diagnosis and treatment of infertility—including four ART attempts—was passed in record time and sent to the governor's desk in June. The original version of the bill was only filed in March of this year.

The surprising and impressive Illinois victory was snatched from the jaws of defeat on more than one occasion. With testimony from RESOLVE members and AFS legislative monitor, Robert R. Kazet, M.D., the bill was passed in the House but met initial defeats in committee and in the full Senate before being amended through a procedure allowing it to be brought back for additional votes. RESOLVE members, aided by an AFS Legislative Alert asking all Illinois AFS members to contact their senators, inundated their legislature with letters and telephone calls. These efforts paid off when the bill passed at the last hour.

Massachusetts has had comprehensive mandated infertility coverage since 1987, but an attempt to eliminate infertility and four other mandates was slipped into the proposed House budget without warning or fanfare. RESOLVE of the Bay State was notified by legislative staff the day the budget proposal was issued and quickly coordinated a successful letter and telephone campaign. Additionally, area IVF centers, physicians, and Serono Symposia USA helped RESOLVE with their mailings, set up a fax tree to update patients and providers, alerted patients, made themselves available to RESOLVE, and provided financial support.

The ultimate result of this cooperative effort was a final compromise provision worked out by a joint House and Senate committee and signed into law by the governor. That provision reinstates mandated coverage for public as well as private employees and directed the state's insurance commissioner to conduct a study of all mandates and make recommendations to the legislature.

The Illinois and Massachusetts experiences illustrate how effective joint consumer and provider efforts can be in both obtaining and keeping fair access to infertility treatment.

Mass. Gen. Laws. ch. 175 §47H; 215 ILCS
5/356m

2.18 Scotland to Fund IVF

June 1992

Scotland's National Health Service announced that it will fund the four IVF centers in that country. This will enable many couples who previously could not afford this option to pursue biological parenting. Details, such as limits on the number of attempts, counseling, and screening have yet to be determined.

Times Newspapers Ltd., 3/8/92

2.19 N.Y. Infertility Insurance Bills Progress; N.J. Governor Vetoes Similar Law
Summer 2000

The New York State Legislature has moved favorably on two bills that would require all group insurance policies and HMO contracts regulated under New York law to include coverage for the diagnosis and treatment of infertility. Early in 2000, the New York State Assembly passed one version of the proposed law [A. 7303], which would require broad coverage of infertility, including medications and a minimum of four ART procedures (plus an additional two cycles if a birth results).

During the same period, the New York Senate passed a more restrictive version of the bill [S.3131-B], which would also provide coverage for infertility drugs and up to four IVF cycles. The Senate version contains other significant restrictions however, including a limitation that patients must be between the ages of twenty-five and forty-four to receive treatment; a maximum lifetime benefit of $60,000 (excluding drugs); and a "conscience clause" allowing employers and insurers controlled by religious organizations to refuse coverage for treatments that would violate their religious tenets. The Senate bill also contains a sunset clause that would eliminate the law in two years unless it is re-enacted.

According to representatives of the American Infertility Association, Inc. (AIA), whose volunteers have been instrumental in the effort to pass an infertility law in New York, infertility insurance advocates, including AIA and ACOG, are currently working with the staff of both houses of the New York legislature in an attempt to draft a compromise bill by early summer. If that attempt is successful, it is hoped that Governor Pataki will sign the new law into effect.

On a related note, in January 2000 an infertility insurance bill passed both Houses of the New Jersey State Legislature, only to be vetoed by Governor Christine Whitman. Infertility advocates have already begun to plan a renewed effort in New Jersey to bring their message directly to the Governor.

> *Note:* In August 2001, New Jersey passed "An Act Requiring health insurers to provide coverage for medically necessary expenses incurred in diagnosis and treatment of infertility."
>
> 2001 N.J. Ch. 236; N.J. Stat. 17:48-6x *et seq.*

2.20 Rhode Island Governor Vetoes Extending Infertility Insurance to Unmarried Women

Fall 2007

As the California Supreme Court considers whether doctors may deny services to women based on their marital status or sexual orientation (in the pending *Benitez* case [2.16]), Rhode Island's governor vetoed legislation that would have extended that state's required infertility insurance coverage to unmarried women. The governor issued a statement that, "[a]s a matter of public policy, the state should be encouraging the birth of children to two-parent families, not the reverse. By removing the marriage requirement, the legislation forces health insurance companies to subsidize out-of-wedlock births. . . . [a]ny further tinkering with this benefit is unnecessary and unwarranted, and allows for even further creeping of cost in our healthcare system."

Providence Journal, 7/20/07

CHAPTER THREE

General Professional Liability Litigation

NOTE: *This chapter is composed of a limited selection of professional liability cases, specifically those that do not fit into any one chapter dedicated to a limited topic. Most of the reported professional liability litigation, including both civil and criminal cases, arises in the context of a specific medical or laboratory procedure, such as donor insemination, embryo transfer (or mis-transfer), or cryopreservation, or within a specific type of claim such as disputes over embryo disposition or custody of born children. Those cases are reported within the appropriate specific chapters.*

❖ MEDICAL COMMENTARY, BY Howard W. Jones, Jr.

THIS CHAPTER RAISES a number of liability-related concerns for medical practitioners.

Multiple pregnancies continue to be an unsolved problem, although improvements have been made in recent years, including a reduction in the number of transferred embryos necessary to create a pregnancy. In any discussion of multiple pregnancies it should be noted that although IVF contributes to the problem, it is by no means the most important or frequent cause of multiple pregnancies. In the United States, the frequency of twins from ovulation induction or ovulation enhancement is four times greater than from IVF, and when it comes to triplets, that figure increases to six times greater than IVF. Nevertheless, public interest has largely centered on the number of embryos to transfer with IVF. The 2009 birth of octuplets following IVF with a multiple embryo transfer far in excess of the current ASRM guidelines may significantly impact this issue. Indeed, proposed laws were introduced in a number of states shortly after the births were announced, putting forth a variety of potential restrictions.

It has always seemed to this practitioner that the law might be able to address—or at least question—situations involving multiple births. In the United States there are professional guidelines from the ASRM but no laws or currently any insurance limits placed on the number of embryos to be transferred. It is surprising, at least to this author, that in the event of the birth of multiples in violation of these guidelines, there has so rarely been any legal questioning or litigation based on the decision of how many embryos to transfer.

This lack of legal action over this issue may be rooted in a case that arose some years ago when the United Kingdom was using guidelines for the number of embryos to transfer, rather than the current situation where the law provides a legal basis for limiting the number to transfer under certain situations. During the guideline era in the U.K., the general medical council (GMC) began disciplinary hearings against an IVF specialist who transferred more embryos than was provided for in the guidelines. After considerable investigation, the GMC dropped its effort to discipline the physician on the basis that the guidelines did not have the status of law and therefore the GMC could not proceed. Whether the prevalence of voluntary professional guidelines, rather than laws, in the United States has prevented litigation associated with multiple pregnancies following embryo transfers above the ASRM guidelines is for lawyers to say, but it is an interesting question to consider.

In other areas, medical practitioners may be exposed to liability even in situations where there are no applicable guidelines or laws. There is a British suit detailed in this chapter in which $2 million was awarded to three surviving quadruplets because gonadotropins, presumably for ovulation induction, were administered in a manner that produced a high-order multiple pregnancy. The reason for this seems to be that there are not any guidelines available to suggest how to use gonadotropins for ovulation induction or ovulation enhancement, let alone any law, in the United States or elsewhere. Given that such litigation has prevailed outside the United States involving a high-order multiple pregnancy resulting from ovulation induction or ovulation enhancement, it is likely only a matter of time before a suit is filed in the United States against a physician or clinic based on higher multiples in violation of the guidelines for IVF, notwithstanding a lack of a legal limit.

In addition to applicable regulations or laws, the existence of any prior consents or agreements—whether oral or written—may also influence the outcome of a case involving multiple births as a result of an ART procedure. The British case noted above involved the Sheffield Fertility Center and a couple who, after having triplets, was awarded child care for the third triplet because they had stipulated ahead of time to have only two embryos transferred. When at the last minute there appeared to be an extra embryo of doubtful quality, there was a verbal discussion with the couple just prior to the transfer in which the clinic director reportedly urged the couple to transfer all three in the hopes of getting a singleton; the couple, after a brief discussion decided to accept the advice. When healthy triplets resulted, the couple sued and was awarded £2 million for the extra child. From a clinical perspective, a physician should be very reluctant—indeed, I would urge, should make it a point never—to raise a previously undisclosed point at the last minute, particularly if there is only a verbal consent from or agreement with the patient. Any such decision needs to be written down. Perhaps the lesson should be that last-minute changes of this kind should not be undertaken unless there is a previous agreement that such a last-minute decision might be necessary. Above all, everything that is done should be clearly agreed upon in writing, by all concerned, prior to the procedure.

This chapter also contains many cases involving mix-ups of gametes in creating embryos, splitting or sharing gamete specimens without prior authorization, and using embryos that were clearly intended for use in another case and for another patient. These mix-ups cannot be tolerated and should never occur.

One very interesting concern from a medical perspective is the appropriate status of malpractice insurance protection for embryological laboratory personnel. When a program is part of or associated with a large hospital or medical school, laboratory personnel should be protected by the institutional policy that covers medical support personnel. However, an increasing number of IVF programs are now free-standing, which opens up the possibility of far more variable practices. Without knowing the facts regarding specific programs, I suspect that malpractice insurance for embryological laboratory personnel in free-standing clinics varies considerably and in many instances may be inadequate.

Another troubling issue is the extent of responsibility of a medical clinic and related professionals to anticipate the welfare of any resultant child, as well as that of the adult participants, prior to a procedure. In the case of *Huddleston v. Infertility Center of America* (1996), for example, the infant of a surrogate mother and single man was murdered by the biological father after the child was born. In the United Kingdom, part of the HEFA regulations necessitate that, before administering care, a clinic should give consideration to the welfare of the child. In the United States, this is usually not considered, but *Huddleston* raises the question of whether in special situations the clinic has some responsibility to screen certain parties. This might arise in situations where surrogacy is involved or even where donor eggs or sperm are involved. This may be particularly so for donor eggs because, unlike donor sperm, complete anonymity is essentially impossible to ensure with donor eggs. The nature of retrieving eggs is such that there is always a medical procedure and many people are involved, so guaranteeing anonymity becomes impossible. In contrast, if anonymity is desired in sperm donation, it can be achieved in at least some instances because, in theory, only two people need to know about it. If, however, donor anonymity is not desired— there seems to be a growing trend away from anonymity—then donors of eggs and sperm can be treated equally.

Another factor that may be relevant to liability is the extent to which patients are screened or counseled before medical procedures are performed. Most clinics spend a considerable amount of time undertaking psychological screening of egg donors, but I suspect very few clinics spend time psychologically screening the recipients of donor eggs. *Huddelston* certainly suggests that there might be merit in doing so where parentage may resemble that resulting from the reproductive process in *Brave New World*. It is also worth mentioning that health care providers treating infertility have at least two, and sometimes three or more, different individual patients to whom they owe a professional duty of care.

When this observer was actively seeing patients, he thought that it was desirable to interview the infertile couple together and also useful to interview the wife and husband separately. This was not always possible, but it seemed useful whenever it was feasible. Usually, the wife was first, and when I discovered that the patient was complaining of infertility, my first question to her was, "Why do you want to have a baby?" This usually brought an incredulous stare and silence. I tried not to break the silence, because I wanted to hear the patient formulate exactly why she wanted to get pregnant. There are many good reasons to get pregnant, but there are some reasons not to get pregnant and it was these "not" reasons that I was listening for. If the patient said something like, "Well, my husband and I do not seem to be getting along very well, and I thought if I got pregnant this would help bring our marriage together," in my view, this was the worst possible answer. Children are a great pleasure, but they are also a trial, and many marriages are strained by children. If a patient indicated to me that he or she was having marital difficulties, my usual response was to outline a course of investigation that would be somewhat prolonged with the hope that the patient would realize that what they were doing might not be in the best interest of all concerned in the long run. This is another example of paternalistic medicine, but this observer happens to be old enough to believe that in certain situations this is appropriate.

∾ LEGAL COMMENTARY, BY Susan L. Crockin

As the medical advances in reproductive medicine and technology outpaced established legal frameworks, professionals providing ART-related services became progressively more exposed to novel legal claims. In addition to traditional claims of medical malpractice or negligence, professionals have found themselves facing claims for breach of contract, violations of privacy, deceptive advertising, and consumer protection violations, to name a few.

The majority of liability cases will be found in the specific chapter addressing the particular medical condition or treatment that gave rise to the legal claim. This chapter discusses those cases that do not fit neatly into any specific topic, such as mixed-up embryos (chapter 1), access to care (chapter 2), or collaborative arrangements gone awry (chapters 4, 5, and 6). Readers interested in professional liability issues will also want to review those chapters to get a more complete understanding of how the law has evolved and continues to respond to these various medical advances.

One notable shift in the law has been the almost complete absence of privacy-related cases since the early 1990s, when two couples sued for breach of privacy over photographs of them published in connection with fertility issues. This change likely reflects a marked increase in the acceptability of both infertility and ART treatment, including IVF, since that time. In one case, a couple pregnant with triplets sued their IVF program and local TV station when their photograph appeared in connection with the program's celebration. The court noted that their participation was a "private matter" and "publicizing the . . . persons who undergo such medical miracles without their consent and without waiver states a (legal) claim."

Today, when popular magazines routinely publish photographs of celebrity parents, their children, and their gestational carriers (but seldom mention the likely frequent use of egg donors) on their covers, it may be hard to recall the years when these medical treatments were undertaken so privately. Indeed, given the proliferation of both professional and popular media coverage of fertility treatments, the public is increasingly aware that many pregnancies are not achieved "naturally."

Another historical anomaly appears to be cases involving deceptive advertising and fraudulent billing practices. Following the enactment of the federal Fertility Clinic Success Rate and Certification Act of 1992 and the Society of Assisted Reproductive Technology's implementation of reporting procedures, claims of inflated or misleading advertising appear to have subsided. As insurance coverage has increased, on the one hand, and ART-related treatments deemed ineligible for insurance coverage (frequently surrogacy and gestational carrier arrangements) have been more clearly labeled, on the other hand, claims of fraudulent billing practices seem to have also subsided.

In contrast, the proliferation of both civil and criminal lawsuits reported here and in specific chapters attest to the increased use of ART and the growing number of individuals involved in creating babies on both the professional and patient sides. While most such suits are brought by patients against physicians and by parents against one another, a small but growing number of civil cases have also been brought against embryologists, attorneys, and others. Some are related to heart-wrenching custody battles over children born from accidentally swapped embryos or gametes or born to divorcing or separating couples or single parents. Divorce cases involving frozen embryos continue to present unresolved legal issues over both control of the embryos and the characterization of cryopreservation documents as consent forms or contracts. Significant legal implications frequently flow from those characterizations.

In one notorious example (*Huddleston v. ICA*, 1996), both a civil case and a criminal case resulted after a single man killed his infant child born to a traditional surrogate. In the civil suit, the most significant legal aspect was the surrogate's claim, initially rejected by the trial court but reinstated by the appellate court. The higher court recognized a novel legal duty owed to the surrogate by the lawyer and others who recruited her, parties that the lower court characterized as "brokers." Even though the surrogate never intended to raise the child, the court found that she was owed a legal duty of care based on the fact of her being recruited into the program. Such legal theories may well have broader applications to other burgeoning areas of collaborative reproduction.

Paralleling developments in ART, genetic testing advances are also straining existing legal frameworks to resolve problems that arise. As genetic testing moves from adults to fetuses (through chorionic villus sampling (CVS) or testing amniotic fluid), to preembryos or embryos (through preimplantation genetic diagnosis of IVF embryos (PGD)), existing tort law and legal theories of "wrongful birth," "wrongful conception," and "wrongful life" will increasingly be put to the test. Additionally, issues involving choice and conflict of laws between jurisdictions where patients live and where tests are performed or reported will be raised, explored, and, one hopes, resolved. One such example is the 2007 decision in *Hood v. LabCorp*, which involved a North Carolina lab misreading its test results for the amniotic fluid of a Maryland couple whose child was born with cystic fibrosis (reported in chapter 9). The company's defense partially relied on the more favorable law of North Carolina, which permits "wrongful conception" but not "wrongful birth," on the theory that it does not want to encourage aborting existing pregnancies. Through a detailed and sophisticated legal analysis, the courts ultimately ruled that Maryland law, not North Carolina law, should apply to protect Maryland residents and that legal liability should not turn on which state the test was performed in. Had North Carolina been the applicable law, a different significant issue could have been presented: whether the outcome of such a case should turn on whether or not the chosen prenatal test was PGD or an amniocentesis, that is, whether an IVF embryo could be treated the same as an in utero fetus for purposes of tort liability. Such cases will likely continue to push the envelope in terms of defining the legal rights and responsibilities of those who order, administer, and receive genetic testing.

Ongoing efforts to standardize medical practice through uniform consent forms (such as have been developed by ASRM in 2008–2009, an effort in which this author took part) or through standardized protocols, voluntary professional guidelines or model laws will likely address some of the more apparent inconsistencies and at the same time create new avenues of responsibility and thus potential liability. To the extent that professional societies establish or recommend uniform practices, they may minimize individual professional liability while simultaneously increasing their own liability if such practices are successfully challenged. At the same time, there is the possibility of increased liability for medical practitioners if the standard of care to which they would otherwise be held in their community (or jurisdiction) is replaced by a higher standard of care through their choosing to adhere to higher uniform standards.

Because ART cases present a unique phenomenon by involving anywhere from two to six patients (in the case of two intended parents, two gamete donors, and a married gestational surrogate), medical and other professionals frequently have multiple and potentially conflicting obligations to those patients. Thus, ART practices can raise unique issues relating to duty of care in the arenas of malpractice and health law. As *Huddleston v. ICA* (1996) and *Stiver v. Parker* (1992) suggested but few subsequent cases have addressed, clear legal standards or duties of care have not yet been established in any coherent or uniform way. Until such time as these issues are addressed and resolved more consistently through guidelines, regulations, uniform laws, or a combination thereof, frequent court cases with varying results in different jurisdictions will continue to proliferate.

Litigation

3.1 IVF Center Celebration Ends in Lawsuit

March 1991

A fifth anniversary celebration commemorating the success of the IVF program at Jewish Hospital of St. Louis led a couple to file suit after they appeared on a television news broadcast of the event. The couple claimed that they were assured there would be no publicity or public exposure.

The couple, who say they had kept their participation in the program a secret, argued that because of the appearance, their privacy was invaded and that they were subjected to embarrassment, ridicule, shame, and humiliation. At the time of the event, the wife was five months pregnant with triplets as a result of IVF.

The suit was filed against the hospital and the television station that broadcast the story. Both initially moved to dismiss the lawsuit. Even assuming the allegations were true, which is required at that preliminary legal stage, they argued that the couple had waived any privacy rights when they attended the event, and that no reasonable person would be ashamed or humiliated by what amounted to a three-second film "clip" of a group of IVF patients within a news broadcast on the subject of IVF.

The trial court agreed and dismissed the suit, but an appellate court refused to dismiss the case. That court ruled: "the in vitro program and its success may well have been matters of public interest, but the identity of the plaintiffs participating in the program was . . . a private matter . . . publicizing the individual persons who undergo such medical miracles without their consent and without waiver states a (legal) claim. . . ."

According to the hospital attorney, the couple was informed that there would be media coverage of the event. This factual issue must now be decided in court. Presently, the parties are engaged in discovery proceedings and are awaiting trial. Ironically, the trial will undoubtedly generate more publicity.

Y.G. v. Jewish Hosp. of St. Louis, 795 S.W.2d 488

(Mo. Ct. App. 1990)

3.2 Privacy Claim of Fertile Couple Rejected

March 1991

Another privacy claim, this time brought in a New York court by a fertile couple, had a different outcome. Ida and Joseph Finger, on behalf of themselves and their six children, claimed that their privacy rights were violated by a photograph of their family that accompanied an article on enhanced fertility. The magazine used the family's picture over a caption referring to "java-spritzed sperm" in an article that described caffeine-enhanced sperm motility in an IVF research project. The family had no connection with the program.

The couple argued that there was a distinction between the newsworthiness of an article about fertility research and the privacy rights of a fertile family who were not related to the reported research study. In contrast to the Jewish Hospital case, the court rejected their claim, finding instead that the couple's ability to have six children, whether naturally or with medical assistance, established a "real connection" to the article's general theme of "fertility."

Finger v. Omni Publications Int'l,
77 N.Y.2d 138 (N.Y. 1990)

3.3 British Physicians Refuse Fertility Treatment to HIV-Positive Couple

September 1991

Citing legal and ethical concerns as well as potential medical risks to staff, London doctors have refused to provide assisted reproductive techniques to an HIV-positive couple. Physicians at St. Mary's Hospital counseled the couple about HIV and pregnancy and performed preliminary infertility investigations. However, they drew the line at assisting in bringing about conception itself. The doctors raised concerns over a "wrongful life" lawsuit by a child born HIV-positive and about helping bring a likely orphan into the world. Legal experts in Britain said it was unlikely a child would succeed in a wrongful birth or life claim, but noted that a negligence action could be brought if physicians failed to warn the woman that pregnancy could accelerate her own condition.

Independent, 6/16/91

3.4 AIDS-Infected Doctor Gives Rise to Infertility Patients' Lawsuit against Medical Centers

December 1991

In what is believed to be the first legal case concerning an infertility center and AIDS exposure, Kelly Wolgemuth and her husband have filed a class action lawsuit on behalf of 400 Pennsylvania infertility patients and their families against Hershey Medical Center and Harrisburg Hospital. Both hospitals employed a resident who had AIDS. The resident, who has since taken a voluntary leave of absence, apparently participated in surgical procedures at the two health centers. Representatives for the medical centers say they took appropriate precautions. The patients' attorney says he hopes the lawsuit will force hospitals into mandatory screening.

Wolgemuth v. Henry and Hershey Medical, 434 Pa. Super. 678, 640 A.2d 481 (1994); *appeal denied*, 538 Pa. 649 (Pa. 1994)

3.5 New York Fertility Clinic Withdraws Brochures

March 1993

Mt. Sinai Medical Center has agreed to stop distributing promotional material that allegedly contained vague, inconsistent, and false statements. For example, the brochures contained the statement that the center's "take-home baby rate" for its IVF patients was a higher percentage than was its actual overall success rate, which was reportedly less than 10 percent. The center's action was taken in response to a charge from New York City's consumer affairs commissioner who claimed that the literature was false and misleading. He has reportedly suggested that although he is pleased that the hospital has ceased distribution of questionable information, it must "still face the legal consequences for deceiving infertility clients in the past." He has not described what those might involve.

The center reportedly reviewed the literature and concluded that the quoted rates were consistent with "subsets" of patients, but that the "overall success rates" could not be confirmed. Consequently, it agreed to permanently withdraw the promotional brochures in question, scrutinize all future promotional materials, and appoint a committee to review any such information reported in the future.

UPI International, 12/08/92

3.6(a) Lawsuits and Investigations Mount against California Doctors (Dr. Asch and Others) and Universities; Embryologists Sued; and Legislation Proposed

Spring 1996

As the number of patients involved rises to a hundred, and the number of separate lawsuits filed by former patients reaches over thirty-two, lawyers for the University of California have requested a six-month stay in their lawsuit against Drs. Asch, Balmaceda, and Stone. In other developments, Dr. Asch was deposed in Tijuana, Mexico, in January; two embryologists have now been sued by a former patient; and two former employees of the Center for Reproductive Health have sued for wrongful terminations. The seven separate investigations continue and new civil and criminal legislation has been proposed in California. The doctors have all denied any intentional wrongdoing.

Former patients have filed at least thirty-two separate lawsuits to date against either Drs. Asch, Balmaceda, and Stone, or the University of California. University officials have said they anticipate twenty-five more such suits. Over a hundred patients are now estimated to have had their eggs or embryos misappropriated and seven children are believed to have been born to nongenetic and/or unintended parents. Dr. Asch was ordered by a Superior Court judge to appear for a January 5 deposition in connection with about a dozen of those lawsuits. He did not appear at the originally scheduled November deposition. At a December court hearing, his attorney, David Brown, stated that Dr. Asch is in Mexico City for a one-year teaching and research sabbatical.

In January, Dr. Asch appeared at a deposition held in Tijuana because of his reported fear of arrest if he returns to the United States. The deposition was scheduled for four days and included attorneys involved in at least twenty-four lawsuits. Dr. Asch reportedly portrayed himself as an "out-of-touch" administrator, whose only role was to perform surgeries. According to his attorney, Lloyd Charton, "It's becoming more and more clear that Dr. Asch depended on the people under him to fill out consent forms . . . if they didn't do that, mistakes were made." The deposition was interrupted by a bomb scare and lost stenographic notes, and resulting searches of the hotel. Some attorneys characterized the proceedings as a "circus" and suggested the interruptions were created to delay the substantive deposition.

On December 18, lawyers for the University of California asked an Orange County Superior Court judge for a six-month suspension of their lawsuit against Drs. Asch, Balmaceda, and Stone, until the conclusion of a federal criminal investigation by the U.S. Attorney's Office. University attorneys said that their suit, which alleges that the doctors misappropriated eggs and embryos, kept funds owed to the university, conducted unauthorized human subjects research, and refused to turn over key documents, is impossible to pursue while criminal investigators hold essential records. Attorneys for the doctors have concurred in the request, leading some patients' attorneys to question the motivation of the university's actions. University spokespersons state it is simply a waste of university money and court time to move forward while critical documentation is unavailable to them.

On the legislative front, bills have been proposed in California that would make it easier to criminally prosecute gamete theft, bring civil suits for misappropriation, and prevent confidential settlements in "whistleblower" cases involving public agencies and funds. The criminal bill, which would not have retroactive application, would define the transfer of eggs or embryos without a patient's consent as theft and battery and be classified as a felony punishable with up to three years in prison and possible loss of medical license. Orange Country Deputy District Attorney Chuck Middleton applauded the bill saying, "It's a deterrent that will be heard loud and clear." Middleton, who also serves on a hospital bioethics committee, suggested that a tough stand by the criminal justice system might also encourage the medical community to increase regulation of the fertility industry.

Two former clinic employees have filed suit claiming wrongful terminations. One claims she was the initial whistleblower; the other claims that she was fired after she questioned instructions to hand over large sums of cash to the physicians and record payments as "adjustments" and not income.

To date, none of the thirty-two lawsuits filed by former patients seek custody of a genetic child, although at least one couple, the Challendars, have stated publicly that while they would not seek custody of the three-year-old twins they claim are their genetic children (a claim that is disputed), they do want an opportunity to follow their "ups and downs" and have reportedly expressed concern over the fact that they are being raised in a Jewish home. The couple are among a number of former patients whose attorney has hired public relations experts to "coach" them for media appearances.

Also among the couples who have filed suit alleging missing embryos are Chrispina and Mark Calvert, whose first child was the subject of a landmark lawsuit in California (*Calvert v. Johnson,* [6.1]) when the woman who had agreed to carry their child attempted to gain custody. The California Supreme Court ultimately ruled that gestational carriers in that state are not mothers. According to the Calvert's present lawyer, they had hoped to have their next child with less publicity.

A third couple has sued two embryologists working at the clinics and two administrators at University of California Irvine (UCI) Medical Center who were fired last summer, in addition to Dr. Asch and UCI. They allege that their egg was misappropriated in late 1993, resulting in the birth of a child to a couple in Mexico, which would have been avoided if UCI officials had properly investigated allegations dating back to 1991 against Dr. Asch. This is believed to be the first case publicly reported to include embryologists amongst the defendants.

One California newspaper, with access to the list of "matched" donors and recipients, has been calling and attempting to put the parties in touch with one another.

Los Angeles Times, Sacramento Bee, Orange County Register, various dates

3.6(b) First Custody Lawsuit Filed Due to Unconsented Egg or Embryo Transfers

Summer 1996

The first child custody suit arising out of the allegations centering around Drs. Asch, Balmaceda, and Stone, and the UCI Center for Reproductive Health was filed in February. A California couple is charging that six-year-old twins born to another California couple were conceived with their eggs or embryos. Both couples were patients at the UCI Center for Reproductive Health in January 1989. Loretta and Basilio Jorge, who never gave birth to a child as a result of their treatments, recently learned their eggs had been "donated" without their consent. They have not yet been able to determine whose sperm was used to fertilize the eggs. They reportedly secretly videotaped and photographed children over a two-month period and have now filed a custody suit in which they seek visitation and genetic testing of the children. To date, the rearing parents have refused the Jorges' requests and have responded to the suit, charging that the Jorges lack legal standing to pursue their claims. The case is pending.

Jorge v. [Name Withheld], Riverside Cty., Sup. Ct. Cal., under seal (1996)

3.6(c) UCI Settles Two Cases Involving Children Born from Stolen Eggs
Winter 1996

The first two settlements of over eighty lawsuits filed involving UCI and Drs. Asch, Balmaceda, and Stone have been approved. Both involve plaintiffs whose eggs were taken without their consent and resulted in the birth of a child. One couple's settlement was for $600,000; the other's for $510,000. The settlements were reached after mediation and end all claims by the two couples against both the university and the physicians. Attorneys for the physicians have objected to being excluded from the settlement talks and decisions. The attorney for the two couples, who likened the experience to a rape and theft, has said his clients are in mourning and needed to take this step to start putting the experience behind them. One of the women has also written a letter to the family raising her biological son.

The settlements were also reportedly motivated in part by the university's desire to establish a "de facto" ceiling on other pending lawsuits. According to published reports, confidential internal memorandum prepared by university attorneys recommended settlement of the cases as a means of providing assistance in "convincing other patients to abandon grandiose settlement claims and evaluate their cases in a realistic manner." Outside legal fees and services for the university, paid by California taxpayers, are reportedly over $2.7 million.

The university also reportedly settled a third suit, for $2,500. That suit involved misinforming a patient about the status and location of her embryos.

Moore v. UCI et al.; Clay v. UCI et al., Orange
Cty., Sup. Ct. Cal.; docket #s752293–7552294
(settlements allowed 8/96)

3.6(d) UCI Files Suit against Doctors to Recoup Settlement Losses and Successfully Defends against Required Defense

Winter 1999

UCI has filed a civil lawsuit against Drs. Asch, Stone, and Balmaceda, attempting to obtain court orders requiring the doctors to repay the settlement costs associated with lawsuits arising from their practice at the university's Center for Reproductive Health. The lawsuit contends that the physicians have refused to provide medical, laboratory, and other records, which has hindered the investigation, and estimates its losses at over $19 million. Two of the three doctors are currently practicing outside of the country.

Note: The Court of Appeal also reversed a trial court order compelling the university's Regents to provide a defense for Dr. Stone, in one of the civil actions against him for unconsented implantation of their genetic material into another woman. The court concluded the conduct the plaintiffs alleged was outside the scope of the physician's employment. At the time, the Regents had before them a clinical panel report concluding egg stealing took place at the fertility clinic.

Stone v. Regents of Univ. of Cal., 77 Cal. App. 4th 736
(Cal. Ct. App. 1999); *Orange County Register*, 9/24/99
(initial published reports of case)

3.6(e) Doctor Arrested in Argentina in 1995 U.C. Irvine–Related Charges

Winter 2000

Dr. Jose Balmaceda was arrested January 18, 2001, in Buenos Aires in connection with pending federal criminal charges in the United States stemming from the alleged 1995 theft of eggs and embryos from the U.C. Irvine clinic where he worked with Drs. Ricardo Asch and Sergio Stone. Dr. Stone was convicted in 1997 for fraudulent billing practices and sentenced to one year of home detention and a

$50,000 fine. Dr. Asch is reportedly living in Mexico and running a medical practice there. Authorities here have encountered difficulties in their attempts to apprehend Drs. Asch and Balmaceda because extradition is difficult from both Chile and Mexico and because neither doctor is a U.S. citizen.

Dr. Balmaceda reportedly eluded authorities for over two years, while living in Chile running a fertility clinic. Federal agents had been monitoring his activities, including traveling to several conferences outside of Chile that he was expected to attend. They were unsuccessful in finding him until his arrest in Argentina after acting on tips that the doctor would be traveling there. Buenos Aires police have reportedly promised to keep him jailed for up to sixty days pending an extradition proceeding. Although U.S. officials predict Dr. Balmaceda will fight extradition, an extradition agreement between the United States and Argentina makes it likely he will be sent to the United States to face charges, including a thirty-count indictment for mail fraud relating to billing practices.

Los Angeles Times, 1/20/01

3.6(f) Former U.C. Irvine Patients' Lawsuit to Determine Twins' Parentage Rejected
Winter 2002

A state appellate court recently upheld the dismissal of a lawsuit brought by a former UCI patient couple to try to determine whether they are the genetic parents of twin girls born to another couple in 1988. The decision affirms a lower court's ruling that both public policy and the state's rules of evidence precluded the lawsuit. The couple initially sought DNA testing and custody. They dropped their custody claim but continued to seek visitation with the now fourteen-year-old girls, reportedly hired private investigators to do surveillance on the family and the girls' school, and threatened to tell the children about themselves. Declaring it hearsay and therefore inadmissible, the lower court refused to accept as evidence a "declaration" from the program's embryologist that records seized by the FBI indicated the second woman had received eggs from the first, resulting in a twin pregnancy. That court also ruled that even if such evidence did establish a genetic connection, it was in the best interest of the children to dismiss the lawsuit.

The plaintiffs had previously received a monetary settlement from the university after learning that their stored embryos had been misdirected. The appellate court found that the couple's rights were vindicated with that settlement, stating "[t]he rights still at issue are not the [couple's] rights. They are the rights of the Does [the rearing parents] and their twins to be free from the interference of strangers who have no standing to pursue their demands . . . and who cannot alter the focus of this issue by characterizing the Does' rights as mere privacy interests that may, under appropriate circumstances, give way to greater rights."

Prato-Morrison v. Doe, 103 Cal. App. 4th 222
(Cal. Ct. App. 2002)

3.6(g) U.C. Irvine Multi-Million Dollar Settlements Disclosed
Summer 2007

More than a decade after the initial scandal, U.C. Irvine has released settlement figures paid out to patients whose eggs were taken without their knowledge or consent through the IVF practice run there by Drs. Ricardo Asch and Jose Balmaceda. A total of $23.2 million was paid to patients whose eggs were either given to other patients— some of which resulted in children—donated for research or which were never found. The total included settlements ranging from about $2,000 to $700,000, the highest resulting from cases where eggs resulted in the birth of a child to an unrelated woman. Despite initial custody claims, none of those approximately twelve cases ultimately ended in a full custody lawsuit, and all of those children were left to be raised by the women who birthed them.

In all, 139 patient lawsuits were filed, sixteen of which were ultimately dismissed. Whistleblower claims were separately settled by UCI, with those settlements also in the millions of dollars, and criminal prosecutions were pursued against the individual physicians who subsequently left the United States.

Orange County Register, 6/26/07

3.7(a) Class Action Status Denied in NewYork Suit against Infertility Clinic

Summer 1996

A New York state trial judge has denied class action status to a lawsuit brought by a couple who claim that an infertility program mis-
represented its success rates and withheld information about health
risks. The plaintiffs, Jayne and Kenneth Karlin, named IVF America,
IVF (N.Y.), Vicki Baldwin, John J. Stangel, M.D., and United Hospital in their suit. The complaint alleges that the program at United
Hospital failed to adequately explain the statistical chances of
achieving pregnancy through misrepresentation of success rates of
various treatments and withheld information about health risks to
mothers and babies. Because the lawsuit was framed as one of consumer fraud, sought money damages for medical expenses and emotional issues, and involved individual issues arising out of the doctor-
patient relationship, the judge ruled that the couple failed to meet
three of the five prongs of the required test under state law for class
action certification and rejected their effort to certify and represent a
class of 4,500 patients. The case will proceed as an individual lawsuit
brought by the named plaintiffs, and the court set up a discovery
schedule for the parties.

3.7(b) Appellate Court Upholds Right to Sue IVF Program under State Consumer Protection Laws

Fall 1999

New York's highest court has upheld a couple's right to sue an IVF
program for false practices and deceptive advertising under that
state's consumer protection laws. It rejected the program's argument
that any claims by its former patients should be limited to medical
malpractice stemming from lack of informed consent, although the
court found those claims could also be brought based on the state's
public health laws. The court distinguished the two types of claims
and interests involved. In contrast to "providing information to individual patients in the course of medical treatment," the court found
that the defendant program's "alleged multi-media dissemination of
information to the public is precisely the sort of consumer-oriented
conduct that is targeted" by its consumer protection laws.

After two and one-half years of unsuccessful treatment, the couple sued, claiming the program disseminated false success rates and mis-represented IVF-related health risks, and thereby "deceptively lured" both patients and referring physicians. The court found the claims fell within the state's consumer protection laws, which it ruled were broad enough to apply to virtually all economic activity. The court also noted that exempting medical services from the consumer protection laws, as the defendant program argued, would be contrary to the scope and history of these laws. Reviewing prior cases, the court noted, ". . . when [physicians] choose to reach out to the consuming public at large in order to promote business, like clothing retailers, automobile dealers, and wedding singers who engage in such conduct, they subject themselves to the standards of an honest marketplace. . . ."

Karlin v. IVF Am., Inc., 93 N.Y.2d 282 (N.Y. 1999)

3.8 "Physician-Assisted Adultery" Claim Brought in Illinois for IVF with Non-Spouse
Spring 1999
BY T. FINESMITH HORWICH

In a case being called "physician-assisted adultery," an Illinois woman has filed suit against her soon-to-be ex-husband, claiming that his participation in IVF treatments with his mistress at one clinic, while the wife was being treated at another, amounted to intentional infliction of emotional distress. Although neither spouse has yet filed separate lawsuits against the medical practices that treated them, both sides say the case raises ethical and practical issues about the extent to which fertility clinics should verify the nature of the relationship between patients being treated together.

Nancy Ledvina was married to Chris Ledvina for almost fifteen years, during which time the couple actively pursued various fertility treatments, including IVF, in the hope that such treatments could bypass the difficulties posed by the fact that Chris was a paraplegic. The treatment was not successful. Toward the end of this period, Chris began seeking IVF treatment at another Chicago area clinic with a different woman, Janet Howe, who was herself married to another man. Chris and Janet conceived triplets as a result of this treatment, two of whom survived after birth. When Nancy accidentally found out about her husband's high-tech infidelity, she began divorce proceedings, and then brought a lawsuit in state court seeking damages for the emotional distress his actions caused her.

In her suit, Nancy claims that Chris actively participated in her IVF treatment, beginning in 1993 and continuing on and off through November 1996. Nancy alleges that Chris encouraged Nancy to go through with at least one cycle, including giving her injections of medication, even though he was already involved with Janet at the time and had already conceived the pregnancy with her through similar treatment elsewhere. According to Nancy, Chris knew Nancy would never have subjected herself to the emotional and physical toll of continued infertility treatment had she known of her husband's infidelity and his impending fatherhood with his mistress. Therefore, given the degree of deception involved, Nancy claims that the unusual claim of intentional infliction of emotional distress is justified.

Not unexpectedly, Chris views his actions very differently. He has denied knowledge that Nancy was undergoing an IVF cycle in November 1996, although he has not denied that his cryopreserved semen was used as part of Nancy's treatment. As to participating in IVF treatment with Janet while still married to Nancy, according to newspaper reports, Chris said, "This happens every day. People are in bad marriages, they fall in love with somebody else and they start a family. I had a medical condition that required assistance to achieve the same thing other people can do in the back seat of a car."

It isn't clear whether the fertility practice that treated Chris and Janet was aware that they were each married to other people at the time, although they claim that they did not deceive the clinic about their marital status, and in fact the treatment was paid for by Janet's husband's insurance policy. Nor is it clear what efforts the program treating Nancy made to verify that Chris consented to continued treatment of his wife with his sperm, raising questions about how much programs verify the identity, relationship, and consent of their patients. Although in this case apparently Janet's husband has not opposed Chris's establishing paternity of the twins, legal battles could easily have been fought about whether Chris was a donor or a father, and whether Janet's husband had any legal rights or responsibilities to the children. According to some ethicists, the case is a signal that fertility clinics need to implement stricter controls to prevent at least this type of obvious case in which conflicts over the child's legal status are a significant risk. Yet others worry that imposing identity checks or relationship standards could lead to arbitrary morality judgments and discriminatory restrictions as to which patients will be allowed to become parents.

In the absence of comprehensive laws or professional guidelines governing these questions, some fertility programs are cautiously edging toward a middle ground that seeks to protect the programs and the children they help create while not unduly burdening their patients' privacy. For example, programs can ask patients (including third-party participants such as donors and surrogates) to provide their marital status in writing as part of their intake and require the patients to inform them of any changes during the course of treatment (including storage and use of cryopreserved material). When the patients' disclosures indicate that a significant legal issue may be presented, they can be referred for legal consultation prior to treatment, just as they are now referred when significant psychological or non-fertility medical issues become apparent. At least in many cases involving third-party participants, a written agreement between the parties could significantly reduce the legal risk to the program as well as to the parties and their children.

Ledvina v. Ledvina, 98 L 12874 (Circuit Ct. of Cook Cty., Ill., filed 11/6/98); *Chicago Tribune*, 12/6/98

3.9 Program Sues Insurer for Libel and Defamation after Being Dropped from Plan
Fall 1999

A Massachusetts IVF program that was dropped from an insurer's health plan is fighting back, in court. The Fertility Center of New England (FCNE) sued Tufts Health Plan and its Vice President and Medical Director, Dr. Robin Richman, for defamation and libel after its contract was terminated for reasons that it alleges differed from those announced publicly by Tufts. The program claims Tufts told their physicians that the program did not meet a requirement that 50 percent of its doctors be board-certified. In media reports, however, Tufts stated the termination, along with two others, resulted from the program failing to meet five new standards of care. Claiming to have lost numerous patients and referrals, and to have been denied loans, the lawsuit seeks triple damages under the state's consumer protection laws.

In its complaint, FCNE alleges it was terminated by written notice that it had failed to meet the newly required 50 percent board certification minimum, which it also alleges it could not meet in part because the termination date set by the insurer was before the next board certification examination and it had been led to believe physicians had five years to become board-certified. The complaint also alleges Tufts defamed FCNE by false statements to the media while publicly considering termination, including comments that it had noted programs' significant differences in success rates, philosophies on patient counseling, how quickly they moved to different techniques, and how honest they were with patients. In one cited example, Dr. Richman allegedly stated that, while patient questionnaires revealed a 90 percent satisfaction rate at six centers still approved, that was "not true for centers no longer on the list." FCNE alleges these statements were false, constituted libel and defamation, could reasonably have been interpreted to apply to FCNE and were harmful to it, were made with "reckless disregard for their truthfulness," and that Tufts knew or should have known that the statements were false and defamatory.

Note: In July 2002, a Massachusetts trial court judge granted summary judgment in favor of defendants on all eleven counts of the plaintiff's complaint.

Fertility Ctr. of New Eng. v. Tufts Associated HMO,
2002 Mass. Super. LEXIS 242 (Mass. Super. Ct. 2002)

3.10 New York Fertility Doctor's Jury Deadlocks in Criminal Fraud Trial
Summer 2000

A mistrial was declared in the federal insurance fraud trial of a prominent New York fertility doctor. The jury was unable to reach a verdict after seven days of deliberations. Prosecutors had alleged that Niels Lauersen, M.D., an obstetrician and gynecologist, had criminally defrauded insurance companies into paying for millions of dollars in infertility treatment services by concealing the fact that many surgeries were performed as part of ART procedures not covered by the insurance policies. According to the indictment, Dr. Lauersen and his anesthesiologist made deliberate misrepresentations on the patients' operative reports about the patients' pre-operative and post-operative diagnoses, symptoms, and the surgical procedures performed. For example, many operative reports allegedly represented ART procedures to be gynecological procedures such as laparoscopy, dilatation and curettage, aspiration of ovarian cysts, or treatment of endometriosis. Dr. Lauersen was also accused of creating false office notes and fraudulent correspondence to insurers to hide the ART procedure, for example by concealing the fact that a patient was taking fertility medications at the same time as the surgery.

The case was being closely watched by infertility doctors, patients, and insurers around the country, particularly since some observers have stated that what Dr. Lauersen is accused of doing is a common, unspoken practice among many physicians. Dr. Lauersen's attorney maintained that his client merely billed insurers for treating the underlying problems that cause the infertility, rather than for the specific infertility treatments themselves. Many of Dr. Lauersen's patients have been vocally supportive of him throughout the indictment process and the trial. Some maintain that Lauersen is a dedicated physician who was unfairly targeted because he speaks out against insurers that deny coverage for infertility.

A retrial is planned. A poll of jurors after the mistrial revealed nine in favor of acquittal and three in favor of conviction. If convicted, Dr. Lauersen, sixty-three, could be sentenced to as much as ten years in prison.

> *U.S. v. Niels Lauersen*, 2000 U.S. Dist. LEXIS
> 7047 *(mistrial; subsequent retrial and
> conviction)*; 348 F.3d 329 (2d Cir. 2003)
> *(affirming and remanding for sentencing)*;
> [ultimate sentence of seventy months]

3.11 Disciplinary Action against British Fertility Doctor Dropped
Summer 2002

Just as disciplinary hearings were set to begin against one of IVF's leading pioneers, Professor Ian Craft, Director of the London Fertility Centre, the General Medical Council (GMC) decided not to proceed. Since last October, the GMC had been investigating allegations that Professor Craft violated government guidelines allowing no more than two embryos per embryo transfer. Since the government guidelines are not laws, doctors can legally use more than two embryos if they believe it can be justified on medical grounds. After finishing the investigation, the GMC decided to drop the case.

London Times, 4/13/02

3.12 British Embryologist Imprisoned for Faking IVF Transfers
Spring 2003

An embryologist at the United Kingdom's North Hampshire Fertility Center and the Hampshire Clinic has been sentenced to eighteen months in jail for faking IVF embryo transfers and falsifying records for eight women between 1997 and 1999. After a three-week trial, a jury found the embryologist guilty of eight counts of "false accounting" and three counts of "assault occasioning actual bodily harm." The embryologist, Paul Fielding, reportedly undertook the deception to clear his debts. At his sentencing, his attorney argued for a non-jail sentence, saying he is already completely disgraced. The court, noting, "[a]s a result of your criminal behavior, every woman going through the anxiety of IVF will be wondering what is going on in the secrecy of an embryologist's lab . . . your crimes were despicable," instead imposed the eighteen-month jail sentence.

A civil action is also pending on behalf of seventy-five men and women, including men who banked sperm before cancer treatments, in what is reportedly the largest compensation claim involving IVF, at least in the United Kingdom.

Independent, 1/16/03

3.13 HFEA Pilots Adverse Incident Alert System
Fall 2003

A pilot program has been introduced in the United Kingdom to reduce the risks of errors and equipment failures in the 110 licensed fertility centers in that country. All clinics will be required to report to the Human Fertilisation and Embryology Authority (HFEA) any "adverse incidents" that may harm patients, which it defines to include anything relating to services that are potentially harmful or actually harms any person, embryos, gametes, or staff. If such an incident occurs, an alert will be sent to all the fertility centers in the United Kingdom, HFEA inspectors, and other professional bodies. The pilot program will be evaluated in the hopes of making it permanent.

> *Note*: After feedback from clinics, an improved system became normal HFEA practice.

IVF.net; BBC News Online, 6/6/03

3.14 U.K. Justice Awards £2 Million to Three Surviving Quads
Fall 2003

A British court has awarded a total of £2 million to the three surviving ten-year-old quadruplets of a woman who claimed she was given too much of the drug Metrodin, resulting in her becoming pregnant with quadruplets born via emergency caesarean section at twenty-six weeks. One child died within two days of birth. Of the surviving quads, one has cerebral palsy, another behavioral problems, and the third is healthy. This is one of the first reported cases awarding compensation to children born from an unwanted multiple pregnancy.

BBC, 6/19/02

3.15 London Fertility Doctor Wins Libel Action and Apology
Fall 2003

A London fertility doctor has successfully sued St. George's Healthcare National Health Service Trust for libel. Geeta Nargund, M.B.B.S., M.R.C.O.G., was suspended in October 2002 from her position as medical director of a reproductive medicine unit following allegations that she was responsible for a "three-way" embryo mix-up involving three patients and was also responsible for the resulting suspension of the unit. The doctor has received a public apology from the Trust for the professional and personal distress caused to her; she has also accepted an undisclosed sum in damages from the Trust.

British Medical Journal, 1/24/04

CHAPTER FOUR

Paternity and Sperm Donation

✦ MEDICAL COMMENTARY, BY Howard W. Jones, Jr.

MANY OF THE DISPUTES about parentage and child support in this section do not involve medical mistakes or mix-ups but sociological mix-ups that occur subsequent to the medical procedure. Many times the procedure involved is also associated with the assisted reproductive technologies, such as donor sperm with surrogacy.

The medical question that these situations raise is whether the medical unit has any responsibility to evaluate the psychological state of the recipients of donor eggs or sperm with a view of trying to assure the welfare of the anticipated child.

In the United States, there is certainly no legal requirement or even professional guideline requirement for programs to do so. In contrast, in the United Kingdom there is an HFEA regulation that requires any clinical program to evaluate the future welfare of the child before undertaking treatment. However, it needs to be said that, to my knowledge, no legal action has ever been taken under this regulation in the United Kingdom.

In the United States, the ASRM's professional guidelines do not require (but "recommend strongly") psychological evaluation and counseling of both sperm and egg donors. Those same guidelines recommend offering counseling to all gamete recipients and require psychological consultation if it appears warranted. As a general practice, medical programs psychologically screen egg donors and, to a lesser extent, sperm donors. This screening is in addition to the medical and genetic requirements set forth by the various regulatory bodies and any such services provided by outside entities that recruit donors. The primary question is whether the recipients of donor material should be psychologically screened by medical programs in an effort to prevent some of the atypical social situations that seem to have arisen in the disputes covered in this section.

As a practical matter, most medical programs confine their screening to egg donors undertaken by a mental health professional trained in this area. The majority of those who are screened out, in the experience of the Jones Institute program, are screened out either for substance abuse or because they have not sufficiently thought through the future implications of being a donor and having helped create a future child for someone else.

One question that naturally arises is whether screening intended parents could be effective. Of course, no psychological screening is required for mating as it normally occurs, and roughly 50 percent of legal marriages in the United States end in divorce. I am not aware of any suitable study that tells us whether the likelihood of divorce is greater or lesser when pregnancy results from donor eggs or sperm than otherwise. It would be extremely helpful to know this figure, but getting the denominator of total pregnancies or total divorces would be almost impossible. Nevertheless, I think the clinician should be alerted when confronted with highly unusual situations, and under those circumstances the least he or she can do is insist that both the donors and recipients be psychologically screened. This is consistent with ASRM guidelines that state: "psychological consultation should be required in individuals in whom there appear to be factors that warrant further evaluation." Further, the procedure should be covered by an informed consent process documenting all the possibilities that might occur, many of which are revealed in the cases in this chapter.

∽ LEGAL COMMENTARY, BY Susan L. Crockin

Since artificial insemination and sperm freezing predate virtually all of the ARTs, both legislatures and courts have had decades of experience with many of the family law issues raised by these "low-tech" procedures. More novel issues have been raised over the years, including physician and sperm bank liability for donor screening and lost frozen sperm (which has been valued from $70,000 to $1.2 million by two different juries in two different states). Both in the United States and internationally, various claims have been brought by or on behalf of the resulting children for a variety of reasons, including medical anomalies and the failure to disclose donor information. There have also been suits charging physicians for noncompliance with statutory requirements and claims for access to both sperm banking and use of banked sperm by various individuals. In addition, in recent years many of the traditional family law issues have taken on a less traditional aspect, as single women and same-sex couples are increasingly having children using donor sperm and seeking legal protections for their resulting families.

Family law remains the province of states: each state determines its own views on parentage, child support, and adoption, for example. The majority of states have some form of statutory law, usually limited to assigning parentage to the man who is the intended father and partner of the woman who is inseminated. Many statutes apply only to married couples. One of the very earliest cases endorsed adoption as a means to ensure a husband's legal parentage. In *Welborn v. Comm.* (1990), the court approved an adoption by the husband of a child born to his wife and conceived through donor insemination, despite a brief donor insemination state law stating that a donor was not the father of such a child since that statute failed to state explicitly that the husband *would* be the child's father. As expected, there are inconsistent court decisions across the many states that have had to confront paternity issues in the context of sperm donation. Additionally, a limited number of cases began to appear in the early 2000s involving children born from mistakenly swapped sperm and eggs, both in the United States and abroad. Most of those cases are reported and reviewed in subsequent chapters.

What may be most surprising and most notable is that many of the challenges and issues raised in the early 1990s continue to be significant and newsworthy today. For example, the very earliest reported cases discussed in "Legally Speaking" (dating from 1990 and reported in the inaugural column) questioned whether a donor insemination law that denied parental status to a sperm donor was unconstitutional as applied to a known donor. Over fifteen years later, *In the Interest of K.M.H.* (2007) raised the virtually identical issue. After extensive briefings by dozens of family law professors on both sides of the issue, the Kansas Supreme Court ruled similarly, rejecting the man's paternity claim. In that case, the man sought to establish his paternity, claiming that he had an oral understanding with his female friend, an attorney, that he would be the father of any resulting child. He was unaware that Kansas law required any such agreement to be in writing, and he did not sign either a written medical consent or any legal agreement. The Kansas Supreme Court ruled the statute did not unconstitutionally deprive a father of his paternity rights and was enforceable. Although the woman had gone to a Missouri clinic for her medical treatment, a state that does not require a written acknowledgment, the court refused to apply Missouri law where both parties were residents of Kansas. In a Pennsylvania case, *Ferguson v. McKiernan* (2008), a known sperm donor who had terminated his personal relationship with a woman but subsequently entered into an oral agreement with her to provide his sperm for artificial insemination in exchange for having no paternal rights or obligations was ultimately found not to be a father by that state's Supreme Court. That court rejected the notion that known donation and single motherhood were against the public policy of Pennsylvania. Thus, in 2007 and 2008, two different state high courts have ruled that single mothers using donor insemination do not violate public policy and constitute an acceptable form of family building.

There is an inevitable overlap between the cases in this section and disputes involving same-sex couples over parentage of children created with donor sperm, which are set out and reviewed at length in chapter 8. Those cases, many of which have wended their way through multiple courts over several years, poignantly illustrate the need to clarify the roles of donors and intended parents at the outset of any arrangement and in accordance with applicable law. That in turn requires a clear understanding of state law and how it may be applied to a specific situation. Even where the law does not require written agreements, it is striking how many arrangements would have benefited from a written record of the various parties' intentions and anticipated roles before any future dispute arose. Time and again, courts have been called on to untangle relationships and intentions based only on inconsistent and unrecorded recollections and the litigants' conduct at various stages of those now unraveling relationships. Issues can also arise over both choice of law at the outset of an arrangement and conflict of laws in the event of a subsequent dispute. Both issues require a sophisticated legal analysis before entering into an arrangement if bitter parentage and other disputes are to be avoided.

Sadly, a number of cases came about because the various parties or the professionals assisting them failed to look beyond the transactional aspect of the proposed arrangement and consider the potential vulnerabilities their contemplated family building plan presented.

Many of the parentage cases, including claims against physicians for failing to obtain written consent from a husband or to meet other statutory requirements, have resulted in varying outcomes as courts struggle with balancing statutes, public policy, and concerns over the welfare of born children. Since many of the reported cases are lower court decisions, they carry no actual value as legal precedent to be followed by other courts within that state or in other states. However, as noted above, the few recent state high court decisions suggest a trend toward recognizing nontraditional, single-mother families and rejecting public policy arguments in favor of two-parent families and exalting the child support to the resulting child over donor status for known donors.

At the same time, the cases also illustrate many recurring and still-unresolved themes and issues. Where the law requires a written agreement by a donor or spouse, there have been numerous claims of fraud or claims that physicians must support the child if their failure to follow legal requirements allowed intended fathers to avoid parentage status and obligations. Regardless of their outcomes, these cases strongly suggest that physicians and their medical programs should have some awareness of the applicable law to medical procedures they perform. As third-party reproduction continues to grow, there will be more cases in which donors come from different states than the intended parents or all patients come from different states than that of the medical program, which complicates applicable law and makes compliance difficult.

Courts have also ruled inconsistently on whether or not donor insemination laws and principles should apply to situations resulting from IVF. In *In the Interest of O.G.M.* (1999), an ex-husband successfully argued for his parentage of a child born to his ex-wife from embryos they had created and frozen during their marriage. The Texas court refused to analogize the man's situation to sperm donation or apply that state's artificial insemination law. In *In re Marriage of Buzzanca* (1998), however, a California appellate court expressly relied on donor insemination principles, including the parental status of children born from donor insemination, to find the intended father of a child born to a gestational carrier with a donated embryo liable for child support based on his original intent to have a child with his former wife. The lack of predictability on this issue illustrates the benefit of enacting legislation, as many of the courts involved in disputes without clear law have requested, to address the actual procedures and parties rather than relying on analogous arguments based on older technologies. At the same time, efforts to enact or update state, uniform, or model ART legislation have had mixed results. Some targeted legislation around the establishment of parentage have been successful, but more ambitious proposals have often been met with conflicting perspectives and lengthy debate, at times resulting in compromise, outdated measures, or proposals that were ultimately unacceptable to lawmakers. Coupled with the rapid pace of medical advances and family-building arrangements, many efforts to provide legislative guidance for third-party arrangements has proved a challenging, if not outright vexing, task.

Screening issues have also given rise to a number of court disputes brought on behalf of parents or their resulting children, with mixed results. In *Higgins v. Mem. Hosp. Jacksonville et al.* (1998), a biracial couple sued their IVF program after they gave birth to Caucasian twins, which was traced to a sperm mix-up. That case was ultimately settled. In *Harnicher v. U. of Utah Med. Ctr.* (1998), the court rejected the parents' claims after the program mistakenly mixed the wrong donor's sperm with the husband's, resulting in healthy triplet boys whose physical characteristics were incompatible with the husband's. The case is a poignant study in contrasting views of infertility, with the majority expressing little sympathy for the couple and holding that the law does not protect a "fiction" (that the husband could have been the children's biological father), while the minority criticized the medical center for failing to properly perform a procedure it offered (sperm mixing) that would have allowed for the possibility of the father's biological paternity.

Genetic anomalies have provided one of the starkest examples of how the ARTs are testing existing legal principles, which is predicted both to continue and to ultimately force new law. Cases involving children born with genetic disorders that were traced to gamete donors (both sperm and egg) have already challenged existing legal theories of "wrongful life," "wrongful birth," and "wrongful conception," as well as product liability. In states where wrongful life (a claim brought on behalf of the affected child, not his or her parents) is rejected, typically on the theory that impaired life cannot or should not be subject to a valuation and that "wrongful birth" depends on direct causation such as a botched abortion or tubal ligation, lawyers for children and their parents have sought to distinguish their claims. Thus, plaintiffs' attorneys have proposed novel legal theories of "negligent pre-conception" wrongs and argued that professionals who selected donors indeed "caused" the children's births. Those latter theories were not accepted in *Johnson v. Superior Court* (2002, sperm) and *Paretta v. Medical Offices for Human Reproduction* (2003, eggs), but liability was found on other grounds in these two seminal cases. Since then, the discovery of a child conceived with donor gametes affected with Tay-Sachs, as well as one affected with Fragile X, confirms that such challenges are likely to continue. In the latter case, a federal district court in 2009 refused to dismiss a product liability claim brought on behalf of a child against a sperm bank from whom the donor had been selected (*Donovan v. Idant Lab,* 2009). In preliminary rulings, the *Donovan* court rejected the mother's claims as time-barred and dismissed the child's "wrongful life" claim but refused to dismiss the child's product liability claim. It also allowed the complaint to be amended to refashion the mother's stricken breach of contract claim as the child's claim under the theory that the child was an intended third-party beneficiary of the contract. It remains to be seen which theories of liability will ultimately prevail in this area of developing law.

As donor insemination becomes less widely used by heterosexual couples due to improved medical techniques in treating male infertility, and more widely used by single women and female couples, many of the legal issues are likely to continue to shift as well. Absent clear legal paths to parenthood for such intended parents, a problem compounded by the mobility of individuals and families and the lack of consistency across state laws, the vulnerabilities and the possibilities of disputes will remain high.

From a legal perspective, donor insemination and related paternity issues have led the way on many of these issues and are likely to continue to raise novel as well as recurring concerns.

Litigation

4.1 Husband to Adopt Wife's Child Conceived by Artificial Insemination
March 1991

A state court in Virginia has raised yet another concern for participants in donor insemination arrangements. Despite Virginia laws
providing that the child of a married woman conceived by artificial
insemination "shall be deemed legitimate" and that, for purposes of
inheritance, the child "shall be presumed" to be the husband's, the
court found that those laws did not sever even an unknown sperm
donor's rights.

As a result, the Virginia court ruled it was necessary and entirely
appropriate for a husband to adopt his wife's twin children conceived
with his consent through artificial insemination, even where the
birth certificate already cited him as the father. While the case
focused on the adoption issue, the court's reasoning would seem to
support a potential claim by a sperm donor to some relationship with
the child, similar to the claims raised in the *McIntyre* case [4.2].

Despite similarly worded statutes in effect in several states, this
appears to be the only court decision ruling that a husband should
adopt his wife's children conceived by artificial insemination.

Welborn v. Commonwealth, 10 Va. App. 631
(Va. Ct. App. 1990)

4.2 Sperm Donors May Have Parental Rights Despite Artificial Insemination Statutes
March 1991

A word of warning and a written contract may be in order for donor
insemination participants, especially single women and couples
using known donors. In a case with potentially widespread implications for other states, an Oregon sperm donor who succeeded in his
initial challenge to a law designed to protect all donor insemination
participants has now reached a court-approved settlement with the
single woman over the child he helped her conceive.

The Oregon law, similar to those in many states, cuts off parent-child rights and responsibilities between sperm donors and the off-spring they help to create. Nonetheless, donor Kevin McIntyre claimed that he donated his sperm to an unmarried woman, part of a lesbian couple, only on the conditions that he remain active in the child's life, participate in important decisions affecting the child, and have visitation rights. The woman denied all of these. The parties did not use a physician for the artificial inseminations. Oregon's law, which is more inclusive than some states, does not limit protection to either individuals using medical assistance or to married recipients.

While McIntyre's initial arguments that the law should not apply to a known donor or to an unmarried woman were rejected, the court found that applying the law to him might unfairly and unconstitutionally deprive him of fathering rights. The court ruled that McIntyre should have an opportunity to prove any understanding between himself and the child's mother.

The case has now settled with the mother and McIntyre agreeing on a number of issues. These include his rights to overnight and extended summer visitation, participation in important decisions affecting the child, child support obligations, renaming the child to have his last name, and a decision concerning custody in the event of the mother's death. McIntyre has also reportedly agreed to have the mother's female partner recognized as a "psychological parent," as permitted by Oregon law.

A number of other state courts have demonstrated a similar reluctance to preclude known donors from asserting that they had expectations or promises of parenting roles. Participants involved in donor insemination would be well advised to check both the laws in their states and all agreements or consent forms that patients and their donors are asked to sign. Single women or couples using known donors may be especially vulnerable. McIntyre's attorney has suggested that the lesson in his client's case may be that individuals should consider entering into a formal written agreement which clearly sets out their understanding of each party's role. Whether and to what extent a court would enforce such an agreement at a future date and on behalf of a future child is unclear.

McIntyre v. Crouch, 98 Or. App. 462 (Or. Ct. App. 1989); *cert. denied*, 495 U.S. 905 (1990)

4.3 Lack of Consent to Donor Insemination May Bar Paternity Determination for Child Support

June 1991

A divorcing husband used New York's donor insemination law in an attempt to avoid support of his estranged wife's child born via artificial insemination. New York law requires the written consent of both spouses as well as the administering physician's certification. In this case, the husband had not consented and the court refused to apply the statute's mandatory presumption of paternity to declare the husband to be the child's legal father. The court also rejected the wife's claim that her ex-husband should be "estopped" from denying paternity, since she had made it clear to him that she was going to undergo insemination with or without his consent.

However, based on his later actions, including letters attempting to reconcile with his wife in which he agreed to support the child, the court found a separate and enforceable agreement to support the child. On the basis of that agreement, rather than the statute, the court ordered the ex-husband responsible for child support.

Anonymous v. Anonymous, N.Y. Sup. Ct. N.Y.
(1/18/91)

4.4 Successful Paternity Suit Brought by "Social" Father

March 1992

In another precedent-setting ruling from California, a court has awarded fatherhood status to Larry McLinden despite the fact that he is neither the biological father of four-year-old Larry McLinden Jr. nor married to the child's mother. McLinden and Karen Hamilton lived together as a couple during the time she gave birth to a son, whom she named after the senior McLinden. His name appears as the father on the birth certificate and he attended the child's delivery. He claims he believed he was the child's father. Hamilton disagrees, arguing that they were not living together at the time of the conception and that McLinden reneged on his promise to marry her. She has since married, and her husband wants to adopt the child.

After a three-week trial, McLinden obtained the novel ruling that he was a "psychological parent" in both his and the child's minds and should therefore be accorded all the rights of a natural parent. A court-appointed psychiatrist who interviewed the child agreed with McLinden's assertions that the boy regards him as a father and that it is in the child's best interest to continue that relationship.

A separate suit to determine whether Hamilton or McLinden will have physical custody is scheduled to begin soon.

McLinden v. Hamilton, CF027259 (L.A. Co., Cal. Super., 1991) (recognizing rights of nonbiological parent)

4.5 Sperm Donor to Be Listed on Birth Certificate
March 1992

Over the objections of the child's mother and her female partner, a California court has ordered the name of a gay sperm donor to be listed as the father of a baby and has ordered the woman to pay part of the man's legal expenses.

Citing the California statute that says sperm must be administered by a physician to preclude a donor's paternity claim, the court ruled that Steve Wittman, who contributed his sperm at the women's home, was the child's legal father and ordered his name listed as such on the child's birth certificate. Wittman, a former co-worker and friend of the women, is separately seeking joint custody of the child. The women claim that they never wanted Wittman to have a parental role in the child's life and that the judge was biased in the case.

The case is similar to an earlier case, *McIntyre v. Crouch* [4.2]. In that case, an Oregon sperm donor claimed that he had parental rights to a child that he helped two lesbian women (including his gay partner's sister) conceive. The state's Supreme Court ruled that its artificial insemination statute was unconstitutional as it applied to McIntyre since it automatically cut off parental rights to which he claimed he was entitled. The case was later settled out of court. McIntyre was placed on the birth certificate and received significant visitation and other rights to the child.

Wittman v. Northrup, Sup. Ct. Cal. (7/91)

4.6 Lesbian Couples Allowed to Adopt Partners' Children
March 1992

Reflecting a different perspective, two courts have recently granted adoptions to two lesbian couples. A District of Columbia court granted joint parental rights to a lesbian couple over each other's child. A Vermont court allowed the co-adoption by a woman of her lesbian partner's adopted child. Both courts stated that their rulings were in the best interest of the children involved. D.C. and Vermont are now among approximately seven jurisdictions to grant such adoption rights to gay or lesbian couples. The courts also each rejected an interpretation of their adoption statute that appeared to require one of the women to first relinquish her parental rights—a common approach within adoption statutes.

In re Adoption of R.C., No. 9088, slip op. at 5-7

(Addison Prob. Ct. Dec. 9, 1991)

4.7(a) Sperm Donor of Eleven-Year-Old Fails in Bid to Obtain Parental Rights
September 1993

A sperm donor who agreed to assist a lesbian couple in having their second child has failed in his subsequent attempt to have himself declared the child's father and to obtain unsupervised visitation with the child. Family law experts say that this is the first such case where the "best interest" of the child was found to supersede a sperm donor's biological connection. In 1979 the women had one daughter with the assistance of another sperm donor. When they wished to have a second child they were referred to the donor "Thomas." The women and Thomas apparently agreed he would not form a parental relationship with either child, but would make himself known to the child if and when she asked about her biological origins, and would treat both children as sisters. Although Thomas and one of the women were attorneys, nothing was put in writing, nor did any party consult an independent attorney.

For the child's first five years, there was no contact. Thereafter, in response to the older child's questions, the women contacted both sperm donors, and Thomas began a relationship with both girls, visiting them several times a year. Desiring a more involved relationship with his biological daughter, in 1991 Thomas sought both a declaration of paternity and unsupervised visitation rights with the child to introduce her to his family.

A New York family court judge rejected those claims on grounds of "equitable estoppel," a common law principle that dictates that parties may be "estopped" from pursuing an otherwise available legal remedy if their previous action or inaction caused the other party to rely on that position to their detriment. Although applicable state statutes provided for a determination of paternity based on blood testing, which was done, the court ruled that Thomas's claim ten years after conception was causing the child anxiety and psychological harm. She reportedly perceived his actions as an attack on her family. The court recognized the existing "functional parent-child bonds" between the women and girls and labeled Thomas an "outsider." While acknowledging that "ideally the recognition of new and complex parenting arrangements is addressed by legislation," the court decided the issue, stating "equitable estoppel has been utilized by the courts to decide paternity proceedings for families whose reality is more complex than a one mother, one father biological model."

4.7(b) Sperm Donor Awarded Paternity Rights to Thirteen-Year-Old Born to Lesbian Couple
December 1994

A sperm donor has now succeeded in his efforts to establish his paternity of a thirteen-year-old girl he fathered for a lesbian couple. The ruling, a three-two vote by the New York Supreme Court's Appellate Division, reversed an earlier decision that the man had no parental rights. The appellate court has now awarded paternity rights to Thomas Steel, a gay California lawyer who had fathered Ry Russo-Young through artificial insemination. The child lives with her mother (also a lawyer), her mother's partner, and that partner's younger daughter by another sperm donor.

In reversing the lower court decision, the appellate court noted: "The notion that a lesbian mother should enjoy a parental relationship with her, but a gay father should not, is so innately discriminatory as to be unworthy of comment."

Whether the women will appeal is still unknown.

4.7(c) Decision Awarding Sperm Donor Paternity Status of Thirteen-Year-Old Appealed

December 1995

A female couple's appeal to New York's highest court succeeded in obtaining a suspension of the intermediate appellate court's order awarding the donor paternity rights pending a final resolution.

Note: The appeal was ultimately dismissed.

Thomas S. v. Robin Y., 209 A.D.2d 298 (N.Y. App.
Div. 1994); *appeal dismissed,* 86 N.Y.2d 779 (N.Y. 1995)

4.8 Artificial Insemination Statute Not Bar to Unwed Father's Child Support

December 1993

A South Dakota man, having helped conceive a child naturally after he and his unmarried friend agreed he would not have child support obligations, has failed to persuade that state's highest court to apply its artificial insemination statute to him to alleviate any child support obligation. The court found the statute inapplicable and ruled that such an agreement could be enforceable only with both a provision for "adequate support" and court approval. Instead, it found the man had parental rights, having conceived the child naturally, acknowledged paternity, and previously paid some support for the now seven-year-old girl. The court then said the man could relieve himself of his parental and support obligations by petitioning the court to terminate his rights. Some would argue, however, that as a matter of public policy courts would be reluctant to terminate one parent's rights in the absence of an adoption or alternate second parent.

Estes v. Albers, 504 N.W.2d 607 (S.D. 1993)

4.9 Divorcing Husband May Not Avoid Child Support Obligation for Child Conceived by Donor Insemination

March 1994

Even without its own statute on donor insemination, an Indiana court has required a divorcing husband to pay child support for a child his wife conceived through donor insemination with his consent. In doing so, the court relied on other states' donor insemination laws as well as its own more general laws on legitimating children.

The Indiana Court of Appeals found that a child conceived by donor insemination was a "child of the marriage." The court made an analogy under its own state laws to children born out of wedlock and adopted during a marriage. It went on, however, to take note that several states have enacted donor insemination legislation that specifically recognizes such children as legitimate. A court's willingness to accept this reasoning in the absence of specific legislation in its own state should offer some encouragement to those involved in newer assisted reproductive efforts. Similar reasoning could protect participants in donor egg conceptions, notwithstanding the absence of a specific statute addressing ovum donation.

> *Levin v. Levin,* 626 N.E.2d 527 (Ind. Ct. App.
> 1993); *superseded by* 645 N.E.2d 601 (Ind. 1994)
> (aff'g father's estoppel from denying paternity
> obligations, granting his petition to transfer)

4.10 Unwed Mother May Not Release Alleged Father from Child Support
March 1994

A single mother's agreement not to seek child support from the alleged father, in exchange for his relinquishing all claims to the child, including guardianship or visitation, has been struck down by the Oklahoma Supreme Court. That court refused to uphold the written agreement, which had been entered into between the two adults shortly after the child's birth. The court took note of similar conclusions reached by courts in several other states. The child's natural conception raised the question of whether agreements between single women and known sperm donors, at least without the protection of a statute, would be similarly unenforceable.

The woman and man, who had denied paternity, entered the agreement in 1979. Ten years later the woman applied for Aid to Families with Dependent Children and listed the man as the father of her child. The state thereafter sought child support from the man, who attempted to rely on the agreement as a bar to any support obligation. The court rejected his argument, stating it could think of no situation in which barring a child's right to support would be in its best interest, and that any such agreements were void as against public policy. The court also noted that to permit unmarried men to escape their child support obligations would discriminate against married men in similar circumstances.

State Dept. of Human Services v. T.D.G., 1993
Okla. 126 (Okla. 1993)

4.11 Swedish Boy Sues Danish Sperm Donor to Establish Paternity
September 1994

In a case of first impression in Sweden, an attorney on behalf of a three-year-old Swedish boy born to a single woman through donor insemination is suing the Danish sperm donor to establish paternity through genetic testing. The attorney, acting in coordination with the child's social workers, is hoping to establish both paternity and child support by having the man legally declared the child's father and not merely a sperm donor.

Because Swedish law restricts donor insemination to women who are either married or cohabiting, reportedly numerous single women desiring donor insemination go to Danish agencies, as did the woman in this particular case. She reportedly met her donor twice in a Danish hotel where he ejaculated into a receptacle; she then performed the insemination without medical assistance.

Although Swedish law requires a sperm donor's name to be available upon request, it also prohibits paternity suits against sperm donors. The boy's attorney is arguing, however, that because the Dane knew the woman was inseminating herself, he was not a donor but the child's father.

The attorney has said that he believes there would be several such suits to follow this one, "[I]f you were single and childless and decided to have artificial insemination, you too might change your mind about the child not having a father a few years later."

Independent, 6/17/94

4.12 Oregon Sperm Donor Fails to Establish Parental Rights
September 1994

An Oregon man has failed in his attempt to establish his parental rights to a child he helped conceive four years ago for a woman and her partner. The man had signed a pre-conception agreement with the couple in which they relinquished any claims against him for legal, financial, or emotional responsibility for the child and he agreed not to bring any claim for custody, paternity, or parental rights to the child.

All parties involved with the agreement acknowledged that after the child's birth, the donor visited the child frequently and made "substantial financial contributions" for the child's benefit and welfare. However, when an earlier dispute arose over the donor's wish to participate more fully in the child's life, the original agreement was both confirmed and re-signed.

The court noted that since there was no evidence of the parties' conduct following their reaffirmation of the agreement, it rejected the donor's claim that the parties had modified, by conduct, their earlier written agreement. The court's ruling emphasizes the advisability of written agreements in these donor gamete arrangements, including a provision that any modification be made in writing and signed by all parties involved in the agreement.

Leckie v. Voorhies, 128 Or. App. 289 (Or. Ct. App. 1994)

4.13 Massachusetts Trial Court Requires Publication Notice of Adoption to Unknown Sperm Donor
Summer 1997

Several states have enacted statutes providing a presumption of paternity to a husband of a woman who gives birth to a child through donor insemination. However, a recent case in Massachusetts illustrates the need to draw upon traditional family laws absent an appropriate statute for certain situations involving assisted reproduction. In this case, a child was born to an unmarried woman through donor insemination. The mother and her female partner filed a co-parent adoption petition in the probate court and requested a waiver of the state adoption law notice requirements. In Massachusetts, when consent to the adoption is lacking from one or both of the birth parents, a petition to dispense with parental consent must be filed, and the court then issues an order of notice to be served by hand on the named parent(s). When the identity or location of the birth father is not known, the notice must be published in a newspaper. Since the mother in this case conceived through artificial insemination from an anonymous donor, she and her partner sought to avoid this additional step. However, the court ruled that the publication requirement may not be waived merely on the ground that the child was alleged to have been conceived through artificial insemination with sperm from an anonymous donor. The court stated that it was not apparent "why this situation is different when the mother has named a source of donated sperm rather than the putative father himself." The court did, however, leave the door open for a renewal of their request, suggesting that the result may be different should they file affidavits from the sperm bank explaining why the donor does not know and cannot learn the name of the recipient of his sperm, and from the mother stating that she did not have sexual intercourse with a man during the relevant period of possible conception. [Such affidavits have subsequently been accepted in lieu of notice.]

In the Matter of a Minor Child, Suff. Prob. Ct.
(*MA Lawyers Weekly*, No.15-003-97)

4.14 Child's Lawsuit against Doctors and Clinic for Failure to Certify Father's Consent to Artificial Insemination Dismissed
Spring 1998

A fertility clinic's failure to have the physician "certify" the husband's written consent to his wife's artificial insemination, as required by California law, does not result in damages to the child, and a lawsuit brought on her behalf by the mother was therefore dismissed. Lorraine and Gordon S. had gone to Pacific Fertility Medical Center in 1992 for artificial insemination. Together they reviewed a donor catalogue, selected a donor, and each signed a three-page consent form which acknowledged that the child would be their lawful child and that neither of them would ever contest the child's legitimacy. The consent form did not provide for certification by the physician as required by California's artificial insemination law and no certification was done.

The couple subsequently divorced and the lower court found the husband had no legal responsibility for the child born to his wife through artificial insemination, accepting his arguments that by signing he intended only to acquiesce to her desire to have a child, that the marriage was essentially ended at the time of the insemination, and the documents were not notarized. Rather than appealing that court ruling, Lorraine sued the physicians and clinic for failing to certify his signature. She argued breach of contract and two claims of negligence: (1) the clinic's failure to obtain her husband's signature deprived Alexandria of one legal parent; and (2) the clinic's negligence resulted in her birth.

The appellate court rejected the claims brought on behalf of the child. It concluded that it would not permit a child to sue for being deprived of a legal parent, noting that a contrary ruling would allow suits by children born to single parents, gay and lesbian parents, or unmarried partners. The court also viewed the claim—that but for the clinic's negligence she would not have been born—as a claim for wrongful life by a healthy child, and refused to recognize it. Finally, the court noted that even if it were to extend civil tort liability to cover these claims, there was no proximate cause of harm by the failure to certify the husband's signature. Disagreeing with the divorce court, the appellate court found that the certification requirement was not necessary to establish the husband's legal paternity and therefore failure to obtain it did not invalidate the husband's consent or his legal obligations. It thus dismissed the suit against both the doctors and clinic.

> *Alexandria S. v. Pac. Fertility Medical Ctr.*, 55
> Cal. App. 4th 110 (Cal. Ct. App. 1997); *review
> denied,* Cal. LEXIS 4831 (Cal. 1997)

4.15(a) Lesbian Couple's Sperm Donor Seeking Parental Rights Challenges Florida's ART Laws
Fall 1998

Florida, one of only a handful of states to have passed comprehensive legislation designed to address the rights, responsibilities, and parental obligations of patients and third parties seeking to create children, is now facing a significant challenge to that law. A lesbian couple who used an acquaintance as a sperm donor has been sued by the man, Danny Lucas, who is seeking to be named the father of the twin boys the women have been raising for three years.

Florida does not recognize same-sex co-parent adoptions, so the women had relied upon the sperm donor provision within the statute and their [three-way] agreement, in which they purportedly agreed to limited visitation and waived child support, and the donor waived any paternal rights.

The women claim they mixed sperm from three different sources: a sperm bank, a married friend, and Lucas. Lucas and the married friend each reportedly signed an "Agreement Regarding Conception," which waived child support and permitted them limited visitation. After appointing a guardian ad litem ("GAL") for the twins, the trial court ordered DNA testing to determine whether Lucas is the biological father. The women objected and that issue is on "interlocutory" appeal (an appeal of only part of a pending case). The parties continue to battle over their contradictory interpretations of the facts and applicable law.

At issue is whether or not Danny Lucas should be considered a father with parental rights, or a sperm donor under the state's assisted reproductive technology (ART) statute. Lucas argues that a man with an ongoing relationship with the child is not a donor under Florida law, but part of a "commissioning couple" under that law, and therefore entitled to parental rights absent a lengthy termination proceeding, which was not undertaken by the parties. Florida law does not require a physician's involvement in sperm donation, states that a sperm donor has no parental rights or obligations, but fails to define the term "sperm donor."

Unlike an anonymous sperm donor, Lucas claims to have visited the children at the hospital at birth, received a photo of them in an "I Love Daddy" frame, and visited them twice weekly until visitation was cut off by their mother when they were a year old. Those actions may make him a father, according to the court hearing the case.

Lucas is arguing he is not subject to the sperm donor statute or that, if applicable to him, that law unconstitutionally denies him the right to assert his paternity. He also maintains the parties' agreement is void as against public policy and has been breached by the mother's refusal to continue visitation. However the case turns out, this test to newly enacted legislation designed to protect the participants of the ARTs will certainly be scrutinized by those attempting to draft such legislation elsewhere.

4.15(b) Florida Sperm Donor's Early Bid for Paternity Testing Denied
Winter 1998

DNA testing must wait until a lower court rules on whether or not Florida's sperm donor statute applies and whether or not a contract between a lesbian couple and the gay, male friend who served as their donor is enforceable. Overturning a lower court order for DNA testing, a Florida appeals court has ruled that Danny Lucas must first establish his right to be considered a father. Traditionally under the common law in most states and based on a bias against disrupting marriages and bastardizing children, men seeking to prove paternity of children born within a legal marriage must first establish a threshold relationship with the mother or child. The higher court's ruling means Lucas's legal claims must be resolved before authorizing any DNA testing.

4.15(c) Florida Sperm Donor Paternity Case Settled; Visitation Agreement Reached
Summer 1999

A closely watched test case of the constitutionality of Florida's sperm donor statute has settled mid-trial, leaving unanswered several troublesome legal questions about parental rights and responsibilities of known sperm donors. Four hours into the trial, Danny Lucas waived any paternity rights in exchange for supervised visitation if a blood test confirms his paternity.

A lawyer appointed for the twins had agreed with Lucas's position that the statute did not govern, stating the adults involved created "a hybrid we don't have laws to govern . . . [the boys] have a right to have a relationship with a mother and a father, even though they have two mothers."

4.15(d) Florida Appellate Court Rules Sperm Donor Has No Parental Rights and Voids Visitation Agreement
Winter 2002

After what it termed "protracted, unnecessary litigation," a Florida appellate court has determined that a sperm donor has no parental rights to twins he helped a lesbian couple conceive and has consequently thrown out the parties' visitation agreement. The case tested

Florida's comprehensive ART statute, which failed to define the term "sperm donor." The court confirmed that both the contract between the parties and the Florida donor insemination statute provided that the sperm donor had no parental rights or responsibilities. The court noted that even though the statute did not define a sperm donor, the contract clearly labeled him as a donor, indicated sperm was the only donation required of him, and explicitly stated he would not have or seek any parental right or obligations. Lucas's attempts to have paternity testing and the visitation agreement were all deemed errors of both the parties and the lower court. Instead, the appellate court labeled him a "statutory stranger to the children" and ruled, "[t]his is a simple case that can be resolved in a one-sentence opinion, to wit: Danny A. Lucas is a sperm donor, not a parent, and has no parental rights. . . ." The case suggests the benefit of clear contracts between parties to collaborative reproductive technology arrangements, even if the law leaves or creates some ambiguities.

Lamaritata v. Lucas, 827 So. 2d 1049 (Fla. Dist.
Ct. App. 2002); *rev. denied, D.A.L. v. L.A.L.,*
835 So. 2d 266 (Fla. 2002)

4.16 Legal Father's Further Appeal Denied; Buzzanca Case Continues to Raise New Issues

Fall 1998

John Buzzanca, the court ordered "father" of a two-year-old born to a gestational surrogate with donor gametes as a result of his and his then-wife's efforts, has failed in his appeal of the most recent court ruling in the case [6.19c]. After over two years of litigation, the California Appeals Court had ruled in March 1998 that John Buzzanca should be considered the child's father as a result of his intention and agreement to create the child. Reversing lower court rulings that the child had no legal parents and it therefore had no subject matter jurisdiction, the appellate court had ruled that entering into the agreement without which the child would not have been born was sufficient to deem John Buzzanca a parent and require him to pay child support. The state's highest court denied further review without comment, letting the Appeals Court decision stand.

In yet another twist to what has already been a most unusual case, the genetic father of the child has also come forward. Reportedly, a Chicago-area lawyer has identified himself as the child's genetic father, as the result of donating "spare" embryos (created with his sperm and donor eggs) after he and his infertile wife completed their family. The couple had been patients at U.C. Irvine and agreed to donate the embryos following their own successful treatment. It is not currently known whether the couple signed consent forms that included the potential donation to a gestational carrier.

Note: For the full case, see 6.19a–d.

In re Marriage of Buzzanca, 61 Cal. App. 4th
1410 (Cal. Ct. App. 1998); *review denied* 1998
Cal. LEXIS 3830 (Cal. Sup. Ct. 1998)

4.17(a) Paternity Suit in Illinois Challenges Donor Insemination Law
Summer 1999

In still another twist to sperm donor laws, an unmarried Illinois woman is suing her former lover for breach of contract for not supporting twins she claims she had at his request using donor sperm. The woman is attempting to apply that state's artificial insemination law, which explicitly covers only married couples. The man denies the allegations. The children were born in 1993 and the couple separated in 1996.

The woman claims her former lover paid for the inseminations, provided support for the children until 1996, and held the children out as his own. She claims she ended the ten-year relationship after learning he was married. The woman is attempting to apply Illinois's artificial insemination law, which holds husbands responsible for their partners' children when they consent and support the partner. The man, who has other children, claims he did not encourage the inseminations and only gave money because he visited her. Her attorney claims that, "[g]iven the availability of this process to unmarried couples who want to conceive, this is going to be the paternity case of the new millennium," while his attorney argues that, "[t]his unmarried woman wants to reach out and tab a married man . . . based on her allegation that certain things existed . . . before we create these obligations on the part of someone who is not the husband or father, you should have more than a relationship he denies."

4.17(b) Parentage Action against Unmarried Partner of Donor Insemination Children Dismissed

Winter 2001

An Illinois trial court has now dismissed this lawsuit to enforce an oral support agreement, ruling that any consent must be in writing and rejecting the woman's claim that the law unconstitutionally discriminated against out-of-wedlock children

4.17(c) Appellate Court Reinstates Mother's Child Support Claims under Common Law

Spring 2003

An appellate court has revisited and reversed a trial court's interpretation of Illinois law, finding that the statute's requirement of written consent did not preclude a woman's common law–based claims of paternity and for child support. Since the statute's requirement of written consent was not met, the court ruled it did not need to decide if that law should be extended to unmarried men. The court added that to protect and promote the welfare of the children, "consistent with this important public policy, cases involving assisted reproduction must be decided based on the particular circumstances presented." "[S]imply put, we cannot accept [the] argument that these children and their mother must be left to fend for themselves."

In re Parentage of M.J., 787 N.E.2d 144
(Ill. 2003) (*aff'd in part; rev'd in part*)

4.18 Utah Appeals Court Reverses Parental Obligations to Child Conceived without Husband's Consent

Spring 2000

The Utah Court of Appeals has ruled that a man whose wife gave birth after continuing artificial insemination following the couple's separation is not the legal father of the resulting child. The child was conceived through artificial insemination performed a month after the couple separated, without the husband's knowledge or consent. The couple had an older child through artificial insemination during the marriage and had attempted to have a second child a year before they separated, agreeing to be jointly responsible for any children they conceived. The husband was unaware his wife was continuing to attempt conception. The couple's divorce agreement, reached prior to the child's birth, did not require the husband to support the child, nor did the wife seek child support before the divorce was finalized two weeks after the child's birth. Four years later, she persuaded a Utah trial court that there had been a "material change of circumstances" and to therefore declare her ex-husband the child's legal father and order him to pay child support.

The Appeals Court has now reversed, holding that Ms. Krambule waived her right to have Mr. Krambule declared the father and ordered to pay support by omitting any such obligations in the divorce agreement. The court rejected her "material change of circumstances" argument, finding the child's birth was entirely foreseeable at the time of the divorce.

Krambule v. Krambule, 994 P.2d 210
(Utah Ct. App. 1999)

4.19 Texas Appeals Court Upholds Divorced Father's Paternity Rights of Child Born from Frozen Embryo

Spring 2000

A Texas appellate court has upheld Donald McGill's legal paternity of a child, born to his ex-wife after a frozen embryo transfer, which occurred with his consent after their divorce. The lower court had previously ruled in his favor as well [1.13]. McGill's ex-wife, Mildred Schmidt, claimed the parties orally agreed McGill was donating their remaining embryos to her while McGill claimed they had agreed he would be the father. McGill is listed on the child's birth certificate, had legally acknowledged paternity under Texas law, and voluntarily paid child support.

The court's detailed analysis of the applicable law is very instructive. First, the court rejected Schmidt's suggestions that the Texas artificial insemination law should apply, stating unequivocally that there was no authority to suggest artificial insemination is analogous to IVF. Next, it rejected both the application of Texas's laws on the parental rights of children born through egg or embryo donation and cases cited by Schmidt, which relied upon the parties' expressed intentions in ART donation cases, concluding that those authorities did not address the narrow facts of a "biological father seeking paternal rights to a child born from his ex-wife through IVF from embryos conceived during marriage."

The court noted that, because of the complexity of legal issues, it wanted to defer to the legislature to enact legislation deciding the rights of parties involved in IVF. It therefore narrowed the issue to granting paternity under the facts presented, specifically a consenting biological ex-husband who wished to retain his paternity rights. Whether the court would have permitted McGill to avoid paternity obligations if he so desired is unclear. The court's reluctance, however, to rely on related but not precisely applicable ART statutes should serve as a cautionary note to all involved in providing or utilizing ART services without the benefit of clear legal guidelines. The court also rejected Schmidt's request for over $300,000 in attorney's fees.

In the Interest of O.G.M., 988 S.W.2d 473, 474
(Tex. Ct. App. 1999); (dismissed 6/15/00)

4.20(a) British Legal Father of IVF / Donor Sperm Child Denied Visitation until Age Three

Summer 2001

A British man has been denied visitation with his one-year-old daughter, conceived through donor insemination and IVF by his ex-wife. Although the law recognizes him as the legal father as a result of his signature on the original IVF consent forms, a High Court judge refused the man access to the child.

The man and the woman first pursued IVF treatment with donated sperm as a married couple in 1996. After the first unsuccessful treatment, the couple divorced, without informing the clinic. A second attempt by the woman after the divorce resulted in the birth of a daughter. Though the British High Court ruled that the man was the girl's legal father, it also ruled that the man's application for parental responsibility, which would include visitation rights, should be postponed until the child turns three. The Court of Appeal confirmed the lower court ruling, rejecting the man's attempt to challenge the ruling.

Guardian, 2/2/01; *Scotsman*, 2/16/01

4.20(b) Paternity Determination of British Former IVF Partner Overturned

Summer 2003

A British appellate court has overturned a determination of paternity for the former husband of a woman who became pregnant through IVF with frozen embryos created during their marriage but implanted and carried after the relationship ended. The man is forty, incapable of bearing biological children, and argued this was his only chance of fatherhood. The court noted "gone are the days when it was always the mother wishing to prove paternity against a man who denied it . . . had this mother been wishing to extract child support from this man, the court would have been slow to adopt a construction (of the Act) which would allow her to do so." The court ruled that under HFEA's definition of "father," paternity is created at the time the embryo, sperm, or egg that results in a birth is placed in the woman, not when the embryos are formed.

BBC News, 2/27/03; *BioNews*, 3/3/03

4.21 Australian Sperm Donor Visitation Fight Lands in Family Court

Spring 2002

An unprecedented sperm donor visitation case is pending in Melbourne's Family Court. The sperm donor of the now-two-year-old boy is reportedly asking for visits every second weekend and alternate holidays, while the lesbian mother and her partner want to limit visits to six hours per year. Experts blame the fact that unmarried women cannot legally be treated in Victorian infertility clinics and so turn to private advertising to find sperm donors for private and unregulated arrangements where the parties may receive little or no pre-donation counseling.

www.news.com.au, 1/29/02

4.22 International Sperm Donors Face Child Support Obligations

Spring 2002

Sperm donors in West Australia and Sweden may be ordered to pay child support for their donor offspring. In January, a Swedish court ordered a sperm donor to pay $555 a month in child support for three children born to the lesbian couple who received his sperm.

The court ruled that a document stating the man was their biological father, which the donor said he signed to ensure the children would know their biological origins and not to accept legal or financial responsibility, was binding. The West Australian Attorney-General has also recently warned that men who donate sperm to single women could be liable for supporting any resulting children. While the current West Australia law provides that a sperm donor is the legal father of any children born to a single woman, proposed legislation to change the law is under consideration by the Legislative Council as part of a gay law reform legislation package.

Other legislation proposed in West Australia would give donor offspring the right to access identifying information about their sperm donor. According to the West Australian Attorney-General, these two issues have created a substantial drop in the number of sperm donors.

Associated Press, 1/31/02; *West Australian Newspapers Ltd*, 2/4/02

4.23(a) British Clinic's ICSI Mix-up Results in Twins and Lawsuit
Winter 2002

Twins born to a patient at the Assisted Conception Unit at Leeds General Infirmary are the result of a mistaken fertilization of her eggs through intracytoplasmic sperm injection (ICSI) with the sperm of another patient. The woman, who is white, gave birth to mixed-race twins earlier this year. The male patient and his wife, who are black, were unsuccessful in their own attempts to achieve a pregnancy. Although the case has been pending for months, and the head of the U.K.'s High Court Family Division has repeatedly said that there is no suggestion the twins would be uprooted from their environment, the court has also just recently ruled it will determine both the legal parentage and custody of the children early in 2003.

BBC News Online, 11/4/02; *BioNews*, 11/4/02

4.23(b) British Biological Father's Legal Paternity Recognized in Twin Sperm Mix-up
Summer 2003

In a sperm mix-up case winding its way through the British courts, a recent ruling has now legally determined paternity of the resulting twins. This recent ruling finds the biological father, "Mr. B," [who is not raising the children] to be their legal father, requiring an adoption if "Mr. A" is to become their legal father.

Reuters, 2/26/03; Sky News, 2/26/03

4.24(a) Washington Appeals Court Finds Sperm Donor Is Not a Father
Summer 2004

In a second ruling by the Washington Court of Appeals, that court has reversed a trial court's order and found that, without a written agreement as required by Washington law, a man is not the father of two children born after he donated his sperm to a woman he was having an affair with while married to another woman. The woman had asked her lover to donate his sperm for artificial insemination, which he provided to her physician, who then performed the inseminations that resulted in the birth of two children in 1998 and 2001. The first child was born during the relationship, and the man signed a paternity affidavit, provided financial child support, and added the child as a beneficiary to his life insurance policy. The second child was born after the relationship had ended, and the man denied knowing that his previously donated sperm had been used for a second insemination. After his wife learned of the affair in January 2002, he stopped providing financial support. In February 2002, the mother filed an action seeking to establish paternity and obtain child support.

The Court of Appeals ruling reversing the parentage determination focused on the artificial insemination statute that was in effect in Washington then. The statute had provided that a sperm donor is treated in law as if he were not the natural father of the child unless the donor and the woman agree in writing that the donor will be the father. The court found that no such written agreement existed.

4.24(b) Sperm Donor Not Father under Washington State's DI Statute
Fall 2004

Under a strict interpretation of that state's artificial insemination statute, the Washington Court of Appeals denied a mother's attempt to establish her sperm donor as the legal father of her two children.

The former Washington statute, in place at the time of the inseminations at issue, provided that when a donor provides semen to a physician for insemination of a woman, the donor is *not* the child's father unless the donor and mother agree in writing that the donor shall be the father. The statute further required the agreement to be signed by the woman and the donor, certified by the physician, and filed with the registrar of vital statistics. The appellate court determined that because the requirements of the statute were not complied with, and notwithstanding the other steps the man had taken to acknowledge paternity, including signing a paternity affidavit and paying child support for the older child, he was not the legal father of *either* of the children and had no obligation to pay child support. A further appeal is possible.

In re Parentage of J.M.K., 155 Wash.2d 374
(Wash. 2005)

4.25(a) Pennsylvania Sperm Donor Ordered to Pay Child Support as Legal Father
Fall 2004

A Pennsylvania appellate court has ordered a man to pay child support as the legal father of twins born using sperm he provided to a then-married woman, Ivonne Ferguson.

According to Mr. McKiernan, following the end of their two-year affair, he agreed to act as an anonymous sperm donor after Ms. Ferguson assured him she would be a single mother and he would have no financial or moral obligations to any resulting child. The court found that while the oral agreement constituted a valid legal contract on its face and found the woman's behavior "despicable," it nonetheless found the contract unenforceable based on "legal, equitable and moral principles." The court rejected the argument that Ms. Ferguson's former husband, who filed for divorce the day of her IVF procedure and was divorced from her at the time of the births, was the children's legal father, notwithstanding any presumption of paternity or that Ms. Ferguson had placed his name on the children's birth certificates. The court further found that the contract was not enforceable because it bargained away a legal right belonging to the children. The appellate court agreed with the trial court that "[a]lthough we find [the mother's] actions despicable and give [her former lover] a sympathetic hue, it is the interest of the children we hold most dear." Media reports indicate that Mr. McKiernan may appeal.

4.25(b) Appellate Court Reverses Child Support Order and Upholds Sperm Donor Agreement between Former Lovers
Spring 2008

The Pennsylvania Supreme Court has reversed two lower courts and ruled that an agreement to donate sperm to a former lover is enforceable and the donor is not liable for child support. . . . The donor and woman had had limited contact following the successful IVF procedure, and the lower court found that the donor "never provided the children with financial support or gifts, nor did he assume any parental identity." Although the two lower courts criticized the woman and recognized that there had been an oral agreement, they had ruled that agreement unenforceable as against public policy.

In reversing, the Supreme Court acknowledged that this was a novel question under Pennsylvania law that potentially affected thousands of Pennsylvania families. The court noted, "the lone question we face is as simple to state as it is vexing to answer. We must determine whether a would-be mother and a willing sperm donor can enter into an enforceable agreement under which the donor provides sperm in a clinical setting for IVF and relinquishes his right to visitation with the resultant child(ren) in return for the mother's agreement not to seek child support from the donor."

The Court noted that a rigorous analysis was necessary to determine whether such an agreement would violate public policy. It took note that the (model) Uniform Parentage Act, not enacted as law in Pennsylvania, does not require anonymity to protect a donor from parentage rights and obligations, and "urges any sperm donor seeking to assert paternity" over any resulting offspring "to execute a writing manifesting that intent." It contrasted "traditional sexual reproduction" in which there is "simply no question" that the parties cannot contract between themselves to deny child support, and "institutional donation" cases where there "appears to be a growing consensus" that no obligations or privileges are conferred on a sperm donor. Recognizing that between these "poles lies a spectrum of arrangements" and that future cases might be difficult to resolve, it found that this was not such a case. "Indeed, the parties could have done little more than they did to imbue the transaction with the hallmarks of institutional, non-sexual conception by sperm donation and IVF. They negotiated an agreement outside the context of a romantic relationship; they agreed to terms; they sought clinical assistance . . . , taking sexual intercourse out of the equation; they attempted to hide Sperm Donor's paternity from medical personnel, friends, and family; and for approximately five years following the birth of the twins both parties behaved in every regard consistently with the intentions they expressed at the outset of their arrangement." The court added, "Assuming that we do not wish to disturb the lives of the many extant parties to anonymous, institutional sperm donation, we can only rule in Mother's favor if we are able to draw a legally sustainable distinction between the negotiated, clinical arrangement that closely mimics the trappings of anonymous sperm donation that the trial court found to have existed in this case and institutional sperm donation, itself. Where such a distinction hinges on something as trivial as the parties' success in preserving the anonymity they took substantial steps to ensure, however, we can discern no principled basis for such a distinction."

The court concluded with an assurance that it takes children's welfare very seriously, despite its ruling that denied support to children who "did not ask to be born into this situation." The court found that absent the agreement, the children would not have been born or would have been born using a purely anonymous sperm donor "who neither party disputes would be safe from a support order."

The implications of this case may be far-reaching. Pennsylvania, like some states, has no sperm donor statute and, like most states, has no egg donor statute. Despite that absence of law, the court was willing to accept that the present state of family building and ART usage includes single parents who wish to access gametes in a variety of settings, and that agreements for those arrangements should not automatically be found unenforceable. The court clearly relied on what it considered the formality of the agreement and the consistency of its terms as a donation, despite it not being in writing. There is little doubt that a written agreement would have avoided the need to cull facts from the parties' behavior and conflicting testimony. In addition, the fact that five years had passed since the donation was helpful in establishing the man's donor status.

The significance of the case should also be considered in light of the recent decision by the Kansas Supreme Court [4.27b], which ruled that a single male friend was a donor, not a father, because he failed to comply with that state's requirement of a written agreement to assume fatherhood status. Read together, both of these cases support permitting single men and women to enter into a binding donor-recipient agreement if they do so by appropriate means. This reasoning, if followed by other states, would give significant comfort as well as helpful guidance to both prospective single parents and those who wish to assist them as donors.

Ferguson v. McKiernan, 940 A.2d 1236 (Pa. 2007)
(reversing and remanding lower court decision)

4.26 Pennsylvania Sperm Donor Ordered to Pay Child Support for Lesbian Couple's Child

Summer 2007

In a somewhat startling ruling, an intermediate appellate court in Pennsylvania has in essence approved a three-way parenting arrangement by ordering a former lesbian couple's sperm donor to pay child support. The man, who was a close friend of the women and had voluntarily contributed financial support for the two children, ages seven and eight, and participated in their lives, was found to be a biological father with obligations to the children that their rearing mothers could not waive. The issue arose when the women separated and a custody case ensued, with one woman seeking child support from the other, as well as from the sperm donor.

The court acknowledged there was no agreement for support but that there was also no need for one and that the donor had showed "constant and attentive solicitude," that he had become "voluntarily, indeed, enthusiastically, an integral part of [the children's] lives" (including being called "Papa"), and as such, should be a party with an allocation of child support assigned. The court affirmed the award of custody, vacated the award of support, and remanded to the trial court with directions that the father be joined as an indispensable party for a hearing at which the support obligation of each litigant was to be recalculated. Unless clarified or reversed by a higher appellate court, it is unclear how or whether a same-sex couple can create a clear donor recipient arrangement with a known donor who plays a role in the resulting child's life.

The donor's subsequent death also left open questions such as whether the children will qualify for social security survivor benefits.

Jacob v. Shultz-Jacob, 2007 Pa. Super. 118
(Pa. Super. Ct. 2007)

4.27(a) Appeal Pending on Constitutionality of Kansas Donor Insemination Law
Winter 2007

The constitutionality of Kansas's donor insemination statute is under scrutiny in a case brought by a known sperm donor who claims the law unconstitutionally deprives him of his parental rights as a biological father. The case is drawing attention from family law scholars around the country, on both sides of the issue. The Kansas statute provides that in cases involving physician-assisted artificial insemination a man other than a patient's husband has no parental rights or obligations unless he and the woman have agreed otherwise in writing. The donor and recipient were single friends who disagree as to whether their understanding was that the man would be a donor or a father. The woman, but not the man, is a lawyer. The mother's position is that, absent a written agreement, he is a donor, not a biological father. Amicus (friend of court) briefs have been filed by groups of law professors on both sides, oral arguments were heard in December, and a decision is imminent.

4.27(b) Kansas Upholds Sperm Donor Law Requiring Written "Opt-Out" for Fatherhood
Winter 2008

A long-simmering appeal questioning the constitutionality of Kansas's sperm donor law has now been resolved, while raising important questions far beyond Kansas. The Kansas statute states that a sperm donor is not a father absent a written agreement between the donor and mother (married or unmarried) acknowledging his paternity. The former friends (the court described the man as "an unmarried male nonlawyer") did not enter into a written agreement prior to the insemination, which took place in neighboring Missouri and resulted in twins.

The man attempted to assert his paternity, claiming the statute, as applied to a known donor, unconstitutionally stripped away his parentage rights in violation of his equal protection and due process rights and that Missouri law, rather than Kansas law, should apply since the insemination process occurred in Missouri, where the law does not similarly presume a donor is not a parent. He also argued that no Kansas doctor would have performed an insemination on an unmarried woman or would have had a duty to discuss the legal implications of the procedure under Kansas law.

The court upheld the constitutionality of the statute as applied to known donors. Even assuming the parties had an oral agreement, the court ruled the legal requirement of a written agreement was not a burden, and that the law was designed to *prevent* the creation of parental status where it was not desired or expected. Rather than taking away a constitutionally protected right, it found that a sperm donor's biological link alone did not rise to the level of a parental right. The court noted that, while it was moved by the set of amicus briefs that argued in favor of policies that promoted two parents, "all that is constitutional is not necessarily wise" and that it was the province of the legislature, not the courts, to weigh such interests and public policies.

The court also rejected the man's argument that Missouri law should apply, finding that the Kansas law was "not only appropriate but constitutional. This choice is neither arbitrary nor unfair; neither party would have been justified in expecting Missouri to have a controlling interest as to any dispute between them." While not the focus of the case, it is interesting to consider the implications of such a statement of choices of law involving collaborative or third-party reproduction where parties and programs often rely on the jurisdiction where the program is located, rather than the state of residence of one or both parties.

In the Interest of K.M.H., 169 P.3d 1025 (Kan. 2007)

4.28 Death Row Inmates Denied Claims to Freeze Sperm

December 1991

The Virginia Supreme Court has denied the appeals of two death row inmates who want to freeze their sperm in an effort to preserve their "bloodline." One man's girlfriend agreed to be named as the legal recipient of his sperm. The other inmate, who is awaiting execution for murdering his male lover, says his girlfriend is considering the possibility. Virginia's Governor Wilder described their arguments as "brazen" and "appalling" and the court characterized them as "frivolous." Rejecting the arguments, the court ruled that it was not unconstitutionally cruel and unusual punishment to execute the men without freezing their sperm for possible future insemination.

Washington Post, 8/18/91

4.29 Workmen's Compensation Covers Artificial Insemination

December 1991

A Pennsylvania couple's expenses for artificial insemination were held to be covered under the state's workmen's compensation law because the husband was infertile due to a work-related spinal injury. A Pennsylvania court reversed the Workmen's Compensation Appeal Board's dismissal of the claim. The court recognized that the procedure was necessary to replace a function that was lost because of an on-the-job injury. Since the wife's participation was essential, her expenses were also held reimbursable.

Tobias v. Workmen's Compensation Appeal Bd. (Nature's Way Nursery, Inc.), 141 Pa. Commw. 438 (1991)

4.30 Death Row Inmates Sue for Right to Father Children

March 1992

Fourteen death row inmates from San Quentin Prison have filed suit in federal court demanding either artificial insemination or conjugal visits with their wives and girlfriends. The inmates' claims, similar to those raised last year by two Virginia inmates [4.28], allege that depriving them of their right to fatherhood and their parents of the right to become grandparents is unconstitutionally cruel and unusual punishment. The suit was filed on behalf of the inmates, their spouses, and their parents. According to one news report, the attorney who filed the suit says some parents are desperate for a grandchild and that "maybe one of the kids would grow up to be a surgeon and save hundreds of lives to help make up for the lives their father took."

California's prison policies permit conjugal visits for some inmates, but not for those on death row. As for artificial insemination, a prison spokesman says allowing an inmate to leave the prison would be unlikely and that prison staff does not have the expertise to collect sperm.

Such claims have received little sympathy. An earlier California suit alleging that these prohibitions violated a Catholic inmate's freedom of religion was unsuccessful, and a similar Virginia lawsuit was dismissed by that state as "frivolous." Lawyers who advocate for death penalty reform expressed concern that the suit could discredit their efforts.

Anderson v. Vasquez, 827 F. Supp. 617 (N.D. Cal. 1992) (court dismissed claims as no right to conjugal visits, *affirmed* by 1995 U.S. Dist. LEXIS 1985 (N.D. Cal. 1995)

4.31 Court Orders Jail to Allow Sperm Storage
June 1993

An unmarried, incarcerated man in Iowa has obtained a court order allowing him to store his sperm for possible use during his confinement. Chris Mabrier, facing up to fifty years for multiple robberies, successfully argued that his opportunity to father a child should not be hindered by his jail term and the state's prison policy, which does not permit conjugal visits. His attorney says any child born would be raised and supported by Mabrier's family and would not become a tax burden.

Mabrier v. Iowa, Mahaska Cty. Dis. Ct. No. CR7203-01931 (2/93)

4.32 British Adult DI Children Seek Identity of Their Sperm Donor "Dads"

Winter 2000

Two adult British half-siblings, Jo and Adam Rose, conceived by the same mother through anonymous donor insemination, plan to file a "test case" through the European Convention on Human Rights seeking to discover the identity of their genetic fathers. Both allege to be suffering an identity crisis and feel they and other children born through donor insemination should be given rights similar to those of adopted children to trace their genetic parents.

news.com.au, 10/8/00

4.33 Britain to Reexamine Laws on Sperm Donor Anonymity

Spring 2001

Britain's public health minister has announced the government's intention to reexamine current HFEA regulations governing sperm donation and is due to release a "consultation paper" on the subject of anonymity for sperm, egg, and embryo donors that will invite public comment. Any changes will be prospective only and the current law would still apply to any children already conceived. Currently British law requires only that after age eighteen, and after counseling, children born via donor insemination have the right to be told they were conceived through donor insemination. There is no requirement that children be given information about their donor's background or physical characteristics. The current law is also being challenged by Liberty, a civil rights organization, on behalf of Jo and Adam Rose, two adult DI siblings who claim the law violates their rights [4.32].

The public health minister, Yvette Cooper, does not want to liberalize the law, expressing concern that it would deter potential donors who would fear being sought out for emotional or financial support. The government has stated its intention, however, to consult on a range of options including: disclosing medical history information regarding donors and their family; allowing donors the choice of giving their names and addresses at the time of donation or making them available to the child upon request. All are increasingly common practices within the United States, and groups in both the United States and Canada are advocating national registries to track donors and offspring. The degree of information to be withheld or disclosed through any such registry has been the subject of much debate.

Interestingly, the British government is reportedly responding to an increasing number of donors raising questions about their rights to privacy, not children or child advocates seeking genetic information.

Note: As of April 1, 2005, the law changed: sperm, egg, or embryo donors after this date may no longer remain anonymous, and donor-conceived people over age eighteen can be given both non-identifying and identifying information about their donor.

Guardian Unlimited, 12/27/00; *National Post,*
12/28/00

4.34(a) Wife and Government Struggle over Smuggled Sperm
Spring 2002

In a particularly unusual case even in this novel area of the law, the federal government has confiscated frozen sperm smuggled out of the Allenwood Federal Penitentiary in New York by a convict's wife who hoped to become pregnant with it. Claiming it is "fruit of the crime" (smuggling), the government seized the sperm from the wife's gynecologist's office and is refusing to release it. The sperm was reportedly smuggled out on at least three occasions over a two-year period of time, with the help of prison guards who accepted bribes to assist the couple. The wife's attorney is arguing that while the bribe money may be properly considered fruit of the crime, "seminal fluids" should not be and the court should allow his client the opportunity to "create a life."

Newsday, Associated Press, 2/13/02; *Boston
Globe,* 2/14/02

4.34(b) Ex-Prison Guard Sentenced for Sperm Smuggling
Summer 2002

A former Allenwood prison guard has been sentenced to twenty-seven months for his role in a sperm-smuggling operation. The guard pleaded guilty last year to charges of bribery and conspiracy after prosecutors alleged he accepted between $200 and $300 per trip to smuggle out the sperm of an imprisoned mobster. The intended father had six months added to his racketeering sentence; his wife, who did not get pregnant, is serving a one-year probation sentence.

Associated Press, 4/19/02

4.35 Sperm Donor Children Begin Case for Access to Donor Information in Britain
Fall 2002

A British High Court action has been brought by a twenty-nine-year-old Australian woman and a six-year-old British child who are seeking non-identifying information about the sperm donors who helped conceive them. They are also pressing for the establishment of a voluntary contact register and the collection and storage of more information about future donors.

Under the current Human Fertilisation and Embryology Authority law in Britain, children have access to non-identifying information about their donors. However, this provision of the Act is limited to children over eighteen and born after the Act came into effect. Lawyers in the case are arguing their claims under the Human Rights Act of 1998, which guarantees the right to form a personal identity, and under the antidiscrimination theory that sperm donor children should have the same rights as adopted children to trace their genetic parents.

BBC Online, 5/22/02; Times, 5/23/02;
Independent, 5/23/02

4.36 Voluntary Gamete Donor Registry Launched in United Kingdom
Summer 2004

A private agency in the United Kingdom has launched a voluntary registry aiming to bring together gamete donors and adult children. Where both parties agree, the exchange of information may include identities and addresses or may be limited to non-identifying information about interests, ages, occupations, and the like. The government in the United Kingdom had earlier ended sperm donor anonymity for children who will reach age eighteen in the year 2023.

BBC, 4/21/04

4.37 Idant Labs and Physician Settle with Widow
Winter 1991

Both the laboratory and doctor involved in a lab mix-up, which resulted in a woman being inseminated with the sperm of a man other
than her now-deceased husband, have settled the lawsuit. Julia
Skolnick claimed damages based in part on the ridicule she and her
daughter experienced as a result of their racial differences and in part
on the emotional distress caused by not having a child biologically related to her deceased husband. While neither admitted fault, the laboratory paid Skolnick $100,000, and reportedly the doctor paid ap-
proximately $300,000. It has now been reported that the physician
was ordered to stop banking semen based on "serious deficiencies"
and his application to resume banking is pending.

Newsday, 7/31/91

4.38(a) Infertility Doctor Indicted for Acting as Sperm Donor
March 1992

Facing a fifty-three-count criminal indictment for wire and mail
fraud, Cecil Jacobson, M.D., formerly of Vienna, Virginia, admits
only to having secretly acted as a sperm donor for his patients on "a
few occasions." Federal prosecutors, on the other hand, contend that
Dr. Jacobson perpetrated two criminal schemes. First, they say that
over a ten-year period, he may have fathered more than seventy children as director of the Reproductive Genetic Center, Ltd., in Vienna.
The second set of charges in the indictment revolves around Jacobson's alleged practice of injecting patients with excess hormones to
mimic pregnancy. Reportedly, he then used false descriptions of ultrasounds to mislead them into believing that they were pregnant
and finally told them that their "baby" had died.

The second set of charges stems from allegations that had earlier
led to several civil suits by Jacobson's former patients (which settled
and formed the basis for the 1989 revocation of his Virginia medical
license).

The more recent incidents alleged in the indictment charge that

Jacobson falsely claimed to have a large sophisticated anonymous donor sperm bank with an elaborate matching system. On two occasions, he allegedly told patients that he could and would match them for religious background and thinness. But clinic employees report Jacobson was the only donor and would produce sperm at his office prior to his patients' arrival for inseminations.

Jacobson contends he used his sperm to ensure his patients did not receive AIDS-infected sperm and because fresh sperm was more effective than frozen. Since he did not reveal the source of the sperm, Jacobson also contends he did not violate his patients' right to privacy and anonymity. Going one step further, Jacobson's attorneys reportedly claim, "It is also ironic that what the government seeks to conceal from these children is that their genetic heritage may, in fact, be superior to what they would have otherwise received . . . the donor could have been a vagrant who carried the HIV virus and who sold his sperm to a 'sperm bank' used by Dr. Jacobson."

The government's attorneys claim that the first family who asked to have their children tested did so based on a tip. Additionally, they say that they have taken extreme measures to be sensitive to the explosive information related to Jacobson's patients. These measures included hiring a psychologist, two social workers, and a geneticist to help inform the families.

Pretrial hearings have so far focused on balancing First Amendment concerns against the government's request to close the courtroom to protect the identities of eleven parents who will testify. The children's ages range from four to fourteen. The judge has refused to close the courtroom, but has agreed to allow the parents to testify under pseudonyms and to be moved in and out of the courtroom in the least public way.

Dr. Jacobson currently lives in Provo, Utah, where he conducts privately funded research on the use of lasers to detect genetic problems.

4.38(b) Cecil Jacobson Convicted on All Accounts
June 1992

On March 4, after a fifteen-day criminal trial, Cecil Jacobson was found guilty of all fifty-three counts of a criminal indictment charging he lied to patients about nonexistent pregnancies and about using an anonymous sperm bank when he was the only donor for as many as seventy-five children. At least one couple had believed Jacobson was performing artificial insemination with the husband's sperm when he secretly used his own. When asked how she would have reacted to the suggestion of donor insemination, the mother of twins fathered by Jacobson testified, "We would have been out of the office in half a second."

Long recognized as a pioneer in amniocentesis, Jacobson was reportedly untrained in obstetrics, gynecology, or infertility. He continued to practice after a 1987 complaint was filed with the Virginia Board of Medicine until a local television investigative report forced him out of practice. The suit resulted when several patients claimed he falsely told them they were pregnant but miscarried by "reabsorbing" the fetus, a widely discredited process. Jacobson agreed to a consent order prohibiting him from practicing in Virginia for five years, the maximum available penalty.

During the investigation, prosecutors called in ethicists, a geneticist, and social workers to determine whether and how to contact parents. The ethicists reportedly agreed that parents had a right to know, and the prosecutors developed a step-by-step approach to informing them. Only if and when they responded to the initial inquiry did parents receive and give more information. Many dropped out along the way. Some elected not to learn the "identity" of their sperm donor after being contacted, a prerequisite to becoming a witness and being told about the case against Jacobson. Some withdrew at later points.

Only seven couples ultimately agreed to have their child submit to DNA testing and to testify at trial. Those parents were permitted to do so under pseudonyms and disguises in an attempt to hide their identities from the children and friends. Their assigned names were taped to the witness stand to minimize the risk of being addressed by their real names.

Jacobson's attorneys have asked for a new trial. They claim the jury did not follow the judge's instructions on motive. The judge instructed the jurors must find Jacobson was motivated by money. Interviewed after the verdict, some jurors said that motive did not factor into their deliberations. Others said they believed Jacobson was perhaps motivated by ego rather than money. Trial evidence indicated some of Jacobson's fees were far below those commonly charged. A videotape of juror interviews was submitted to the court to support Jacobson's motion for a new trial. However, most legal observers would agree that overturning jury verdicts based on deliberations is extremely difficult and rare.

The case has also raised questions about the responsibility of physicians to act as "whistleblowers" against colleagues. Just days after the verdict, a *Washington Post* article questioned the responsibility of other area physicians over the decade-long period of Jacobson's scheme. The prosecutor suggested the case should "send a message to the local medical community to do a better job of policing itself." A Virginia obstetrician, who saw one of Jacobson's patients, said he informally reported his concerns to a few members of the state's Board of Medicine but was advised to "back off" or risk a possible defamation claim by Jacobson. Another gynecologist, who said he told patients to avoid Jacobson as early as 1982, wonders now if he should have done more. Several doctors apparently reported concerns to the chair of the Ob/Gyn department of Fairfax Hospital and Jacobson's reported "mentor." That doctor testified that the handful of complaints was insufficient to seek formal action against his former student.

The case has been cited as an example of the need to further regulate assisted reproductive technology clinics and physicians.

4.38(c) Cecil Jacobson Sentenced to Five Years in Prison and Subject of $5 Million Civil Lawsuit

September 1992

Dr. Jacobson was sentenced to five years in prison without parole and $116,000 in fines and restitution. The court allowed Dr. Jacobson to remain free on bond pending appeal.

A former patient, who testified against Jacobson at his criminal trial, has now filed a $5 million malpractice suit against Jacobson for fathering her two children (as proved by DNA testing) by using his own sperm instead of her husband's during artificial insemination procedures.

4.38(d) Cecil Jacobson's Criminal Conviction Appealed (and Affirmed)
June 1993

Cecil Jacobson's attorneys have appealed, arguing he was wrongly convicted based on mistakes rather than fraud and on the testimony of doctors who disagreed with his unorthodox medical practices. A decision is expected shortly.

> *Note:* The conviction was affirmed later in 1993. Several families subsequently filed civil suits against Dr. Jacobson, whose professional liability insurance coverage was found to apply to his actions.
>
> *United States v. Jacobson,* 1993 U.S. App. LEXIS
> 22534 (4th Cir. 1993) and *St. Paul Fire &*
> *Marine Ins. Co. v. Jacobson,* 1995 U.S. App.
> LEXIS 3089 (4th Cir. Va. 1995)

4.39 Sperm Bank Controversy Headed to Administrative Law Hearing
September 1992

Two staff members at Mt. Sinai Medical Center have been charged by the state of New York with running an unlicensed sperm bank using their own fresh sperm, misleading doctors and patients about the number of donors, and profiting by $9,000. Attorneys for one of the two, a medical resident, claim the state has "perverted" the definition of a sperm bank, and their client was simply an occasional sperm donor.

The medical center has denied allegations that it was involved in any sperm bank scam and the matter is pending before an administrative law judge.

> *Note*: Mt. Sinai was cited for operating an unlicensed sperm bank, since the bank operated on its premises, and was also required by the New York State Department of Health to submit an application for its egg donation program, which the state ruled was not covered by the program's prior application, which it found was limited to sperm.
>
> *Newsday,* 4/26/92 and 5/7/92

4.40 Physician Sued for Child Support and Damages
March 1993

A Minnesota woman has sued the physician who performed donor insemination without her husband's written consent.

Doreen and Marvin Johnson separated and filed for divorce between the time she conceived through insemination and delivered a baby girl. Marvin has refused to support the child on the grounds that he did not give his written consent to the insemination procedure and, therefore, has no paternal obligation.

The Minnesota law on donor insemination requires a husband's written consent and then assigns paternal responsibility for any resulting offspring. Ms. Johnson is seeking financial support lost from her ex-husband and compensation for legal fees and mental anguish.

The suit may be the first against a physician for failing to follow a state's consent requirement for donor insemination. It is not, however, the first time an estranged spouse has attempted to use such a law to avoid support obligations for a child conceived through DI. In a small number of cases, divorcing husbands have raised such arguments based on failure to comply with various technical statutory consent requirements. In one similar case, a South Carolina court rejected the argument and ruled that a former husband's cooperation in the procedure and his acting as the child's father for a number of years "estopped" him from denying his paternity and support obligations to the child. However, since this case involves a separation before the child's birth, the Minnesota court may be more willing to assign responsibility to the physician.

Johnson v. Petrini and Park Nicollet Med. Center,
Hennepin Cty., DC CA#92-23348

4.41 Fertility Clinic Ordered to Pay Couple over $70,000 for Lost Sperm
June 1993

A jury awarded a couple $73,975 from a clinic that lost two of three vials of sperm that had been banked by the husband prior to his vasectomy and divorce from his first wife. The couple claimed the three frozen samples were an important factor in his current wife's decision to marry him. The loss was discovered after the first, and now only, artificial attempt the couple underwent. The clinic's attorney minimized the loss and emphasized the relatively small chance of achieving a pregnancy with only two remaining samples.

Casas v. Fertility Center of CXA, Orange Cty.,
Sup. Ct., Cal. 1/12/93

4.42 Doctor and Clinic Sued by Donor Insemination Recipients Who Contracted HIV

September 1994

At least two women who were inseminated with sperm later found to have come from a donor who has AIDS have sued a Los Angeles physician who performed the insemination and the clinic where the insemination took place.

Mary Orsak, who was inseminated in 1984 and 1985, has sued Dr. Jaroslav Marik and the Tyler Medical Clinic of West Los Angeles. She claims that they are liable for having imposed "little or no screening procedures" on donors at that time. Orsak and the other plaintiff are the only two of forty-six women located who were inseminated with the same donor's sperm who have tested positive.

The women are reportedly two of five women known to the Centers for Disease Control who have contracted the virus through donor insemination. All five were inseminated before the HIV antibody test was licensed in 1985, and none conceived from the infected sperm.

The cases have renewed criticism in the popular press over screening practices for donor insemination. The CDC has responded by saying that voluntary industry and CDC guidelines issued in 1988 regarding freezing, testing, and quarantining sperm are now standard practice and are adequate safeguards against infection.

Interviewed after the suits were filed, Dr. Marik noted that his clinic has always tested for HIV as the technology permitted, and acknowledged that "this is a tragedy for everyone concerned . . . [t]hat donor was used in the early 1980s. There was no way to test him."

Los Angeles Times, 5/22/94

4.43 Nonconsenting Husband May Sue Doctor over Donor Insemination of Wife

March 1995

Although Ohio's donor insemination statute does not spell out a remedy in the event a physician breaches his duty to obtain consent from the husband, the Ohio Court of Appeals has ruled that a nonconsenting husband's lawsuit against the physician is appropriate. Moreover, the court noted that the alleged violation could be considered to interfere with the husband's constitutionally protected right not to procreate.

After learning his wife was pregnant following a donor insemination procedure to which he did not consent, Philip Kerns moved out of his marital home and sued the physician who performed the procedure. The couple thereafter divorced, and Kerns was ordered to pay child support. The divorce court did not address his claim that the child was not his child because of his lack of consent to the insemination.

The physician attempted to end the suit by claiming that the statute did not provide a remedy for any physician breach and therefore no such remedy was available to the father. The appellate court disagreed and pointed out that although the purpose of the statute was to protect recipients of donor insemination from claims by nonspousal donors, Kerns's fraud claim should proceed.

Kerns v. Schmidt, 94 Ohio App. 3d 601
(Ohio Ct. App. 1994)

4.44(a) Couple Sues Hospital Alleging Switched Sperm Sample Led to Birth of IVF Twins
Spring 1997

A now-separated couple has sued Jacksonville Memorial Hospital, claiming the hospital inadvertently used another man's sperm to fertilize the wife's eggs in an IVF procedure that resulted in twins. Elizabeth and Michael Higgins, a biracial couple, gave birth to Caucasian twins in 1996 with B positive blood types. The parents are both O positive. Subsequent DNA testing confirmed that the twins are the biological children of Elizabeth, but not Michael. The couple has separated, with the children's paternity cited as the main reason. According to the couple's attorney, "the hospital is really the father, and . . . should be the one financially responsible for the support of these children."

Michael Higgins, appearing on the national news show *20/20*, has said he simply cannot bond with the children. Elizabeth Higgins and the children have moved out of the family's Florida home and are staying with her parents.

The lawsuit seeks an unspecified sum for damages, including emotional and mental distress. Among other allegations, the couple's complaint alleges the hospital held itself out as "providing state-of-the-art and skilled assisted reproductive and IVF services and that it maintained a zero tolerance standard for assuring accurate identification of patient samples and specimens used in in vitro fertilization." According to published news reports, the hospital lab director initially suggested the couple had been given the wrong embryos altogether, and a former embryologist had prepared a written report outlining concerns about sloppy procedures, the ways in which samples were labeled and stored, and being overworked at the hospital.

The hospital has denied any wrongdoing and has moved to dismiss the case. Unless dismissed (or settled), the suit is scheduled for trial next year.

4.44(b) Couple's Lawsuit against Florida Hospital for Sperm Switching Settled

Winter 1998

A now-divorced couple's lawsuit against Jacksonville Memorial Hospital has been settled for a confidential monetary sum. The court must still approve the parties' settlement and appoint guardians to supervise the monetary award for the benefit of the children.

Higgins v. Mem. Hospital Jacksonville, Inc., and
Memorial Healthcare Group, Inc., No. 96-01810
(Fla. Cir. Ct. 1998)

4.45 Hospital Sued for Lost Sperm

Spring 1997

A Scarsdale, New York, couple with two children has sued Mt. Sinai Hospital, claming it disposed of sperm samples the couple intended to use to attempt to have a third child. Published reports of the amount of damages sought by the couple range from $65 to $70 million. The court complaint, filed in a state court in Manhattan, alleges the hospital was given the sperm to maintain and protect for future IVF attempts and that, through its "negligence, carelessness, and recklessness," instead permitted the sperm to be destroyed without the couple's consent. In the interim, the husband underwent chemotherapy, which precluded use of his sperm. The lawsuit seeks both actual or compensatory damages and punitive damages.

It is unclear whether the missing sperm was part of the sperm apparently lost last year when temperature changes in storage tanks at Mt. Sinai resulted in lost samples. In January 1996, Mt. Sinai and New York City agreed to dismiss an action brought by the city in which the hospital acknowledged it had failed to check nitrogen levels in a semen storage tank or maintain proper temperatures and agreed to pay a $2,000 fine.

Anonymous v. Mt. Sinai Hospital, N.Y. Sup. Ct.

(Manhattan) filed 12/3/96

4.46 Lost Sperm Valued in Malpractice Case

Winter 1997

An Oregon jury has awarded $1.25 million to a man who had banked his sperm before undergoing chemotherapy in 1985. Finding the sperm irreplaceable, the jury found the defendant hospital's sperm bank, which lost the sperm, liable and responsible for damages.

Eubanks v. Legacy Emanuel Hospital; AP Wire,

10/12/97

4.47(a) Anonymous Sperm Donor Passes on a Genetic Disorder

Summer 1998

A recent controversy and lawsuit involving an anonymous sperm donor has been reported in the media. A sperm donor allegedly passed on polycystic kidney disease to at least one child and possibly many other children. The child's parents want the sperm donor tested to confirm the child's diagnosis. The clinic providing the semen does not want to disclose the donor's identity nor compel him to undergo testing.

Disclosure of the donor's identity will not provide additional relevant information for the child's medical treatment and the clinic has raised concerns over the potential harm in disclosing the donor's identity. It does, however, raise a serious question about whether other children were born using this donor's sperm and whether the parents of such children should be contacted.

This situation points to the need for clinics and sperm banks to maintain accurate records for use of donor gametes and to maintain up-to-date medical information about gamete donors, including change in donor medical status.

Johnson v. Superior Court, 80 Cal. App. 4th 1050
(Cal. Ct. App. 2000); *Los Angeles Times*,
August 9, 1997 at A1

4.47(b) "Anonymous" Sperm Donor Forced to Testify in Suit against Sperm Bank
Fall 2000

The California Supreme Court has upheld an order that an anonymous sperm donor may be forced to testify in a lawsuit brought against the sperm bank by the parents of a child whose serious kidney disease they allege resulted from the donor's sperm. The court rejected arguments that the donor had a right to privacy that superseded any claim by the girl's parents, although it did say that his identity should, "to the fullest extent possible," remain undisclosed. According to the appellate court, California Cryobank failed to properly test and screen the donor or, despite his familial history, to investigate further, and falsely represented to the couple that the sperm had been tested and screened for infectious and genetic diseases. At the time of the donation, there was no genetic test available for the disease in question. Attorneys for the defendant sperm bank have stated that the court's facts and analysis are wrong, that the decision is harmful and will dissuade potential donors.

The case involves an eleven-year-old girl diagnosed with ADPKD (autosomal dominant polycystic kidney disease). The donor, #276, reportedly began donating sperm in 1986 while a law clerk and, over five years, made approximately 320 deposits for which he received a total of $11,200. According to a deposition from a counselor at California Cryobank, the donor was reportedly "retired" in 1991 based on "new medical information." In his initial questionnaire the donor reportedly indicated his aunt had kidney disease, and marked an "X?" on a question as to whether his mother had kidney disease. The court found that in 1995 California Cryobank informed the child's physician that the donor's aunt had ADPKD and a kidney transplant, that his maternal grandmother had died from the disease combined with heart failure, that his mother had the disease and was in good health, and that the donor was in good health.

The court rejected the privacy arguments, ruling the donor's privacy rights were "substantially diminished" because of his multiple donations. These, in the court's words, represented "a substantial commercial transaction likely to affect the lives of many people." The court also rejected the notion that the doctor-patient privilege applied, finding that the donor was not a patient. It added that the bank's contract, which assured the donor of anonymity under any circumstances, went too far, since under California law discovery rules attorneys in a lawsuit may obtain such information for "good cause."

4.47(c) Sperm Bank Falls under California's Health Care Provider Law
Winter 2002

A California appellate court has ruled that a sperm bank is a "health dispensary" and therefore a "health care provider" protected from punitive damages under California law absent proof of malice or fraud. The family claims that they were never informed of the donor's family history of kidney disease and would have chosen a different donor.

The Court of Appeals also ruled that the child could not recover general damages or lost earnings, rejecting that claim as a form of "wrongful life," a legal concept rejected by California and many other state courts. The reasoning behind such a principle is that it is impossible either to find that being born with an impairment is worse than never being born at all or to calculate such damages. The family's attempt to distinguish the case, by claiming that the defendants "caused" the injury, was rejected. Despite the fact that the couple would have chosen another donor, the court ruled it was the donor's genetic abnormality, not the defendants' alleged misconduct, which literally "caused" the impairment. Despite denying petitioners' motion for reconsideration of a summary adjudication on the issue of fraud (and therefore punitive damages) as untimely, the court noted that evidentiary issues had been raised about the source of handwritten notations on a page of the Donor Profile and whether the original page was deliberately withheld from petitioners, and that the lower court had discretion to allow discovery on that issue.

Johnson v. Superior Court, 101 Cal. App. 4th 869
(Cal. Ct. App. 2002); *review denied,* 2002 Cal.
LEXIS 8341 (Cal. 2002)

4.48 Utah Supreme Court Rejects Liability for Use of Wrong Sperm Donor
Winter 1998

Parents of healthy triplet boys failed in their attempt to hold the University of Utah Medical Center liable for allegedly using the wrong sperm donor to achieve their pregnancy. The couple, David and Stephanie Harnicher, claimed they were extremely reluctant to use any donor sperm, but were encouraged by the Center to mix both husband and donor sperm in an ICSI procedure, and then carefully selected a donor with the same blood type and hair color as the husband. After birth it was determined that the children did not have the same blood type or physical appearance as the husband and likely resulted from Donor #83 and not, as the couple requested, Donor #183. The couple sued, claiming negligent infliction of emotional distress by the Center. At the trial level, the court granted summary judgment for the Center, effectively dismissing the case. A divided state Supreme Court affirmed.

On appeal, the majority of the justices found against the couple, concluding that they failed to prove their case and that destruction of the "fiction" that the husband was the biological father of the children was not a recognizable harm. The two dissenting justices criticized the Center for promoting a procedure (sperm mixing) that had been scientifically rejected, and chastised the majority of the justices for refusing to attribute liability to the Center for "... destruction of the very circumstances [it] counseled the couple to seek and promised to provide. . . ." or to recognize the couple's loss.

The two opinions in the case make a fascinating study of very different perspectives of infertility, as well as demonstrate the limitations of tort law. Applying common law principles of Utah tort law, the majority of the court ruled that the couple failed to prove physical injury or illness (physical or mental) to support their claim of negligent infliction of emotional distress. They noted that in their depositions the Harnichers did not claim "bodily harm," but only after consulting a clinical psychologist (which the court suggested they did only to avoid the lawsuit's dismissal) did they allege such conditions as sleep disturbances, fatigue, impaired concentration, loss of appetite, crying spells, cold flashes, muscle tension, and diminished work productivity. The majority also rejected the Harnichers' claim of emotional distress "to the point of mental illness" based on the fact that the children did not match the husband's blood type or appearance. "Exposure to the truth about one's own situation cannot be considered an injury and has never been a tort. Therefore, destruction of a fiction cannot be grounds for either malpractice or negligent infliction of emotional distress." The court also noted that the couple did not claim any racial or ethnic "mismatch," without explaining why that might create a recognizable claim.

The dissent criticized the majority for a biased reporting of the facts and an insensitivity to the human losses associated with infertility. Other facts it claimed were overlooked or minimized by the majority included: the Harnichers' detailed explanations of their apprehension over not having a child of the husband; their careful selection of the one donor acceptable to them; and the fact that they would not have undergone donor sperm IVF unless they were assured they would never need to know whether or not the husband had a "biological bond" to any resulting child. "Had it not been for the University's negligence in mixing sperm from the wrong donor with David's, the 'fiction' would never have been labeled a fiction; it would simply have been an 'alternative reality' for the Harnicher family. In fact, in a sense, it was this alternative that the Harnichers negotiated for in their contract with the University, and that the University destroyed through its negligent act." The dissenting justices cited Barbara Eck Menning and others to support their sympathetic view of infertility and its losses. They also noted that the experienced clinical psychologist's unchallenged findings of clinical depression were consistent with a sufferer's lack of insight into their condition and were based on extensive testing on the couple.

The appellate ruling ends the case, concluding that no legally recognizable harm resulted from any negligent act of sperm switching that may have occurred and leaving unaddressed the question of whether there was negligence in the sperm donation process.

Harnicher v. University of Utah Med. Ctr.,
962 P.2d 67 (Utah 1998)

4.49 New York Court Allows IVF-Sperm Mix-up Lawsuit to Proceed Against Embryologist and Program
Spring 2007

An apparent sperm mix-up involving a 2004 IVF procedure is the subject of an ongoing lawsuit filed by the girl's rearing parents. The couple initially became concerned after the child's birth when she appeared to have darker skin than either the wife, who is Hispanic, or the husband, who is Caucasian. After three DNA tests confirmed that Thomas Andrews is not the girl's genetic father, the couple sued the clinic and professionals involved. The sperm is purportedly from an African-American sperm donor. The couple has also expressed concerns over whether the husband's sperm may have been used to create another child. The trial court recently allowed the case to proceed against the New York Medical Services for Reproductive Medicine, the physician who owns the practice only in that capacity, and the program's embryologist who purportedly fertilized the wife's eggs. The court dismissed claims against the physician who performed the embryo transfer and rejected the couple's claim of mental distress, ruling that the birth of a healthy but unwanted child is not a recognizable injury under New York law, but allowed other aspects of the case, including the malpractice claims, to continue.

Andrews v. Keltz (and N.Y. Medical Services), 838
N.Y.S.2d 363 (N.Y. Sup. Ct. 2007); *Guardian,* 3/27/07

4.50(a) Court Allows Product Liability Suit against Sperm Bank to Proceed
Fall 2009

Ruling that sperm is a product and its sale subject to strict liability under New York law, a federal court in Pennsylvania has refused to dismiss a product liability claim against Idant Labs. The suit was brought by a Pennsylvania mother and her thirteen-year-old mentally retarded daughter who has Fragile X and was conceived through allegedly improperly screened donor sperm from that sperm bank. In its preliminary ruling on the various legal theories presented, the court struck the mother's claims under the applicable statute of limitations, dismissed the child's "wrongful life" claim as one not recognized in New York, but allowed her product liability claim to proceed as well as her amended breach of contract claim (as an intended third-party beneficiary) even though her mother's claim was time-barred. This is another instance where choice of law may be outcome-determinative. While both states have "blood shield statutes" which prohibit product liability suits for blood and blood products, Pennsylvania includes other human tissues so a product liability claim would be barred under that law. The case is likely to take many more twists before a final ruling is reached.

Donovan et al. v. Idant Laboratories, 2009
U.S.Dist. LEXIS 44350 (E.D.Pa. 2009)

4.50(b) Trial Court Reverses; Dismisses Strict Liability Claim against Sperm Bank

Winter 2010

A federal district court has reversed itself on a motion for reconsideration by the defendant sperm bank, Idant Labs, and struck the remaining claims brought against it by a mother and child who claimed defective sperm had caused the child's Fragile X.

After originally dismissing all but the child's strict liability and breach of warranty claims, the court was also persuaded it could not allow those under New York law. Since the only resulting "injury" was the daughter's impaired life, it concluded even that claim amounted to a "wrongful life" action, which New York does not recognize. Quoting from a New York appellate decision, the court found: "[a] cause of action based on 'wrongful life' seeks to put the child in the position of having not received the defective sperm, thereby depriving the infant plaintiff of [her] very existence." Although economic injuries or loss are permitted under strict product liability law, "here it is impossible to distinguish plaintiff's economic injuries from those of a claim for wrongful life," and thus could not be applied in this case. In dismissing the child's breach of warranty claim, the court noted New York law permits only personal, not economic, injuries, and because the only injuries she could state to avoid "wrongful life" issues were economic ones, that claim also failed.

Donovan et al. v. Idant Laboratories, 625
F.Supp.2d 256 (E.D.Pa. 2009) (6/10/09)

CHAPTER FIVE

Maternity and Egg Donation

❖ MEDICAL COMMENTARY, BY Howard W. Jones, Jr.

FROM A MEDICAL PERSPECTIVE, egg donation is very different from sperm donation. Sperm donation has been common practice for over fifty years, requires but a few minutes and little medical intervention, and brings no medical complications; in addition, sperm can be readily frozen and reliably thawed. Nonetheless, anonymous sperm donation has been complicated by the appearance of infectious disease, including HIV. Because of infectious disease, the FDA has intervened and now considers egg and sperm donation like other tissue transplant situations and has created rules for their use. In the case of sperm, FDA regulations require most sperm be quarantined for six months; the donor must then be retested and found to be free of specified diseases before the quarantined sperm can be released for use.

Eggs are more difficult to freeze and thaw than other reproductive tissue. Until that changes, the six-month quarantine is impractical for eggs, so the quarantine requirement has been waived. Donors are tested for HIV and many other diseases. Presumably, when the oocyte can be frozen and thawed efficiently, the same quarantine and retesting requirements will apply to eggs as well as sperm. The current waiver makes some biological sense. Present technology allows sperm of HIV-positive males to be washed and thus be HIV-negative, since the virus is transmitted in the seminal plasma and not in the sperm itself. There have been a number of cases reported of HIV-positive men whose sperm has been used by HIV-negative women without any complications. I know of no cases of transmission under this circumstance. It therefore makes biological sense that the oocyte itself probably is not involved; at a minimum, the current HIV six-month quarantine waiver for eggs is appropriate.

Dr. Jacob Mayer, director of laboratories at the Jones Institute, an executive member of SART, and a liaison to the U.S. Food and Drug Administration regarding tissue regulations, is very familiar with the FDA's requirements. His comments follow:

Currently, federal regulations require testing for a number of infectious diseases, including HIV 1 and 2, HTLV1 and HTLV2. The FDA tissue transplant regulations prescribe specifically the types of tests that have to be done and when they have to be done (generally within seven days of tissue collection) on any kind of transplanted cells or tissue, including cornea transplants, heart valves, skin, and semen. Semen donors must be tested within seven days of the actual semen collection. In addition, because semen has the advantage of being easily frozen, the FDA's regulations essentially adopted the existing industry standard: a six-month quarantine and then a retesting. A Donor semen sample can only be used if the results from both the initial testing and the six-month retesting are all negative.

The FDA regulations are a two-tier system of both "**testing**" and "**screening**" for all tissue. In addition to the testing described above, the FDA requires facilities to screen out individuals with certain risk factors for infectious diseases. These are often behavioral factors, such as "men who have engaged in sex with other men" or "IV drug users" and are the same sort of screening factors as applied to potential blood donors. All tissue for use in transplantation in the U.S., whether donated within the U.S. or imported into the U.S., must meet these regulations.

Oocytes present a unique situation. Because oocyte donors usually are matched to their recipients and begin the expensive "stimulation treatment" far in advance of when the actual tissue (oocytes) is collected, the FDA made an exception to the "seven-day testing" rule and allows up to 30 days between the time of oocyte collection and the time of "Oocyte Donor"–testing (The same exception applies to hematopoietic cells.) Unlike sperm, there is no requirement for a six-month quarantining and subsequent re-testing of Oocyte Donors.

The FDA also makes an exception in its regulations for the transplantation of tissue from a "directed donor." With informed consent, a recipient can choose to use a "directed donor's" tissue even if it tests positive for disease or for a known risk factor, and would otherwise be ineligible. This rule was put into place primarily for hardship cases where, for example the only compatible tissue for a necessary tissue transplant is from a family member who may be ineligible due to some behavioral risk or problem in their testing or screening. This allows a recipient who knows the tissue donor to accept that risk and go forward with the transfer from an ineligible tissue donor. Thus, according to the FDA regulations, with informed consent a recipient can use sperm or oocytes from an HIV positive "directed" donor (or any other disease).

Gametes from sexually intimate partners are also exempted by the FDA from tissue transplant screening and testing. The FDA reasoned that such individuals were already at risk for transmission of infectious diseases and the tissue transplant procedure did not represent any addition risk.

In contrast to donor eggs and donor sperm, surrogacy presents a very different situation from the FDA perspective. There is no specific FDA requirement for testing gestational surrogates. Under current FDA definitions, a gestational surrogate is a recipient of tissue. Because the FDA's regulations have been aimed at testing/screening the donors of tissue to prevent transmission to the recipient, to date it has not put into place any requirement to test the gestational surrogate, or her partner, for any transmissible disease. The FDA has not yet acknowledged or addressed the concerns of disease transmission from the recipient (surrogate) to the transplanted tissue (embryo) in the case of reproductive therapies.

Complicating the picture, States may also have their own laws or regulations in place about infectious disease including HIV positive tissue semen or blood. Typically these regulations were written in the late 1980s when HIV contamination in the blood supply and in sperm banks was a substantial concern and they usually addressed only semen and blood. Most have not kept up with the technology and treatments, and simply preclude any use of a positive HIV sample. If a state law is more restrictive than the Federal law, the more restrictive law always applies and clinics in those States need to meet these additional requirements.

To date, egg freezing has been inefficient. Using standard slow freezing techniques as might be applied to sperm, a limited number of pregnancies and births have been reported. Using the faster technique of vitrification, the live birth per frozen egg is more efficient and reported to be in the 5 percent range per egg frozen. From a practical point of view, therefore, cryopreservation of oocytes is still considered a developing technology, although it is one that is developing rapidly amidst significant interest due to its potential both to make egg donation a more predictable process similar to frozen sperm donation and to preserve female fertility. A 2007 ASRM Practice Committee Report considers cryopreservation for preserving a woman's own fertility to be an experimental procedure that should not be "offered or marketed" as a means to defer reproductive aging.

As noted in the legal commentary, problems may arise in egg donation aside from any medical issues or mix-ups. Once again, the question arises whether the IVF program has any responsibility in trying to forecast and, therefore, prevent these sociological mishaps. One example that comes to mind is the California case involving the child Jaycee Buzzanca. Discussed in chapter 6, a gestational surrogate was asked to carry a donor egg fertilized by donor sperm for a married couple. When the husband decided to divorce his wife during the pregnancy, he attempted to avoid child support and paternity obligations by claiming that he was not the child's biological or legal father. It took several appeals and a number of years before he was found to be legally responsible for the child's support. Troubling situations like this raise difficult questions for the medical profession.

Does the IVF program have any responsibility in trying to identify such situations? While it has become rather routine practice to psychologically examine or screen egg donors and surrogates, I don't believe all programs psychologically examine or screen prospective parents either routinely or in unusual situations. It seems to me that a program that wishes to dot all the i's and cross all the t's would be alert and perform whatever screening is available in atypical situations. Unfortunately, there are no clear data in this area that support whether it should be done, whether it could be done, or what the results would signify. Doing it is simply common sense.

One of the difficult situations in egg donation is where there is a split or shared donation, as when a woman is not able to afford her own IVF treatment so agrees to split her eggs, donating some of her eggs to another couple, who then share part of the financial burden for the procedure. Problems can arise when one but not both of the women become pregnant. Because egg quality is routinely assessed, splitting eggs is never a biologically equal undertaking. It goes without saying that in any informed consent process, all of these various outcomes need to be considered thoughtfully and documented carefully so that the patient who chooses to go forward understands and accepts the resultant whims of nature.

∾ LEGAL COMMENTARY, BY Susan L. Crockin

Egg donation ushered in a new era of collaborative or third-party reproduction, significantly expanding the number of patients who could now hope to achieve a pregnancy and give birth to a child biologically related to one spouse or partner. From both a medical and legal perspective, it also carried obvious parallels with sperm donation. Sperm donation provided an initial conceptual framework for both providers and patients contemplating this new option for family building as well as a legal basis for arguments that equal rights or protections required treating gametes and donors of either sex alike. At the same time, distinguishing characteristics also soon became apparent.

Sperm donation, which predated the ARTs by decades, has had longstanding laws in approximately thirty-five states that at a minimum clarify parentage in many contexts. Almost all such laws apply to married couples; less frequently, they may also cover unmarried recipients and explicitly relieve donors of any parental rights or obligations. A number of those laws also include requirements such as physician involvement and oral or written consent by the nonbiological husband.

The medical distinctions between male and female donation have strained the application of sperm donor laws and created challenges to the developing law and practice surrounding egg donation. In contrast to the minimal medical role involved in sperm retrieval, female donors undergo a relatively lengthy medical procedure from screening to retrieval and are exposed to the risk of ovarian hyperstimulation and the potential but unknown risks of repeated hormone stimulations. Moreover, egg donation still requires careful cycle coordination between donor and recipient, whereas the evolution to almost exclusive use of frozen, quarantined sperm has eliminated any need to coordinate sperm donation with recipient cycles.

At the same time that egg donation was rapidly expanding, the increasing use of ARTs by single women and men and by same-sex couples meant that more intended parents did not fit within the protections of existing laws, whether they were using donated male or female gametes or not. Recruitment and compensation for egg donors rose quickly, far outpacing sperm donation fees, and became a hotly debated issue. Attempts to limit reproductive donors' compensation through voluntary professional guidelines have met with limited success. Despite ASRM guidelines, compensation amounts continue to rise, and both anecdotal and documented reports of compensation far in excess of these guidelines by some intended parents and some recruiting programs continue to proliferate. The advent of embryonic stem cell research and the need for donor eggs to create research embryos have fueled a very public debate. On the research side, both voluntary guidelines and a few state laws were put in place to deny payment to research donors as a way of addressing concern over potential undue influence on prospective donors or commodification of their eggs. In contrast to reproductive donors, those restrictions have to date been followed so strictly that many stem cell programs have reported an inability to recruit donors. The discrepancies between regulatory paradigms for reproductive and research donors have been the subject of ongoing debates within the scientific and legal communities; from a legal perspective, they are certainly difficult to justify.

Thus, for multiple reasons, as egg donation proliferated the legal stage was set for novel disputes and conflicting resolutions across the country. The advent of egg-freezing technologies and their already commercial applications create the very real likelihood that in the future, frozen donor eggs, like sperm, will become widely available for procreation. This developing technology will require yet another rethinking of some of the current principles and policies surrounding egg donation.

Readers should also be mindful that the relative novelty of egg donation means that the related legal issues are still in their own infancy; the law surrounding egg donation is still evolving. In contrast to very common sperm donation statutes, only a handful of states (eight at last count) have enacted statutes that explicitly define parentage of children born through egg donation. Despite the predictably few cases to date, a number of issues, sometimes overlapping in the same scenarios, have emerged: (1) maternity of children born from donor eggs, including children born to lesbian women and gestational surrogate carriers; (2) regulation, screening, and related protocols surrounding donation procedures; (3) reconciliation of frozen donor egg protocols and practices with existing professional standards; and (4) professional liability surrounding use and misuse of donated eggs.

For married couples using donor eggs where the wife carries the pregnancy, the relatively sparse litigation suggests that these children will be seen much as children born from donor sperm are, that is, as the children of the couple and specifically the married woman. Attempts by two ex-husbands to gain custody based on being the only genetic parent were summarily dismissed in both New York and Ohio (*McDonald v. McDonald* and *Ezzone v. Ezzone*). Failure to screen out an egg donor who was a cystic fibrosis carrier (*Paretta v. Med. Offices*) was analyzed much like a sperm donor case in which the donor had an undisclosed family history of a kidney disorder (*Johnson v. Sup. Ct.*). In both cases, the courts refused to apply or extend legal principles of wrongful birth and wrongful pre-conception screening while allowing other theories of liability to proceed. Similarly, the relatively small number of reported egg mix-ups are likely to be addressed and resolved under the same principles as sperm or embryo mix-ups in terms of both custody and professional liability. In one mix-up case, a child born to a single woman who had thought she was using a donor embryo but was mistakenly implanted with a married couple's embryo created by the husband and an anonymous egg donor was ruled by the court to be the child of the single woman and husband. The wife's intention to be the mother of any child born from those embryos was rejected by the court as a valid basis for determining maternity (*Denise v. Robert and Susan B.*). The degree to which intended parenthood plays a role in deciding contested parentage disputes continues to be an unpredictable factor in many of these cases and one that merits careful legal attention in the creation of these arrangements in the hope of avoiding such disputes altogether.

Cases that particularly test the ability of courts to define parenthood involve donor eggs and gestational carrier pregnancies, raising the possibility of three mothers (genetic, gestational, and intended). In the relatively infamous California case of a "parentless child," which first came to light in 1998, a child born to a gestational carrier using a donor embryo was quickly seen as the child of her intended mother when neither carrier nor egg donor attempted to claim maternity. Multiple appeals took place before the intended father who did not want paternity obligations following a divorce was deemed the legal father (*In re Jaycee B.*). On the other hand, in another highly publicized set of interrelated cases several years later, unmarried intended parents battling with their gestational carrier over triplets conceived with donor egg and the intended father's sperm proactively sought out their previously anonymous egg donor to assert maternity rights in a litigation strategy aimed at trumping any maternity rights the carrier was asserting (*Flynn v. Bimber* (2005) and the related proceeding *Rice v. Flynn* (2005)). Both of those cases illustrate the complexity and novelty of the legal issues, the lengths to which parties will go to establish or deny parentage, and the critical need for legally clear arrangements from the outset. Absent clearly applicable law, consent forms and legal agreements will bear the burden of attempting to clarify parentage consistent not only with the parties' initial expectations but also with existing analogous laws and public policy.

As egg donation has evolved, legal agreements between donors and intended parents have been introduced as an alternate means of attempting to clarify the respective intentions, rights, and obligations of the parties. No court has yet ruled on the enforceability of such agreements. They were initially designed over a decade ago (by this author, among others) in the hope that they would help protect both donors and intended parents who, together with independent counsel, could negotiate a mutually protective legal agreement. In one series of cases, an egg donor who had not authorized splitting her eggs between two recipient couples and who had entered into a legal agreement with only one couple successfully sued to halt a physician's attempt to share her eggs until the issues were ultimately settled to her satisfaction (*Options v. Allon et al.*). As stand-alone recruiting programs continue to proliferate and at times direct the legal arrangements, it remains to be seen whether these agreements will indeed be found to protect the parties, as was initially envisioned.

Same-sex couples have also presented unique legal issues. As discussed in chapter 8, professionals should be mindful that female same-sex couples who intend to have a child together are at risk of being characterized as egg donors or gestational carriers, especially if medical consent forms and other written documentation do not accurately reflect their intentions. Thus, well-meaning professionals whose documentation has not been updated or customized to reflect newer forms of family building or who do not refer such patients to knowledgeable legal counsel to review and supplement that documentation may inadvertently contribute to legal complications and vulnerabilities for these families and, consequently, themselves. One such case involved twins born to a lesbian couple using one woman's eggs while the other woman carried the pregnancy (*K.M. v. E.G.*, 2005). Although the decision was ultimately reversed, two courts initially ruled against the genetic mother based on the women's conflicting testimony bolstered by the IVF program's boilerplate consent form, which treated the genetic mother as an anonymous egg donor. Such lengthy and in many instances heartbreaking litigation is likely best avoided by medical programs and intended parents seeking to clarify and record intentions prior to any medical treatment.

Egg freezing is too recent a development to have fostered litigation in the United States to date, but the growing interest in commercial egg freezing for both fertility preservation and donation will inevitably present challenges to those administering, regulating, offering, or hoping to receive such genetic material. Medical professional guidelines currently consider egg freezing to preserve a woman's own reproductive potential to be experimental and express caution about the need to ensure that such women are fully informed about a process still considered experimental. Voluntary professional guidelines currently make clear that donors are to be compensated only for their time, discomfort, inconvenience, and risks associated with the donation process, not for the eggs themselves. Compensation to donors and payments by intended parents; the issue of quarantining frozen eggs and retesting donors; the flow of personal information among donors, intended parents, and future children; and the possibility of donors changing their mind about eggs that have been donated and frozen but not yet thawed or fertilized—all of these will be among the many challenging issues that this evolving field is likely to face.

Litigation

5.1 Gamete Donors Continue to Make News

September 1992

CNN reported that a thirty-five-year-old Jewish woman, whose ancestors were Holocaust victims, says she wants to help repopulate the world: "As far as I'm concerned . . . my egg is a Jewish egg and the child that is born from my egg is Jewish."

By strict tradition, children are only considered Jewish if their mother, or birth mother if they are adopted, is Jewish. Otherwise a conversion is required. Some religious scholars therefore question whether or not a child resulting from a Jewish donor's egg would be Jewish.

CNN, 7/5/02

5.2 Egg Donor Dispute Ends in Settlement

September 1992

According to local New York media sources, a New York City infertility center and a former egg donor have resolved their compensation dispute. The thirty-three-year-old donor was reportedly told she could no longer donate eggs by the Center for Reproductive Services at Mt. Sinai Medical Center after she developed an ovarian cyst while being stimulated. The Center initially refused to pay her any portion of the $1,500 fee on the theory that she did not participate in the most difficult part (retrieval). After she objected, the Center reportedly offered $350, then ultimately paid her $1,000 despite its policy to only pay upon completion and its claim that it needed to absorb the cost of the drugs.

The donor reportedly contacted the media after seeing an article on the Center's donor egg program and recruitment of anonymous donors.

Newsday, 5/8/92

5.3 Two States Pass Enlightened Donor Egg and Embryo Legislation

September 1993

ART professionals, together with RESOLVE members and lawyers with expertise in reproductive technology, have drafted and successfully lobbied for egg and embryo donation laws in Florida and Texas. In Florida the effort was headed by Stan Williams, M.D., chief of reproductive endocrinology and infertility at the University of Florida Health Science Center in Gainesville. In Texas, the effort was headed by legal scholar John Robertson, J.D., and Ruby Fisher, a nurse practitioner and IVF clinic coordinator. These laws, which are similar in concept to sperm donation provisions found in many states, provide significant legal clarification in this emerging area. Oklahoma passed an egg donation law in 1990.

According to Robertson, the legislatures in Texas and Florida have enacted legislation that gives legal recognition to children born of egg and preembryo donation. In Texas, the new law treats the offspring of egg and preembryo donation the same as children born of donor insemination: if the wife consents to placement of a donor oocyte that has been fertilized with her husband's sperm in her uterus, any resulting child is the legitimate child of the couple, and not the child of the oocyte donor. A similar provision applies to children born of preembryo donation. In either case, the consent of the husband and wife must be in writing. The law does not address gestational surrogacy.

In Florida, the law states that any child born within wedlock who has been conceived by means of donated eggs or preembryos shall be irrebuttably presumed to be the child of the recipient gestating woman and her husband. Both parties must consent in writing to the use of donated eggs or preembryos. The Florida law also contains provisions for legal recognition of the rearing intentions of the parties in gestational surrogacy.

Passage of these laws illustrates that state legislatures are willing to deal with the legal issues presented by egg and embryo donation. By making clear that the recipient couple are the legal parents for all purposes, and that the donor has no parental rights or duties, the legal uncertainty surrounding rearing rights and duties in egg and embryo donation procedures is now removed. Physicians and others interested in having egg and embryo donation legislations passed in their state will find that either statute is a workable model for such legislation.

Fla. Stat. 742.11 (2007); Tex. Fam. Code Ann.
160.702 (2007) [current citations]

5.4 First Dispute Reported Involving Egg Donation
June 1994

A divorcing husband has failed in his initial attempts to wrest custody of his twin daughters away from his wife on the grounds that they are "illegitimate." He claims to be their only genetic parent because they were born as the result of egg donation. Related lawsuits brought by the husband against his wife and the medical center that performed the egg donation / IVF procedure are also pending.

Robert and Olga McDonald, a New York couple who married in 1988, underwent IVF with donor eggs at Mt. Sinai Hospital Fertility Clinic, resulting in the birth of twin girls in early 1991. Robert subsequently sued to divorce Olga, and sought custody of the children on the grounds that he was "the only genetic and natural parent available" to them and that his custody claim was therefore superior to his wife's.

The divorce court rejected Robert's claims, as did the higher court to which he appealed, each finding that Olga was both the children's legally presumed and intended mother. The appellate court relied heavily on the California Supreme Court's decision in *Johnson v. Calvert* [6.1g]. Although the Johnson case involved a gestational surrogate's unsuccessful claim to the child she had carried for his genetic parents, the California Court ruled that the parties' intentions controlled. It also distinguished Johnson's situation from "the true egg donation situation," in which the court said it would recognize the birth mother as the natural mother. The New York court recited that analysis and language with approval and concluded that New York law similarly provided ample support for finding the wife to be the natural mother.

The husband was also unsuccessful in his bid to obtain all medical records regarding the children's birth. The court first noted that the physician-patient privilege was not a bar since the records were his wife's and were sought in a custody lawsuit. However, it agreed with the wife that the husband's real purpose was to obtain information about the egg donor and therefore rejected the request.

The husband was more successful in having the children's birth records revised to replace his wife's maiden name with his last name, a change which the court noted "merely reinforces the principle of legitimacy."

Separate suits brought by Robert McDonald are reportedly pending against both Mt. Sinai and his wife, arising from his claims that his consent to the egg donation / IVF was not properly obtained.

McDonald v. McDonald, 196 A.D.2d 7 (N.Y. App. Div. 1994)

5.5 British Debate Donor Cards for Ovaries and Eggs
September 1994

A new controversy has erupted in Great Britain, this time over the endorsement by the British Medical Association to allow young women to carry donor cards permitting their ovaries or eggs to be used in the event of their death. The British Medical Association considered permitting such cards to be issued to and signed by girls as young as twelve.

Criticism has ranged from the concept of donating eggs and ovaries after death to the application of it to girls of such a young age. An infertile Korean woman is already reportedly pregnant through an ovary transplant from such a deceased donor.

The British Medical Association's position is part of its response to the consultation that HFEA has been conducting for the past six months and that includes the debated use of fetal eggs and ovaries as well. A report by that group is due out shortly.

Glasgow Herald, 7/6/94; *Independent*, 7/1/94

5.6(a) Second Father Claims Custody of Twins Based on Egg Donation
Spring 1997

The father of four-year-old twins is attempting to get custody of them over his estranged wife on the grounds the children were conceived using eggs donated by his wife's sister. The husband, who is a lawyer, is arguing that his wife is the stepmother and an aunt, but that he is the only biological parent and therefore should be given custody. A similar claim was rejected by a New York court two years ago (*Mc-Donald v. McDonald*, [5.4]). Because Ohio has no statute on egg donation, the husband claims his wife has no legal claim to motherhood. Ohio does, however, have a sperm donation statute and equal protection arguments may be applicable and ultimately persuasive. In addition . . . he signed two contracts at the time of the IVF procedures stating his wife would be recognized as the legal and natural mother, and the twins' birth certificates reflect her as the mother. The husband is attempting to rely on an earlier, uncontested, Ohio case to support his position that genetic parenthood trumps gestational parenthood. In that case (*Belsito v. Clark*, 67 Ohio Misc. 2d 54, 1994), an Ohio judge agreed with the parties that the genetic mother was entitled to have her name on the birth certificate of the child carried for her by her sister as a gestational carrier. That decision, which centered on the accuracy of a birth certificate, may have limited application to a contested divorce and custody case.

5.6(b) Mother Wins Custody Fight over Donor Egg Twins
Winter 1997

A divorcing father's efforts to obtain custody of the couple's now five-year-old twins conceived through egg donation, on the grounds that he was their only genetic parent, has failed. The court awarded custody to the mother; her sister had been the egg donor. The court ruled that any other decision would violate both state and federal equal protection clauses, since it would have placed women needing donor gametes to create their families in a different, and worse, position than men, and thus be unfair and discriminatory. The court also noted the wife had given birth to the twins and her name appeared on their birth certificates as a result of an earlier legal action brought by the couple for that purpose. The father has not yet decided whether he will appeal.

> *Ezzone v. Ezzone*, Ct. Common Pleas, Dir. Dom.
> Rels, Lake Cty., Ohio No. 96 DR 000359 (1997)

5.7 Frozen Eggs Withheld from British Patients
Spring 2000

A woman being denied the use of her frozen eggs by HFEA is suing, and a London clinic storing eggs for fifty other women is considering similar legal action if its negotiations with HFEA are unsuccessful. Although HFEA has been permitting freezing since October 1999, it still prohibits thawing and use of the eggs out of concern over the unknown impact on the resulting children. The Assisted Reproduction and Gynaecology Centre, the only British clinic licensed by HFEA to store eggs, is negotiating with HFEA to allow its patients, all cancer survivors, to access their eggs. The clinic's director, Dr. Taranissi, has pointed out that the treatment currently banned in the United Kingdom has been successfully used in the United States, Australia, and Italy, and should be available to Britons. HFEA representatives maintain they do not believe the scientific data supports the use of frozen eggs and "will not permit women to be experimented on."

Daily Telegraph; Guardian, 12/16/99

5.8(a) Litigation Erupts in Texas over Egg-Sharing Donation
Winter 2002

According to published reports, an egg donor has sued two couples who shared her eggs, seeking to stop their usage by anyone without her written consent and asking for money damages. In turn, the second couple, who had sought to use four remaining embryos created with the donor's eggs and husband's sperm, has sued the egg donor, the doctor, and the clinic. The interlocking disputes involve an anonymous donor located through the California-based Options National Fertility Registry, two infertile couples who shared her eggs to create embryos, Michael A. Allon, M.D., and Obstetrical and Gynecological Associates of Houston, Texas.

According to their lawsuit, the second couple, the McBrides, claim the doctor recommended the egg-sharing arrangement to them, but when they went to use their second set of frozen embryos (after an initial miscarriage), the doctor then told them that he did not have the donor's permission. His attorney has been quoted as saying the doctor had relied on the donor's initial permission and Texas law.

The donor claims she only authorized the first couple to receive her eggs and at no time was asked, informed of, or agreed to her eggs being used by any other couple. The McBrides are claiming the embryos are "children in waiting" whose fate should be determined on a "best interest of the embryos" standard. There was reportedly a legal agreement in place between the donor, who was represented by separate legal counsel, and the first, but not the second, recipient couple outlining their mutual understandings.

These interrelated cases challenge the assumption of many programs and intended parents that they are free to use donated gametes or embryos as they wish, despite a lack of clarity in the law or documentation. Whatever their outcome, these cases suggest a need to review the sufficiency of existing protocols, consents, and documentation in light of the current uncertainties in the law in most states.

Houston Chronicle, 5/31/02

5.8(b) Jury Verdict in Options National Fertility Registry Litigation
Summer 2005

A jury trial between a donor egg recruitment agency and the medical professionals arising out of an egg-sharing arrangement has concluded. The agency, physician, and medical program were ultimately the only remaining parties in a trial that concluded in January 2005 with the jury finding the defendants liable for failing to comply with their agreement with the agency and for interference with the agency's business, but not liable on a charge of intentionally interfering with the agency's contract with its own clients.

Options Nat. Fertility Registry v. Dr. Allon, et al.,
and related cases (Jud. Dis. 190th, Harris Cty.,
Tex., 1/10/05)

5.9(a) Court Refuses to Recognize Genetic Mom Following Lesbian Partners' Breakup
Fall 2003

In a case that may have IVF programs reviewing their consent forms, a lesbian woman who supplied the eggs for her partner's pregnancy has reportedly been denied legal parenthood following the couple's split. Although the women had reportedly presented to the IVF program as a couple, they were apparently given standard donor egg consent forms. The form signed by the genetic mother, K. M., reportedly characterized her as an egg donor and contained language acknowledging she was giving up any parental rights as a donor. Her partner, E. G., became pregnant, delivered twin girls in 1995, and the women reportedly reared them as a couple until they separated in 2001. The case was heard over a four-day period during the fall and winter of 2002, with a decision coming down recently.

According to published reports, the trial court rejected the genetic mother's argument to recognize her as a legal parent, relying instead on her former partner's having carried the children as a basis to recognize her as their birth mother and the consent form as a basis for the genetic mother having given up any parental rights she had as an egg donor. The genetic mother's attorney had argued that the women had an agreement between themselves to create a child together and that the consent form was a contract of "adhesion," i.e., one that the genetic mother was forced to sign if she wanted to undergo the IVF-ET treatment. The court found against the genetic mother, and her attorney plans an appeal.

The women's respective medical conditions were reportedly the basis of their doctor's recommending this course of treatment: one had fibroid tumors; the other had difficulties with egg quality. In at least a few states, including Massachusetts, some courts have been willing to legally recognize both women as mothers when a lesbian couple has created a child together in a similar manner, with one contributing the genetic component and the other the gestational component [8.8].

With more and more nontraditional couples and single parents accessing ART treatments, programs may want to review their consent forms and procedures to ensure that they accurately and adequately address their patients' situations. Programs may find it protective for both their patients and themselves to refer patients to a knowledgeable attorney before proceeding with such medical treatment. Revisions, or at least personalized addendums to consent forms, may be in order to accurately reflect atypical circumstances. At a minimum, both patients and programs should be aware of the contents and any limitations of their standard documentation.

5.9(b) California Court of Appeals Denies Parental Status to Egg Donor
Summer 2004

A California Court of Appeal has upheld a trial court's ruling that the woman whose eggs created twins born to her former lesbian partner is not a legal parent. The court followed the "intention test" sent forth in the 1993 case *Johnson v. Calvert* and found that "substantial evidence" supported the trial court's finding that only E. G. intended to bring about the birth of a child whom she intended to raise as her own. The court cited evidence that K. M. orally agreed before the children were conceived that E. G. would be the sole legal parent and had signed a donor consent form expressly waiving any parental rights, showing she understood her relinquishment of parental rights.

The court rejected K. M.'s argument that her conduct after the birth in actively parenting the girls should be seen as a rescission of any agreement that E. G. would be their sole parent, rejecting the idea that intent to parent should be assessed and reassessed over time. It interpreted the *Johnson* test to focus on the intentions at the time the child was conceived: "The law requires a fixed standard that gives prospective parents some measure of confidence in the legal ramifications of their procreative actions." The court thus rejected K.M.'s argument for co-parentage because she played a joint parental role in raising the children. The court concluded, "[f]unctioning as a parent does not bestow legal status as a parent."

Lastly, the court also rejected the application of a "best interests of the children" standard, finding such a standard applicable to custody, but not parentage determinations.

5.9(c) Reversal: Genetic Mother Deemed Second Parent of Twins Born to Former Partner
Winter 2008

The California Supreme Court has reversed an intermediate appellate court's ruling that had deemed the genetic mother of twins born to her former partner an egg donor, largely in reliance on the medical program's standard donor consent forms and waiver of parental rights contained in that form. The state's high court relied on undisputed facts that the couple lived together and both intended to bring a child into their joint home; it distinguished the case from a true gamete donation situation, and rejected the applicability of California's sperm donor statute even assuming it should be extended to egg donation.

The Court also distinguished the often-cited *Johnson v. Calvert* decision [6.1], where it had rejected a compensated gestational carrier's attempt to establish maternity, ruling that California law "recognized only one natural mother" and made an intent-based determination that the married woman whose egg had been used with her husband's sperm was the child's legal mother. In contrast, here the Court found that because there were not three competing parentage claims, and because K. M. did not claim to be a mother instead of E. G., it did not need to apply a similar intentionality test and its final ruling made both women mothers based respectively on genetics and gestation.

K.M. v. E.G., 2005 Cal. LEXIS 9066

5.10 Parents' Claims against Program and Doctors for Failing to Reveal Egg Donor's Cystic Fibrosis Carrier Status Meet with Mixed Judicial Reaction
Fall/Winter 2003

A New York trial court dismissed all but one claim involving an IVF program's failure to advise parents that their egg donor had been tested, and found to be a carrier, for cystic fibrosis. After the child was born with cystic fibrosis, the husband was tested and also found to be a carrier. The child was born with severe physical symptoms, necessitating two months in intensive care, several surgeries, a colostomy bag, and lifelong medical care. Shortly after the child's birth, one of the defendant physicians wrote the parents, acknowledging the donor's positive CF screening results and expressing regret that the results had not been given to the couple earlier.

The parents and child sued for medical malpractice, alleging failure to: properly screen the donor; inform plaintiffs of the positive screen; or test plaintiff father prior to conception. The plaintiffs sought punitive damages for the defendants' allegedly "egregious, grossly negligent and reckless conduct."

The court followed New York's law disallowing wrongful life claims brought on behalf of a child under a public policy rationale that a child's life cannot be valued or devalued as compared to not having been born, and dismissed most, but not all, of the plaintiffs' claims. The plaintiffs had argued that the child's complaint did not rely on a wrongful life theory, but stated a relatively new legal claim for "negligent preconception and preimplantation counseling" and that preimplantation genetic diagnosis of the embryo should have been performed. The court rejected the argument and also rejected damages for the parents' emotional distress. It allowed damages necessary to reimburse actual expenses necessitated by the child's disease that it found flowed from the defendants' alleged breach of a duty to the prospective parents.

The court also rejected an argument that the doctors were actually responsible for the child's conception by manipulating the egg and sperm during the IVF procedure. It ruled it would be unfair if IVF children or their parents could recover for emotional distress if their naturally conceived counterparts cannot. Finally, however, the court stated that the parents might still be able to recover punitive damages, having alleged grossly negligent or reckless conduct. The court found that the defendants' alleged conduct, failing to disclose genetic test results or to test the intended father, might certainly constitute at least gross negligence.

The court noted "it is hard to ignore defendants' alleged role in Theresa's illness. Indeed, it is difficult to conceive that parents, concerned about whether the egg donor had freckles and with the size of her eyes and ears, would not have expected full disclosure of information regarding whether she carried cystic fibrosis. Thus, the Parettas will be permitted to vigorously pursue recovery."

In 2002, a similar case was decided by the California Appeals Court involving a child born with a serious genetic disorder (polycystic kidney disease) after her parents unknowingly received affected donor sperm from a sperm bank (*Johnson v. Sup. Ct.*, [4.47]). The California court similarly rejected claims for general damages and lost earnings as based on a wrongful life theory and also applied state statutory protections designed for health care providers.

Both courts also refused to adopt the distinction and theory urged by the plaintiffs—that the defendants had caused the child's genetic abnormalities by approving the donor. Rather, the courts noted it was the donor's genes that had literally caused the abnormalities.

> *Paretta v. Med. Offices of Human Repro. et al.*, 195
> Misc. 2d 568, 760 N.Y.S.2d 639 (2003); *Appeal*
> *withdrawn*, 6 A.D.3d 1249 (N.Y. App. Div. 2004)

5.11 New Zealand Reviews Frozen Egg Request

Fall 2006

A New Zealand woman is seeking permission from that country's Health Minister to have the first child conceived in New Zealand through frozen eggs. Two earlier attempts by other women were unsuccessful. Both predated last year's Human Assisted Reproductive Technology Order, which banned the use, but not the freezing, of frozen eggs, stemming from safety concerns over current freezing and thawing techniques. The request is under consideration by an advisory committee to the Health Minister. New Zealand's approach to egg freezing contrasts with that in the United States, where an increasing number of private medical and donor programs have been considering and developing egg freezing options for both donors and intended mothers, for both medical and social reasons (although this is regarded as experimental by ASRM).

> *Note*: In July 2008, New Zealand's Advisory Committee on Assisted Reproductive Technology (ACART) proposed to recommend to the minister that the use of frozen eggs become an established procedure for: (1) individual treatment purposes; (2) donation for treatment purposes; and (3) donation for use in research. If approved, it will be ACART's responsibility to collect information to monitor the health outcomes of children born as a result of the use of frozen eggs.

> *nzherald.co.nz*, 8/23/06

5.12 Donor's Maternity Rights Raised in Triplet Gestational Surrogacy Controversy

2006

> *Note:* A complex set of interrelated, multi-state custody claims arising out of a highly unusual, multi-state gestational carrier arrangement appears in chapter 6 [6.33]. Readers of this chapter should note that this case presents a unique egg donor issue. The genetic father and his fiancée sought out and located their previously anonymous egg donor, who agreed to assert her maternity rights to support their custody claims over those of the carrier and her husband. The triplets were ultimately returned to the genetic father.

> *J.F. v. D.B.*, 2007 Ohio LEXIS 3330, and
> *J.F. v. D.B.*, 589 Pa. 739 (Pa. 2006)

CHAPTER SIX

Traditional and Gestational Surrogacy Arrangements

✦ MEDICAL COMMENTARY, BY Howard W. Jones, Jr.

IN LEGAL PARLANCE, *surrogate* and *gestational carrier* are often used as synonyms. From a medical perspective, though, they present very different situations. A traditional surrogate is a woman who supplies both the egg, that is, the genetic component, and the gestational role of carrying the pregnancy. ART is not necessarily a part of this arrangement; indeed, usually it is not. Instead, artificial insemination is typically sufficient to establish the desired pregnancy. A gestational surrogate or gestational carrier supplies no genetic material and simply gestates the conceptus. ART (IVF) is always required for this type of arrangement. Until the science of IVF made it possible to decouple genetics from gestation, these distinctions were impossible. Although some legal observers and courts attempt to make this distinction between traditional surrogates and gestational carriers—and I think it is one well worth making—others do not.

The landmark case of the gestational carrier, Anna Johnson (*Johnson v. Calvert*, 1993), who sought custody of the child she carried, raises the question of whether the bonding between gestational carrier and fetus is more than merely psychological. Although bonding was one of Johnson's principal arguments, from a medical point of view there is certainly no current evidence of a biological basis for bonding. It is entirely a psychological connection, although it may be a very strong one.

Another example of a gestational carrier who claimed and at least initially won custody of triplets is the case involving Danielle Bimber (*Flynn v. Bimber*, 2005). The sperm of the male partner of the intended parents and the egg of an anonymous egg donor were used. The intended parents were not married. The gestational carrier was reportedly unhappy with the treatment accorded the triplets at birth by the biological father and therefore sought custody, which the lower court granted. Although this ruling was ultimately reversed, this is another example of the intensity of bonding, which, as already noted, is not biological.

A major problem in making a medical comment in some of these surrogacy cases is that it is often not clear whether the surrogacy was medically required for reproduction or socially elected. This distinction is critical in some of the more atypical cases.

Of all the nontraditional family arrangements made possible by ART, those involving surrogacy, whether of the traditional or gestational type, seem to give rise to more litigation than sperm or egg donation. This again raises the question whether the medical providers have a special responsibility to psychologically screen or at least counsel the prospective parents prior to the procedure. This is especially a concern when there might be a possibility that the surrogacy is being pursued on a sociological, rather than a medical, basis.

The current generation of medical providers is very reluctant to practice paternalistic medicine. The patient these days has a large say in his or her own treatment, so the question is a particularly sensitive one. Consider the case, however, of James Austin, a twenty-six-year-old single male who sought assistance to arrange for a traditional surrogate, Phyllis Huddleston, to bear a child created with his sperm. This was duly accomplished, and the child was turned over to him after birth. However, within six weeks, the child was hospitalized and died from a skull fracture and internal head injuries. Austin was convicted of criminal homicide in connection with the infant's death, and the surrogate sued the professionals involved (*Huddleston v. ICA*, 1996).

This case represented a clear sociological indication for surrogacy. This old-fashioned practitioner, for one, cannot help but believe that health care providers should practice paternalistic medicine in unusual situations like this. According to the court, the young man had no parenting experience and had recently experienced the death of his own mother. Whether the tragedy just recounted could be prevented by psychological examination of the intended recipient, of course, is a matter of uncertainty, but surely an effort to analyze and understand the patient's motivation in a situation as curious as this one seems consistent with good medicine.

Or consider the 1998 case of Jaycee Buzzanca, who was born to a gestational surrogate under an agreement with a married couple using both anonymous sperm and anonymous eggs. After the implantation and pregnancy commenced, the couple separated and the husband filed for a divorce shortly before the child's birth. This scenario certainly falls into the category of unusual situations where, I believe, medical personnel should investigate further before proceeding. We are not simply technicians.

It is, of course, desirable to follow the patient's wishes; however, the attentive and proactive physician tries to develop the patient's insight into an unorthodox situation so that the patient can recognize it as such and take steps to resolve as many of the vulnerabilities as is possible. This is time-consuming for the physician, so the physician often is apt to suggest a referral to a mental health professional, a suggestion that sometimes causes the patient to disappear—in other words, the next appointment is not kept.

More and more, mental health professionals are playing a role in sorting out atypical situations in reproductive medicine. Indeed, many large practice groups incorporate one or more medical psychologists or social workers to help with these situations.

As a last resort, there is a longstanding tradition that a physician can refuse treatment. However, in this situation, it has long been held that the physician is obliged to suggest to the patient other sources of therapy, and the law suggests that any refusal to treat cannot be based on a categorical refusal to treat a patient because he or she is part of a legally protected class of persons.

Fortunately, these situations are really quite rare, but they do occur, as a number of the cases reviewed in "Legally Speaking" and analyzed in this chapter illustrate.

～ LEGAL COMMENTARY, BY Susan L. Crockin

Both traditional surrogacy and gestational carrier arrangements (also called gestational surrogacy) have challenged longstanding family law principles and presumptions, with varying and often inconsistent results from state to state. Before the advent of IVF and gestational surrogacy, it was literally impossible for a woman to deliver a child without being the biological mother. In recent years, medical advances have forced courts to define parentage in light of, or in contrast to, existing adoption and parentage laws (in the context of both disputed and consensual parentage or custody claims); to determine the constitutionality of statutes intended to restrict or govern such arrangements; to decide forum-shopping or jurisdictional disputes when multiple states or countries are involved; and to assess liability for the myriad of professionals who help navigate these new ways of making babies and families. The litigation reflects the vulnerabilities of some of these arrangements, the often contradictory views of many judges and courts, and the resulting patchwork quilt of legal guidance found across the various states. For lawyers and recruiting programs involved in this growing area of third-party ART, the transactional steps and agreements needed to create these arrangements may be the most predictable ones. They may even seem deceptively straightforward to the untrained eye. However, to establish legally secure families in light of the changing and variable state of the law, the learning curve can be steep; the vulnerabilities attendant to these arrangements should be recognized and addressed before any attempts to establish a pregnancy are taken.

This is also an area where choice of language has often been determinative. Defining motherhood when the components of genetics, gestation, and intention can be found between or among two or even three women has perplexed both courts and legislatures. Even more challenging are claims such as that made by a single intended father that he is the sole legal parent of a child born to a gestational carrier using his sperm and a donor egg. This author and others have obtained court rulings in a handful of such cases, with courts concluding the child has no legal mother at all, but outcomes cannot be reliably predicted. Perhaps more than any other chapter, the cases reported here illustrate an expanding story of ever-increasing creative family building efforts and the vulnerabilities these efforts may give birth to.

There is currently no consensus within the United States on parentage of children born through any type of surrogacy arrangements, and the cases—arising from arrangements both within the United States and from abroad—illustrate the need for parties to these arrangements to be vigilant and well-informed of the legal vulnerabilities that may surround them in a particular jurisdiction. The seminal 1993 case of *Johnson v. Calvert*, which established the legal maternity rights in California of the intended genetic mother over that of a gestational carrier, has been often cited, but not always followed, in other scenarios in which a donor egg or a same-sex couple is involved. This author has filed two amicus briefs in Massachusetts appellate court cases (*RR v. MH*, 1998, and *Culliton v. BIDMC*, 2001) in an effort to assist the judiciary in understanding the *medical* distinctions between gestational and traditional surrogacy, thereby helping to provide courts with a basis to analyze, distinguish, and apply the law more precisely. Such efforts can be of significant assistance to judges who may have a limited understanding of or exposure to novel medical treatments. The results can be both helpful and gratifying, as when the Massachusetts court accepted the distinction in *Culliton*. Lower courts in that jurisdiction now routinely make the legal distinction between a traditional surrogate and a gestational carrier, treating a traditional surrogate as a birth mother under standard adoption laws and principles, and a gestational carrier as a nonmother, as in *Johnson*.

As medical professionals are well aware, traditional surrogacy requires a simple donor insemination procedure, usually using the intended father's sperm, resulting in the surrogate having both a genetic and gestational connection to the child. Many courts have found that connection sufficient to legally categorize the traditional surrogate as a birth mother, with all of the legal protections and regulations of the adoption paradigm squarely applicable. Other states have placed more emphasis on the intentions of the parties. A number of state courts have expressed concern over, or flatly rejected, the exchange of money where a woman is the biological parent of the child she is carrying. In a somewhat surprising court decision, a 2007 Maryland court recognized a single man as the sole legal parent of a child carried by a gestational carrier but went out of its way to comment on the statutory prohibitions in that state against exchanging money for a child, leaving many legal professionals to question whether the state had flagged concerns about paid gestational carrier arrangements (*In re Roberto d. B.*, 2007).

In contrast to traditional surrogacy, in most states gestational surrogacy or gestational carrier arrangements have been interpreted more liberally. A woman carrying a pregnancy that does not involve her genetic material has been less likely to be legally deemed to be the mother and instead is usually allowed to contract or agree to having the genetic mother and father (or in a smaller number of states, the intended mother and genetic father where an egg donor was used) recognized as the legal parents of the child. Increasingly, state courts have recognized the value of parentage orders (allowed before birth in some states), at least for genetic, intended parents and often even for intended parents using donor gamete(s). Cases involving both donor sperm and donor egg have raised more legal questions than situations where only one of the two is used. A few statutory developments have been reported. Illinois has enacted limited legislation that authorizes the intended genetic parents (but not intended parents who use donor sperm or egg) of a child carried by a gestational carrier to be recognized and entered onto the child's birth certificate without a court proceeding. Outcomes are still very much state- and fact-specific and can be dramatically affected by both choice and conflict of law issues.

Courts have also struggled with the degree to which existing laws such as those addressing donor insemination and adoption are applicable in various contexts, including gestational carrier arrangements involving parentage and custody disputes over born children. This is another area where courts have frequently emphasized the paramount importance of the child's interests and issued calls for legislative action.

A more nuanced issue arises, however, over whether the traditional family law principle of "the best interest of the child" applies if the court is being asked to determine who qualifies as a parent, not which of two legally recognized parents is the better custodian. Delving into those issues often highlights the differences between adoption and ART law, with hundreds of years of adoption precedent of varying applicability to ART families. At least two states, Connecticut and Illinois, have enacted legislation that makes establishment of parentage and access to birth certificates easier in some situations. Constitutional challenges to statutes prohibiting surrogacy have also been brought and won (in both Arizona and Utah) by couples and gestational carriers arguing that the statutes violated their constitutional rights.

One of the most serious and still unsettled areas of the law involves the applicable standard of care, and the roles and obligations of various professionals—not just medical doctors—who help create these arrangements. While doctors have routinely been drawn into these cases, other

professionals, including lawyers, mental health professionals, and recruiting programs (at times referred to as "agencies," "centers," or "brokers") have also been sued. These cases involving relatively novel roles
and duties of care raise profoundly important issues.

Two significant reported cases have addressed the unique obligations
and vulnerabilities of nonmedical professionals. Both cases (*Stiver v.
Parker,* 1992, and *Huddleston v. ICA,* 1996) were brought by traditional
surrogates. In both, the attorneys who recruited the surrogates as part of a
surrogacy business were found to owe them a high duty of care, as both a
federal and state court rejected the lawyers' claims that they owed no
obligations to the surrogate. Those courts were adamant that recruiting
healthy women for profit exposed these attorneys and their affiliated
professionals and businesses to an affirmative duty of care. More recently,
cases have been filed against the attorney in a three-state triplet controversy (*Bimber v. Flynn,* 2005) involving a gestational carrier and donor
eggs for allegedly failing to clarify within the agreement the designation
of legal maternity where the intended mother was not married to the
genetic, intended father. This is an area of the law that remains highly
unsettled and is likely to grow with the proliferation of collaborative ART
arrangements that cross state lines and involve multiple parties.

Finally, international developments in this field are also notable, with
some countries imposing age and marital restrictions, and court cases
illustrate the degree to which reproductive tourism has proliferated. Reported cases involving Kuwait, Italy, India, Japan, Germany, and England show the problems that arise when intended parents and gestational surrogates attempt to create international pairings. More recently,
the phenomenon of Americans traveling abroad for collaborative arrangements (including for gestational surrogacy in India, with and without donor eggs) is likely to generate novel legal issues. Reports of those
arrangements include clinics where women serving as gestational carriers and intended parents do not meet, where the women are not always
given information about the intended parents' marital status or sexual
orientation, where illiterate carriers sign agreements with a thumbprint,
and compensation—a fraction of that paid Western women—is still several times higher than the local annual income figures in India. In at
least two cases involving Indian surrogacies, unanticipated problems
arose when the genetic parents attempted to bring the children out of the

country, resulting in delays and legal entanglements before the children were permitted to leave. These cases are dramatic illustrations of the need for professionals involved in creating these unusual family building arrangements to understand and anticipate the legal steps that will be necessary to create not just a child but also a legally secure family under any applicable laws.

Establishing parentage will always be a critical element of any surrogacy arrangement, whether traditional or gestational. For those arrangements that also involve donor gametes, nontraditional couples, single parents, or any parties from more than one state or country, the complexities and vulnerabilities are likely to be significantly greater. Moving forward without a clear plan to establish parenthood should be both avoidable and avoided by any professional offering services to would-be parents in this ever-changing field. One mantra that this author has found useful is always to "start at the end" and recommend that clients undertake an arrangement only when the path to parenthood has been thoughtfully analyzed and vetted with appropriate consultations as needed (including local counsel and judicial clerks in the relevant jurisdictions for novel situations) and proceed only after that path has been clearly identified, illuminated, and cleared (and an alternative identified, if needed).

Without a consensus as to (1) what legal standards make a parent (intent, gestation, genetics, or some combination of these elements); (2) if and how gestational surrogacy arrangements should be regulated; and (3) how and when legal parentage should be determined—pre- or post-birth, by contract, court order, or adoption—litigation in this area will continue to explore and attempt to resolve these issues with various and inconsistent outcomes.

Litigation

TRADITIONAL AND GESTATIONAL SURROGACY/ CARRIER ARRANGEMENTS

6.1(a) Gestational Surrogate Loses Claim to Child
December 1990

Refusing to create a "three-parent, two natural mom" situation calling it "ripe for crazy making," a California trial judge has now awarded the genetic parents sole custody of a baby boy born a month earlier to an embryo transfer [gestational] surrogate. In doing so, Judge Parslow compared embryo transfer surrogate Anna Johnson to a foster parent when he ruled that "a surrogate carrying a genetic child for a couple does not acquire parental rights." The decision ends round one of the first lawsuit involving a gestational surrogacy arrangement. Johnson's attorneys have appealed.

Johnson, reportedly a co-worker of the biological mother, had initially sued to establish her parental rights and to share custody of the then-seven-month-old fetus she was carrying by agreement with its biological parents, Crispina and Mark Calvert. Johnson claimed the Calverts had lost interest in the pregnancy and had breached the contract she had signed with them. Moreover, she claimed that she and the fetus had bonded. The Calverts countered, arguing that Johnson had made repeated demands for payments ahead of the agreed-upon schedule for her $10,000 fee and that she was "kidnapping" their child.

In addition to denying Johnson any parental or visitation rights, Judge Parslow went on to comment more broadly and favorably about embryo transfer surrogacy. Even if Johnson had any parental rights, Parslow ruled, she waived them by entering into a valid contract with the Calverts. The judge added that such contracts are not against public policy and are valid and enforceable. He also ruled that the $10,000 payment was for the discomfort or "pain and suffering" of carrying the child, not for the child itself, and therefore acceptable. Furthermore, he stated that legislative attempts to outlaw such agreements entirely would run afoul of the constitutional rights of those involved.

Comparing the case to the now-infamous *Baby M* case, which involved a "traditional" surrogate's custody claim, the court commented that the procreative rights involved here are those of the genetic mother, not the "carrying person."

Finally, noting that, ". . . clearly the in vitro fertilization genie is out of the bottle and you can't put it back. . . ," the court called on the California legislature to take steps to avoid future litigation.

Both Johnson's appeal and request for visitation rights during the appeal are now pending.

6.1(b) Gestational Surrogate's Fight May Shift Focus to Doctor and Lawyer

March 1991

Anna Johnson has at least succeeded in expediting her appeal. The intermediate appellate court's ruling may come by mid-spring, and an appeal to the California Supreme Court is a virtual certainty.

Johnson's attorney, Richard Gilbert, said he expects to win any and all appeals: "I don't think they're [the courts] going to stand for women being set back a thousand years and turned into cows." Should he lose, Gilbert claims to have a backup plan. He intends to sue both Attorney William Handel, who drafted the surrogacy agreement, and Ricardo H. Asch, M.D., who performed the IVF/ET procedure for "intentional and negligent infliction of emotional distress, medical malpractice, battery, and other torts." Dr. Asch, who says he performed the procedure only at the direct request of both women and only after fully reviewing the case and finding no reason to deny the requested services, warns other doctors of the possibility of being sued after performing an appropriate, requested, consented to, and successful medical procedure.

6.1(c) Gestational Surrogate Now Sues Doctor, Clinic, and Lawyers

June 1991

Gestational surrogate Anna Johnson has followed through on her threat to sue the doctors and lawyers involved in the surrogacy arrangement she entered into with Crispina and Mark Calvert. Ricardo Asch, M.D., the Center for Reproductive Health, and UCI Medical Center, have all been named as defendants in the lawsuit, which charges medical malpractice and battery among other claims. Johnson charges that the medical defendants failed to inform her of the physical and emotional risks of IVF, acted in excess of her consent, and "knew or should have known" she was "susceptible to mental distress because of her prior history of miscarriages and stillbirths" (facts she had not disclosed).

Johnson also sued her lawyer who drafted the surrogacy agreement, charged her own former lawyer with malpractice, and sued various "Does," including a therapist who met with Johnson and recommended her for surrogacy.

In addition, Johnson's lawsuit claims $5 million damages for intentional infliction of emotional distress by all the defendants, whom she claims knew that their acts were likely to result in "illness and mental distress."

6.1(d) Gestational Surrogate Loses Again on Appeal
December 1991

Anna Johnson has now lost on appeal. Johnson's claims of fetal bonding were met with charges that she repeatedly sought additional monies, threatened to induce labor at five months, and failed to disclose several earlier problem pregnancies and miscarriages.

A unanimous California appellate court upheld the lower court's ruling and found that the state's laws were clear: "If a blood test shows a woman is not the natural mother of the child, the case must be decided accordingly." The court applied California's paternity testing statute to the question of maternity, rejected the claim that giving birth to the child created a constitutionally protected liberty interest, and declined to decide whether the agreement was enforceable. It rejected Johnson's attorney's argument that the California law's presumption of maternity favored Johnson and foreclosed further inquiry into the question of who was the child's mother.

Johnson has since remarried and is again pregnant, and reportedly considering a further appeal to the state's Supreme Court. In the meantime, Chris Calvert, the child, has celebrated his first birthday.

6.1(e) Landmark Gestational Surrogacy Appeal to Be Heard
Summer 1992

A recent court ruling has revived the hopes of Anna Johnson, who made legal history as the first gestational surrogate to sue for custody of the child she bore for its genetic parents. The lower courts rejected her claims, but the California Supreme Court has set aside those rulings and agreed to hear Johnson's appeal.

6.1(f) Gestational Surrogate's Appeal Argued
June 1993

During arguments before the California Supreme Court, the court's bias against the surrogate was apparently so clear that her attorney urged, "I pray that one of your number will pen a dissenting opinion," presumably to strengthen an intended appeal to the U.S. Supreme Court. The judges questioned Johnson's ethics and perceived motivation of greed.

6.1(g) Gestational Surrogate Found to Have No Parental Rights

September 1993

The California Supreme Court has rejected all claims brought by Anna Johnson. The court ruled that Crispina Calvert, the genetic and intended mother, is indeed the child's legal mother. The court looked to its state Uniform Parentage Act (UPA), which has provisions for determining maternity based on both delivering a child and proof of genetic parentage. Finding that both "mothers" had presented legally acceptable methods of proving their maternity, the court ruled that the parties' intent should control and was clear: to create a child of and for the Calverts. The court found there was no intent to create a child for Anna Johnson, and thus her constitutional right to procreate was not implicated. The court went on to hold that surrogacy arrangements did not violate the state's public policy or deprive gestational carriers of any constitutional rights.

The 1975 UPA law, which provided that any interested party could prove a mother-child, as well as a father-child, relationship, could not have contemplated its application to surrogacy, which was virtually unknown at the time. Nonetheless, concluding that courts are frequently called upon to construe statutes in factual settings never contemplated at the time of a law's passage, the court ruled:

"[W]hen the two means of establishing a mother-child relationship (genetic consanguinity and giving birth) do not coincide in one woman, she who intended to procreate the child—that is, she who intended to bring about the birth of a child that she intended to raise as her own—is the natural mother under California law." The court added, in a "true 'egg donation' situation," where the intent was that the gestational mother raise the child, the gestational mother would be recognized as the natural mother under California law.

The court rejected the argument that the situation should be analogized to that of sperm donation, noting that the Calverts never intended to donate a zygote to anyone. Similarly, it refused to apply adoption laws, which prohibit payments to birth mothers, finding gestational surrogacy "differs in crucial respects from adoption" by virtue of the voluntariness of the agreement in advance of the pregnancy.

The court rejected Johnson's constitutional arguments as well. It ruled that she was not a mother and thus had no constitutionally protected right as such. It went so far as to say that any constitutionally protected right to procreate in this situation was found in the couple who intended to "exercise their right to procreate in order to form a family of their own, albeit through novel medical procedures," not in the woman who carried a couple's zygote by agreement. The court was similarly unpersuaded that surrogacy amounted to unconstitutional involuntary servitude or exploitation of poor women. The court even noted that "the 'limited data available' seem to reflect an absence of significant adverse effects of surrogacy on all participants."

The court did not explicitly address traditional surrogacy arrangements, and it is unclear how broadly the decision may be read. One judge dissented and urged the application of a "best interest of the child" standard. Johnson's attorney has now asked the U.S. Supreme Court to hear an appeal

6.1(h) Supreme Court Refuses to Hear Further Appeal
March 1994

The U.S. Supreme Court has refused to consider Anna Johnson's appeal, leaving in place the California Supreme Court's decision that she has no maternal rights to the child she bore for the child's genetic parents. Every court to which Johnson appealed rejected her claims, and the California Supreme Court affirmed that the Calverts were the sole legal parents of the child.

Johnson v. Calvert, 5 Cal.4th 84 (Cal. 1993);
cert. denied 510 U.S. 874 (U.S. 1993)

6.2(a) New Surrogacy Fight Begins in California
June 1991

California courts are once again in the eye of a surrogacy storm. Only months after the nation's first "gestational surrogacy" case was filed there, a unique three-way custody battle is underway. The case involves a "traditional" surrogate, the biological father, and his estranged wife (the couple separated a few months after the child's birth). All three potential "parents" are vying for custody of a ten-month-old child conceived under an agreement that is now in dispute.

Phase one of the trial began April 8. Four lawyers, one for each of the adults and one whom the court appointed for the child, initially argued over which woman was the child's legal mother. The court declined to enforce the surrogacy agreement, declaring it to be "contrary to public policy," and treated the case as a custody dispute. In the first of many decisions that are certain to be appealed, the trial judge ruled that the surrogate is the child's legal mother and that the potential adoptive mother who helped raised the child has no legal rights. That court will decide next whether the surrogate or the biological father should be given custody and has suggested it will also consider whether the pre-adoptive mother should be given visitation rights under a law designed for stepparents. That phase of the trial is scheduled for June; in the meantime, the father has the child and the surrogate has been granted visitation three days a week.

Elvira Jordan, forty-two, claims that the surrogacy agreement she entered into was based on an understanding that the child she bore would be reared in a stable, caring, two-parent home. Jordan was about to give birth when she learned from Cynthia Moschetta, fifty-one, that she and her husband Robert, thirty-five, planned to separate. Reportedly, Jordan then refused to relinquish the child until, at Jordan's insistence, another agreement was reached where she set conditions for the Moschettas to take the newborn home. These included marital counseling for one year, permission for Jordan to visit their home at any time, and payment of the remainder of Jordan's surrogacy fee while accepting her refusal to sign a final adoption agreement for one year. It's unclear why, but only Jordan signed the new agreement. The child went home with the couple following her birth in May 1990.

Jordan subsequently signed documents that, Robert Moschetta contended, relinquished the child to him. The court agreed with Jordan's attorney that the relinquishment, which was signed without the benefit of legal counsel, was invalid under California law. According to her attorney, Jordan believed she was signing a receipt for her surrogacy payment. Moschetta's attorney testified that she had refused to draft the document, believing it was unethical and improper.

When Robert Moschetta moved out of his marital home with the child in November, the arrangement moved to the courtroom. Since the stepparent adoption was never commenced, Cynthia Moschetta's status was unclear. She had signed the surrogacy agreement, intended to adopt the child, taken maternity leave, and contributed an estimated $26,000 to the cost of the surrogacy arrangement. Her attorney argued that she should be considered an equal parent based upon all of these factors as well as her rearing role in the child's life. A somewhat similar claim by a *gestational* surrogate, Anna Johnson, based on her *pre-birth* rearing role (without evidence of intent to parent), was rejected at the trial level.

In rejecting Cynthia Moschetta's parental claims, the trial court relied on another recent California case, which resolved a similar question in favor of the biological mother (*Nancy S. v. Michele G.*, Cal. Ct. App. 3/21/91). In that case, a lesbian couple, who separated after a fifteen-year relationship and rearing two children together, were unable to agree on custody arrangements. Even though the nonbiological partner performed the insemination, was listed on the birth certificate as the father, and fully participated in the two children's lives as a parent, an appellate California court recently ruled that the woman had no legally recognizable parental status. Regardless of the "relatively straight-forward" facts about the intent of the natural mother to create a parental relationship with her former partner, that court ruled that "expanding the definition of a parent ... could expose other natural parents to litigation brought by child care providers, longstanding relatives, successive sets of stepparents, or other close friends of the family." Furthermore, the court noted that to expand the definition even narrowly would invite more litigation and less certainty into matters with complex social and policy ramifications.

Family law experts agree that the Moschetta case raises difficult legal and philosophical questions: specifically who is, and what makes, a mother. Ultimately, all of these cases and the novel questions of parenthood they raise will most likely be decided by higher courts.

6.2(b) Joint Custody Ruling in Three-Way Surrogacy Battle Questioned
December 1991

A judge's ruling in a three-way custody battle has raised as many questions as it answered. Robert Moschetta, who left his wife and took the child with him six months after her birth, has argued that the child does not need a mother.

The court's initial ruling excluded Cynthia Moschetta as a potential parent. A new ruling orders Robert Moschetta and Elvira Jordan to share joint custody. This court-ordered arrangement has left more than one observer skeptical. Awarding what one commentator has called "day-care provider status" to Elvira Jordan, she is to have custody weekdays from 8:00 to 4:00. Moschetta has custody the rest of the time. Holidays are alternated, and each parent has a four-day vacation with the child. Robert Moschetta has vowed to appeal his claim for sole custody. In the meantime, he seems to have found something few working parents today can claim—free day care. Both Elvira Jordan's and Cynthia Moschetta's appeals are still pending.

6.2(c) Custody Ruling Challenged in *Jordan v. Moschetta*
June 1992

The parties to a widely questioned award of "joint custody" were back in court recently. Moschetta's attorneys attempted to have Jordan held in contempt of court, claiming she returned the child late on three occasions and violated the arrangements.

The court dismissed, finding no evidence she had "willfully" violated the arrangement . . . two times were holidays. Her attorney argued the arrangement was unclear and the charges brought for harassment. Meanwhile, according to the father's attorney, two-year-old Marissa occasionally has "screaming fits at night" and the two parents have "significant communication problems," while Jordan's attorney said that the parents' biggest problem is "deciding what kind of shoes the child should wear."

In two related developments, Robert and Cynthia Moschetta's divorce was finalized, and Jordan has now reportedly sued her therapist for malpractice. Cynthia Moschetta, who helped raise Marissa for her first nine months, was awarded neither custody nor visitation rights to the child. Jordan's new lawsuit claims her therapist should have known she was susceptible to mental distress when she recommended her for surrogacy. The suit charges the therapist with negligence and infliction of distress.

6.2(d) California Court Voids Traditional Surrogacy Contract; Reverses Joint Custody Award
September 1994

Yet another round of appeals have been initiated by Robert Moschetta in an effort to gain sole custody of his now-five-year-old daughter, Marissa. His ex-wife, who was stripped of any parental rights, has since reportedly developed a close relationship with Jordan and Marissa and continues to support the court's joint custody award.

In a separate development, Jordan was convicted in 1992 of welfare fraud for failing to report the $10,000 payment from the Moschettas as income, placed on probation and ordered to repay the government $8,500. Her attorney at the time said that she had been told by the surrogacy broker that the money was for medical care and legal aid, and was not considered income.

Relying on the California Supreme Court's ruling in *Johnson v. Calvert* [6.1] that gestational surrogacy agreements do not violate public policy, Moschetta argued that traditional surrogacy agreements should also now be deemed enforceable according to their terms, that California's Uniform Parentage Act should be read to make his former wife, Cynthia, the child's legal mother, and that the surrogacy agreement should be interpreted as a binding consent to adoption by Jordan.

An intermediate court has rejected both arguments, but nonetheless remanded the case to the lower court to review the custody arrangement. The court squarely rejected the claim that traditional surrogacy agreements had been endorsed by the *Johnson* decision and distinguished the two types of surrogacy. In contrast to *Johnson*, it found that here, "the two usual means of showing maternity—genetics and birth—coincide with one woman" and thus there was no dispute under California law over who the child's genetic mother was and no "tie" to break as there had been in that case.

The court found, however, that the lower court had improperly considered and penalized Robert Moschetta for both the circumstances surrounding the surrogacy itself and his arguments that Jordan was not the child's legal mother. The court acknowledged that only because this was not a "run-of-the-mill" custody case, but one of first impression, it decided to remand to the lower court to determine whether or not Robert Moschetta should be given primary physical custody.

The court ordered the lower court to disregard Moschetta's "predisposition to Johnson, the fact that he knowingly married an infertile woman, or his tactics and position in this case up to now," but to give consideration to his "present willingness" to allow Jordan visitation.

The court also distinguished the *Johnson* case on financial terms, commenting that wealthy couples can afford more complicated but legally more protective gestational surrogacy arrangements while those who cannot afford such procedures must rely on traditional surrogacy and applicable adoption laws. In the court's words "[f]or them and the child, biology is destiny . . . [t]he result is disquieting."

In re Marriage of Moschetta, 25 Cal. App. 4th
1218 (Cal. Ct. App. 1994); *rev. denied* by 1994
Cal. LEXIS 5623 (Cal. 1994)

6.3 France Outlaws Surrogacy

September 1991

France's highest court has now outlawed surrogate motherhood, calling it a "subversion of the institution of adoption." Agreeing with the solicitor general who argued that "certainly it is necessary to fight the terrible unhappiness of sterility, but there are other solutions," the court invalidated all surrogacy contracts. The solicitor general cited legal problems and specifically legal cases in the United States where surrogates had changed their minds. The high court rejected the lower court's ruling that surrogate motherhood, without concern for profit, was an "expression of free will and individual responsibility." It did not, however, order the subject of the lawsuit, a child born in 1988, returned to the surrogate. Also in 1988, the government ordered the three main surrogate associations in that country dissolved.

New York Times, 6/2/91

6.4(a) Surrogate Seeks to Overturn Agreement, Obtain Parental Rights and Visitation

September 1991

Another California case, now pending on appeal, may ultimately establish whether traditional surrogacy agreements for money are legal there. At issue are parental and visitation rights to a five-year-old boy, conceived under an agreement between Tim and Charlotte Myers and former surrogate Nancy Barrass.

Ms. Barrass, who originally answered an agency's surrogacy advertisement, was artificially inseminated with Tim Myers's sperm and gave birth to a child in 1986. Two months later, she consented to the boy's adoption, and even threw a champagne party for the couple, but in 1987 filed a suit to overturn that adoption. Barrass claimed the contract was illegal and her consent invalid. She now seeks to void the adoption, establish her parental rights, and have court-ordered visitation with the child.

At the recent oral argument before the California appellate court, at least one of the judges on the three-judge panel apparently questioned those rights, noting that Barrass voluntarily sought out a surrogacy position when she answered the ad back in 1984.

While Barrass recognized that the child's custody is unlikely to be disturbed, the court will need to decide on her visitation rights and more broadly whether such agreements are presently or should be enforceable.

6.4(b) California Surrogacy Decision Avoids Enforceability Issue

December 1991

A California appellate court, which was expected to decide the question of the legality of surrogacy contracts, has instead sidestepped the question.

Without deciding whether such agreements are enforceable, the court found that the child should remain with the couple that had raised him from birth, based on the "best interests of the child," a traditional legal standard in family law. One judge added that, if necessary, he would hold surrogate parenting contracts illegal under present law. The entire court called on the legislature to pass laws to govern the issues of surrogacy agreements.

While the surrogate's attorney criticized the decision and is preparing an appeal to the state's Supreme Court, the couple's attorney praised the decision for illustrating the court's ability to award custody to the adoptive couple even if a surrogacy contract is deemed illegal or unenforceable.

Adoption of Matthew B., 284 Cal. Rptr. 18
(Cal. Ct. App. 1991); *petitions for rehearing*
and review denied (1991)

6.5 Israeli State Attorney Approves Embryo Surrogacy for Couple
September 1991

An Israeli couple has received approval from the state's attorney and the Ministry of Health to undergo an IVF retrieval at Assuta Hospital in Tel Aviv and then to have the fertilized eggs flown to the United States for implantation in a surrogate.

Daniel and Ruth Nahmani went to the High Court of Justice for approval of the procedure and are now awaiting a written permit from the Ministry of Health, which is expected shortly. Ruth Nahmani had a hysterectomy after being diagnosed with cancer. The Israeli hospital is providing the services free of charge.

The Health Ministry also announced that the Ministers of Justice and Health will establish a joint panel of experts to review all aspects of surrogacy. The chair of the Israeli Medical Association's Ethics Committee cautioned that surrogacy should be used only in exceptional cases.

Note: See case 1.9 for 1996 developments pertaining to the couple's frozen embryos following their divorce.

Jerusalem Post, 3/8/91

6.6 Healthy Twins Born to Grandmother Acting as a Gestational Surrogate
March 1992

The headline-making grandmother who acted as a gestational surrogate for her daughter (*New York Times*, 8/5/91) gave birth to healthy twins on Oct. 31, 1991. While medical ethicists debate the appropriateness of the arrangements, Arlette Schweitzer, forty-two, of Aberdeen, South Dakota, simply says, "If you can do something to help your children, you do it." Before the procedure, a psychiatrist screened Ms. Schweitzer and her daughter, who was born without a uterus.

6.7 Michigan Court Upholds Ban on Paid Surrogacy
September 1992

Three infertile couples and two potential surrogates have lost their challenge to Michigan's law banning paid surrogacy. The group, which included a couple hoping to have their second child via surrogacy, had argued that the 1980 law was an unconstitutional invasion of their right to privacy and procreation.

The court noted the law required relinquishment of parental rights, and ruled that the state's interest in preventing baby-selling and exploitation of poor women overrode the couples' and women's rights.

According to the ruling, "Whatever sense of idealism may motivate the fertile woman into choosing a pregnancy for an otherwise infertile couple is rendered asunder by the introduction of the profit motive . . . [A]s overwhelmingly repugnant as the thought may be, unbridled surrogacy-for-profit could encourage a commodity approach to babies."

The director of the state's ACLU predicts the case, which had been widely watched, will now be appealed to the state's Supreme Court.

Doe v. AG, 194 Mich. App. 432; 487 N.W.2d 484 (1992)

6.8 Paid Anti-Surrogacy Law Passes in New York
September 1992

By a vote of 104 to 39, the New York state assembly has passed into law a bill banning surrogate parenting for pay, which is now on the governor's desk. The legislators cited the case of a Michigan surrogate who gave birth to twins for a couple who wanted only a girl and placed the boy in foster care. After a legal battle funded with her surrogacy fee, the surrogate, Patty Nowakowski, ultimately gained custody of both children.

An earlier bill also designed primarily to prevent paid surrogacy included overly broad language that declared that "all in vitro preg-

nancies" were against public policy and any agreements to create
such a pregnancy were unenforceable. That bill was ultimately
defeated.

N.Y. CLS Dom. Rel. 124(passed into law 1992;
eff. 7/93)

6.9(a) Surrogacy Broker, Lawyer, and Doctors Sued for Failing to Protect Surrogate from CMV Transmission
December 1992

In a case that could have significant implications for professionals
performing ART procedures, a federal appeals court has ruled that
surrogacy broker Noel Keane, as well as doctors and lawyers he employed, may be liable because a traditional surrogate's child was born
with cytomegalovirus (CMV). Although the surrogacy consent form
listed CMV as a risk, the case is now headed to a jury trial.

The case arose out of a 1982 surrogacy arrangement "brokered" by
Keane and his center (Michigan has since outlawed paid surrogacy).
The surrogate, Judy Stiver, was inseminated with the untested semen
of Alexander Malahoff. Although not relevant, Stiver's child was later
found to be her husband's, not Malahoff's.

The lower court initially rejected Stiver's lawsuit, which charged
negligent acts against Keane, the doctors who performed the procedure, and the lawyer he engaged to review the contract. The federal
appellate court for the Sixth Circuit reversed, stating that the
defendants—whom they described as "entrepreneurs pioneering in a
new field . . . [who] expected to profit from their roles"—owed the
surrogate, child, and contracting father an affirmative duty of protection and a "high degree" of diligence. Because of that "special relationship," the court ruled the defendants had a duty to protect the
participants from "foreseeable harm."

The question of whether or not that newly recognized duty of care
was breached now returns to the lower court for a jury's consideration. The jury will deliberate on whether the design of the program
amounted to a breach of the defendant's duty. The court noted several potential deficiencies. First, the surrogate had no meaningful opportunity for counseling because she first met with professionals only
a week before the procedure. She was also expected to sign a multi-

page contract the same day she had a single brief meeting with a lawyer selected by Keane. Furthermore, she was only given a copy of the contract after the insemination, and the doctors who inseminated her were found to have little knowledge about fertility. Finally, the contracting father was not required to submit to testing. The fact that the surrogate signed a consent form in which CMV was "buried in the middle" of several hundred potential infections and diseases in a "boiler plate addendum" was unpersuasive.

The court noted that this was a unique case, and it looked to the subsequent passage of Michigan's law banning paid surrogacy, the prohibition against organ selling, and the state's disallowance of adoption-related expenses that were not court-approved as relevant policy considerations.

One judge disagreed, arguing that the court was imposing "strict liability" on professionals and implementing social policy rather than a legal standard. That judge argued that an attorney should not be liable for a medical procedure unless he failed to procure adequate medical treatment. He also claimed that doctors should not be held to a higher standard for surrogacy than that imposed for other artificial insemination procedures.

The court's ruling could be applicable to doctors, lawyers, and other professionals involved in counseling, arranging, or performing other ART-related procedures. Consequently, a court following this reasoning might determine that an affirmative duty of care is owed by those performing these services to those receiving them. Whether Keane and associates will be found negligent is undecided.

6.9(b) Surrogacy "Broker," Lawyer, and Doctor Pursue Appeal
March 1993

The appeal process revolving around a surrogate's child born with severe birth defects as a result of CMV continues. Following the child's birth, the intended father brought a breach of contract suit after the child's father was discovered to be the surrogate's husband, as well as complaints filed against Attorney Noel Keane, the doctors, and the surrogate's lawyer. The Sixth Circuit (appellate) court found Keane was a surrogate "broker," who, together with his legal and medical assistants, owed the surrogate a higher standard of care, which should be applied in the upcoming trial. Keane and associated professionals have appealed that ruling and petitioned for a rehearing "en banc" (by the entire appellate court).

Stiver v. Parker, 975 F.2d 261 (6th Cir. 1992);

reh'g denied

6.10(a) Suit Filed to Clarify Status of Child Born to Gestational Surrogate

December 1992

A Washington state couple has filed suit in Virginia to be declared the legal parents of a child born to a gestational surrogate for them in that state. The surrogate is in agreement, and all parties are represented by a single attorney, who says the suit is necessary because under current Virginia law, the woman who gives birth to a child is considered the legal mother unless the couple proves they are the child's parents. Recently passed Virginia legislation will permit such agreements to be brought before a court to determine the child's parentage pre-birth.

Washington Post, 11/7/92

6.10(b) Virginia Court Approves Gestational Surrogacy Agreement

March 1993

A Virginia court has now ruled that the man and woman whose two-month-old biological child was carried by a gestational surrogate are, indeed, the child's parents and that their names should be placed on the child's birth certificate.

Legislation passed in Virginia will, in the future, make the process of establishing legal maternity and paternity in surrogacy cases easier. The parties to either a traditional or gestational surrogacy arrangement will be able to present their agreement to a court *before* the child's birth and obtain an order establishing legal parenthood of the child.

Without this type of proceeding, parties to gestational surrogacy arrangements face adoption proceedings, despite the fact that the child is their biological child.

Baby Doe v. Doe, 15 Va. App. 242 (Va. Ct. App. 1992)

(guardian's suit); Va. Code Ann. § 20-49.1 (2009)

6.11 New Jersey Bioethics Commission Recommends Criminalizing Surrogacy

December 1992

A report prepared by the New Jersey Bioethics Commission in response to that state's now-infamous *Baby M* case recommends that: paid surrogacy be a crime; all contracts voided; and unpaid surrogacy between relatives or close friends discouraged. The report also favors giving the woman who gives birth, including gestational surrogates who have no biological link to the child, a strong presumption of custody in any contested case. The report found that surrogates were typically poorer, less educated, and therefore at a disadvantage in any arrangement with a contracting couple. "Putting a monetary value on women, pregnancy, and the children of surrogacy has a negative impact on societal value and perception in general," concluded the Commission's executive director.

UPI, 9/21/92

6.12(a) Surrogacy Legislation Progresses in California

June 1992

In the wake of two landmark surrogacy cases (*Johnson v. Calvert*, [6.1] and *In re Marriage of Moschetta*, [6.2]), and at the urging of the two judges who heard them, the California legislature is actively at work on legislation to allow paid surrogacy. If enacted, the law would become the first in the country to comprehensively legislate paid surrogacy. It would require surrogates be at least twenty-one, have had at least one child, and receive counseling both before and after the birth. It does not require a surrogate be married, or if married require her husband's consent. Payment would be capped at $15,000 with an inflationary clause. The law would distinguish between a traditional and gestational surrogate, allowing the former, but not the latter, to change her mind after birth and have a coequal right to seek custody to the genetic father. Children born to traditional surrogates would need to be adopted, while children of gestational surrogates would automatically be deemed the children of their genetic parents.

The bill is progressing through the California legislatures with both strong support and opposition. It is sponsored by the Beverly

Hills–based Center for Surrogate Parenting, which estimates that there have been 4,000 surrogacy births nationwide with 500 of those in California. It reports sixteen known surrogacy disputes nationwide, six of which took place in California.

6.12(b) California Surrogacy Legislation Vetoed

December 1992

Governor Pete Wilson of California vetoed legislation that would have allowed and regulated surrogacy. Despite heavy backing from the Center for Surrogate Parenting, and support from the state bar, a broad coalition of opponents succeeded in scuttling the law. The chief opponent of the law has said she plans to sponsor legislation next term that would back paid surrogacy and make adoption laws, which prohibit payments other than for expenses, apply to surrogacy.

UPI, 9/21/92; *Recorder,* 9/29/02

6.13(a) New York Court Refuses to Acknowledge Mother in Gestational Surrogacy Arrangement

June 1993

A New York court has refused to recognize a "maternity action" brought in an attempt to establish the genetic mother of twins born to a gestational surrogate as their legal mother. The parties were all in agreement. After reviewing the HLA tests and evidence submitted about the IVF procedures, the court recognized the genetic father as the legal father and entered that order. It also noted the state legislature had enacted a law to cover children born via DI but not IVF. It concluded New York law did not allow an order establishing maternity and that the state legislature, not its courts, must be asked to expand the law to cover "technological advances."

"[C]learly the legislature could have enacted similar legislation to protect the rights of biological parents involved in a fertilized ovum implantation procedure." The court also rejected the argument that its ruling unconstitutionally discriminated against women and concluded that the mother was "not without a remedy" since she could adopt the children. That perspective ignores potential problems if adoption procedures are applied to arrangements not designed for the purpose. Depending on the adoption laws of a particular state, a child's legal status could be unclear for several months and thus leave all the parties vulnerable until an adoption finalization could be accomplished.

Unless reversed, the decision will force New York parents to adopt their own children. Assuming the genetic father is placed on the birth certificates, a time-honored tradition that the courts and statutory scheme have long recognized, a stepparent adoption will be necessary to place the genetic mother on the birth certificates.

6.13(b) Genetic Mother Declared Legal Mother of Twins Born through a Gestational Carrier
June 1995

A New York court has now allowed the genetic parents, the Arredondos, to be recognized as the legal parents of twins born to Judith Nodelman, a married gestational carrier, and place their names on the children's birth certificates. Although the original birth certificates had listed the children's last names as Arredondo, they listed the gestational carrier as their mother and did not list a father. The Supreme Court found that genetic tests excluded Mrs. Nodelman as the mother and noted there was no dispute between the parties as to either genetic parentage or custody.

Arredondo v. Nodelman, 163 Misc.2d 757;
1994 N.Y. Misc. LEXIS 616

6.14 Surrogate Parenting Contract Upheld
December 1993

A Maryland trial court has ruled in favor of a surrogacy agreement in which the surrogate received $12,000 from the intended parents. Because a stepparent adoption was necessary to legitimize the intended mother's status, the court was required by its adoption statutes to review any payments made to the surrogate mother. The court acknowledged that the adoption statutes prohibited payments for a child but declined to apply those laws since it found no criminal intent as required under those provisions.

Moreover, the Maryland trial court found that a significant number of states with similar "baby-selling" statutes had nonetheless enacted legislation either resulting from or prohibiting surrogacy. The court thus concluded that, without a specific statute expressly prohibiting surrogacy agreements in its state, and "given the ambivalent history of surrogacy contracts both in and outside the state, the court simply cannot conclude that such surrogacy agreements are so patently offensive to the public good that they must fail as a matter of public policy."

In re Petition of MSM for Adoption of Infant,
Md. Cir. Ct., Montgomery Cty. (8/20/93)

6.15(a) Court Dismisses Eight Surrogate Adoptions

June 1994

In a case that highlights a problem with applying adoption laws to traditional surrogacy arrangements, a District of Columbia court rejected eight adoption petitions filed by nonresident couples for children born through surrogacy. Under District law, the courts only have jurisdiction over an adoption if the child is in the legal custody of a licensed child-placement agency located within the District.

Although in each of the eight cases the surrogate mother had relinquished her legal rights to a D.C. agency, the biological and intended father had expressly retained his rights, while consenting to the adoption by his wife, and the court concluded that there was no legally effective transfer of legal rights to the agency and dismissed all eight petitions.

It was apparent that the parties had been looking for a friendly forum. The court noted that surrogate parenting arrangements were "not looked on with favor" in at least three of the five jurisdictions in which the petitioning adopters resided (Michigan, New York, and New Jersey) and their status was "murky at best" in the remaining two (Israel and Ontario). The court also noted that the petitions were filed prior to the passage of a law in the District that now makes such contracts illegal.

6.15(b) D.C. Court of Appeals Rejects Adoption Petitions Filed in Surrogacy Arrangements

December 1995

BY K. ZIESELMAN

Although adoption laws continue to be applied to traditional surrogacy arrangements to enable a wife and intended mother to legally adopt her husband's biological child, the D.C. Court of Appeals has recently upheld the lower court's decision dismissing the adoption petitions of several such wives. The court ruled that since none of the parties are D.C. residents in any of the cases, a D.C. court does not have legal jurisdiction. The Appeals Court also agreed with the lower court that none of the children were ever in the complete legal care, custody, or control of the D.C. agency and thus that court did not have jurisdiction to hear the adoption petitions. The court did not address the legal status of the children in the absence of the requested adoptions.

In re S.G., 663 A.2d 1215 (D.C. 1995)

6.16 Arizona's Surrogate Parenting Statute Declared Unconstitutional
March 1995

Arizona's surrogate parenting law violates equal protection principles because it prevents a biological mother from proving maternity while allowing a biological father to do so. Designed to prohibit surrogacy contracts, the statute defines a surrogate (traditional or gestational) as the legal mother for all purposes. Although the surrogate's husband is also presumed to be the legal father, his presumption is rebuttable.

The issue arose when Ronald and Pamela Soos had three embryos implanted in a gestational carrier, and then filed for divorce during the carrier's pregnancy. Thereafter, Ronald Soos established his paternity under the statute and obtained temporary custody of the triplets. Pam Soos then attacked the constitutionality of the law, which precluded her from establishing her maternity. The lower court agreed with her, and also ordered she be allowed visitation. The appellate court affirmed, ruling that the disparate treatment between the two parties, because it involved childbearing, must meet the most stringent test for constitutionality, "strict scrutiny," and failed to do so.

Soos v. Superior Ct. of Arizona, 897 P.2d 1356
(Ariz. Ct. App. 1994); *reh'g denied*

6.17 Surrogate and Intended Mother Bring Novel Joint Custody Claim against Father

March 1995

After Frank Swenson reportedly took off with his six-month-old child while his wife, Jan, was in the shower, she enlisted the help of the surrogate who bore the child to attempt to regain custody from her husband. The unique custody battle, initially filed in California, will now be decided in Connecticut where the couple lived before deciding to separate.

Jan and Frank Swenson initially entered into a traditional surrogacy arrangement with surrogate Anna Benedict through the Center for Surrogate Parenting in Beverly Hills, California. After the Swensons agreed to separate within months after the child's birth, Frank Swenson reportedly left the country with the child. Jan Swenson then approached Benedict, and they have jointly sued for custody of the child, now eleven months old. In partial response, Frank Swenson has reportedly sued Anna Benedict for child support. The Connecticut judge has also recently imposed a "gag" order on the trial, prohibiting the parties from discussing the case publicly.

Although other surrogacy disputes have arisen around the country, this case is unique in joining together the intended mother and surrogate to attempt to establish custody. Because the intended mother's legal rights had not yet been finalized through a stepparent adoption, under traditional legal principles she has little basis for a claim to the child. There are some similarities with the *Moschetta* custody fight [6.2], where the couple also separated shortly after the child's birth. In that case, however, each of the three parties attempted to obtain sole custody of the child, with that court ultimately ruling that the intended mother had no legal rights, and awarding joint custody to the father and surrogate, with the father being awarded custody of the child nights and weekends and the surrogate having her on weekdays.

In this case the surrogate has taken the position that she intended to relinquish her rights to the couple, not the father alone, and has said that if she and Jan Swenson win custody of the child, she intends to have Swenson raise the child and will visit once a month. The Center for Surrogate Parenting, which created the arrangement, is also considering bringing a claim against Frank Swenson for breach of their surrogate contract. At present, the child is living in Boston with her father, who has recently agreed to allow the two women a ten-day visit with the child.

Swenson and Benedict v. Swenson, Sup. Ct.,
New London, Conn. (filed 12/94)

6.18(a) Father Charged with Murdering His Five-Week-Old Infant Conceived by Surrogate

June 1995

BY A. JAEGER

James Austin, a twenty-six-year-old single male, paid $30,000 to the Infertility Center of America, an Indianapolis clinic directed by Noel Keane, to arrange for a (traditional) surrogate mother to bear a child created with his sperm. The surrogate gave birth to a boy on December 8, 1994, and turned him over to Austin the next day. The baby was hospitalized a month later and died January 17 from a skull fracture and internal head injuries. Austin was charged with criminal homicide. Austin admitted he repeatedly shook the baby and hit him with a plastic coat hanger to stop him from crying. The surrogate claimed the body of the infant and arranged for his funeral.

This incident clearly raises questions about whether clinics should psychologically screen potential parents and the need for greater regulation of surrogate parenting arrangements. On one hand, screening potential parents may identify potential abuses and prevent such tragedies. On the other hand, people who have their own biological children are not screened or licensed. Such cases of egregious abuse of a child conceived through a surrogate parent are rare, and probably less frequent than abuse of children born without the aid of reproductive technology.

6.18(b) Single Father of Surrogate Infant Sentenced; Surrogate Files Additional Civil Lawsuits

Spring 1996

James Austin has been convicted and sentenced to twelve and a half to twenty-five years in prison, the maximum term for third-degree murder, for shaking his child to death a month after the child's birth.

The surrogate, Phyllis Huddleston, has sued both Austin and ICA in state courts in Indiana. Huddleston's suits allege that ICA billed itself as the premier surrogacy program in the United States but failed to include safeguards to ensure the child's well-being by performing psychological testing or providing parenting classes to the intended father. She also claims she received no counseling, and seeks financial compensation for the infant's death.

In the criminal case, the judge who sentenced Austin noted, "[t]here is no question that this child was bred for the purpose of sale." Austin's uncle also noted at the sentencing that society, by permitting an untrained, single young man to "buy a day-old baby is partly to blame for his crime. . . ," which he termed a "tragedy."

In Huddleston's civil suit, ICA attorneys argued that it had no contact with her, acted only as a mediator between her and Austin, and thus neither owed nor breached a duty of care to her. ICA's attorney also argued that the physicians who performed the insemination procedure were not affiliated with ICA. Similar arguments were made, and ultimately rejected, in a 1991 lawsuit brought by another surrogate against Noel Keane and related professionals in Michigan in the *Stiver v. Parker et al.* case [6.9]. A federal district court initially dismissed that surrogate's claim, but a federal appeals court reversed, ruling that the Michigan center, its principals and associated lawyers and doctors should all be held to an affirmative duty of protection and heightened diligence in connection with the alleged transmission of cytomegalovirus to a surrogate resulting in the birth of a child with severe birth defects. That court relied on the fact that the surrogate was a healthy woman who had been "enticed" into the surrogacy program by "brokers" motivated by "profit."

6.18(c) Surrogate Mother's Wrongful Death Suit Dismissed; Broker Not Obligated to Ensure Father's Parental Fitness

Winter 1996

Ruling that a surrogacy broker has no obligation to the surrogate to evaluate intended parents' fitness, a Pennsylvania court has dismissed Phyllis Huddleston's suit against Infertility Center of America, Inc.

In a sixty-page decision, the court found that the surrogacy center acted only as a mediator and did not have a contract with the surrogate. It therefore created no relationship with, or any fiduciary duty to, the surrogate. Furthermore, the court ruled that any negligence claim on the child's behalf would fail because the father's actions were not foreseeable. The court did not address the seeming "Catch-22" its ruling created in finding the father's actions unforeseeable after finding there was no duty to investigate or evaluate the father's parenting abilities.

In reaching its decision, the trial judge partly based his decision on the lack of surrogacy laws in Pennsylvania and his review of the mother-child relationship in issue. Noting that "wrongful death" actions brought by parents or children require the existence of a family relationship, he found that Huddleston's contract with the father made it clear she never intended the child to be a part of her family and explicitly agreed not to form a parent-child relationship. Huddleston, however, on learning of the child's injuries, had contacted the center to stop the custody proceedings and had planned to raise the child if he survived. The court also reviewed surrogacy laws from other jurisdictions and concluded that no state regulating surrogacy arrangements requires psychological counseling of a biological father for the benefit of either the surrogate or intended child. The decision is on appeal.

6.18(d) Traditional Surrogate's Case against Broker Reinstated
Winter 1997

In a surrogacy case with potentially widespread implications for other professionals practicing in the area of collaborative reproduction, a court has ruled that a surrogacy business operating for the sole purpose of conceiving a child and profiting from that endeavor has a "special relationship" and therefore an affirmative duty of protection to the adults and child. The decision reverses a lower court ruling, which had dismissed the action.

In reinstating the negligence claim, a Superior Court judge found that a "special relationship" existed between the surrogacy business, its clients, and the child conceived through their efforts. It specifically found that the question was not, "whether it is foreseeable that a sperm-donor father would brutally murder his child, the actual issue is whether it is reasonably foreseeable that child abuse could result in a surrogacy situation." Answering that question in the affirmative, the court ruled that a jury should therefore decide whether it was foreseeable in this case. The court upheld the dismissal of other claims brought by the surrogate.

In reaching its decision, the court relied on a 1992 federal appellate decision, *Stiver v. Parker* [6.9b], where a traditional surrogate contracted CMV and gave birth to an affected child after artificial insemination with untested sperm of the intended father. That appellate court ruled that the surrogacy business, by undertaking to provide a special and sometimes perilous service for profit and having controlled all of the details of that process, created a "special relationship with the adults involved and the resulting child," to all of whom it then owed an affirmative duty of protection. In echoing the *Stiver* opinion, which had not been previously relied upon by other courts, *Huddleston* suggests a possibly emerging, and very high, standard of care for professionals involved in collaborative ART treatments.

Huddleston v. Infertility Ctr. of Am.,
700 A.2d 453 (Pa. Super. Ct. 1997)

6.19(a) "Parentless Child" Born to Surrogate Brings Call for Regulation
Summer 1996

In a case described by a California court as the "most extraordinary" surrogacy case ever, a child has been conceived and born with no legal parents. The girl, Jaycee Buzzanca, was born to a surrogate under an agreement with a couple using anonymous donor sperm and donor egg. The couple separated two weeks after signing the agreement, and the husband filed for divorce shortly before the child's birth. The wife, who has physical custody of the child, has sought temporary child support from her soon-to-be ex-husband. In granting the temporary support while deferring the question of permanent support, the three-judge panel also asked state legislators to provide better regulation in the area.

Luanne and John Buzzanca had been married for over six years, lived together for three years before marriage, and had spent Luanne's $200,000 inheritance on five surrogates attempting to have a child prior to the birth of Jaycee Buzzanca in April 1995. The couple specifically used a donor egg to avoid the surrogate having any genetic connection to the child. The couple and surrogate reportedly signed a contract prepared by the Center for Reproductive Alternatives of Southern California, the validity of which John Buzzanca's attorney questions. The agreement did not provide for the possibility of divorce.

Luanne Buzzanca's initial claim for temporary support was denied by a trial judge on the grounds that the court had no jurisdiction to even hear the matter until the legal parentage of the child was established and reasoned that the wife needed to obtain a court decree of adoption for the child. As the appellate court noted, the lower court judge did not address the fact that a court could not force the husband to sign adoption papers. Recognizing that the case was one of first impression, and that he had put the wife in a "Catch-22" position, the judge also acknowledged that the child might have independent rights to support and appointed an independent lawyer for the child to challenge his decision.

The appellate court reversed and, on a temporary basis, ordered the husband to pay child support. It first analyzed the couple's signed surrogacy agreement, which explicitly noted that the embryo was to be created with "donated genetic material unrelated to any of the parties." It then analogized the case to older paternity cases in which husbands denied paternity yet were required to pay temporary support pending the ultimate legal determination of their parentage. Here, the appellate court found, the critical question was: "given the admission he [the husband] signed the surrogacy agreement, is it likely that John will ultimately be held to be the father?" It then relied on the California courts' decisions in *Johnson v. Calvert* [6.1] and *Moschetta* [6.2] for help in answering that question in the affirmative.

The appellate court noted that the earlier surrogacy decisions did not go so far as to find the agreements "enforceable per se," but did find that the parties' intentions, as manifested in their agreement, could break any tie between two women who could rely on different parts of California law to claim parentage. Finding that in this case the anonymous genetic parents will not likely be held to be the legal parents, the court then noted that, "to rule that the birth mother in a gestational surrogacy arrangement is the natural mother is to burden her with responsibilities she never contemplated and is directly contrary to her expectations" (court quoting from *Johnson v. Calvert*). It concluded that at least for the purposes of its order for temporary support, it would look to the intention of the parties as to both parents and found "it is enough that John admits he signed the surrogacy agreement which, for all practical purposes, caused Jaycee's conception every bit as much as if he had caused her birth the old fashioned way."

In issuing its ruling for temporary support and reversing the lower court, the court stressed that it was working with a sense of "extreme urgency" and noted that the husband could appeal its order but that the law should not provide an incentive to recalcitrant intended parents to delay support. "Jaycee cannot wait for the slow, deliberative processes of the judicial system to ponder a case of first impression." In conclusion, the court said, "once again, the need for legislation in the surrogacy area is apparent . . . we reiterate our previous call for legislative action." An attorney representing the child noted he hopes the ruling will prompt John Buzzanca to pay more child support and said that "It would be nice if Jaycee had two parents who loved her." Until the case is finally resolved however, legally speaking, she has none.

6.19(b) New Order in Parentless Child Case
Winter 1997

Jaycee Buzzanca continues to be the subject of legal battles. The Court of Appeals has now issued an order granting a "writ of supercedeas," allowing the appeal to proceed. In the meantime, the gestational carrier had filed a petition to establish her parentage, which the intended mother responded to by filing a petition to terminate her rights. The gestational carrier thereafter agreed to having her petition dismissed with prejudice, meaning she cannot bring such a suit at any time in the future. This leaves Luanne Buzzanca, the intended mother and the woman with physical custody of the toddler, fighting only with her estranged husband over issues of parentage and child support.

6.19(c) Court Rules That Intent of the Parties Should Govern in Collaborative Reproduction

Summer 1998

On appeal, the California Appeals Court has held that the John and Luanne Buzzanca, as the intended parents of Jaycee, are her legal parents because without their intention to initiate and consent to the fertilization of an embryo and transfer to a gestational carrier the child would not have been born.

In its reasoning, the court first found that the wife was the lawful mother of the child. The court then found the husband to be the lawful father of the child. In doing so, the court compared this situation to artificial donor insemination (AID—later changed to DI to avoid confusion with AIDS) within a marriage. The court noted that AID statutes are a well-settled area of law, namely that if the husband consents to AID, he is the legal father of the child. In both AID and gestational carrier situations, procreation of a child is by consent to a medical procedure by someone who intends to raise the child but who otherwise does not have any biological tie to the child. Just as a husband is deemed to be the lawful father of a child unrelated to him because he consented to the donor insemination, so too a wife who consents to the use of a donor egg and transfer of an embryo to a gestational carrier is deemed the lawful mother of the resulting child. The fact that Luanne did not give birth to the child was irrelevant to the court.

The court's rationale for relying on the parties' intent was the presumption in favor of finding legal parenthood where possible and avoiding the need to resort to adoption as a default determination. The court found this promotes certainty and stability in families and "correlates significantly" with the child's best interests.

The court was quick to note that AID statutes did not anticipate current medical technology allowing IVF and ET, but found there is "no reason to distinguish between husbands and wives" since both are equally situated in their ability to consent. It followed the *Johnson v. Calvert* decision, which allowed maternity testing to establish a maternal genetic link, the same as paternity testing.

The court also discussed the role of the gestational carrier contract. It was not concerned with the enforceability of the oral and written contracts. Rather, the court was concerned with the agreement that set into motion a medical intervention that resulted in a child, looked to the intent of the parties to create a child and found the clear expression of that intent in the gestational contract. The court likened the contract to "procreating conduct," the same as the act of sexual intercourse. The court's reliance on the parties' intentions raises the stakes around obtaining informed consent and expressing intent through written agreements.

Finally, the court noted that artificial insemination, traditional surrogacy, gestational carriers, cloning, and gene splicing are part of the future. It suggested that even if all ARTs were outlawed, courts would still be called upon to decide who the lawful parents are and who must provide the child with maintenance and support. The court joined others in calling "on the Legislature to sort out the parental rights and responsibilities of those involved in artificial reproduction. Courts can continue to make decisions on an ad hoc basis without necessarily imposing some grand scheme. Or, the Legislature can act to impose a broader order which, even though it might not be perfect on a case-by-case basis, would bring some predictability to those who seek to make use of artificial reproductive techniques."

6.19(d) Father's Further Appeal Denied; Case Continues to Raise New Issues
Fall 1998

John Buzzanca, a court-ordered "father," has failed in his latest appeal, when the state's highest court denied further review without comment, letting the Appeals Court decision stand.

In yet another twist to what has already been a most unusual case, the genetic father of the child has also come forward. Reportedly, a Chicago-area lawyer has identified himself as the child's genetic father, as the result of donating "spare" embryos (created with his sperm and donor eggs) after he and his infertile wife completed their family. The couple had been patients at U.C. Irvine and agreed to donate the embryos following their own successful treatment. It is not currently known whether the couple signed consent forms that included potential donation to a gestational carrier.

Jaycee B. v. Superior Ct., 42 Cal. App. 4th 718
(Cal. Ct. App. 1996); *In re Marriage of Buzzanca*,
61 Cal. App. 4th 1410 (Cal. Ct. App. 1998), *rev.*
denied by 1998 Cal. LEXIS 3830 (Cal. 1998)

6.20 Surrogate Carrying Fetuses of Two Different Couples
Summer 1997

BY K. ZIESELMAN

A thirty-five-year-old Italian surrogate mother is reportedly carrying two fetuses for two different couples. The embryo transfer procedure was done in Switzerland, where the woman plans to give birth. Apparently, the children will be matched to their parents through blood testing at birth. The surrogate is a mother of two and claims to be receiving only reimbursement for expenses. The Italian Health Minister has called for new laws to regulate surrogate motherhood, and the Italian physicians association is pursuing disciplinary action against the doctor.

Associated Press, 3/7/97

6.21(a) Massachusetts Hears Test Case on Traditional Surrogacy
Winter 1997

A traditional surrogacy dispute has put Massachusetts into the forefront of legal arguments over the enforceability of such agreements, with a surrogate attempting to get custody of the child she birthed. The case is pending before the state's highest court, which took the case on direct and expedited appeal. This author has filed an amicus (friend of the court) brief jointly on behalf of the Boston Fertility Society [now the New England Fertility Society] and RESOLVE of the Bay State for the purpose of distinguishing the significant medical and legal differences between traditional surrogacy and gestational carrier arrangements. A decision is expected shortly.

6.21(b) Massachusetts Finds Paid Traditional Surrogacy Agreements Unenforceable; Distinguishes Gestational Surrogacy
Spring 1998

Massachusetts, having entered the legal debate over surrogacy, has announced that it comes down squarely on the side of . . . the children. After a traditional surrogate in Massachusetts attempted to keep custody of a child she had agreed to bear for a Rhode Island couple, they sued and succeeded before a lower court both in being awarded physical custody of the child and a ruling that they were likely to prevail under the surrogacy contract. The contract provided for the surrogate to relinquish physical custody of the child to the father or repay all funds she'd received; it did not address the relinquishment of parental rights.

The state's highest court took the case on direct and expedited appeal. Despite the parties' subsequent custody settlement (agreeing the child should remain with the father, with visitation by the surrogate mother), which negated the necessity of a court decision, the court decided on its own to rule on the contract issue.

While finding there was "nothing inherently unlawful" in a traditional surrogacy arrangement, the state's highest court flatly refused to impose a contract analysis on surrogacy arrangements. It found the payment of $10,000 and a pre-birth agreement to relinquish physical custody (if not legal parentage) to the father "troubling." Ruling that a mother and father may not make a private, binding agreement as to a child's custody or adoption, it determined that such a decision must be subject to a judicial determination based on the best interests of the child.

This author's amicus brief, filed on behalf of the Boston Fertility Society and RESOLVE of the Bay State, outlined to the court the medical and legal distinctions between traditional and gestational surrogacy and argued that the latter was not precluded or governed by existing Massachusetts adoption laws. Responding to that point, the court acknowledged that gestational surrogacy presented "considerations different from those in the case before us" and cited *Johnson v. Calvert* [6.1] as enforcing such a contract and noted that in *Calvert* the mother was recognized to be the egg donor and not the surrogate. As these groups had hoped in filing a brief, the recognition of this distinction should prove important in allowing parties to more reliably enter into enforceable gestational surrogacy contracts in Massachusetts.

Regarding *traditional* surrogacy, the court ruled that a surrogate mother must have time after birth to change her mind and that eliminating payments beyond undefined "pregnancy-related expenses" was the only way to ensure against economic pressure on a woman to act as a surrogate. The court noted that potential surrogates may be less economically well situated than infertile couples. Essentially, the court applied adoption standards to the arrangement, including the minimum four-day post-birth requirement before a birth mother may relinquish her parental rights. Although this contract was carefully drafted to avoid any reference to relinquishment of parental rights by the surrogate, the court found the agreement to give physical custody to the father sufficiently similar to apply the same standards. The court reviewed the state's artificial insemination statute, which it referred to as "surrogate fatherhood," as well as its adoption laws, in reaching its decision.

The court then went further and offered essentially a "blue-print" for the legislature. It suggested its concerns would be alleviated if, in addition to no compensation and a change of mind period post-birth, the surrogate's husband consented in advance, the surrogate was an adult who had delivered at least one live child, all parties had been evaluated for their "soundness of judgment and capacity," the intended mother was "incapable of bearing a child without endangering her health," the intended parents were suitable to be parents (inferring an adoption-like home study might be required), and all parties had legal representation. Finally, after surveying other states' approaches to surrogacy, the court noted that both New Hampshire and Virginia provided for pre-conception judicial approvals, which it noted "might be a better procedure."

While not prohibiting traditional surrogacy, Massachusetts's highest court has clearly issued a cautionary note for couples and professionals considering traditional surrogacy there. No matter how any agreement is worded, a father can have no assurance he will ultimately get custody of his child. For those pursuing gestational surrogacy on the other hand, the court's ruling suggests such agreements may well be enforceable.

R.R. v. M.H., 689 N.E.2d 790 (Mass. 1998)

6.22 Divorce Court to Decide Custody of Fourteen-Year-Old Child Born to Surrogate and Never Adopted
Fall 1998

The Connecticut Supreme Court has reversed a divorce court's ruling that it did not have jurisdiction over a custody dispute between a divorcing couple where the wife had never formally adopted the fourteen-year-old child the couple conceived through traditional surrogacy. Although it agreed that the wife was not a parent because the child was not a "child of the marriage" as that is defined under Connecticut law, the appellate court ruled she may pursue her claim for custody as an "interested third party." Such parties are permitted under Connecticut law to attempt to rebut the presumption that it is in a child's best interests to be placed with his/her biological parent. The decision culminates seven years of litigation, and the court noted that 1) raising the child together for her first eight years, 2) the husband's having participated in a "public ruse" that the wife was the child's birth mother, and 3) the child having lived with the wife for over seven years thereafter were sufficient to rebut the legal presumption that it was in the child's best interest to be in the father's custody.

The court accepted the lower court's ruling that, having failed to adopt the child, the wife was not within the law's definitions and protections of a "child of the marriage," which it noted included a child born through artificial insemination or a child born to either spouse and adopted by the other. While the decision therefore confers what is known as "subject matter jurisdiction" on the trial court to decide whether the girl is better off with the wife or husband, it does not award the wife status as mother. To retain custody, she must ultimately meet the standard of proof set out for "interested third parties." Three justices dissented from the court's opinion, arguing that the child should be considered to come within the law's definition of "a child of the marriage." A similar issue was recently debated by the California courts in the widely reported case of Jaycee Buzzanca [6.19].

Doe v. Doe, 244 Conn. 403 (Conn. 1998)

6.23 Illinois Enacts Gestational Surrogacy Legislation
Winter 1999

Illinois has enacted legislation that amends existing Illinois law to permit individuals who undertake a gestational carrier arrangement and birth there to be deemed the legal parents of the child and to have the child's birth certificate issued accordingly without the necessity of litigation or adoption. Applicable only to cases in which both intended parents are also the genetic parents (excluding arrangements involving traditional surrogates or egg or sperm donation), the new law requires all parties, including any husband of the carrier, as well as a physician, to sign certified statements as to the child's genetic parentage prior to birth. The form statements being promulgated will require neutral witnesses and must be placed in the carrier's medical file. If the process is not completed prior to birth, the carrier and her husband are presumed to be the parents of the child and court action is required to transfer those parental rights. In many states, stepparent adoptions are currently employed to establish legal parentage after the genetic father is placed on the birth certificate through legally established methods of determining paternity. The Illinois law should simplify the ability of genetic parents there to be legally recognized as such.

750 Ill. Comp. Stat. 47/25 (West 2005)

6.24(a) Money Damages Sought in British Medical Malpractice Suit for Surrogacy Treatment
Spring 2000

After being rendered infertile at age nineteen by an emergency hysterectomy following two unsuccessful emergency caesarean sections in one year, British citizen Patricia Briody is now suing the British health authority for her resulting infertility. Last year the court found the health authority guilty of negligence in her 1973 care. Ms. Briody is now reportedly the first person to seek money damages to cover surrogacy as treatment for infertility. Because her ovaries are still intact, IVF, coupled with the use of a gestational carrier may be a viable option, though experts testifying before the court disagreed as to the probability of success.

Guardian Newspapers Unlimited, 12/7/99

6.24(b) British Woman Left Infertile by Medical Negligence Denied Damages for Surrogacy ·
Fall 2001

BY N. ELSTER

In a recent decision in the United Kingdom, a woman rendered infertile by what the court determined was negligence by that country's health authority was denied damages to cover the cost of surrogacy. ... Ms. Briody had sought damages to cover the costs of a commercial surrogacy arrangement in which she had planned to participate in California, since commercial surrogacy arrangements are illegal in England. The court found that "[o]n any view of our law the claimant seeks an award of damages to acquire a child by methods which do not comply with that law. . . . It is one thing for a court retrospectively to sanction breaches of statute in the paramount interests of an existing child, it is quite another to award damages to enable such an unenforceable and unlawful contract to be entered into." Additionally, the judge ruled "the chances of success are so low that it is in my view unreasonable to require the defendants to fund the enterprise." Her appeal of that decision was subsequently denied by the Court of Appeal in June 2001.

During her twelve-year legal battle for compensation, Patricia Briody spent more than £50,000 in an attempt to conceive a child. Although denying her claim for damages to cover the expenses of surrogacy, the court did recognize that under some circumstances, such an award might be appropriate. However, as Ms. Briody's chances of a successful pregnancy using her own eggs were so slim, less than 1 percent according to some experts, the justices reasoned that it would be unreasonable to expect the National Health Service to pay for the service. Additionally, a surrogate pregnancy using donated eggs would not be "in any sense restorative." Rather, it would be "seeking to make up for some of what she has lost by giving her something different. Neither the child, nor the pregnancy, would be hers."

Briody v. St. Helen's and Knowsley Health Authority,
2 FCR 13 (1/2000); *Independent,* 6/30/01

6.25 New Jersey Trial Court Denies Pre-Birth Parentage Order in Gestational Surrogacy Agreement
Fall 2001

On May 21, 2001, a New Jersey Superior Court denied a request by petitioning biological parents, supported by the gestational surrogate [the mother's sister], to be listed as the legal parents in a pre-birth order. The surrogate, "Gina," agreed to carry and give birth to a child created with Andrea's egg and the sperm of Andrea's husband, "Peter." Plaintiffs unsuccessfully sought a pre-birth parentage order citing the granting of similar orders in California, Massachusetts, and Florida.

The court ruled that, "although Gina is extremely likely to surrender her rights as planned, she must not be compelled to do so in a pre-birth order." New Jersey law requires that the woman who gives birth to the child must be recorded as a parent on the birth certificate, however, such certificate can be issued within five days of the birth of the child. Additionally, under the state's parental termination law, a woman must be given seventy-two hours after the birth of the child to surrender her parental rights. In light of these two statutes, the court reasoned that, "the gestational mother may surrender the child seventy-two hours after giving birth, which is forty-eight hours before the birth certificate must be prepared. If Gina does choose to surrender the infant, and certifies that she wishes to relinquish all rights, then the original birth certificate will list the two biological parents, Andrea and Peter, as the baby's parents." In the court's opinion, this resolution most closely accommodated the parties' wishes while complying with existing statutes and public policy concerns raised in the *Baby M* case.

A.H.W. et al. v. G.H.B. et al.; 772 A.2d 948
(N.J. Super. Ct. 2000)

6.26 French Siblings Become Parents Using Egg Donor and Surrogate
Fall 2001

A storm of controversy has been swirling over the French village of Draguignan since the May 14 birth of a baby boy to sixty-two-year-old Jeanine Salomone. Jeanine is the oldest Frenchwoman to have given birth; fertility treatments to postmenopausal women are illegal in France. However, the controversy continued when several weeks later it was learned that Jeanine's brother, Robert, was the child's biological father. As the story unfolded, it became known that Jeanine and Robert traveled to the United States seeking the services of an egg donor and a surrogate. They did not inform the clinic that they were siblings; they allowed the program to believe that they were a married couple. The "couple" then selected an egg donor whose eggs were fertilized with Robert's sperm. Embryos were then transferred to Jeanine and the donor who had also agreed to be a surrogate. Jeanine gave birth to a boy and eight days later in California, the surrogate gave birth to a girl.

Jeanine and Robert are now raising the two children as their own. Officials in Draguignan are concerned with the Salomones' ability to parent and are currently investigating the situation. A senior prosecutor in the town has called the case one of incest, "not biological, but social." Suggestions have even been made that the siblings sought to have the children in order to secure their eighty-year-old mother's multimillion-dollar fortune when she dies.

The case has caused an ethical uproar in Europe and in the United States. In fact, the California program where the Salomones received treatment, distressed by the pair's deception, now insists on seeing marriage licenses before proceeding with IVF.

Agency France Presse, 6/21/01; Daily Mail,
6/22/01; Time Europe, 6/22/01

6.27 Massachusetts High Court Rules on Parentage in Gestational Carrier Arrangements

Winter 2001

The Massachusetts Supreme Judicial Court has affirmed the practice of issuing pre-birth court orders declaring genetic, intended parents the legal parents of their child when there is no dispute between any of the parties. This ruling solidifies the court's earlier indication that it would support such a determination and practice and is intended to protect children created through such arrangements. The ruling reversed a lower court that had denied a petition to establish parentage of twins being carried by a gestational carrier for genetic intended parents, after questioning whether it had legal authority to issue such a pre-birth order. Most Massachusetts trial courts had used their equity powers to grant similar orders on numerous occasions, but the legal authority to do so had not been explicitly articulated by the high court.

The court noted it had previously suggested the Probate Court develop a procedure for such cases in its 1999 *Smith v. Brown* decision (this author's case), 430 Mass. 1005 (1999).

Presented here with its third "reported case" (an appeal not by a losing party but from the lower court seeking clarification) on the same issue, it decided to explicitly address the sole issue of parentage. It did so by essentially affirming the use of equity petitions pre-birth upon sufficient proof of parentage. The court went on to note, however—as have most courts faced with novel legal issues in ART cases—that the legislature would be the "most suitable forum to deal with the questions involved in this case, and other questions as yet unlitigated, by providing a comprehensive set of laws that deal with the medical, legal, and ethical aspects of these practices."

The high court determined that neither Massachusetts adoption laws, paternity laws for out-of-wedlock children, nor its artificial insemination statute applied to gestational carrier arrangements. Instead, the court concluded that where: "(a) the plaintiffs are the sole genetic sources of the children; (b) the gestational carrier agrees with the orders sought; (c) no one, including the hospital, has contested [objected to] the complaint or petition; and (d) by filing the complaint and stipulation for judgment the plaintiffs agree that they have waived any contradictory provisions in the contract (assuming those provisions could be enforced in the first place)," the Probate and Family Court judge has authority under its equity jurisdiction to consider the merits of the parentage petition.

In its opinion, the court emphasized the importance of establishing the rights and responsibilities of parents as soon as practicably possible to avoid potential detrimental consequences of delays in establishing parentage. Among possible negative consequences, the court listed potential interference with a child's medical treatment, inheritance disputes, difficulty in the collection of Social Security benefits, and undesirable custody or support obligations.

The court also emphasized the need to provide accurate reporting of pregnancy and birth information to the Registry of Vital Records and Statistics (a concern raised in a separate brief submitted by the state), which is mandated by law to gather such data for every birth. To meet that concern, the court ruled that parties to a parentage action must notify the state registrar of both the commencement of the action and of any court orders or judgments. This effectively gives the state the opportunity to file an appearance and object in any case in which it feels its interests are not served or its concerns met. Amicus (friend of the court) briefs were filed on behalf of the Massachusetts Women's Bar Association (WBA) and RESOLVE, Inc. (by the author and another) and others. In a subtle, but significant, linguistic victory, the Court accepted one of the points made by the WBA / RE-SOLVE brief in distinguishing traditional surrogates and gestational carriers.

Citing works by ASRM members Drs. Susan Cooper, Ed.D., and Andrea Braverman, Ph.D., amongst others, the brief clarified the medical and therefore legal distinctions between "traditional surrogacy" and "gestational surrogacy" or "gestational carrier arrangements," and urged the use of the more accurate terms: "gestational carrier" and "gestational carrier arrangements." The court's opinion adopted the gestational carrier language and refrained from referring to the carrier as a surrogate or the procedure as gestational surrogacy. That distinction, if followed by other courts, should both help develop a more sensitive terminology and move legal debates away from older cases involving traditional surrogacy, characterizations of "surrogate mothers," and arguments that all surrogates should be viewed as "birth mothers" and subject to adoption laws.

In refusing to adopt a broader "intent-based" test for parentage as urged by plaintiffs, the Court left unanswered how it would decide a case involving donor eggs or sperm or same-sex intended parents. It also left unanswered questions as to whether gestational carrier agreements are enforceable and how it would decide a case where genetic parents and a gestational carrier disputed parentage.

Culliton v. Beth Israel Deaconess Medical Center,
756 N.E.2d 1133 (Mass. 2001)

6.28 Connecticut Approves Pre-Birth Parentage Orders for Gestational Carrier Agreements, Rules Agreement Enforceable
Spring 2002

On January 1, 2002, a new law went into effect in Connecticut that permits the Superior Court to issue pre-birth parenting orders in gestational carrier cases. The new law applies only to gestational carrier arrangements, and not to traditional surrogate arrangements, which will still require termination of parental rights and stepparent adoption proceedings. In the first action under the new law, a Connecticut court reportedly not only issued the pre-birth orders, but also found the Agreement valid and enforceable.

2001 Conn. Acts 01-163 (Reg. Sess.)

6.29(a) Utah Surrogacy Law Challenged

Summer 2002

Genetic parents of twins and their friend who acted as an unpaid gestational carrier have filed a lawsuit in the U.S. District Court in Utah,
asking the court to declare that state's surrogacy statute unenforceable. The parties are also seeking to validate their contract with each
other and to order the state's Office of Vital Records and Statistics to
issue birth certificates listing the twins' genetic parents as their legal
parents. Under Utah's surrogacy statute, contracting with a woman
to carry a child for profit is a misdemeanor. While unpaid surrogacy
and gestational carrier arrangements are not illegal, they are not recognized and cannot be enforced. The law also requires both the surrogate or carrier's name be listed on the birth certificate as the child's
legal mother, and, if she is married, her husband's name as the child's
legal father. Since the carrier in this case was unmarried, the genetic
father's name was able to appear on the birth certificate as the twins'
father. At present, however, his wife's parental rights will only attach
through an adoption.

The parties are hoping their case will pave the way for others in
similar situations in Utah. A few states, including Massachusetts and
Illinois, have resolved these issues through litigation or legislation
[6.23 and 6.27].

6.29(b) Federal Court Strikes Part of Utah's Surrogacy Law

Summer 2003

A federal court in Utah has now ruled part of that state's surrogacy
statute unconstitutional. Struck from the law is a provision that requires the surrogate or gestational carrier and her husband to be
listed as the child's parents on his or her birth certificate. Since the
couple here did not pay her, the part of the same 1989 statute that
precludes enforceable contracts to pay a woman to carry a child was
not implicated and still stands. The court ruled that "J.R. and Mr. R's
fundamental liberty interests in their parental relationship with their
children arises from the fact of biological parent-child relationship,
independent of any grant of right, privilege or designation of status
by the state . . . [e]ven as it is called upon to consider new questions
thrust upon it by the advent of new technology, the Legislature, no

less than the court, must keep the fundamental liberty interests of the people clearly in mind." That liberty interest superseded the state's designated status. A similar ruling declared Arizona's surrogacy statute unconstitutional on the same point in 1995 [6.16].

J.R. v. Utah, 261 F. Supp. 2d 1268 (D. Utah 2003)

6.30 British High Court Decides Gestational Carrier Is Mother of Twins
Summer 2002

An international legal fight continues in a highly publicized gestational carrier arrangement between a California couple and a British woman who carried the couple's genetic twins. The agreement was to give birth in California with the genetic parents taking immediate custody upon birth. Problems arose when the genetic parents requested a selective reduction procedure, the carrier refused, and the genetic parents threatened not to pay her. The carrier then decided to keep the twins. The American couple applied to a British court for a declaration of international abduction, arguing the twins were residents of California based on the biological father's residence there. The British High Court has now rejected the argument, ruling that under British law the carrier is the mother of the twins and the only person with parental responsibility. The genetic parents are expected to appeal.

Times, 2/26/02; *Guardian, Daily Telegraph*,
2/19/02

6.31 Woman Escorted out of Kuwait by Canadian Embassy after Surrogate Procedure
Fall 2002

After entering into a gestational carrier contract with a Kuwaiti couple, a Canadian gestational carrier traveled to Kuwait for the embryo transfer. The plan, facilitated through a California attorney and an Internet website, was for the woman, Shani Russell, to wait until confirmation of the pregnancy, return to Canada, and give birth in California. She was to be paid $10,000.

The plans went awry when an apparent family tragedy prompted the carrier to request an early return home, prior to pregnancy confirmation. According to Ms. Russell, but denied by the intended parents, the couple threatened to hold her against her will. She also allegedly feared arrest in Kuwait, where a "fatwa," an Islamic legal ruling, bans this type of surrogacy, a fact that she claims not to have known prior to the July procedure. After her frantic emails to Canadian governmental authorities pleading for help getting out, Canadian embassy officials escorted her from her hotel in Kuwait City to the airport for a flight home. Since returning home, Ms. Russell has had a negative pregnancy test. According to her mother, Ms. Russell had hoped to use some of the money for her own in vitro fertilization as she has no fallopian tubes; her mother reports she is now considering egg donation instead.

ABC News Internet Ventures, 6/23/02

6.32 Dueling Insurance Companies Dispute Coverage for Gestational Carrier and Child
Winter 2003

A federal court stepped in to resolve the question of which of two insurance companies was required to cover the pregnancy, complications, and two months of neonatal hospitalization costs of a child, referred to as "Brenda Roe," born through a gestational carrier arrangement between two sisters. It appears there was no dispute between any of the adults, with all seeking the maximum coverage for their various expenses. Mid-South, the insurer for the carrier's husband and his dependents (defined as "spouse and children"), balked at covering both the maternity complications costs and the newborn costs for the premature infant. Celtic Insurance, which covered the genetic, intended parents, refused to cover the child.

In what appears to be the first reported case dealing with this issue, the court split the coverage obligations in what was a predictable outcome for those familiar with these issues. Less predictable were the lengths the parties were willing to go to try to get insurance by characterizing the child as that of the carrier. The court found that the carrier's pregnancy and medical complications were covered by her husband's family policy while the child, whom the surrogacy agreement acknowledged would be the child of the genetic, intended parents, should have been covered by their policy had they registered her, as that policy required for coverage to extend to a dependent child beyond the thirty-first day of life. The court held that the genetic parents' ultimate adoption of the child did not negate her legal status as their daughter prior to the adoption.

The court recognized the Mid-South policy covered the gestational carrier's husband and his dependents, with "child" defined to include "natural child, step child, or adopted child." The court found "no reasonable person" could interpret the term "natural child" to mean Brenda Roe, instead finding it obviously meant "biological child" and, since the carrier's husband was the policyholder, no reasonable language interpretation could make her his natural child. The court denied the term "natural child" was ambiguous because of the unusual nature of a surrogate pregnancy. Nor did the fact that the genetic parents sought an order of adoption for their child dissuade the court from recognizing the facts of the child's parentage. Any other construction would have flown in the face of the parties' expressed understanding of the child's parentage and the language of the policies.

Mid-South was less successful in arguing that it did not have to cover the carrier's pregnancy complications. The court rejected both arguments the company raised, finding the expenses were not for the benefit of a third party and were at least in part to protect the carrier's own health; and finding the surrogacy agreement's statement that the intended, genetic parents would pay for any "maternity and birth costs" if "health insurance is not available. . . ," was clearly contingent on lack of coverage under the policy, not in lieu of it.

However, the court refused to find Mid-South acted in bad faith, since given the unusual circumstances of a surrogate pregnancy, it was reasonable to seek a declaration of rights.

Finally, the court found the child was not covered under her genetic, intended parents' policy after thirty days post-birth, since they failed to inform the company of her birth, as the policy required for all dependent children.

The decision is likely in line with both the expectations and experience of those who have been involved in gestational carrier/surrogacy arrangements. Indeed, the parties' arguments to the court that the child should be seen as the child of the gestational carrier and her husband for purposes of insurance coverage would seem not only ineffective but also potentially make a family—perhaps one not involving sisters—vulnerable to claims of a legal parent-child relationship between the carrier and the child.

Mid-South Ins. Co. v. Doe, 274 F. Supp. 2d 757 (D. S.C. 2003)

6.33(a) Pennsylvania Trial Court Awards Custody of Triplets to Gestational Carrier
Summer 2004

According to news reports, a Pennsylvania trial court has awarded custody of infant triplets to a gestational carrier, with instructions to work out visitation arrangements with their biological father. The children were conceived with donor eggs, pursuant to a surrogacy contract between the biological father and carrier. His fiancée was not a party to the contract but intended to adopt the children, according to the father's attorney. After the triplets were born, the carrier reportedly became unhappy with the biological father's treatment of them, including accusations that he only spent one hour with them after birth then disappeared for days, that he failed to name the children for at least a week, and that he said he was too busy to take the triplets home from the hospital the day they were ready to be discharged. Because the father had not provided the hospital with a court order, the hospital allowed the carrier to take them home. She and her husband have three children of their own.

The trial court invalidated the surrogacy contract because it failed to name a legal mother, ruled that the fiancée could not be considered a legal mother because she was not married to the father, and allowed the carrier to maintain custody of the triplets. The biological father has appealed, claiming the carrier did not have legal standing to assert legal rights to the children.

6.33(b) Gestational Surrogate Awarded Legal Custody of Triplets in Pennsylvania; Father and Egg Donor Press Suit in Ohio
Spring 2005

In an ongoing custody battle involving two states and three potential parents, a Pennsylvania trial court has awarded legal custody of triplets to the gestational surrogate, Danielle Bimber, who has been caring for them since birth. A separate action brought by James Flynn, the Ohio father, and the Texas egg donor remains pending in that state. The donor has reportedly not pursued her suit, said to have been filed solely in an attempt to assist the father in gaining legal custody.

In its recent ruling the Pennsylvania court found Bimber was the better parent. The court noted that although Flynn makes more money and lives in a bigger house, he had not bonded with the children, did not offer to pay child support voluntarily, and did not take off time from work when the children were with him for twelve days over the summer. The court awarded weekend custody to the father and ordered the boys' last names to be Flynn, but their first names to be those chosen by the surrogate.

An appeal is anticipated.

6.33(c) Donor's Maternity Rights Debated in Triplet Gestational Surrogacy Controversy

Summer 2005

The formerly anonymous Texas egg donor involved in a triplet surrogacy gone awry has now asked a Pennsylvania trial court to reject a petition to terminate her maternity rights that was filed by the gestational carrier. The donor, twenty-three-year-old Jennifer Rice of Texas, is attempting to maintain her parentage status both by filing suit in Ohio and defending the current action brought by Bimber. The donor has acknowledged that her legal fees are being paid by the children's father, that she does not want custody, and that she is willing to relinquish her maternal rights if the father's fiancée (and originally intended mother) is permitted to adopt the children. The Pennsylvania court also took testimony from experts who testified that inserting a new "parent figure" into the sixteen-month-old boys' lives would likely be detrimental to them. The court ordered the parties to submit legal briefs on the case and a ruling is expected shortly.

In the wake of this litigation, Pennsylvania has proposed a law that would require court approval of any surrogacy contracts, as well as counseling for all parties.

A separate lawsuit was filed in late May by the intended parents against the Indiana attorney and agency who brokered the arrangement. The couple's suit, for negligence and breach of contract, claims attorney Steve Litz and Surrogate Mothers Inc. of Indiana failed to

file documents to give Flynn, as the genetic father, sole legal custody
or to inform them their contract could not be enforced in Pennsylvania, which has no surrogacy laws. Litz has reportedly responded that
he always warns clients some states do not recognize surrogacy
agreements and has called the lawsuit "meritless."

Pittsburgh Post-Gazette, 4/6/05;

Associated Press, 5/19/05

6.33(d) One Trial Court Deems Gestational Carrier Mother of Triplets; Second Court Allows Donor Maternal Status
Winter 2005

A Pennsylvania trial court has ruled that Bimber, the gestational carrier, is the legal mother of the triplets, while an Akron, Ohio, judge
has ruled the egg donor does have a parent-child relationship with
the triplets, but declined to decide who has parental rights, leaving
that to the Pennsylvania court to decide. A decision from the Pennsylvania court is expected soon.

Pittsburgh Post-Gazette, 11/10/04

6.33(e) Carrier Ordered to Turn Triplets Over to Father and Return Payments
Summer 2006

Two further court actions in this ongoing, tri-state legal battle have
resulted in the return of two-and-a-half-year-old triplet boys to their
father from the gestational carrier who has been raising them since
birth, as well as an order to return her $20,000 fee for carrying them
(the fee issue has been stayed with orders for the lower court to revisit that question). In March, an Ohio appellate court ordered the
carrier to return funds, claiming she violated the contract to surrender the children to the father. In April, the Pennsylvania Superior
Court overruled a lower court's decision and ordered the children returned after finding that the carrier, together with hospital officials,
kept the couple from visiting the children in the hospital and incor-
rectly told the couple the children had been discharged when they
were still in the hospital. The most recent court found that the carrier's actions in obtaining custody of the children were "fraught with
impropriety." More litigation is anticipated.

6.33(f) Ohio and Pennsylvania Courts Rule: Reverse Custody; Award Donor Maternity Rights, Find Surrogate Breached Valid Contract and Damages Award to Be Reviewed.

Spring 2008

The Ohio appellate courts have now ruled that the egg donor, Jennifer Rice, was the mother of the children, that Bimber breached the surrogacy contract, and that surrogacy contracts are not against the public policy of Ohio, but declined to uphold the damages award against the Bimbers premised on breach of contract without a lower court review of that issue.

The Pennsylvania appellate court has vacated the prior Pennsylvania custody order in favor of Bimber, reversed the order terminating the egg donor's parental rights, and awarded the father full physical and legal custody of the triplets. On appeal of a second action brought by the father to recover child support payments he paid, the reviewing court upheld the trial court's determination that a person caring for a child had standing to seek child support regardless of whether she had been granted custody.

J.F. v. D.B., 589 Pa. 739 (Pa. 2006); and *J.F. v. D.B.*, 116 Ohio St. 3d 363 (Ohio 2007)

6.34 British Surrogate's Death Triggers Custody Battle

Spring 2005

A custody battle is reportedly brewing over a child born to a British traditional surrogate who died ninety minutes after the child's birth from a ruptured aorta and heart attack. The surrogate, Natasha Caltabiano, was twenty-nine, engaged to be married to her longtime partner, and the mother of two. The baby, who weighed eleven pounds at birth, was placed with the commissioning Irish couple in Northern Ireland, but Ms. Caltabiano's mother, fifty-six-year-old Marilyn Caltabiano, says she wants the child placed with a younger, childless couple. The commissioning couple are fifty-two and forty-eight and have five children from previous relationships.

The parties apparently met after Ms. Caltabiano created a website to advertise her willingness to be a surrogate, and the inseminations were reportedly done without a physician's assistance. The couple is reportedly refusing to pay the remainder of the expense payments, claiming they have incurred significant legal bills due to Ms. Calta-biano's death. The couple had bought a life insurance policy, in accor-dance with the surrogacy agency's procedures (standard for most sur-rogacy arrangements), which will reportedly be used to buy a home for Ms. Caltabiano's children and mother.

Marilyn Caltabiano has criticized the surrogacy system, arguing it encourages women such as her daughter to put themselves at risk through a pregnancy and has been quoted as saying it would feel like a "complete waste of my daughter's life" to give the baby to an older couple with other children. Caltabiano's former fiancé, Paul Brazier, gave a published interview to *The Mirror* and has a different perspec-tive: "Surrogacy did not kill Tasha, being pregnant did—and that was the risk she decided to take." Unlike Marilyn Caltabiano, Brazier claims the child is where his deceased fiancée chose and would want him to be and that she would have no regrets. He is currently es-tranged from her family following her death.

Under British law, the surrogate and any consenting partner are the legal parents until and unless they transfer their parental rights to the commissioning couple or the couple adopts the child. With Ms. Caltabiano's death and her fiancé's reported estrangement from her surviving family, who, if anyone, is the child's legal guardian is unclear.

BioNews, 2/21/05; *Weston Mercury*, 2/4/05;
Mirror.co.uk, 2/3/05

6.35 Trust Provisions Benefit Children Conceived through Gestational Carrier and Donor Egg Arrangement

Summer 2005

In a novel court case, a New York court has ruled that twins born through IVF / ET using donor eggs and born to a gestational carrier are entitled to inherit from the estate of their maternal grandfather and that an exclusion for adopted children did not apply. The case in-volved a trust created in 1959 for the benefit of the settler's eight chil-dren or their children's descendants with the stated exception that "adoptions shall not be recognized."

In 2002, one of the adult children had twins born in California and, under that state's laws, obtained a parentage judgment. The issue before the New York court was whether or not those children were entitled to inherit. New York law does not recognize surrogacy contracts. The case arose when the trustees asked the court to determine whether or not the exclusion applied.

The court found that the children were not adopted and that the adoption language in the trust should not be extended to apply to them. The court noted that no adoption occurred, that under California law a judgment for parental relationship is a totally distinctive proceeding and governed by a different part of California statutory law. Given that the trust was created in 1959 before these technologies were available and used, the court also found that there could have been no intent to exclude ART-conceived children.

Interestingly, the court was indifferent to the use of donor egg and relied on the California court's legal determination of parentage based on intent and found that, "no reasoning justifies a denial of full faith and credit to the judgment. . . . [I]t is clear that in California the twins were not adopted. . . ."

In the Matter of John Doe, 793 N.Y.S.2d 878

(N.Y. Misc. 2005)

6.36 Utah Legislation Approves Surrogacy Contracts, Streamlines Birth Certificates

Summer 2005

Governor Jon Huntsman has signed into law a surrogacy law that permits court-approved contracts and sets out procedures for obtaining birth certificates for children born to gestational carriers. The law is limited in its application to married infertile couples and gestational carriers (who are not using their own eggs). Prior to this, Utah law prohibited any form of surrogacy and any traditional surrogate or gestational carrier, regardless of whether she was a genetic parent, was required to go on the child's initial birth certificate. Despite some legislative opposition, the law passed and goes into effect July 1, 2005.

Utah Uniform Parentage Act, 2005 General

Session, Utah Code Ann. 78-45g-801

6.37 Non-Residents Entitled to Massachusetts Gestational Carrier Pre-Birth Order

Winter 2005

The Massachusetts Supreme Judicial Court determined that Massachusetts both had jurisdiction and was a proper choice of law to determine parentage of a child born in that state even though all the parties were out-of-state residents. The intended, genetic parents lived in Connecticut; the gestational carrier and her husband lived in New York. The only Massachusetts connections were the prenatal care and birth. Noting the equity statute's absence of a residency requirement, the hospital's status as a Massachusetts corporation, and the carrier and her husband's agreement to submit to the court's jurisdiction, the Court determined Massachusetts had proper personal and subject matter jurisdiction to grant the relief requested, a pre-birth parentage order.

The Court also upheld the contract's choice of Massachusetts law provision, finding Massachusetts had a "substantial relationship" to the transaction and that the result would not be contrary to Massachusetts public policy. In reaching that conclusion the court considered whether another state had a stronger connection to the transaction, and thus considered the laws of both New York and Connecticut. Both states address gestational carrier and traditional surrogacy arrangements, but with contradictory policies (pro- and anti-surrogacy), which made the Massachusetts court's decision easier to reach. The Court also noted it had not been asked to, and would not, express any opinion on the validity, construction, or enforceability of any other provision of the agreement. Thus, the opinion clarifies that nonresidents may seek parentage orders in Massachusetts at least where pre-natal care occurs there, the child's birth is planned and occurs there, and their contract provides for such.

Hodas v. Morin, 442 Mass. 544, 814 N.E.2d 320 (2004)

6.38 Gestational Carrier Loses Temporary Custody of Own Children

Winter 2006

The estranged husband of a gestational carrier has gained temporary custody of their two children, ages seven and two, and a Kentucky court has denied both her attempt to regain joint custody or to have a custody evaluation of both of them, as well as her request to have another judge appointed to decide the case. A permanent custody decision, originally scheduled for January 2006, has been postponed indefinitely. Jack Bendschneider filed for divorce and took temporary custody of the children because, he told a local newspaper, a surrogacy arrangement his wife, Arletta Bendschneider, entered into with author Jaquelyn Mitchard and her husband had, "consumed his wife to the detriment of her own children." The children are reportedly being cared for by Jack Bendschneider and his parents, who have moved into the family's home. Bendschneider also refused to sign the Massachusetts court documents denying his parental rights of the child his wife was carrying, and under Kentucky law was presumed to be the legal father of any child born to his wife.

The baby boy was born on November 1, 2005, and is with Mitchard and her husband. A determination of legal parentage was delayed because of Bendschneider's refusal to consent, but ultimately issued.

Lexington Herald-Leader, 12/16/05; *Advocate-Messenger,* 1/11/06 and 1/19/06

6.39 British Gestational Carrier Fights to Keep Twins
Spring 2007

In a legal first for England, a forty-two-year-old single mother is fighting to keep legal custody of twins she bore for a married couple from their frozen biological embryos after changing her mind during the first trimester. The twins are currently living with her and her two teenaged sons, with court-ordered weekend custody for the biological parents. Under British law, she is considered the legal mother and must be found unfit to remove custody from her. Because the biological father is deemed the legal father, he and his wife have been granted court-ordered weekend custody while the case moves forward. The parties found one another through COTS, a British surrogacy agency, and used the couple's previously frozen embryos to establish a pregnancy. The gestational carrier reportedly passed both medical and mental health screenings.

According to a published interview with the woman (the couple declined to be interviewed), she became upset when the warm, personal relationship she expected with the couple—including contact with the child—became more businesslike, including being told the couple, who are Asian, did not want their family to know the children had been carried by a white woman and did not want a continuing relationship with her. She was also reportedly angered when, after expressing her reservations about carrying a twin pregnancy, she was immediately scheduled for a termination without further input or discussion. She has returned the money she had received and expressed her willingness to continue the present arrangement with the twins essentially having three parents. A hearing in January decided the temporary custody arrangements while the case is pending.

Mail on Sunday, 12/17/06, 1/25/07

6.40 Maryland Court Upholds Birth Order, Questions Baby Buying Restrictions
Summer 2007

More questions were raised than answered by an intermediate appellate court's ruling that a single man may obtain a birth order without a mother being listed for twins carried for him by a gestational carrier and created with the help of an egg donor. There was no disagreement by the parties and the court found that state law, and specifically its equal rights act and paternity statutes, supported equal treatment for women denying maternity and thus the gestational carrier's right not to be legally treated or listed as the twins' mother. That conclusion falls into line with a number of other states that are increasingly issuing pre- or post-birth orders for children born to gestational carriers.

The court went further, however, suggesting that surrogacy arrangements may be vulnerable under that state's laws: "It requires noting that surrogacy contracts, that is, payment of money for a child, are illegal in Maryland," and noted that the courts have enforced two statutes that prohibit payments not only for adoption, but for custody, as well as in exchange for a waiver of child support. Strongly worded dissenting opinions were also filed, referring to ART births as creating new ways of "manufacturing children." Subsequent clarification of Maryland law as to both traditional and gestational surrogacy arrangements may be anticipated.

In re Roberto d. B, 399 Md. 267; 2007 Md.
LEXIS 269 (5/16/07)

6.41 Rising Interest in International "Reproductive Outsourcing" Generates Legal and Ethical Concerns

Spring 2008

The growing interest in "reproductive tourism" and "reproductive outsourcing," including a dramatic rise in Indian gestational surrogacy, has generated both legal and ethical concerns. The attraction is frequently described from a monetary perspective: the entire process can cost $25,000, which includes airfare, accommodations, and the surrogate's fee (typically $7,500 or less than 50–75 percent of the fee for arrangements within the United States, but the equivalent of ten to fifteen years of normal income for the carrier) and significantly lower medical costs. Surrogacy is legal in India, and the carrier's name does not appear on the birth certificate. Many of the women live together in a group setting, physically attached to the IVF clinic. Some programs also offer egg donors.

According to one recently published profile of Rotunda—the Center for Human Reproduction in Mumbai, which offers both surrogacy and egg donation, does not allow any of the parties to meet, and recently coordinated a process with a gay male Israeli couple, an Indian egg donor, and an Indian gestational surrogate. The gestational surrogate was not told she was carrying a child either for a same-sex couple or foreigners. The article profiling the arrangement noted that "on some contracts, the thumbprint of an illiterate surrogate stands out against the clients' signatures." Other concerns have been raised about: the carriers' level of understanding including whether their lack of knowledge as to whom they are contracting with undercuts any agreement; whether donor egg information is adequate for recipients; and whether immigration and citizenship issues are clearly and reliably established. The only clear issue is that, financially speaking, Indian surrogacy is a bargain for those who are seeking it out.

New York Times, 1/3/08, 3/10/08;
Washington Post, 1/2/08

6.42 Indian Surrogacy Twins' Birth Certificates Create Visa Problems for Parents

Summer 2008

As interest in surrogacy arrangements in India continues to grow, a German couple living in the United Kingdom were refused visas for their twin sons born in India through a gestational carrier and donor eggs because the wife's name, and not the gestational carrier's, had been listed as the mother on the boys' birth certificates. They were also given the wife's surname. The arrangement was reportedly facilitated by Dr. Naina Patel, who had registered the children's births with the Anand municipality where they were born.

The United Kingdom consulate refused the children visas. The father then petitioned the court to change the children's surname to his, and to remove his wife's name. The father also submitted testimony that under German law the woman who delivers a child, rather than the woman for whom she delivers it, is considered the mother. The court directed the municipality to make the changes to reflect the carrier and not the wife as the twins' mother.

In its order the court made reference to the "National Guidelines for Accreditation, Supervision and Regulation of ART Clinics in India," acknowledging that an amicus (friend of the court) brief "rightly submitted" that a "number of areas perhaps are required to be addressed, more particularly, on the legal issues involved."

Some proponents of Indian surrogacy have argued that it is both easier and less expensive than in the United States, with advocates and couples specifically promoting the lack of legal "red tape" as a reason in favor of pursuing surrogacy in India.

This case recognizes that determining legal recognitions of parentage for children born in India may be more complex than simply registering them as the children of the intended parents and suggests that there may be procedural steps that need to be addressed to properly protect those involved in these overseas arrangements.

Times of India, 4/6/08

6.43(a) New Controversy Involves India's "First Surrogate Orphan" or "Stateless Baby"

Fall 2008

A Japanese father has run into both controversy and legal obstacles in trying to take his infant daughter out of India where she was born via egg donation and surrogacy in July. The father and his wife divorced a few weeks before the birth. In a somewhat ironic twist, India has been a destination chosen by many seeking a simpler, less expensive, and less legally regulated surrogacy arrangement, but has now become a legal quagmire for this father. The child remains in India two months after her birth as both countries struggle to resolve her nationality and thus passport and visa issues to permit her to travel from India to Japan. Her paternal grandmother from Japan has arrived to care for her.

The issue revolves around the child's citizenship and the respective citizenship rules of India and Japan. At birth, the child's birth certificate was registered with only the father's name. India permits a child to have Indian citizenship if either parent is an Indian citizen, but the gestational surrogate does not want to be recognized as the child's legal mother, so the child cannot be given an Indian passport. Japan recognizes nationality if either mother or father is Japanese and married at the time of birth. A child can reportedly still acquire Japanese citizenship if only her unmarried father is Japanese, as is the case here, but without an adoption in India he is not recognized as the legal father. Japan has asked for an Indian court order regarding paternity but if the child is considered an Indian child, India law does not allow adoption by a single man. The current result is that the child has neither Indian nor Japanese citizenship and no permission to leave India or enter Japan.

The case has focused attention on Indian surrogacy, with calls for legislation in that country similar to those long familiar in the United States, but no action to date. Indian surrogates are reportedly often paid $7,500 to carry a child, a huge sum in comparison to typical annual income figures in that country but a fraction of the cost in the United States and elsewhere.

Daily Yomiuri, Associated Press, 8/17/08;
China Daily, 8/7/08

6.43(b) Japanese Baby Born to Indian Gestational Surrogate Heads Home
Spring 2009

After two months of delays, an infant born to an Indian gestational surrogate in India and conceived from a donor Indian egg and sperm from her now-divorced Japanese father headed home to Japan. During the delays, her grandmother cared for her in India.

The court in India and passport office ultimately authorized the baby to travel, despite an appeal by an entity in India to gain custody of the baby.

India Today, 10/14/08; *CNN.com,* 11/02/08

6.44 Traditional Surrogate Granted Full Custody of Child
Winter 2008

In an informal surrogacy arrangement between a married Florida couple and their traditional surrogate gone sour, the surrogate, Stephanie Eckard, has been awarded full legal custody of the baby girl she delivered in May 2007. The court denied child support from the biological father, Tom Lamitina, ruling he was a sperm donor under Florida law. According to the reported circuit court opinion handed down in October, the parties—all of whom had prior surrogacy experience, reportedly used an agreement the surrogate got off a surrogacy website, which only she then signed prior to the insemination. There were also allegations that during the pregnancy the father (whom DNA later confirmed is the biological father) had questioned his paternity, and that the surrogate had both raised financial issues and cancelled any agreement. The circuit court ruled that under Florida's surrogacy and artificial insemination laws, there was no enforceable legal surrogate agreement and the intended father was considered a sperm donor with no parental rights or responsibilities. The court also noted that "the services of an experienced attorney who was familiar with the [law] may have adequately protected" the father and his interests. The couple's attorney has vowed to appeal.

Eckard v. Lamitina, OrlandoSentinel.com,
Florida Times-Union, 10/11/07

6.45 British Twins Born to Ukraine Surrogate Also Allowed to Go Home
Spring 2009

Another international surrogacy case raising legal uncertainties due to conflicting laws has been resolved. Twins born to a married Ukraine gestational surrogate through a surrogacy arrangement with a British couple, who had used the husband's sperm and an anonymous egg donor, had reached a standstill with the twins having no right to enter the United Kingdom. Under British law, which does not allow compensated surrogacy, a married surrogate and her husband are considered the child's legal parents. Under Ukraine law, which recognizes surrogacy, a surrogate has no parental rights or responsibilities. Thus, the children had no legal parents absent a court order, and for a time there were suggestions the children be placed in a Ukraine orphanage.

As of December 11 however, a British court has issued a "parental order," which recognizes the British couple as the parents, notwithstanding limitations in that country's laws. Another British court had earlier issued a special discretionary clearance that allowed the children to enter Britain while their legal status was resolved.

Couples considering such international surrogacy arrangements will want to gain a clear understanding of how they will ensure any children they conceive in another country will obtain citizenship and travel approval since any discrepancies between the two countries' laws may have a dramatic impact on those plans. The British couple had been advised to look overseas because Britain does not allow paid surrogacy. In the wake of the case there have been calls for a review and overhaul of British surrogacy law.

Bionews, 12/16/08

Posthumous Reproduction

Access and Parentage

❖ MEDICAL COMMENTARY, BY Howard W. Jones, Jr.

O N THE ISSUES of posthumous reproduction and the parentage and support of resulting children, the courts rarely state the exact method of obtaining or using the decedent's sperm. In only two of the abstracted cases is it specifically stated that IVF was involved. Nonetheless, it is apparent that medical assistance was required either to obtain and freeze the sperm posthumously or to thaw and transfer sperm or embryos previously created and frozen during the decedent's lifetime.

These cases are rare, but once again, even within these few cases are a few extremely unusual situations. For example, consider the situation brought about by Lance Smith's fatal car accident. Although healthy at the time of the death, Smith had stored sperm and left written instructions allowing his fiancée to use the sperm to have a child in the event of his death. This was unusual enough, but her decision to rule out having such a child made the case even more so. Smith's parents asked the hospital to turn the sperm over to them so that they could create a child to carry on the family line. Smith's father was quoted as saying, "We threw ourselves into this because we thought Lance could live on through the child." The abstract of the case does not state how the parents intended to use the sperm for carrying on the lineage. More recent cases sound similar themes, suggesting these issues need to be addressed prospectively.

Clearly, not all posthumous uses of sperm can be foreseen. The practical point seems to be, however, that a medical provider must be prepared, if asked, to store sperm for future use in the event of a patient's subsequent infertility (such as following a course of successful chemotherapy) or possible death (following an unsuccessful course of treatment or the increasingly common situation of military personnel storing genetic material before going overseas). The medical provider should have a consent form that spells out as many of the possible user situations as possible, especially those involving posthumous use. Such a form would require a legal expert, but it probably would be worthwhile in view of these situations, including the curious case abstracted above.

The question can be asked whether sperm stored for use in anticipation of a long absence (but not death) might also be used if the sperm depositor dies. This situation could easily arise. We often store the sperm of military personnel whose wives might benefit from intrauterine insemination, but the possibility of using fresh insemination treatments are obviously handicapped by the fact of the serviceman's imminent deployment overseas. In such a case, the sperm are banked and the inseminations are carried out in the absence of the husband (with the proper consent forms in place, of course). If the serviceman should be killed in action and the wife nevertheless wishes to proceed with the insemination but the consent form does not specifically address posthumous use, what should be done?

Many clinics in this situation have suggested a suitable waiting period of perhaps six months. I agree with this, and I also think that many such cases would benefit from the inclusion of a mental health professional, who can review the entire situation and make a recommendation as to the suitability of continuing with the process. If these requirements are fulfilled, I would be inclined to honor the wishes of the widow and carry out the program that had been originally planned, even if it did not expressly include use after death.

~ LEGAL COMMENTARY, BY Susan L. Crockin

Long before the existence of ART, children have been born after the deaths of their biological fathers. The law, therefore, is no stranger to the need to clarify the legal status of posthumous-born children. Most states have longstanding statutory or case law recognizing the paternity of children born within a prescribed time following the death of their presumed or alleged father—often a year to ensure a time period of sufficient length to encompass the length of any possible pregnancy resulting from a pre-death conception. Cryopreserved sperm and, more recently, cryopreserved embryos and eggs have created novel opportunities for conception through the use of the cryopreserved genetic material of deceased men and women by an ever-expanding group of would-be progenitors. Since parentage and intestate inheritance principles have always been issues governed by state law, each state is free to resolve disputes that arise within their borders as they see fit. The results have been inconsistent rulings from state to state.

A second legal issue involving posthumous reproduction has to do with access: when and under what conditions surviving spouses, family, or friends may gain access to genetic material after the death of the patient who preserved it. Cases have arisen both where the deceased left explicit approval and instructions to use his or her genetic material and where no such clear directives were provided. This has raised novel issues of informed consent and public policy principles as to who should have access to the material, and what legal control or relationship—if any—the deceased should have over the material and to any resulting offspring.

A third, less common issue involves posthumous *extraction* of genetic material, and what rules and parameters should be in place—including informed consent and legal parentage—to allow surviving relatives to have sperm or eggs retrieved from the corpse of their loved one in the hope of creating a child. Unlike cases dealing with use or parentage of children resulting from cryopreserved genetic material, posthumous extraction cases typically arise under extraordinary time constraints. With the need to make immediate, consensual (one hopes) decisions, they seldom make it to a reported or appellate court decision. Instead, physicians, families, ethics boards, and lawyers are more likely to reach a decision involving some form of consensual agreement to extract and freeze the deceased's genetic material or, on occasion, obtain an emergency court order to do so. Those agreements or orders often require a subsequent judicial authorization for the desired future use or a further agreement to release the professionals from liability in exchange for doing the family's bidding. Such cases seem to be becoming more prevalent, possibly a reflection of the increased awareness of available medical and ART options. In early 2009, for example, a trial court judge in Texas approved a mother's request to harvest her twenty-one-year-old son's sperm after he died unexpectedly; a trial judge in New York granted a fiancée's similar request. In both cases the grieving mother and fiancée spoke of their desire to carry on their loved one's legacy.

Another novel access issue that has yet to be litigated is whether current FDA regulations that impose strict testing and quarantining requirements on genetic material to be distributed to a "non-intimate" partner may preclude distributing genetic material of some deceased individuals to those who seek to use it.

Over the past fifteen years, at least nine courts have resolved issues involving children whose biological fathers died before their conception through either artificial insemination of cryopreserved sperm or implantation of cryopreserved IVF embryos.[1] Most arose over a child's qualification for Social Security survivor benefits, a federal entitlement provided to those who, under applicable *state* law definitions, are considered a decedent's legal heirs. Thus, courts have for the most part been called on to interpret, apply, and in some cases extend existing state laws that long predate IVF to decide if a child is considered the legal child of the deceased for purposes of intestate (without a will) inheritance. A few courts have also been confronted with the question of whether or not to release the sperm of a deceased man to enable an attempt at pregnancy.

Two reported cases involving whether to release a deceased man's sperm to his former fiancée or girlfriend for her to attempt a pregnancy reached opposite conclusions. In California, William Kane's banked sperm was posthumously released to his fiancée, with the court overruling objections from Kane's former wife and grown children and finding that Kane's written intention was clear and that posthumous conception was not against the public policy of California (*Hecht v. Superior Ct.*, 1993). In the second case, a Louisiana court affirmed a preliminary injunction against a former partner's use of a deceased's sperm where evidence was conflicting as to his intentions for posthumous use. His extended family—including his adult son, sister, and mother—all objected; he and his

---

1. Conception, as used throughout this book in the context of ART or artificial insemination of sperm refers to the point of insemination or the transfer and implantation of embryos into a woman's uterus, a definition that reflects the views of most courts and scientists. It should be noted, however, that this is another instance where language may be outcome-determinative: if conception were to be legally defined as occurring upon fertilization of the female egg, that would impact numerous issues regarding the legal status of the embryo, as discussed more fully in chapters 1, 7, and 9.

female partner had not been actively undergoing inseminations at the time of his death; and a written "Act of Donation" crucial to her case had been drawn up by her law partner rather than a disinterested professional (*Hall v. Fertility Institute of New Orleans*, 1994).

In Britain, Diane Blood succeeded after a lengthy court battle in gaining access to her deceased husband's stored sperm and then in having him legally recognized as the father of the two resultant children she conceived after his death. Her efforts ultimately resulted in a London High Court judge ruling that the 1998 European Convention on Human Rights overrides inconsistent language in Britain's 1990 Human Fertilisation and Embryology Act, which stated that a man is not the father of a child created posthumously with his sperm. HFEA supported the Human Fertilisation and Embryology (Deceased Fathers) Bill of 2003, which allowed a man to consent to his name being recorded on the birth certificate of a child born as a result of posthumous fertility treatments. As of 2009, proposed amendments to that Act are pending.

Several federal and state courts have ruled on the legal parentage of posthumously born children. In Massachusetts, New Jersey, Louisiana, and Arizona, the children were found to be the legal children of the deceased. In Arkansas, California, and New Hampshire, the courts rejected posthumous parenthood. In Arkansas the court rejected both Social Security benefits and workers' compensation benefits for posthumously born children. A 2009 federal appellate decision denied benefits under California law absent a deceased's express consent to both create and support a posthumously conceived child.

The first case involved a child conceived three months after her father died from cancer, using sperm he had banked for that purpose. Because Louisiana law recognizes parentage only if a child is born during or within several months of the father's lifetime, the Social Security Administration initially denied Judith Hart benefits, but later reversed, acknowledging that the case "raises significant policy issues that were not contemplated when the . . . Act was passed many years ago." "[R]ecent advances in . . . the field of reproductive medicine necessitate a careful review of current laws and regulations to ensure that they are equitable in awarding Social Security payments" (*Hart v. Chater*, 1996).

Following that groundbreaking case, a lower New Jersey court recognized the paternity of IVF twins born eighteen months after their biological father's death: "Once a child has come into existence . . . a fundamental policy of the law should be to enhance and enlarge the rights of each human being to the maximum extent possible, consistent with the duty not to intrude unfairly upon the interests of other persons." The court emphasized that while this new technology could be applied in positive ways, it also creates ethical, legal, and social policy problems. Thus, the court also ruled, prospective parents should consider carefully the consequences of using posthumous conception technology, and "[t]he law should certainly be cautious about encouraging parents to move precipitously in this area" (*In re the Estate of William Kolacy,* 2000).

Massachusetts was the first high appellate state court to rule on this issue. In *Woodward v. Commissioner of Social Security* (2002), that court identified three critical proof requirements for inheritance eligibility: (1) genetic paternity; (2) the decedent's actual consent to posthumous reproduction; and (3) proof of his actual consent to support any resulting children. In requiring this "double consent," the court found that the mere act of storing sperm to preserve fertility during a man's life does not necessarily indicate an intention to father children after death. Some commentators at the time questioned why the court would require proof of intent to support the resulting children, something that is not required of living fathers regardless of whether they even intended to reproduce. The court may have been alluding to the possibility that a man might be willing to have his sperm used as a posthumous donor but not as an intended posthumous parent. The court also required notice to existing heirs and noted that any decision would partly rest on whether those heirs would be harmed by the result. A number of reported cases followed a similar path to allowing benefits but, in 2007 and 2008, both the New Hampshire and Arkansas Supreme Courts rejected these theories.

In *Khabbaz v. Commissioner, Social Security Administration* (2007), New Hampshire refused to allow a child conceived through artificial insemination after her father's death to inherit from the father as his surviving issue under that state's intestacy law. Rejecting every argument made on behalf of the child under various New Hampshire statutes, the court relied solely on its intestacy statute, interpreting the term "surviving issue" to preclude any child not born prior to the decedent's death. The court rejected a broader reading of the statute and refused to find persuasive facts that had swayed the Massachusetts court in *Woodward* (in *Khabbaz*, the decedent had explicitly consented both to posthumous reproduction and to support any resulting children). It did, however, agree with other courts that clarifying legislation is needed to address important public policy considerations.

In *Finley v. Astrue* (2008), Arkansas also refused to recognize a deceased man as the father of a child born to his widow following an embryo implantation a year after his death. The court refused to interpret state statutes on legitimacy, and thus entitlement to Social Security benefits, for children "conceived" prior to death to include the point of embryo fertilization. It ruled "conception" referred to the point of implantation; if death occurred prior to implantation of a cryopreserved embryo, the child did not meet the intestacy laws. The court added that public policy changes were for the legislature, refusing to read any of its laws more broadly. It did not address whether its artificial insemination law, wherein a child born to a married woman after donor insemination with the consent of her husband is entitled to intestate succession, could apply posthumously. The "conception at fertilization" argument is somewhat novel, as no other court considering posthumous reproduction has yet to address or rule on that point, and could have broad implications for other areas of reproductive law. A related decision also denied the child workers' compensation benefits which require a child be "wholly and actually dependent" on the deceased. The court rejected the argument that embryo storage fees could be considered evidence of dependency, even assuming the embryo could be considered a "person," an argument the court said it need not review. It also refused to consider the novel argument that children conceived through IVF were, as a class, unconstitutionally discriminated against since it was not raised at trial. Such contradictory rulings make it virtually impossible to predict what other courts faced with these issues will do.

In *Vernoff v. Astrue* (2009), the federal Ninth Circuit, after having allowed benefits in an earlier decision under Arizona law (*Gillett-Netting*, 2004), ruled that under California law genetics does not determine a parent-child relationship. Where the deceased's sperm was not only used but *removed* posthumously, and with no evidence he intended to or consented to be a parent, the mother failed to establish either a parent-child relationship or dependency under California law and the court denied the child benefits.

The war in Iraq has raised new legal issues related to posthumous reproduction. With sperm banking more common prior to deployment, at least three children are reported to have been conceived using the sperm of dead military personnel, and there are likely more on the way.

Of note from both a medical and a legal perspective, some ART programs recommend surviving widows or partners wait an informal time period, often set at six months, before attempting a pregnancy with sperm or embryos created by their deceased loved ones. Many such programs report that a number of these women changed their minds after their initial grieving period and did not seek to conceive. This likely sound medical advice could have an unintended and unfortunate legal consequence if the time frame is extended too far for either a particular court's comfort level or a specific state's law to recognize legal parentage. Medical programs and their legal counsel should therefore be hesitant to make recommendations or policies in the absence of a clear understanding of the potential legal implications for any resulting child; women seeking to use the genetic material should always be referred to an attorney who can analyze those issues on her behalf. Ideally, any consent process involving the storing of genetic material should include the possibility of posthumous reproduction and clearly record the depositor's intentions and desires regarding any such usage. This author has represented parties facing imminent death or other medical uncertainties that would likely affect their future procreation and has drafted protective documents, including supplemental medical consents, detailing as clearly as possible the patient's or couple's respective wishes and intentions.

Anecdotal evidence and cases (some handled by this author) suggest that such situations are not as rare as one might think. Despite having no specific consent for posthumous use, requests have been made by surviving widows, fiancées, mothers, or other relatives seeking access to and use of the sperm of a deceased individual. In one such case, a decedent's mother sought to use the sperm with a donor egg, planning to carry the pregnancy herself. In another case, parents of a deceased single male sought to use his banked sperm with donor egg and a gestational carrier to create a biological link to their deceased child. Such cases raise extremely sensitive and complex issues regarding the nature and scope of a decedent's informed consent, the survivorship of such consent if it does not expressly address posthumous use, and the potentially opposing (or in some cases unknown) desires and rights of the deceased and extended family to control genetic material. Some have argued that the deceased have no right to control their genetic material, while others take the position that posthumous use of genetic material without an explicit consent to do so violates rights that survive death. These cases can also raise significant professional liability issues for those who control access to such genetic material. There are a few reported cases in which medical programs have obtained indemnification and releases of liability from parents of deceased men in exchange for releasing sperm to them.

If and as frozen embryos are made available for donation and egg freezing becomes more common, issues of posthumous parenthood will expand to maternity. These issues are certain to continue to arise in ever more complex constellations and require even more delicate balancing than courts have attempted to date.

Litigation

7.1(a) Inheritance Contest Creates Debate over Frozen Sperm
March 1993

In a California inheritance contest, Deborah Hecht, thirty-seven, is seeking to keep and use fifteen vials of sperm willed to her by her fifty-three-year-old partner, William Kane, before he took his own life. Hecht wants to be inseminated with the sperm and bear Kane's child. In his will, Kane reportedly willed the sperm to her and left selected names for a boy and a girl.

Kane's former wife and two grown children are contesting his will and have filed a wrongful death case against Hecht. They claim she knew Kane was suicidal and assisted him by not attempting to prevent the death.

On December 9, 1992, a probate court ruled against Hecht, citing the lack of legal precedent on disposition of sperm in a contested estate, and suggesting an appellate court decide the case.

Kane's daughter is represented by his ex-wife, an attorney. His son's attorney claims the court's rejection of Hecht's claim recognizes that a dead man's sperm is not ordinary property and raises issues concerning law, ethics, and public policy. If Hecht does gain access to the sperm and bears Kane's child, novel inheritance issues could also arise from that child's potential claim to a portion of his or her pre-deceased father's estate.

The case now appears headed to an appellate court.

7.1(b) Deceased Man's Frozen Sperm May Be Inherited
December 1993

Sperm may indeed be willed and used to inseminate an unmarried woman according to California appellate courts. The appellate court concluded that Kane's interest in his sperm was "in the nature of ownership" and that he had "decision-making authority" over it. It cited with approval the AFS Ethical Statement on in vitro fertilization that donors have "sole discretion" over the disposition of their gametes.

The court also rejected the adult children's other objections, ruling that it was not against California's public policy to inseminate an unmarried woman or permit insemination with stored sperm of a deceased man. The court noted California's DI law does not restrict its protections to married women (as many states do), and quoted approvingly from the recent California gestational surrogacy decision, *Johnson v. Calvert* [6.1g]: It is not the role of the judiciary to inhibit the use of reproductive technology when the legislature has not seen fit to do so; any such effort would raise serious questions in light of the fundamental nature of the rights of procreation and privacy." The court concluded that it had no legal right "to make the value judgment as to whether it is better for such potential child to be born." Whether and when Kane's lover will gain access to the sperm is still undecided because his children are also contesting the will itself.

7.1(c) California Court Orders Estate to Immediately Release Deceased Man's Frozen Sperm
December 1995

BY K. ZIESELMAN

A court order directing the estate of a deceased man to release three vials of his frozen sperm to the woman with whom he had been living before his death has been ruled by a California appeals court to be immediately enforceable. Despite a pending appeal of that decision by Kane's adult children, the Appeals Court agreed with Hecht that at age forty her chances of becoming pregnant are declining, and thus ordered the sperm distributed to her immediately.

Hecht v. L.A. Cty., Superior Court, 1997 Cal. LEXIS 131 (Cal. 1997) (real parties in interest's petition for review denied)

7.2 Male Accident Victim's Sperm Unavailable
March 1993

In London, a young wife has been denied permission to take sperm from her comatose husband on life support following a car accident. Although sympathetic to the wife, hospital authorities say that HFEA forbids sperm storage without a donor's consent, but permits donors to bank sperm and leave instructions for its use after death. The public and drafters of the law are calling the outcome a "tragic" and unintended consequence, and an amendment is being considered for future cases.

Independent, 12/20/92

7.3(a) Widow Seeks Social Security Benefits for Child Born from Deceased Husband's Sperm
March 1995

A Louisiana widow has filed what is believed to be the first U.S. lawsuit aimed at obtaining benefits for a child conceived after her father's death. The three-year-old child, Judith Christine Hart, was conceived three months after her father's death through a GIFT procedure with sperm he had stored earlier that year after being diagnosed with esophageal cancer. Her mother, Nancy Hart, says this was her husband's desire and she wants to both legitimize her child and obtain benefits for her. Her husband also left two adult children from another marriage. They reportedly recognize Judith as their half-sister and an heir to their father's estate, but Louisiana law does not. For inheritance purposes, state laws typically define children of a decedent as those born during the father's lifetime or within several months after his death (and presumably conceived before his death). The case presents some of the same issues as the California dispute involving William Kane's stored sperm [7.1], where a California court declared it was not against public policy to use sperm to create a posthumous child. Because no child was conceived and born, however, that court did not face the issues of legitimacy, inheritance, and benefits that three-year-old Judith Hart presents.

7.3(b) Child Born from Deceased Man's Sperm Ruled Legal Heir and Entitled to Benefits
September 1995

An administrative law ruling has reversed the Social Security Administration's (SSA) earlier rejection of Nancy Hart's claim on behalf of her daughter Judith born a year after her father's death through stored sperm.

Federal law provides survivor benefits to a dependent child of a deceased person who contributed to Social Security through taxes on his or her income. However, the determination of who is a dependent child and thereby eligible for the federal funds is determined by state intestacy or inheritance laws. Louisiana, where Judith and Nancy Hart live, defines an heir as a child conceived before his or her parent's death.

Nancy Hart has also filed a federal lawsuit in Louisiana claiming the federal SSA and Louisiana's state inheritance laws violate both federal and state constitutional guarantees of privacy and equal protection and that the state laws governing inheritance discriminate based on the circumstances of one's birth. That case is pending.

7.3(c) Social Security Benefits Allowed for Child Born from Deceased Father's Sperm
Summer 1996

Ending a four-year court and administrative battle, the Social Security Commissioner has now agreed to provide $700 in monthly Social Security survivor benefits to Judith Hart. In reversing its position, the Social Security Commissioner issued a statement acknowledging that the case "raises significant policy issues that were not contemplated when the Social Security Act was passed many years ago . . . recent advances in modern medical practice, particularly in the field of reproductive medicine, necessitate a careful review of current laws and regulations to ensure that they are equitable in awarding Social Security payments in cases such as this." In his own statement, one of the Harts' lawyers suggested this was a policy statement, not a legal decision, and that the Social Security Administration "just caved in. [Judith] is too cute."

A week following the final decision of the Social Security Administration, which was delivered in a press release, the federal case was dismissed.

Hart v. Chater Comm'r Soc. Sec., No. 94-3944
(E. Dis. La. 1996) (*entry of stipulation of dismissal* 3/18/96)

7.4(a) British Widow Wins Partial Victory over Husband's Sperm
Spring 1997

England's Court of Appeal has now ruled in a widow's appeal on a decision by HFEA not to release her deceased husband's sperm to her, and ordered HFEA to reconsider its refusal to allow her to take the sperm to Belgium where a clinic has offered to inseminate her. Diane Blood had appealed to the court after HFEA reconsidered but ultimately upheld its own earlier decision denying her use of the sperm either in England or abroad. The HFEA has said it will reconsider its ruling, as well as whether it will appeal the court's ruling, by February 27. Blood failed to persuade the court that HFEA did not have the authority to restrict access to treatment outside the country.

The couple had been trying to conceive before the husband contracted meningitis. While he was in a coma and on life support, doctors agreed to his wife's request to retrieve and freeze his sperm. Her subsequent request to use the sperm was refused because her husband had never given written consent as required under the British Act. When doctors in the United States and Belgium offered to treat her, HFEA reconsidered whether it would authorize release of the sperm, but then affirmed its earlier decision. It was this decision that Diane Blood unsuccessfully appealed to the High Court.

She returned to court once again in mid-January, arguing to Britain's Court of Appeal that HFEA improperly classified cases where a husband dies as donor insemination and thereby requiring written consent and moreover, that under European law's guarantee of free access to medical treatment in other member states, she has a right to be inseminated at a Belgium clinic if denied the right to treatment in Britain. After having reserved judgment at the hearing to consider the "difficult points" raised by the case, the court ruled on February 6. One of the justices noted that the decision should not create a significant precedent since the sperm should not have been frozen without the husband's consent. The court also ordered HFEA to pay Blood's legal expenses, which had reportedly cost over £50,000 and necessitated Blood mortgaging her home and raising donations. Following the ruling, the British government announced it had ordered a comprehensive review of the law and issues associated with the case.

R v. HFEA ex parte Diane Blood [1997] 2 All
ER 687; *Guardian*, 10/18/96, 11/23/96,
and 2/7/97

7.4(b) British Government to Change Law to Allow Deceased Fathers on Birth Certificate
Winter 2000

Britain is rethinking its policies following the highly publicized 1998 case of Diane Blood, a widow initially denied access to her deceased husband's sperm and, after going abroad with it to conceive, prohibited from listing him as the father of her child. Following this high-profile case, the government organized a review to examine the issue of posthumous conception. As a result the British Minister for Public Health has recently announced plans to change the law to reflect the right of such children to have their fathers listed on their birth certificates.

BBC, 8/25/00

7.4(c) Human Fertilisation Parentage Measure Stalls in British House of Commons
Summer 2001

In Britain, House of Commons debate on the proposed Human Fertilisation (Deceased Fathers) Bill has been postponed, effectively barring any chance that it will become law this session. This bill would have allowed Liam Blood to have his biological father's name on his birth certificate. Liam was conceived after Diane Blood's three-year fight for the right to use her deceased husband's sperm without his written consent. Ms. Blood has not ruled out the possibility of bringing a legal test case against the government on the basis that the current laws discriminate against Liam's right to identify himself, his background, and his parentage. At least two similar cases have arisen in the United States. In both the child was ultimately recognized as the child of their deceased father, but without an appellate decision.

Daily Telegraph, 4/29/01

7.4(d) British Widow Expecting Second Child of Deceased Husband; Challenging Paternity Laws
Spring 2002

Diane Blood has recently achieved a second pregnancy with her deceased husband's sperm and is now preparing to litigate the rights of both children to be recognized as the legal children of her deceased husband. Blood has reportedly given the government a deadline before she commences litigation and intends to argue that denying her children this legal status is a breach of her family's human rights.

Reuters, 2/8/02; *Scotsman,* 2/9/02

7.4(e) Posthumous Parentage Case Filed in Britain
Summer 2002

Three-year-old Liam Blood is beginning his own court battle, with lawyers on his behalf filing a challenge to HFEA's restriction that a man who fathers a child through the use of his sperm after his death is not the child's legal father and therefore cannot be listed on the child's birth certificate. The lawyers argue that HFEA is incompatible with Liam's right to respect for private and family life as guaranteed by the Human Rights Act and discriminates between children conceived after their fathers' deaths and others born as a result of fertility treatments.

This case follows on the heels of the first state high court opinion in the United States involving posthumous reproduction (*Woodward v. Commissioner of Social Security,* [7.9]. That court found that twins born to a widow using her deceased husband's cryopreserved sperm may be entitled to inherit from him under Massachusetts law and therefore be entitled to survivors' Social Security benefits if certain criteria are met. Even if all criteria are established, the Massachusetts court noted that there may still be issues of timeliness or competing interests of other heirs (including children already in being) that would preclude inheritance.

Guardian, 4/16/02

7.4(f) U.K. Victory for Diane Blood and Posthumously Conceived Children
Winter and Summer 2003

After protracted challenges by widow Diane Blood and other women who also became mothers using their deceased husbands' preserved sperm, recent changes in British law now allow a deceased father, including the father of Blood's two sons, to appear on the posthumously conceived child's birth certificate. The space for the child's father's name had previously been left blank. The new law, the Deceased Fathers Bill, applies not only to deceased biological fathers, but also to deceased social fathers, i.e., to children born through artificial insemination to women, married or unmarried, whose former partner did not himself provide the sperm. In that respect, the law mirrors the same position given social fathers in the Human Fertilisation Act. Blood estimates there are forty to fifty existing families who will be affected and another five to ten such births a year.

The government was reportedly forced to pass the new law after an English court suggested that the former law was incompatible with Article 8 of the European Convention on Human Rights. In contrast, in the United States, individual women have brought court challenges in only a handful of states (including Massachusetts, New Jersey, and Louisiana)—with mixed results—to attempt to have posthumously conceived children recognized to be the legal children of deceased biological fathers.

Tizzard, J., Progress Educational Trust; Bionews
226:22/9/0; BBC News and Reuters, 2/28/03

7.5 Australian Widows Seek Use of Deceaseds' Sperm
Summer 1999

Australian papers report at least seven women there have had sperm drawn from their deceased husbands or lovers and are considering attempting pregnancies. One woman last year received court approval to remove her dead lover's sperm in Victoria, where its use is prohibited. The court also ruled that the Infertility Treatment Authority allows taking sperm to another Australian state or another country. Now, a year later, she is reportedly going through formal channels to request that the Infertility Treatment Authority permit her to remove the sperm from Victoria. Her lawyer says a number of other women in similar circumstances have since sought his advice on the subject. A British widow, Diane Blood, gave birth to a child from her dead husband's sperm after winning a three-year battle for permission to take the sperm to Belgium for insemination.

Herald Sun, 3/17/99

7.6 Dead Man's Sperm Withheld from Parents in Britain
Spring 2000

An English couple is attempting to create a child using their deceased son's sperm. Lance Smith was killed in a car accident last year. Although healthy at the time of his death, Smith had stored sperm and left written instructions permitting his fiancée to use the sperm to have a child in the event of his death after reading about the case involving Diane Blood's fight to use her dead husband's sperm [7.4]. After she decided she did not want to go forward, the hospital storing the sperm refused to release the sperm to the man's parents without a court order. Unlike Diane Blood, who ultimately won the right to use her dead husband's sperm, Smith had no specific consent in place for his parents' using his sperm as now requested. The hospital claims it has been advised that releasing the sperm to Smith's parents would be illegal and that it also has concerns because Smith did not undergo counseling before banking sperm as required by HFEA rules about the welfare of any resulting child. Mr. Smith's father has been quoted as saying, "[w]e threw ourselves into this because we thought Lance could live on with a child." With the only means of parenthood specifically authorized by the dead man unavailable, the case brings up increasingly familiar and troubling issues of lack of consent and posthumous reproduction.

BBC, 12/20/99; *Telegraph,* 12/20/99;
Guardian, 12/19/99

7.7 First Birth from Posthumously Obtained Sperm
Summer 2000

In mid-March, a woman gave birth to a baby girl conceived with sperm taken from her husband more than a day after he died. Although posthumous extraction of sperm has been performed a number of times, this is apparently the first time that the procedure has resulted in a child. [According to published reports, this was also the longest post-death sperm collection attempted. Because death occurred on July 3, the body was in the morgue but inaccessible until after the July 4 holiday.]

In 1995, Cappy Rothman, M.D., extracted the sperm from Bruce Vernoff at the family's request, after Vernoff had died suddenly from a reaction to prescription medication. He had not executed any sort of written consent to such use of his sperm, but Dr. Rothman has said that he expressed his general desire to have children in a video. After one unsuccessful attempt to use the sperm for fertilization, Gaby Vernoff became pregnant.

Currently, there is no federal or state law regulating posthumous reproduction in the United States. Since few men execute a written consent to posthumous reproduction or retrieval in anticipation of their death, physicians or courts have been left to decide on a case-by-case basis whether to undertake posthumous sperm retrieval. Dr. Rothman, who performed the procedure, suggested laws should limit the use, but not the extraction, of such sperm. This birth is likely to rekindle the ethical debate over whether posthumous reproduction—including retrieval—is a private decision that the family of the deceased are entitled to make, or instead a violation of a deceased's individual right to make a deliberate decision whether or not to reproduce.

Note: See 7.15 for related case.

New York Times, 3/21/00

7.8 Posthumously Conceived IVF Twins to Inherit in New Jersey
Fall 2000

Twins born eighteen months after the death of their biological father as a result of IVF using his frozen sperm have been held to be his legal heirs by a trial judge in New Jersey. A lawyer sought the state ruling on the children's behalf after a federal administrative law judge denied them benefits. He hopes to use the state court ruling in appealing the federal case. The father died intestate (without a will) and without any estate to pass on to his heirs. Thus, Social Security Survivor benefits were the only source of potential funds available to pass on to the children. The government argued unsuccessfully that the court lacked jurisdiction on what it deemed a federal, Social Security matter.

In re Estate of William J. Kolacy, 332 N.J. Super.
593, 2000 N.J. Super. LEXIS 275

7.9 Massachusetts High Court Rules Posthumously Conceived Twins May Be Legal Heirs of Genetic Father

Spring 2002

The Massachusetts Supreme Judicial Court has ruled that twins born to a widow using her deceased husband's cryopreserved sperm may be entitled to inherit from him under current state law and therefore entitled to survivors' Social Security benefits if certain criteria are met. The children were born two years after their father's death from cancer. As this is the first state appellate court to decide this issue, the court's concerns and rulings may provide guidance to ART programs looking to ensure that their gamete and embryo disposition consent forms best protect their patients and their programs.

The court identified three critical requirements for inheritance eligibility under Massachusetts law: (1) proof that the children are the genetic children of the deceased; (2) proof that he affirmatively consented to posthumous reproduction; and (3) proof that he affirmatively consented to support any resulting children. The court emphasized the "double consent" requirement was necessary because, while a man facing medical treatment that may leave him sterile may want to preserve the possibility of having children later in life, the mere act of storing sperm does not necessarily indicate an intention to father children after death. Even with such evidence, there may also be issues of timeliness or competing interests of other heirs (including children already in being) that preclude inheritance. The court made it clear that widows or other representatives of such children seeking inheritance rights will need to go to court to establish paternity and consent, and must formally notify "every other interested party," including other potential heirs.

It is likely that programs' consent processes and forms may be drawn into such cases as evidence of the deceased patient's intent, and failure to obtain appropriate consents may entangle ART programs in these court actions. Programs will want to ensure that patients cryopreserving genetic material clearly record their intentions as to all subsequent authorized uses of it. Consents may also need to state clearly that programs cannot guarantee that any resulting children from the medical procedures will be considered heirs or entitled to other benefits and recommend patients seek outside legal and estate planning advice.

Woodward v. Commissioner of Social Security,
435 Mass. 536 (Mass. 2002)

7.10(a) Arizona Federal Court Denies Posthumous Social Security Benefits
Spring 2003

Two children conceived more than ten months after their biological father's death with his frozen sperm are not entitled to receive Social Security survivors' benefits, according to a U.S. District Court's interpretation of Arizona inheritance law. At least one similar case has come to the opposite conclusion, based on a different state's laws.

Soon after their marriage, Rhonda Gillett and Robert Netting began fertility treatments after failing to achieve a pregnancy on their own. After being diagnosed with cancer, Netting banked sperm before beginning chemotherapy treatments. According to both his widow and her doctor, although not put in writing, Netting knew and agreed that his sperm could be used to impregnate his wife after his death.

After artificial inseminations failed, Ms. Gillett ultimately became pregnant through IVF using the stored sperm. Following the birth of twins, she filed a claim on their behalf for Social Security survivor's benefits. Under Arizona's intestate succession provisions, only a child who survives the deceased parent or was in gestation at the time of death may inherit. Because the twins had not yet been conceived at the time of death, the Social Security Administration and court found the twins were not entitled to benefits under the Act. The court also rejected the argument that the children's equal protection rights had been violated.

The court recognized its decision was at odds with a similar case decided under Massachusetts law, *Woodward v. Commissioner of Social Security* [7.9]. In that case, however, Massachusetts's intestacy laws did not explicitly limit succession to children "in gestation" and, unlike Arizona's laws, were written a century before assisted reproductive technologies were available. . . . [t]he court also distinguished a similar case in New Jersey (*Kolacy*), where a lower court decision allowed the benefits, as having interpreted underlying New Jersey law. Until and unless uniform or model ART legislation (such as the Uniform Parentage Act) is widely adopted by states, courts will be required to interpret varying inheritance laws of individual states and inconsistent rulings are likely to continue in this area.

Gillett-Netting v. Barnhart, 231 F. Supp. 2d 961
(D. Ariz. 2002)

7.10(b) Appellate Court Reverses: Awards Children Benefits
June 2004

The Ninth Circuit has reversed a federal district court's ruling and found the Gillett-Netting twins are legitimate under state law, and therefore did not have to prove either dependency or their legitimacy under federal law. The court noted Arizona had abolished legal distinctions based on legitimacy and found that under that state's law, "Netting would be treated as the natural parent of Juliet and Piers [the twins] and would have a legal obligation to support them if he were alive, although they were conceived using in-vitro fertilization, because he is their biological father and was married to the mother of the children" and cited Arizona's artificial insemination statute. It went on to add that, "[a]lthough Arizona law does not deal specifically with posthumously conceived children, every child in Arizona, which necessarily includes Juliet and Piers, is the legitimate child of her or his natural parents." The court's willingness to adapt and apply older statutes to newer forms of family building resulted in the reversal.

Gillett-Netting v. Barnhart, 371 F.3d 593 (9th Cir. 2004)

7.11 New York Finds Two Posthumously Conceived Children Entitled to Inherit

Fall 2007

In a case of first impression in that state, a New York court has ruled that two children born to their widowed mother from her deceased husband's sperm are legally considered his children and as such, entitled to inherit from their grandfather's estate. What makes the case particularly unusual was that the children were born several years after both the deaths of their biological father and grandfather and that the sperm was left to the man's widow simply with instructions to do with it what she saw fit.

The seven trusts were created in 1969 and directed funds be distributed to the grandfather's "issue" and "descendants." The trustees sought direction from the court, which found that although the facts could not have been contemplated at the time of the trusts, it was clear that the grandfather wanted his sons and their families to inherit equally, and therefore, "a sympathetic reading . . . warrants the conclusion that the Grantor intended all members of his bloodline to receive their share."

Somewhat paradoxically, New York recently amended its laws on wills to exclude "post-conceived" children from a parent's estate unless there was a specific provision in that individual's will. The court noted that not only was the new law expressly limited to parent-to-child wills, but also involved different issues such as when a class of beneficiaries is defined for purposes of probating an estate (raised by deciding whether a decedent was a parent of the posthumous child) rather than distributing it as was the case here. Former Governor Mario Cuomo, the guardian ad litem for the children, has applauded the decision and suggested it should help the legislature in addressing these issues.

In the Matter of Martin B, 841 N.Y.S.2d 207
(Surr. Ct. of N.Y. 2007)

7.12(a) Arkansas Court Rejects Posthumous Parentage Claim

Summer 2008

The Arkansas Supreme Court is the latest high state court to weigh in on the legitimacy of posthumous born children. The case involved a child born to a widow from a frozen embryo implanted a little less than a year after her husband's death. The court refused to recognize the legitimacy of the child for purposes of inheritance or Social Security benefits. Instead, it adopted a literal interpretation of a 1969 Arkansas statute, in acknowledged contrast to some of the other states that have faced this issue. The Arkansas statute in question reads: "[p]osthumous descendants of the intestate conceived before his or her death but born thereafter shall inherit in the same manner as if born in the lifetime of the intestate." The widow's attorney argued that the child was "conceived" at the time the embryo was created and frozen, but the court rejected that argument or any other interpretation of the law in her favor. The court also refused to apply or extend the state's artificial insemination statute, which recognizes a child "conceived following artificial insemination of a married woman with the consent of her husband shall be treated as their child for all purposes of intestate succession."

The court could have, but declined to, read the statutes more broadly or to adapt them to technologies that did not exist when the statutes were passed. It ruled that to define the term "conceive" would be making a determination with multiple public policy implications, a role that it found should be the exclusive province of the legislature. It concluded its opinion, as have many courts resolving ART disputes, with a plea to the state legislature to "revisit the intestacy succession statutes to address the issues involved in the instant case and those that have not but will likely evolve."

While the court could have perhaps reached a different conclusion by extending the reasoning of a statute that predated the technology, if it had accepted the principle that conception occurs in an IVF embryo upon fertilization and freezing the court would have created significant and widespread implications far beyond the inheritance issue at hand.

Finley v. Astrue, 2008 Ark. LEXIS 2 (1/10/08)

7.12(b) Arkansas Court Now Denies Workers' Compensation Benefits to Posthumous Born Child; Rejects Embryo Storage Fees as Basis for "Dependency"

Fall 2009

Having lost a court battle for Social Security survivor benefits earlier in 2008, an Arkansas widow has now also lost her attempt to have her son receive workers' compensation benefits as a "dependent child" of her deceased husband.

The case now decided by the Arkansas intermediate appellate court presented a somewhat unusual fact pattern: a few weeks after Amy and Wade Finley Jr. underwent an IVF procedure and embryo transfer (which was unsuccessful) and cryopreservation of four embryos, Wade Finley Jr. was killed in an employment-related accident. Eleven months later, Amy Finley used two of their remaining embryos, gave birth to Wade III, and then sought both Social Security and workers' compensation benefits.

Amy Finley made more novel arguments in her effort to obtain benefits, including that because the couple had paid storage fees for their fertilized embryos, "the embryo was wholly and actually dependent" on Wade Jr. at the time of his death. The Court of Appeals decided it need not determine if the embryo was a "person" because it did not find the embryo "wholly and actually dependent" on Wade Jr. at the time of his death. The court rejected Finley's argument that frozen embryo storage fees were the types of support contemplated by the law. "Though [frozen embryo] storage fees are akin to housing, we decline to adopt this creative reading of the statute."

Finley also attempted to argue that Wade III's constitutional rights were violated by depriving a "whole new class of children" rights because they "were not conceived and born in a 'normal' or 'accepted' manner." Since she had not made that argument in the lower court as required, the appellate court refused to consider it.

Finley v. Farm Cat., Inc., 103 Ark.App. 292

(Ark. Ct. App. 2008)

7.13 New Hampshire Court Denies Paternity in Posthumous Birth
Winter 2008

The Supreme Court of New Hampshire has added its views to a growing body of law involving parentage of children conceived with frozen sperm from a decedent. In doing so it rejected the reasoning of a number of other courts deciding similar cases. The New Hampshire court ruled its state intestacy law precluded a child conceived after her father's death via artificial insemination from eligibility to inherit from him as his surviving issue. Rejecting a series of arguments made on behalf of the child, which were based on a number of other New Hampshire statutes, the Court concluded that the question was governed solely by its intestacy statute, and interpreted the statute's term "surviving issue" to preclude any child who was not born prior to the decedent's death. Although the facts were very similar to the Massachusetts court decision, *Woodward v. Commissioner of Social Security* [7.9], where the decedent had affirmatively consented both to posthumous reproduction and to support any resulting children, the New Hampshire court declined to read the statute more broadly or follow the ruling or rationale of *Woodward*. It did, however, emphasize the need for clarifying legislation to address the important public policy considerations at stake. With this most recent court decision, the states are now clearly divided on this issue.

Khabbaz v. Commissioner, Social Security Administration, 930 A.2d.1180 (N.H. 2007)

7.14 Two Trial Courts Allow Posthumous Harvesting of Sperm without Prior Consent

Trial court judges in Texas and New York have both approved posthumous harvesting of sperm at the request of one dead man's mother and the other's fiancée. Both men died unexpectedly. Neither left written instructions or other records or evidence of any desire to create a child posthumously. In the Texas case, Marissa Evans persuaded a judge to harvest her twenty-one-year-old son's sperm after he died in a street assault. She said her son, Nikolas, always wanted to have children, had frequently spoken of having three sons, and that she would attempt to create a child with the assistance of a surrogate, saying, "I want him to live on" and "I want to keep a piece of him." In New York, thirty-one-year-old Johnny Quintana's sperm was harvested after he collapsed and died suddenly. A judge approved the harvesting at the request of his fiancée, who is the mother of a two-year-old that he had fathered. She said they had talked as recently as the day before he died about having another child, and said this is "the last thing I can do for him."

Austin American-Statesman (4/08/09);

BBC News (4/19/09)

7.15 No Social Security Benefits for California Child Born from Posthumously Retrieved Sperm

Summer 2009

The federal Ninth Circuit has upheld a denial of Social Security benefits for a ten-year-old California girl born three years after her biological father's accidental death with the use of sperm extracted from his body posthumously [see 7.7]. In a careful analysis of California law, the court distinguished its decision from one it made just months earlier under Arizona law allowing such benefits to posthumously conceived twins (*Gilllet-Netting v. Barnhart*, [7.10]).

It found the California couple had no other children and "no evidence to suggest that Bruce consented to the [posthumous extraction] procedure, or had ever contemplated having a child postmortem," whereas the Arizona husband had delayed cancer treatment to deposit sperm and before he died confirmed he wanted his wife to use it to have their child.

In contrast to Arizona's emphasis on biology, the court ruled that parentage under California law requires intent to create and willingness to support a child, as well as dependency on the deceased at the time of death. It also ruled that denying benefits to *this* posthumously conceived child was not an equal protection violation against all such children. Interestingly, it did not question the widow's posthumous extraction and use of the sperm without consent. That issue will need to wait for another day.

Vernoff v. Astrue, 568 F.3d 1102 (9th Cir. 6/17/09)

CHAPTER EIGHT

Same-Sex Parentage and ART

❖ MEDICAL COMMENTARY, BY Howard W. Jones, Jr.

ART BY DEFINITION is technology that requires the laboratory processing of gametes from both a male and a female. In the case of lesbian or gay couples, ART may or may not be required. Generally speaking, in the case of lesbian couples, ART is often not used, on the assumption that the only requirement is a sperm donor. Some lesbian couples obtain fresh semen samples informally and inject the semen with a syringe into the vagina of the partner who is to carry the pregnancy. This can be medically dangerous as it predisposes to sexually transmitted diseases. If sperm are obtained from a licensed andrology laboratory, the sperm donor and the sperm will have been screened and tested to try to eliminate several diseases as specified by the FDA. Furthermore, the sperm must be quarantined for six months and the donor found to be free of HIV before the sperm can be thawed, released, and used. Sperm donors to licensed laboratories do not usually know (except in special cases or certain labs) who the recipient will be, and historically most donors have not wanted to know.

While the medical facts are not discussed in many of the cases abstracted in this chapter and seem to be of little interest to the courts, it seems likely that in the case of many lesbian couples, the donors were socially recruited with no medical assistance required. While this may have no legal significance in the outcome of a dispute, it certainly has medical significance and may reflect a lesser degree of sophistication on the part of the participants regarding the medical risks associated with fresh semen. As the cases illustrate, it can also contribute to confusion over the status of the male as a donor or intended parent. On the other hand, for some lesbian couples, ART is required or desired, as for example when the egg of one of the partners is used with donor sperm to transfer the resultant conceptus into the uterus of the other lesbian partner.

In the case of male same-sex couples, ART is frequently used, although ART can be avoided if a traditional surrogate can be found who will accept the semen of one of the partners. Sometimes the semen of both partners has been mixed for injecting into the traditional surrogate or for fertilizing eggs in vitro for an ART procedure. ART is always required if a gestational surrogate carrier is used with donor egg and the semen of one or both of the men is used.

Medical personnel, regardless of the combination of steps or events toward parenting that can occur in lesbian and gay partnerships, eventually will become involved in trying to achieve or maintain a pregnancy. Therefore, the ethical aspects of the participation of medical personnel in gay and lesbian parental attempts come sharply into focus.

The Ethics Committee of the American Society for Reproductive Medicine has considered the matter of homosexual couples involved in procreation. An ASRM ethics report published in November 2006 available on ASRM's website (www.asrm.org) addresses this matter and is titled, "Access to Fertility Treatment by Gays, Lesbians, and Unmarried Persons." It points out that unmarried persons and gays and lesbians have an interest in having and rearing children and concludes that ART programs should treat all requests for assisted reproduction equally without regard to marital status or sexual orientation. This conclusion was based on a study of the literature in which it was found that there was no persuasive evidence that children raised by single parents or by gays and lesbians are harmed or disadvantaged by that fact alone.

Thus, it seems to be the view of the Ethics Committee that ART programs should treat all patients with all due diligence and respond to their requests. However, it should be pointed out that the law trumps ethical considerations. Many states have laws bearing on surrogacy, for example, and it behooves any program faced with a request from a lesbian or gay couple to familiarize itself with the law that applies in that particular state, especially if a surrogate or gestational carrier is involved. Furthermore, as pointed out in one of the legal cases reported on in this chapter (K.M. v. E.G., 2005), programs should be very careful in ensuring that their consent forms conform to the situation at hand. Specifically, if one of the lesbian partners is to contribute an egg to be gestated by the other partner, it is not enough to use the program's standard donor egg consent form, as such forms usually indicate that the donor is relinquishing all parental rights. In these particular situations, it is important to pay careful attention to any state law that may be applied; as these are quite variable, it is necessary to have a consent form that applies to the particular situation. As cases involving same-sex parents are still relatively rare, it is important to seek out the legal advice of a professional experienced in this area in drawing up such consent forms.

∿ LEGAL COMMENTARY, BY Susan L. Crockin

The law's responses to the increasing use of ART procedures by same-sex couples has profoundly affected, and in many respects transformed, family law. Nowhere is the interplay between existing law and the new technologies more pronounced or had a more significant impact. The laws of adoption, custody, presumptions and recognition of parentage (including both donor insemination and ART statutes, as well as common law presumptions), child support, conflict of laws, comity, full faith and credit, and the federal Defense of Marriage Act (DOMA) have all been implicated.

Long before the advent of assisted reproductive technology, lesbian women have adopted as single parents or used artificial insemination, with sperm obtained from both anonymous sperm banks and known sperm donors. Frequently, the couple's inability to undertake a co-parent adoption and/or the lack of a biological tie for one partner left the resulting family unrecognized and unprotected in the eyes of established family law principles in most states.

The growing acceptance of same-sex families, as exemplified in the recent and dramatic increase in the number of states recognizing same-sex marriages, is bringing sweeping changes to how family law is interpreted, applied, and in some cases simply reversed when addressing the status of same-sex families. Same-sex marriages have been recognized by courts in Massachusetts (2004), California (2008; subsequently reversed by referendum, with litigation ongoing), Connecticut (2008), and Iowa (2009); by state legislatures in Vermont, Maine, and New Hampshire (2009); and by the District of Columbia for out-of-state marriages

(2009). Even without legal marriage—or before it in these few states—courts and legislatures have been increasingly confronted with the realities and resulting need to address the many legal issues surrounding same-sex families.

The cases in this chapter reflect these challenges and dramatic changes. Starting in 1993, two state appellate courts (Massachusetts and Vermont) became the first to recognize the legality of same-sex couple adoptions. In 1995, two more jurisdictions (New York and Washington, D.C.) followed suit, as did California in 2003. During those years, thousands of lower courts in many states allowed such adoptions, regardless of whether their appellate courts had pronounced these relationships legally binding under state law. Most of the courts found existing adoption laws sufficiently expansive to recognize these families. A few notable exceptions still include Florida, which bans same-sex adoptions, a ruling whose constitutionality was upheld on appeal, subsequently rejected by two lower courts in 2008 and in 2009, and is once again before an appellate court.

With the advent of IVF, an increasing number of female couples began sharing pregnancies, with one partner supplying the eggs and the other carrying the pregnancy. Some of these situations arose from medical needs, others by the choice of the couple. In a groundbreaking decision in 2000, a Massachusetts court found that both partners of a female couple were legal parents based on their respective genetic and gestational ties to the resulting child—without the need for an adoption. Since then, similarly positioned female same-sex couples in many states have obtained pre-birth orders recognizing both of them as legal parents.

Unfortunately, in a society where approximately 50 percent of marriages end in divorce, same-sex couples also separate and have inevitably challenged existing laws when they disagree over parentage, custody, and child support. These cases have at times stretched over years and across multiple states; many cases turned on judicial interpretations of older laws and "best interest of the child" standards. In a few such cases, it was apparent that medical consent forms and oral informal agreements between the former partners and between the former couple and their sperm donors have added layers (and years) of uncertainty and litigation, with the children inevitably caught in the middle of these struggles.

Former partners moving from one state to another have also created the need to resolve sometimes conflicting laws—and brought esoteric legal concepts such as "full faith and credit" and "comity" into sharp focus in these highly emotional arenas. Thus, when two women who had been in a legally recognized Vermont civil union separated and the biological mother moved to Virginia, it set off a series of court decisions in both states that have stretched over five years as of this writing. The Virginia Supreme Court finally ruled that that state was required to recognize the Vermont civil union under constitutionally based principles of "full faith and credit," regardless of its own disapproving views of such unions. By that point, the child was four years old and had not seen her second mother for three years. Despite that ruling and two subsequently denied applications for review to the U.S. Supreme Court, the girl's biological mother, who has since renounced her homosexuality and has the backing of several interest groups, has continued to resist visitation, facing contempt charges, and ongoing court hearings (*Miller-Jenkins v. Miller-Jenkins*, 2008).

Sperm donors have also played a significant role in the development of the law involving same-sex couples and their families. In some cases, known donors have succeeded in having themselves recognized as a legal parent, with visitation rights and child support obligations. In others, courts have ruled that they have no parental rights or obligations under existing donor insemination statutes or as a matter of constitutional law and public policy. In one case (*Lamaratita v. Lucas*, 2002), ironically involving a challenge to Florida's relatively recent ART statute, a known sperm donor claimed that he was instead part of a "commissioning couple" under that statute (which does not explicitly define the term *donor*) and thus entitled to recognition as a father. After multiple levels of court hearings, which exposed the vulnerability of even progressive statutes aimed at addressing ART families, the man's claim ultimately failed.

In many of the cases involving parentage of children born to same-sex couples, the courts have carefully attempted to glean the parties' intentions based on any existing written documents (including consent forms and private agreements) and the parties' actions, pointing out the advisability of parties memorializing their true intentions at the outset. Courts have also noted that medical programs must ensure that their consent forms are current and accurate as applied to a specific set of patients. Although ultimately reversed, both a California trial and intermediate appellate court initially ruled against the genetic mother of twins born to her former same-sex partner, largely based on the gestational mother's contention that her former partner had been simply an egg donor as their boilerplate medical consent forms reflected (*K.M. v. E.G.*, 2006).

Inevitably, same-sex couples have cited existing laws to attempt to avoid as well as to assert familial status and obligations. Thus, in two cases a former partner argued that since she had no biological or legal connection to the child, she should not be held to child support obligations (an argument similarly made, unsuccessfully, by a married man, John Buzzanca, in a case involving gestational surrogacy). In one case the woman succeeded, having left the relationship before the child's birth as the court ruled that her promise was only to stay in the relationship, not specifically to support the child financially (*T.F. v. B.L.*, 2004). Again, the benefit of clear, written agreements is apparent. Indeed, that case also points up the potential malpractice issues for legal professionals who counsel same-sex couples in states that do not recognize such unions. Had that couple had an agreement to support any resulting child financially, the court's ruling suggests that commitment would have been enforceable.

The groundbreaking Massachusetts case recognizing same-sex marriage (*Goodrich v. Dept. Public Health*, 2003) has had some unexpected, and ironic, implications. After passage of DOMA (the federal Defense of Marriage Act, which allows a state to disregard a marriage from a state that conflicts with its own public policy), legally married same-sex couples faced a novel legal conundrum. Within Massachusetts they did not need an adoption or pre-birth order, or indeed any additional legal steps, for both partners to be fully recognized as parents of a child born to one of them. They could instead rely on a gender-neutral interpretation of that state's artificial insemination statute (Massachusetts does not have a donor egg statute). Outside of Massachusetts, however, if their marriage was not legally recognized, one member of the couple would have virtually no legal rights to their child. Thus, in a somewhat ironic twist, but one endorsed and strongly recommended by lawyers and courts in that state, the vast majority of same-sex, legally married couples in Massachusetts are *also* legally adopting their child after birth. By taking that additional legal step in reliance on the oldest adoption laws in the nation, these couples ensure legal recognition of their parent-child relationship in any state. In that same vein, a few states have failed in their attempts to refuse to recognize adoptions by same-sex couples who return home after adopting in a state that endorses such adoptions (*Finstuen et al. v. Edmondson et al.*, 2007). In 2009, both individual couples and the Massachusetts attorney general sued to prevent DOMA's reach into Massachusetts.

Male same-sex couples face additional legal issues, since they cannot physically produce eggs or carry and deliver their own child. Thus, male same-sex couples have found themselves either working with a traditional surrogate, with all of the inherent legal vulnerabilities or, more frequently, both an egg donor and a gestational carrier, at considerable additional cost and complexity. In the latter instance, although there is little appellate law, many such male couples are either obtaining pre-birth orders of dual parentage or undergoing a co-parent adoption after their child's birth—or both—for the same reasons female same-sex couples do. There has been far less litigation involving custody or rights to children by same-sex male couples than female couples. This may reflect both the more recent entry into parenthood in large numbers by same-sex male couples and the more complex path they must take to parenthood. Since men cannot casually obtain an egg and achieve a pregnancy, as their female counterparts are able to do with sperm, informal arrangements, and the vulnerabilities they may give rise to, are less common. Unless a male couple is working with a traditional surrogate, they have likely undergone a significantly more complex series of steps to achieve parenthood, including entering into formal agreements with an egg donor and gestational surrogate, with all the legal protections and counseling that forming such arrangements bring.

Notwithstanding the many advances in this area, same-sex couples of both sexes remain more vulnerable as parents than traditional, married, heterosexual couples. As a result, both courts and commentators continue to emphasize the need for and the benefits of informed, written records of intentions (including consent forms and legal agreements) and sound legal advice. Until such time as same-sex marriage is more widely recognized in more states and so long as DOMA remains in effect, it is critical that couples recognize and take advantage of all available legal steps to secure their rights and those of their children.

Litigation

8.1 Lesbian Couples Allowed to Adopt Partners' Children (Vermont, D.C.)
March 1992

Two courts have recently granted adoptions to two lesbian couples. A District of Columbia court granted joint parental rights to a lesbian couple over each other's children. A Vermont court allowed the co-adoption by a woman of her lesbian partner's adopted child. Both courts stated that their rulings were in the best interest of the children involved. Washington, D.C., and Vermont are now among approximately seven jurisdictions to grant such rights to gay or lesbian couples. The courts each rejected an interpretation of their adoption statute that appeared to require one of the women to first relinquish her parental rights—a common approach to addressing biological parents' rights in adoption statutes.

In re Adoption of RC, No. 9088, slip op. at 5-7

(Addison Prob. Ct. Dec. 9, 1991)

8.2 Same-Sex Co-Parent Adoptions Recognized in Two High State Courts (Massachusetts, Vermont)
December 1993

In two closely watched cases, the Vermont and Massachusetts Supreme Courts recently became the first two state high courts to recognize co-parent adoptions between two unmarried adopters. In both cases, the adopters were two women partners in longstanding monogamous lesbian relationships. Each high court ruled that their adoption statutes could be interpreted liberally enough to permit a co-parent adoption without first requiring the biological parent to relinquish her parental rights.

In the Vermont case, the court ruled that the couple's adoption of the two children born to one of the women from the same anonymous sperm donor would be in the children's best interest. "Deborah," as she was known in the court papers, sought to adopt "Jane's" two children, without simultaneously terminating Jane's parental rights.

The lower court in Vermont had refused either to allow the adoption or to consider the children's best interests since it ruled that the adoption statutes first required the termination of the biological mother's rights, and found the "stepparent" exception inapplicable. Under that exception, a biological parent does not have to relinquish parental rights to have his or her child adopted by their spouse.

The Vermont Supreme Court took a more flexible approach, finding that the intent of the adoption statutes as a whole was to "clarify and protect the legal rights of the adopted person at the time the adoption is complete, not to proscribe adoptions by certain combinations of individuals." Although recognizing that the adoption statutes were never drafted with same-sex adoptions in mind, the court nonetheless held that the legislature could not have meant to terminate the parental rights of biological parents who intended to continue raising their child with a partner, and thus approved the adoption.

The Massachusetts court reached a similar ruling in a case involving breast cancer specialist Susan Love, M.D., and her partner. The Massachusetts court found that it was in the best interest of Dr. Love's biological child, Tammy, to be adopted by both women, and determined that no parental rights needed to be terminated to accomplish the co-parent adoption.

Like the Vermont court, the Massachusetts court recognized that its adoption statutes did not contemplate this form of adoption at the time they were passed. Nonetheless, the court found nothing that prohibited nonmarried or same-sex partners from adopting together and therefore approved the adoption.

As the Vermont court stated: "It is not the courts that have engendered the diverse composition of today's families. It is the advancement of the reproductive technologies and society's recognition of alternative lifestyles that have produced families in which a biological and therefore a legal connection is no longer the sole organizing principle. But it is the courts that are required to define, declare and protect the rights of children raised in these families. . . ."

Adoptions of B.L.V.B. and E.L.V.B., 160 Vt. 368
(Vt. 1993); *Adoption of Tammy*,
416 Mass. 205 (Mass. 1993)

8.3 Homosexual Adoptions at Center of More Legal Battles (New Jersey, Florida)

March 1994

Lower courts in New Jersey and Florida have reached opposite conclusions about homosexual couples adopting. A New Jersey court approved the adoption of a twelve-year-old child by her mother's long-time lesbian partner, concluding that the adoption was in the child's best interest. That court relied on the recent Vermont Supreme Court's decision [8.2] and compared the adoption to that of a step-parent, which does not require the biological mother to first relinquish any rights.

In contrast, a Florida court has upheld that state's ban on homosexual adoptions. Florida is currently one of only two states with such a ban. The Florida court ruled that its ban was not unconstitutionally vague, but restricted only those who engage in homosexual activity from adoptions. It further found that adoption was a privilege and not a right, which could be withheld from those who voluntarily elect to engage in and disclose their homosexual activity.

> *Matter of Adoption of a Child by J.M.G.*, 267 N.J.
> Super. 622 (Ch. Div. 1993); *Dept. Health & Rehab.*
> *Servs. v. Cox*, 627 So. 2d 1210 (Fla. Dist. Ct. App. 1993);
> *aff'd* (with partial remand), 656 So. 2d 902 (Fla. 1995)

8.4 New Jersey Court Permits Lesbian to Adopt Partner's Twins

December 1995

BY K. ZIESELMAN

A New Jersey Court of Appeals has ruled that a woman may legally adopt her lesbian partner's three-year-old twins born via artificial insemination. In a split decision, the majority decided it was in the best interests of the children to allow the forty-seven-year-old woman they call "Mom" to adopt the twins. Their biological mother, whom they call "Mommy," has lived with her lesbian partner for fourteen years, and the women have shared the twins' rearing. The decision overturns a lower court ruling and may establish legal precedent in New Jersey. There appear to be an increasing number of state court decisions granting adoption rights to same-sex couples, including fairly recent decisions in Washington, D.C., Illinois, Massachusetts,

Vermont, and Washington [8.2 and 8.3]. However, the Wisconsin Supreme Court rejected such an adoption petition last year.

In re Adoption of Two Children by H.N.R., 285 N.J. Super. 1 (App. Div. 1995)

8.5 New York's Highest Court Rules Same-Sex Couples May Adopt

December 1995

BY K. ZIESELMAN

New York is now the third state (joining Vermont and Massachusetts, as well as the District of Columbia) whose highest court has ruled that homosexual couples may legally adopt children. . . . Patricia Irwin gave birth to her daughter five years ago after being inseminated with sperm from an anonymous donor. She and her lesbian partner have been together for nineteen years. Overruling a lower court decision, the Court of Appeals decided, by a vote of four to three, that since single adults can legally adopt, the right to adopt must be extended to qualified unmarried couples, regardless of their sexual orientation.

In the Matter of Jacob, 86 N.Y.2d 651 (N.Y. 1995)
[consolidated cases]

8.6 Legal Status of Twins Born in California to British Gay Couple Uncertain

Spring 2000

A gay British couple, after being denied treatment in England, have fathered twins with the help of an American egg donor and an American gestational carrier. The children were born in California, and through a California court order obtained birth certificates listing the two men as their parents. The couple, Barrie Drewitt and Tony Barlow, reportedly had been denied in their earlier efforts to adopt in England. Both men's sperm were used and they have declined to disclose DNA test results. Upon the babies' entry to the United Kingdom, British immigration officials reportedly told the couple that the babies do not qualify for automatic residency and confiscated the babies' passports. Arguably Britain is not required to recognize the U.S. court order or that either of the men is a parent and the government has suggested the couple should now go through adoption proceedings there to ensure their children's parentage and nationality. The men noted that their previous five years of adoptive efforts in Britain were unsuccessful. The children have been granted a one-month temporary stay in Britain. The couple's next step is not yet clear. Their options include: applying for an extension of the temporary stay to begin a possibly long and uncertain adoption process; asking Britain's Home Secretary to intervene and grant the children residency; applying for entry clearance rather than citizenship for the twins (who would then remain American nationals but be allowed to live in the United Kingdom); or take the case to the European Court of Human Rights alleging discrimination against the children of gay couples. Meanwhile, some British commentators have said that the American gestational carrier and her husband are, under British law, the only legally recognizable parents of the children. The carrier, who has four children of her own, has said that she is willing to act as a gestational carrier for the couple again if they wish to pursue another child with any of their remaining twenty frozen embryos.

Sacramento Bee, 12/12/99; *Boston Globe*, 1/9/00

8.7 Israeli Court Recognizes Two Mothers under Comity Principles
Fall 2000

Israel's High Court of Justice has ordered the government to register both members of a lesbian couple as the mothers of the two boys they are raising together. In doing so, the court ruled that the recognition is of legal, not biological, parentage. The women are dual U.S. and Israeli citizens, and the nonbiological mother adopted one of the children under California law.

The couple successfully argued their case on the narrow legal principle of comity. Under that principle, countries recognize and respect foreign determinations even if such determinations are not recognized under their own laws. Thus, the women prevailed on the argument that Israel recognizes the legal standing granted to its citizens abroad, even if it doesn't recognize the same standing in Israel. The decision was denounced by the Orthodox legislators as judicial overstepping.

H.C.J. 1779/99 *Berner-Kadish v. Minister of Interior*, 54 P.D. 368 (2000) (Israel High Court of Justice); *New York Times*, 6/3/00

8.8 Massachusetts Trial Court Allows Two Mothers to Be Listed on Birth Certificate

Winter 2000

A trial court in Massachusetts has ordered the names of a lesbian couple be placed on their child's birth certificate without requiring a co-parent adoption where it found both had a biological connection to the child. One of the women gave birth to the child conceived through IVF using her partner's egg and anonymous donor sperm. In its decision, the Court employed a two-part test for legal parenthood: (1) the intention to create a child together; and (2) a biological connection to the child through birth or genetics. Under these facts, the court found that each woman had a sufficient connection to the child to establish her legal parenthood and ordered the child's birth certificate to so reflect that without the necessity of a co-parent adoption. The decision does not appear to open the door to parental recognition of a partner without either such a biological connection or a co-parent adoption.

Knoll v. Beth Israel Deaconess Med. Ctr., No.
00W-1343 (Mass. Suff. Prob. & Fam. Ct. 2000)

8.9 Colorado Supreme Court Denies State's Appeal of "Two-Mom" Birth Certificates

Winter 2000

The Colorado Supreme Court has denied an appeal by its Department of Public Health and Environment of seven cases where two District Court judges allowed lesbian couples to place both mothers' names on their children's birth certificates. In contrast to the Massachusetts case (*Knoll v. BIDMC*, [8.8]), only one of the women in each couple was the genetic and gestational mother; the other had no genetic connection to the child. The state agency argued that the judges lacked the legal authority to create a new kind of nontraditional parent-child relationship, and that such lawmaking should be left to the legislature. Lawyers for the lesbian couples, on the other hand, claimed that banning same-gender parents from a child's birth certificate would be discriminatory and contrary to the child's best interests.

Colorado Dept. of Public Health & Env. v. E.C.V. et al., Colo. S. Ct.
No. 00SA-272 (unpublished opinion); *Denver News*, 8/22/00

8.10 Three-Way Minnesota Custody Battle Appealed to U.S. Supreme Court

Spring 2001

An eight-year-old girl is at the center of an unusual custody battle between her biological mother, her mother's former lesbian partner, and the known sperm donor who had successfully sought to be recognized as her father. Minnesota's law on artificial insemination, like the majority of such statutes, only applies to married couples. The child's biological mother, Denise Mitten, has now appealed her case to the U.S. Supreme Court.

According to Mitten, she and her then-partner, Valerie Ohanian, intentionally chose a friend, Mark LaChappelle, to be the child's sperm donor. In December 1990, LaChappelle reportedly signed an agreement waiving any parental rights. Shortly after Mitten became pregnant, however, he expressed a desire to be part of the child's life. The three then signed another agreement, which they termed "an agreement in the best interests of the child." There they agreed that LaChappelle would have a "significant relationship" with the child. The girl was born in January 1993 and legally adopted by Ohanian. What those terms and agreement mean are now in dispute.

The women sought court intervention to limit LaChappelle's role and he sought full legal status as the child's father. The court voided the adoption on the grounds that it had been misled about the father's presence and granted LaChappelle's request for parental status in 1997. The women then broke up and, with court permission and an award of visitation for both the former partner and now-legal father, the biological mother and child moved to Michigan. The monthly visitation arrangement involved flying the child to the Twin Cities and the father and former partner flying to Michigan in alternating months.

After complaints from Ohanian and LaChappelle that the distance was impairing their relationship with the child, in 1999 the court ordered full custody to Mitten on the condition she move back to the Twin Cities. The court then appointed a "special parenting panel" to help the three adults work out their various disagreements outside the court. According to Mitten, the three were in court twice a month. The child currently has twice-weekly visitation with the other two adults in her life, and all three share important decisions for the child, including education, religion, and health care.

The three-way arrangement has not been smooth. According to Mitten, "Nothing has been as scary, as out of control, as once you go to court." She has now challenged the order that she live in the Twin Cities to the U.S. Supreme Court for possible consideration. Few such cases, however, are taken by the highest court. The arrangement, which many would advocate for nontraditional families, may highlight some of the difficulties for such families without clear legal protections.

LaChappelle v. Mitten, 607 N.W.2d 151
(Minn. Ct. App. 2000); 2000 Minn. App. LEXIS 226

8.11 Delaware Court Orders Lesbian Ex-Partner to Pay Child Support
Summer 2002

A Delaware Family Court has ordered a woman to pay child support for the child she and her former lesbian partner created together through fertility treatments. The women separated after the child's birth. Karen, the biological mother, sought mandatory child support after Carol was awarded permanent visitation rights. Carol argued against the child support order, arguing that she had no biological or adoptive connection to the child and that Delaware does not legally recognize same-sex couples. Under a broad interpretation of the Delaware Parentage Act, the court ordered support despite the absence of any biological connection between Carol and the child.

Chambers v. Chambers, No. CN99-09493, 2005
Del.Fam.Ct. LEXIS (Del. Fam. Ct. 1/12/05)

8.12 Co-Parent Adoption Recognized in Child's State of Birth (Mississippi)
Summer 2003

A child born in Mississippi and adopted by a lesbian couple in Vermont is entitled to an accurate birth certificate that reflects both of his mothers. The women ran into problems when they attempted to send their Vermont adoption decree to Mississippi to obtain an "amended" birth certificate reflecting them both as the child's parents. Since nothing in the Mississippi birth certificate laws required two parents to be of different sexes, the Mississippi court ruled that its State Bureau had no discretion to refuse to issue the certificate. The challenge, brought by the Lambda Legal Defense and Education Fund, challenged the law on constitutional and other grounds. Similar challenges have arisen in other states, with couples attempting to have their adoption or parentage court decrees given "full faith and credit" in the child's state of birth. Results have, to this author's knowledge and experience, been mixed. Mississippi has since outlawed adoptions by gay couples so it is unclear whether a similar challenge would now succeed. The couple has other adopted children and reportedly have been sought out as adoptive parents by Vermont officials for special-needs children.

> *Perdue v. Miss. State Bd. of Health* (Civ. No.
> G-2001-1891; Hinds Cty., Miss.); *Burlington*
> *Free Press*, 4/7/03

8.13 California Supreme Court Affirms Second-Parent Adoptions
Winter 2003

The California Supreme Court has judicially affirmed its practice of allowing second-parent adoption proceedings and reversed a lower appellate court, which had thrown the legitimacy of same-sex or other unmarried couples' adoptions into question by interpreting California's adoption laws to require a birth parent relinquishment prior to any adoption. That practice has not been routinely followed in the estimated 10,000 to 20,000 second-parent adoptions in California where the first legal parent typically consents to the partner's adoption without relinquishing his or her own parental rights. In a separate opinion, concurring in part and dissenting in part, one judge suggested that by waiving the statutory requirement of relinquishment, the majority of the court had opened the door to unlimited multiple-party adoptions, a charge the majority denied.

The court also noted that, "[u]nmarried couples who have brought a child into the world with the expectation that they will raise it together, and who have jointly petitioned for adoption, should be on notice that if they separate the same rules concerning custody and visitation as apply to all other parents will apply to them." This decision suggests the significance of clear clinical consent forms, especially for nontraditional couples, which accurately reflect the parenting intentions of the parties.

Sharon S. v. Sup. Ct., 31 Cal. 4th 417 (Cal. 2003);

cert. den'd, 540 U.S. 1220 (U.S. 2004)

8.14(a) Constitutionality of Florida's Ban on Gay Adoptions in the Courts
Spring 2004

The United States Court of Appeals for the Eleventh Circuit has upheld the constitutionality of the Florida statute that prevents adoption by practicing homosexuals. Multiple gay foster parents filed suit after being rejected as adoptive parents for the children under their care. They made three constitutional arguments on appeal: (1) that the statute violates their rights to familial privacy, intimate association, and family integrity under the due process clause; (2) that the statute impermissibly burdens a fundamental right to private sexual intimacy recently recognized by the U.S. Supreme Court (in striking down a Texas sodomy law); and (3) that the statute violates the equal protection clause by categorically prohibiting only homosexual persons from adopting children.

The court rejected all three constitutional challenges, finding that the statute does not violate any fundamental rights. The court found that Florida had valid rational bases for the legislative classification, including the legitimate state interest in encouraging optimal family structure by seeking to place adoptive children in homes that have both a father and a mother. "The State of Florida has made the determination that it is not in the best interests of its displaced children to be adopted by individuals who 'engage in current, voluntary homosexual activity . . .' and we have found nothing in the Constitution that forbids this policy judgment."

8.14(b) U.S. Supreme Court Declines to Review Florida Law Banning Gay and Lesbian Adoption
Spring 2005

The United States Supreme Court has refused to hear an appeal of the lawsuit brought by the ACLU. The case was brought by four gay men who are raising foster children but prohibited by Florida law from adopting; the law was upheld in 2003, and both the full Eleventh Circuit and now the U.S. Supreme Court declined to reconsider that decision. As a result, the adoption ban remains in place.

Lofton v. Sec'y of the Dep't of Children & Family Servs., 377 F.3d 1275 (11th Cir. 2004); *cert. den'd*, 543 U.S. 1081 (U.S. 2005)

8.14(c) Florida Trial Court Strikes Down Florida's Ban on Gay Adoptions
Fall 2008

A trial judge from the Key West area of the state has found Florida's ban on gay adoptions law violates the state constitution, and ruled that a gay man who has been a child's foster parent, and since 2006 his permanent guardian, may adopt him. The now-thirteen-year-old boy has special needs and learning disabilities. By essentially ruling out an entire group of prospective parents without any opportunity to examine what is in an individual child's best interest, the court found the statute impermissibly violated the separation of powers by prohibiting the courts and child welfare officials to perform their functions. A home study recommended the adoption by the man and his partner. Florida is one of only two states that ban gay adoptions.

In refusing to follow the law, the judge ruled that, "[c]ontrary to every child welfare principle, the gay adoption ban operates as a conclusive or irrebuttable presumption that . . . it is never in the best interest of any adoptee to be adopted by a homosexual."

The law has previously been upheld, and unless this ruling is appealed and affirmed, it will have no precedential effect on the current Florida law. However, it does reflect the discomfort some lower courts have with the current law. A similar case is reportedly pending in Miami.

In the Matter of John Doe, Monroe Cir. Ct., Fla. (9/08)

8.14(d) Second Florida Trial Court Finds Gay Adoption Ban Unconstitutional
Spring 2009

A second Florida trial judge this year has now ruled that the state's longstanding ban on gay and lesbian adoptions unconstitutionally violates the equal protections rights of both foster children and their prospective adoptive parents. Florida has had a statutory ban on gay adoptions since 1977 and is one of only a very few states to explicitly ban adoptions (but not foster parenting) by gay and lesbian parents. The statute has been upheld by a federal appeals court, and the state has said it will appeal this most recent decision.

This case arose in connection with an adoption of two foster children, now eight and four, by Frank Martin Gill, a single man and experienced foster parent who has been raising the boys with his partner for the past four years. The children, deemed abandoned and neglected, were initially placed with the men by the state on a temporary basis. The court held over fifty hearings, heard expert testimony from both the state and Gill. It rejected the state's expert testimony that there is a higher incidence of drug and alcohol abuse, and less stable relationships, amongst same-sex couples, as well as a social stigma for their children; instead it sided with the adoptive father and his experts.

In her fifty-three-page opinion, the judge wrote: "[b]ased on the evidence presented from experts from all over this country and abroad, it is clear that sexual orientation is not a predictor of a person's ability to parent." Sexual orientation no more leads to psychiatric disorders, alcohol and substance abuse, relationship instability, a lower life expectancy or sexual disorders than race, gender, socioeconomic class, or any other demographic characteristic. The court also focused on the rights of the children to be adopted, finding the ban denied them the right to permanency, which may present an issue on appeal.

The state has also said Gill was a wonderful foster parent but must enforce state law.

Note: As of publication, an appeal of that ruling is pending before the intermediate appellate court. Regardless of the outcome, further appeals to the Florida Supreme Court or beyond are anticipated (Fla. Ct. Apps. 3rd Dis. [oral arguments heard 8/26/09]).

In the Matter of the Adoption of John Doe and
James Doe, 11th Fla. Jud. Cir., 11/25/08;
New York Times, 11/26/08

8.15(a) Massachusetts Rules in Favor of Gay Marriage
Spring 2004

The highest state court in Massachusetts has declared that barring an individual from the protections, benefits, and obligations of civil marriage solely because that person would marry a person of the same sex violates the Massachusetts Constitution. The court stayed entry of judgment for 180 days to permit the state legislature to take "such action as it may deem appropriate in light of this opinion."

While homosexual marriages may not be recognized outside of Massachusetts, this ruling should have significant implications for the parentage of children in families who marry once the court's judgment is entered. In Massachusetts, a child is generally presumed to be the legal child of the person to whom the child's mother is married. Therefore, in cases where a lesbian woman gives birth following donor insemination or IVF, her partner may be presumed to be the child's legal parent if the women are legally married. This may also alleviate the need for co-parent adoptions, which are frequently and routinely performed in Massachusetts. The full implications of the court's decision and its effect on related areas of law, such as parentage, have yet to be explored.

Goodridge v. Dept. of Public Health,
440 Mass. 309 (2003)

8.15(b) Massachusetts Courts Double-Up Protections for Married Same-Sex Couples' Children

Fall 2005

Having passed the one-year anniversary of the *Goodridge* decision, which recognized same-sex marriage in Massachusetts, courts in that state are now facing novel issues when these newly recognized couples create families. For almost a decade preceding that decision, co-parent adoptions for same-sex couples were recognized and regularly authorized by the Massachusetts courts. Following the groundbreaking decision, married female same-sex couples using donor insemination may now rely directly on that state's donor artificial insemination statute, which presumes the husband or spouse of a married couple is the child of the marriage. By extension and application of the state's equal rights laws, some courts have acknowledged that the same presumption should also be available to same-sex male couples. Under that analysis, married couples are entitled to recognition as the legal parents of a child born to one of them, regardless of whether or not the child was born with the assistance of either or both donor egg or a gestational carrier. Pre-birth orders to that effect are regularly presented to, and allowed by, the appropriate probate courts.

In a somewhat ironic "twist," in several recent cases the probate courts have gone one step further. While recognizing the joint paternity of a male same-sex married couple or the joint maternity of a same-sex female married couple, and issuing pre-birth orders to that effect, these courts are also strongly recommending the couples return to court following the birth of the child and undergo a "traditional" co-parent adoption in accordance with pre-*Goodridge* procedures. The courts' articulated rationale is that the pre-birth order and recognition of parentage based on Massachusetts's recognition of same-sex marriages may have no effect in states without such a law, and particularly in so-called "DOMA" (the 1996 federal Defense of Marriage Act) states. DOMA defines marriage as a legal union between one man and one woman for federal purposes and permits states not to recognize same-sex marriages from another state. The majority of attorneys involved in the field in Massachusetts (including the author) are routinely recommending this additional, traditional legal step as an added precaution and protection for these legally novel families

Multiple Massachusetts Probate Ct. rulings,

2004–2005

8.16(a) Washington Appellate Court Grants Lesbian Co-Parent Standing to Seek Parental Rights

Summer 2004

The Washington Court of Appeals ruled that a woman may proceed with an action for recognition as a "de facto" or psychological parent and, in the alternative, for third-parent visitation of a child she raised with her former partner for six years. The child, L.B., was conceived in 1994 by Sue Ellen Carvin's partner, Page Britain, through donor insemination with a known donor who was a gay friend of the couple. The women had been living together since 1989, and Carvin actively parented the child for the first six years of her life. After the couple separated, Britain cut off Carvin's contact with the child. Carvin filed a petition for parental rights and/or visitation. Thereafter, Britain married the sperm donor, signed an acknowledgment of parentage with him, and had his name added to the child's birth certificate.

The Court of Appeals reversed the trial court's ruling (that Carvin had no cause of action for a determination of co-parentage or third-party visitation). The appellate court first found that Carvin could not pursue her claim under the 2002 Uniform Parentage Act, as she does not fit into any of the specific, unambiguous categories of persons listed in the Act as having standing to adjudicate parentage. However, the appellate court permitted Carvin to proceed under Washington common law with her action to establish that she is a de facto or psychological parent, or alternatively for visits with the child under Washington's third-party visitation statute. The case was remanded to the trial court for proceedings consistent with the appellate court's opinion.

8.16(b) Washington Appellate Court Allows Former Partner to Proceed with Parentage Claim Only
Winter 2005

The Washington Supreme Court subsequently upheld the lower appellate court decision that the trial court should determine whether a former partner was a de facto parent, but reversed the appellate decision that the former partner could petition for [third-party] visitation.

> *In re Parentage of L.B.*, 155 Wash. 2d 679 (Wn. 2005); *cert. den'd sub nom; Britain v. Carvin*, 547 U.S. 1143 (2006)

8.17 Lesbian Partner's Maternity Disputed under "Intent"-Based Parentage Order
Fall 2004

In a case with potentially wide-ranging implications, a former lesbian partner's legal maternity of a two-year-old child conceived by her former partner through artificial insemination is in dispute. The facts are undisputed: the former couple had obtained a pre-birth order that both would be the child's mothers, as well as a birth certificate reflecting their joint parental status, and jointly raised the child for two years prior to separating. At issue is the sufficiency of the legal steps they took to secure their joint parentage. The appellate court has voided their prior order but allowed the nonbiological parent an opportunity to attempt to establish parentage under California's family law code in the case, which involves both disputed custody and visitation following the couple's breakup.

While still together and pregnant, the couple secured a pre-birth order of joint maternity based on a "stipulation" or agreement. They did not present any other evidence to the court nor did they subsequently undergo a co-parent adoption. After their separation, the biological mother challenged the pre-birth order she and her former partner had obtained, arguing the court lacked jurisdiction to render such a judgment based [only] on the parties' agreement. The appellate court agreed and rejected any notion that parentage can be established simply by agreement or intention, separate from following established statutory law. Despite arguments submitted from multiple "amici" ("friend of the court") briefs that hundreds, if not thousands, of parentage cases had been processed and allowed based on intention, including *In re Marriage of Buzzanca* [6.19], the court found that intention alone did not suffice to create parentage.

However, the court ruled that a gender-neutral application of California's Uniform Parentage Act provided a separate basis to establish legal parentage of a nonbiological parent—by demonstrating that she had held herself out as a parent and received the child into her home. The court rejected the biological mother's argument that permitting such evidence would invade an intact family unit, finding that the family unit had allegedly been comprised. The case was remanded to the trial court for a factual hearing.

Note: Following multiple appeals and hearings, the initial reversal was itself reversed. The court's final ruling held that the biological mother was estopped (prohibited) from challenging the stipulated judgment of joint parentage and that the court did have subject matter jurisdiction. Further, the court declared that the child had two parents and that any other ruling would be unfair to both the child and second parent.

Kristine H. v. Lisa R., 37 Cal. 4th 156 (Cal. 2005)

8.18(a) Federal District Court Voids Oklahoma's Anti-Gay Adoption Law
Summer 2006

In a lengthy ruling, with potentially wide-ranging impact on inter-state adoptions and other collaborative reproduction arrangements, an Oklahoma federal district judge has voided an anti-gay amend-ment to that state's adoption law as unconstitutional. An appeal by the state is likely. The 2004 amendment prevented Oklahoma from recognizing final adoptions by same-sex parents from other jurisdic-tions. The statute explicitly required giving what is known as "full faith and credit" (FF&C) to foreign judgments: "[T]he courts of this state shall recognize a decree, judgment or final order creating the re-lationship of parent and child by adoption" from other states or countries as their own. The 2004 amendment, however, added: "Except that, this state . . . shall not recognize an adoption by more than one individual of the same sex from any other state or foreign jurisdiction."

Three same-sex families sued on four constitutional grounds: FF&C, equal protection, due process, and right to travel, and won on all but the last ground. Two had moved to Oklahoma after adopting their children in states that permit same-sex adoptions. The third couple, California residents, wished to travel to Oklahoma to visit their child's birth mother, as their open adoption agreement pro-vided. The court found the state could not justify denying legal recog-nition to these families under either a "rational basis," equal protec-tion basis, or a "fundamental" due process rights basis, finding the law violated the right to "care, custody, and rearing" of one's child.

The court rejected the state's arguments that adoption decrees are not the types of judgments to which the FF&C clause applies, and that to force it to recognize these adoptions would impermissibly al-low another state to dictate Oklahoma's policy on same-sex adop-tions. In its ruling, it quoted the U.S. Supreme Court that there is "no roving public policy exception" to FF&C for foreign court judgments.

The court also found it irrelevant that Oklahoma law does not per-mit same-sex adoptions and refused to characterize the issue as whether there is a fundamental, constitutional right to adopt or not (one of the arguments Florida relied upon in successfully refusing to allow same-sex adoptions there). Instead, it ruled the law's effect was to "refuse legal recognition of certain parent-child relationships that have been legally formed in a different state" and that it would unconstitutionally deny the children certain legal rights, including inheritance and child support.

In the court's words, "[t]he very fact that the adoptions have occurred is evidence that a court of law has found the adoptions to be in the best interests of the children. . . . To now attempt to strip a child of one of his or her parents seems far removed from the statute's purpose and therefore from Defendants' asserted important government objective."

The decision, unless overturned on appeal, lays out a comprehensive rationale for constitutionally requiring states to recognize judicially established parent-child relationships from other states. That analysis could apply equally to other court orders, including pre-birth or post-birth parentage orders for children born to gestational carriers, donors, or same-sex parents.

8.18(b) Appeal of Oklahoma Law's Refusal to Recognize Out-of-State Same-Sex Adoptions
Winter 2007

In yet another example of the inconsistencies between state laws and the impact it can have on families, a federal appeals court has heard arguments on whether Oklahoma may refuse to recognize same-sex adoption decrees from three same-sex couples impacted by the law. The appeal raises, in the adoption context, another example of the conflict of laws principles and potential vulnerabilities that can arise when more than one state is involved in family building arrangements.

> *Note:* The Tenth Circuit affirmed the district court's order and judgment declaring the statute unconstitutional and directed issuance of a new birth certificate for one of the children. The court reversed on the issue of standing of one of the sets of parents and directed issuance of a new birth certificate for those parents.
>
> *Finstuen v. Crutcher,* 496 F.3d 1139 (10th Cir. 2007)

8.19 Virginia and Texas in Same-Sex Birth Certificate Controversies
Winter 2006

As nontraditional ART and adoption arrangements continue to proliferate, two states have come to different conclusions as to whether to recognize out-of-state adoptions by same-sex couples. In Texas, based on a statute explicitly prohibiting its Vital Records department from issuing birth certificates except to a female and male parent, that state has refused to issue a birth record for a child adopted in Oregon despite the Oregon decree ordering a new birth certificate to issue. In Virginia, three test cases ended up in that state's Supreme Court with a ruling that the out-of-state adoption decrees must be honored and new birth certificates issued. Most recently, in January, Virginia's Division of Vital Records agreed to issue a new birth certificate for one of those couples listing them as "Parent One" and "Parent Two," instead of "mother" and "father."

Tex. Health & Safety Code § 192.008 (2009);
Davenport v. Little-Bowser, 269 Va. 546 (Va. 2005)

8.20(a) Two-State, Same-Sex Custody Battle Saga Continues
Winter 2007

The most recent ruling in a two-year, two-state ongoing custody battle between a former lesbian couple points up the critical role conflicts-of-law can play in family custody battles. The case involves a four-year-old girl born to one of the women while they lived in Vermont in a legally recognized civil union there. After the couple separated, a Vermont court affirmed parentage by both women and awarded visitation for the nonbiological mother. The biological mother moved to Virginia and obtained sole legal custody despite the first court's order. The issue became whether Virginia must recognize, or give "full faith and credit" to, the Vermont ruling, despite having very different family laws, with no recognition of civil unions or other legal protections for same-sex couples. Granting full faith and credit to a court order is a longstanding principle, regardless of whether or not such a decision would have been reached under that state's laws. In November, a three-judge panel of the Virginia Court of Appeals reversed its lower court, ruling Vermont has legal jurisdiction over the case because it was first filed there. Further appeals are reported likely.

8.20(b) Virginia-Vermont Lesbian Couple's Civil Union Dissolved

Summer 2007

After a year-long, two-state custody battle, a Vermont judge has now dissolved the civil union between two women whose custody dispute over their five-year-old daughter sparked a national debate over states' rights and same-sex couples. The U.S. Supreme Court refused to hear an appeal of the Vermont court decision in April of this year, but Miller is reportedly considering an appeal of the new visitation order so the most recent decision may not be the end of the legal or emotional sparring over the child's status.

> *Miller-Jenkins v. Miller-Jenkins*, 2006 Vt. 78;
> Nos. 2004-443/2005-030; *New York Times*,
> 6/19/07; *Rutland Herald*, 6/19/07

8.20(c) Vermont High Court Reaffirms Parental Status Based on Civil Union

Spring 2008

Refusing to reexamine its earlier ruling, the Vermont Supreme Court has let stand a custody decision over a now-five-year-old child that has been bitterly contested in two states by a former lesbian couple. The case illustrates the significance of choice of law and the strength accorded principles of full faith and credit since the Virginia courts were ultimately ordered by that state's high court to respect the Vermont court's orders on parentage and custody stemming from the civil union.

The Vermont Supreme Court has now refused yet another attempt by the biological mother to deny her former partner access to the child, finding her most recent appeal to be "nothing short of disingenuous" and her conduct "contemptuous." The Virginia Supreme Court is expected to rule in April on the question of whether it can be required to enforce the Vermont custody and access orders.

Note: The Virginia Supreme Court upheld its Court of Appeals ruling that Vermont law and court decisions must be upheld.

> *Miller-Jenkins v. Miller-Jenkins*,
> 912 A.2d 451 (Vt. 2008);
> Associated Press; *Boston Globe*, 3/15/08

8.20(d) Inter-State Custody Battle Enters Fourth Year for Same-Sex Couple and Child

Spring 2009

Despite appellate court rulings in two states (Vermont and Virginia) that Janet Miller is not entitled to withhold visitation privileges from her former civil-union partner, Lisa Jenkins, visitations problems continue. Miller's second attempted appeal to the U.S. Supreme Court was rebuffed in December 2008. Trial dates in January over Miller's compliance with court-ordered visitation have been set.

After several years of litigation (in which Miller has been aided by national conservative groups), the Virginia Supreme Court ultimately confirmed that Vermont's civil union laws and the co-parent relationship that flowed from them must be respected, rejecting lower courts' rulings that had wrongly attempted to apply Virginia law. Miller, who has since renounced her homosexuality and become very active in the Baptist Church in Virginia, continues to refuse to allow her former partner to have unsupervised visitation, for which she faces potential contempt charges.

Newsweek, 12/15/08; *Miller-Jenkins v. Miller-Jenkins*, 661 S.E.2d 822 (Va., 2008)

8.21(a) California Finds Same-Sex Marriage Protected on State Constitutional Grounds, Potentially Widespread Implications

Summer 2008

The California Supreme Court has become the most recent state to find a constitutionally protected right to marry for all individuals, including same-sex couples. In its May 15 ruling, the court reversed a lower court to strike down a state statute that allowed only opposite-sex couples to be designated as married. Enacted in 2000, the law in its entirety reads, "[o]nly marriage between a man and a woman is valid or recognized in California."

In a lengthy opinion, with two dissenters, the court found two fundamental constitutionality problems with the statute's prohibition. First, the court ruled it violated the equal dignity and respect that the court said is a core element of the fundamental constitutional right to marry. Secondly, it found that the statute violated California's equal protection clause. The decision is noteworthy for many reasons, not the least of which is that California already had in place a "domestic partnership" law that the court acknowledged "affords . . . virtually all of the same legal benefits and privileges, and imposes upon the [same-sex] couple virtually all of the same legal obligations and duties" as marriage. Thus, the issue before the court was squarely whether the designation of "marriage" could constitutionally be reserved for one group of individuals and not another.

The court first clarified the level of scrutiny that the law must pass, the initial question in any constitutional analysis. Depending on the issue or inequality alleged, a statute challenged as denying equal protection under the law is held to different standards. Where there is no "suspect" or protected class involved, a law will be upheld if it has a "rational basis." Where there is a protected, suspect class—such as race and gender—alleging a discriminatory impact, the highest standard applies. A law that is being challenged as discriminating on a "suspect classification" or impinging on a "fundamental right" must be reviewed under a "strict scrutiny" test and, to pass constitutional muster, must be found to be necessary to protect a "compelling state interest" and to also be drafted as narrowly as possible to meet that interest. The California court was unequivocal in stating that the marriage statute must meet the highest standard. Critical to the court's decision, with potentially widespread future implications, is its finding that the sexual orientation rises to the same level of scrutiny and protection as race and gender. In the court's words, the statute in question "must be understood as classifying or discriminating on the basis of sexual orientation, a characterization that we conclude represents—like gender, race and religion—a constitutionally suspect basis upon which to impose differential treatment."

The court also made clear that it was *not* deciding policy, but only interpreting constitutional law and thus deciding that having two official names for relationships based on sexual orientation was unconstitutional. The court reviewed the court cases involving the "right to marry" and concluded that under the state constitution, the "constitutionally based right to marry properly must be understood to encompass the core set of basic substantive legal rights and attributes traditionally associated with marriage that are so integral to an individual's liberty and personal autonomy that they may not be eliminated or abrogated by the Legislature or by the electorate through the statutory initiative process." The court rejected the Attorney General's argument that as long as the substance was the same, the form or name of the two relationships could be different. Instead, the court ruled that denying same-sex couples and their children the "familiar and highly favored designation of marriage is likely to cast doubt on whether the official family relationship of same-sex couples enjoys dignity equal to that of opposite-sex couples." It also found that it would perpetuate the general premise "now emphatically rejected by this state—that gay individuals and same-sex couples are in some respects 'second-class citizens' who may, under the law, be treated differently from, and less favorably than, heterosexual individuals [in] opposite-sex couples."

The decision, as expected, has opened a floodgate of same-sex marriages in California. While the full impact of the court's decision will not be known for some time, what is now abundantly clear in California is that distinctions based on sexual-orientation will be held to the highest level or scrutiny, and that anything short of full marriage for all couples, in form as well as substance, is unconstitutional and will not be allowed.

In re Marriage Cases, Supreme Ct. Cal,

2008 Cal. LEXIS 5247

8.21(b) "Prop. 8" Sends California Gay Marriage Back to Court
Fall 2009

California's Supreme Court has again addressed the status of same-sex marriage after the November passage of "Prop. 8," a one-sentence constitutional amendment designating "marriage" as a union between a man and a woman. The referendum overrode its prior ruling guaranteeing same-sex marriages under the state constitution. Three lawsuits were filed the day after the vote.

The court issued a consolidated decision in May, upholding Prop. 8 as a valid, but limited, constitutional amendment. It noted the law "carves out a narrow exception [to the state's equal protection clause] applicable only to the *designation* of the term 'marriage'" and, quoting its own opinion in the *Marriage Cases* [8.21], not to "any other of the core set of basic *substantive* legal rights and attributes traditionally associated with marriage," such as a legally protected relationship with the person of one's choice or the right to raise children within that legally recognized family. It ruled sexual orientation remains a suspect classification subject to strict scrutiny review and the amendment should not be read more broadly to limit any of those protections. As the amendment was not retroactive, the court also ruled the existing 18,000 same-sex marriages remain legally recognized.

Strauss v. Horton, 93 Cal. Rptr.3d 591; *reh. den'd*
2009 LEXIS 5652 (6/17/09)

8.22 Multiple Efforts to Repeal DOMA Underway
Winter 2010

Two federal lawsuits pending in Boston challenge the constitutionality of section 3 of DOMA, which authorizes the federal government to ignore any same-sex marriages for purposes of federal laws and programs. Section 2 of the 1996 law (permitting states to draft their own same-sex marriage policies and not recognize any state's conflicting laws) is not being challenged. GLAD sued on behalf of several married couples and surviving spouses, arguing DOMA violates their Equal Protection rights for income tax, Social Security and federal employment benefits, and essentially creates national marriage laws—improperly intruding into a traditional area of state law. The Massachusetts Attorney General's lawsuit alleges section 3 unconstitutionally creates second-class marriage status for the state's 16,000 same-sex married couples by denying them federal benefits and federally funded state benefits. Other suits around the country have also been filed. The government has moved to dismiss GLAD's case largely on the grounds that federal benefits are not a fundamental right, while acknowledging it believes the law is discriminatory and wants it repealed. With several states now recognizing same-sex marriages, the number of couples impacted by the law and legal challenges to it are growing rapidly.

Gill v. OPM, No.1:09 cv-10309 (D. Mass. 2009)
(mtn. to dismiss filed 9/18/09); *Comm. v. Dept.*
Health & Human Services (D. Mass. filed
7/8/09)

CHAPTER NINE

Genetics (PGD) and ART

❖ MEDICAL COMMENTARY, BY Howard W. Jones, Jr.

DUE TO MISCONCEPTIONS about what preimplantation genetic diagnosis (PGD) is, and what its capabilities are, the procedure must be defined precisely. PGD is usually done on a single cell removed from an embryo of about eight cells in development. An analysis is done on the removed cell. If there is no adverse diagnosis on that cell, the embryo's remaining seven cells continue to divide and can be used to transfer and give rise to a child without a specific genetic defect if that particular embryo is selected. It should be noted that generally several of a crop of embryos are eliminated by an adverse diagnosis. Thus, the pool of embryos for embryo transfer following PGD is smaller than for traditional implantation, and the pregnancy expectation in these cases is not as great as it would be if the pool of embryos had not been reduced. Thus, in its use, it must be understood that pregnancy expectation following PGD is somewhat less than for IVF in general.

It is important to understand what PGD cannot do. It cannot be used routinely to screen every embryo with the notion that you could thereby identify those embryos that are "normal." PGD identifies a specific defect. It cannot be used for making a designer baby.

PGD can identify specific gene defects. Examples are cystic fibrosis or Tay-Sachs disease or some two hundred other diseases that have been identified by examination with suitable technology. It anticipates the discard of those embryos that turn out to show the specific defect, which has troubled some people who believe that personhood begins with fertilization.

PGD can also identify the sex of the embryo. This has a number of uses. Certain diseases are sex-linked. If one is dealing with such a disease, it would then be possible to select the sex that would be unaffected, but this also may result in the discard of the remaining embryos, again raising ethical concerns for some. PGD also could be used for social sex selection. Indeed, some programs offer this service, but aside from any ethical concerns, PGD is generally frowned upon as a technique solely for sex selection because it is expensive and cumbersome and not without risk.

PGD can be used to identify the chromosomes in the removed blastomere. This is useful where there is a balanced translocation and the technician identifies the embryo with an unbalanced set of chromosomes. One then chooses those embryos that have normal chromosomes or those that have a balance translocation, assuming that the patient understands and accepts that this would transmit the balance translocation to the child.

This technology has also been used in patients who have a high risk for miscarriage or in older patients where the chromosomes are more likely abnormal to select those that have normal chromosomes. This then eliminates the apparent abnormal or aneuploidy chromosomes, assuming that the biopsied blastomere is representative of the blastomeres that remain behind in that embryo. This assumption does not always appear to be correct. When PGD is used for this purpose, it is often referred to as preimplantation genetic screening (PGS). The process has been used widely for this purpose, but it is controversial, as many studies have indicated that the use of PGS does not improve the end result. Some suggest that the embryo may subsequently self-correct and that the appearance of the embryo at the time of the screening may be misleading. At the present time, the use of PGS for this purpose remains very experimental, as a 2007 ASRM Practice Committee Opinion states.

It goes without saying that informed consent for PGS should reflect the uncertainty of its usefulness as expressed in the literature. The consent form should include the fact that the total reproductive potential of a single egg harvest with PGS is less than the usual pregnancy rate for an IVF cycle without PGS, since the pool of transferable fertilized eggs is necessarily reduced by the elimination of those preembryos screened out because of aneuploidy or other abnormal findings.

There are also more unusual or "out-of-the-box" uses that need to be mentioned. Sometimes a child will have a disease which requires a bone marrow transfusion and there is no suitable donor. It is possible to select an embryo to create a child who will be compatible for the use of bone marrow transfusion for its sibling. A number of cases of this type have been reported ("savior siblings"), and it always gives rise to a controversy and usually some form of ethics review prior to moving forward with the goal of hoping to reassure all involved that the sibling is not being created for the sole purpose of saving the life or improving the health of the existing child.

PGD has also been requested to select for a defect, particularly deafness. Deaf couples have, in a few instances, reportedly requested that their child be deaf and this sometimes can be identified when the deafness is on a genetic basis. This has also given rise to significant controversy and ethical debate.

PGD and PGS need to be distinguished from those screening and diagnostic tests that are applied to pregnancies already established within the uterus. Nuchal translucency testing is one test that occurs once pregnancy is established. This test, performed between the eleventh and fourteenth week of pregnancy, uses ultrasound to measure the clear space in the folds of tissue behind the developing fetus's neck. Nuchal translucency testing correctly detects Down syndrome about 80 percent of the time. It is non-invasive, but all such tests raise cost issues. Another screening test is the "triple screen." These tests measure the quantities of various substances in the mother's blood and, together with the woman's age, estimate the likelihood that her baby has Down syndrome. These are usually offered between the fifteenth and twentieth week of pregnancy. These procedures are screening tests and, as they are non-invasive, can be applied to all pregnancies. They are rapidly being incorporated into standard obstetrical care, but due to their cost, both patient and physician must evaluate the risk/benefit ratio. If these screening tests prove to be positive, it is usually advised that a diagnostic test—either amniocentesis or chorionic villus sampling (CVS)—be confirmed before taking action, such as termination of the pregnancy.

In sum, PGD and intrapartum tests are currently competitive. Any condition that can be tested by PGD can also be tested by amniocentesis or CVS. The decision rests with the patient largely because the patient needs to decide, if she is at risk, whether it would be better, from a medical perspective, to get pregnant, be tested intrapartumly, and have an elective termination of the affected child. A number of patients are opposed to an elective termination and therefore elect PGD in order to eliminate the affected fertilized eggs prior to implantation. However, this involves an IVF procedure, with the attendant costs and risks, so the decision or judgment is not simple but must be made with consideration of all the factors mentioned above.

Needless to say, this is a very cursory outline, but it may serve the purposes of explaining briefly what presently PGD and PGS can and cannot do and providing a backdrop for a better understanding of current and future legal issues.

∾ LEGAL COMMENTARY, BY Susan L. Crockin

The legal responses to the developments in the field of genetics over the past decade have been nothing short of revolutionary. With the advances of reproductive genetics (or what some refer to as "reprogenetics"), including newer genetic testing technologies such as PGD (preimplantation genetic diagnosis), existing legal frameworks and concepts, such as wrongful birth, wrongful conception, statutes of limitation, definitions of "illness," "conception," and what is considered "medically necessary," as well as choice and conflict of laws principles have all come under scrutiny. Access to care and insurance coverage issues have also emerged as these technologies become more available, acceptable, and helpful in diagnosing genetic conditions.

As courts are forced to interpret and apply longstanding legal distinctions between concepts such as "wrongful birth" and "wrongful conception" in the context of PGD testing of IVF embryos, policy implications over when life begins may find a new forum for debate and deliberation. "Wrongful birth" and "wrongful conception" are both tort theories of civil liability that may be brought by parents of an affected child or, in other contexts, parents of a child they did not want or expect (traditional fact patterns for such claims include failed tubal ligations or missed diagnoses of genetic anomalies in older siblings or parents). The majority of states recognize some form of these claims, although they vary widely as to what forms of damages are appropriate. Some states limit damages to out-of-pocket costs (for example, reimbursement of a tubal ligation fee), while others allow larger damages for the costs of raising an affected child or the loss of the companionship of an unaffected child. In contrast, "wrongful life" theories of liability belong to the child themselves and require courts to weigh the value of an affected versus a normal life. Thus, for example, a child would sue for being born with a serious anomaly for which the physician failed to properly diagnosis or screen out. The majority of courts reject wrongful life claims, on the theory that courts cannot be properly asked to evaluate the reduced value of an impaired life over no life. All of these theories have been reinvigorated and retested, however, in light of genetic advances, with mixed results to date.

As the field of genetics continues to offer newer and earlier information to would-be parents and families, and as patients and professionals increasingly rely on ART related techniques such as PGD to obtain that information, issues involving "reproductive wrongs" are likely to proliferate in courts across the country. (For readers interested in a deeper discussion of these legal issues, the "Overview of Reproductive Genetics," written by this author for the Genetics and Public Policy Center, can be accessed at www.dnapolicy.org.)

The cases begin with a 1996 decision recognizing that a genetic predisposition to cancer may be considered an illness and treatment for it "medically necessary" (*Katskee v. Blue Cross/Blue Shield of Nebraska,* 1994). The courts can be seen starting to analyze genetic susceptibility statistics. Also outside the field of ART, in the mid-1990s courts began to grapple with the scope of the "duty to warn" when doctors uncovered a genetic condition that might affect a patient's extended family. One of the earliest such cases resolved the issue by ruling that a physician's warning to his patient about the genetic nature of her cancer would serve as meeting any duty he owed to her family members (*Pate v. Threlkel,* 1995). As PGD became more available, both American and international courts and ethics committees have confronted and wrestled with issues of "savior siblings" and sex selection for nonmedical reasons such as "family balancing."

More recently, fascinating cases have looked at how prenatal testing errors should be analyzed and whether "wrongful birth" or "wrongful conception" theories apply, a distinction that is recognized only in some states and can be outcome-determinative as to both liability and damages. While the majority of states have recognized "wrongful birth" claims, some states have traditionally rejected them on policy grounds to avoid any valuation of life or diminution of value based on a child's health condition that could have been avoided by an abortion. Yet some of those same states have been willing to recognize and assign liability under a "wrongful conception" theory, since that would not involve termination of an ongoing pregnancy. Thus, despite Minnesota's ban on "wrongful birth" liability, a groundbreaking case found liability where a negligent failure to diagnose a child's Fragile X condition resulted in his mother conceiving (naturally) a second child with the same condition (*Molloy v. Meier*, 2004). Interestingly, the court recognized a duty to the mother but not to her second husband, the father of the second, affected child. Another significant implication of such a ruling is the expansion of the time frame for legal liability by the professionals involved. The court noted that these types of genetic developments may throw statutes of limitation (often set by state statute at two to three years from the time of the mistake or its discovery) out the window, as undisclosed genetic conditions can stay hidden for several years until a subsequent child is conceived and born. A conflict among the laws of different states can also be outcome-determinative, similar to some of the third-party ART disputes reviewed in prior chapters. In a 2006 case involving a national North Carolina–based lab's misreading of an amniocentesis result for a Maryland couple, a federal court rejected the defendant lab's suggestion that North Carolina law should apply based on the lab's physical location. Instead, the court found liability under Maryland law where the couple resided and tragically, in reliance on the report, conceived and gave birth to a second child with cystic fibrosis. They had sought the testing after their first child was born with cystic fibrosis and after they had terminated their second pregnancy following an accurate amniocentesis that revealed an affected fetus. These facts were important to prove that the couple would have aborted had they received accurate test results. The critical legal distinction was that North Carolina recognizes only "wrongful conception" but not "wrongful birth," and since the mother was obviously pregnant at the time of the amniocentesis, there would have been no damages under that state's law. Ironically, had the couple relied on IVF and PGD instead, there would have been a significant question raised, with both constitutional and policy implications, over whether or not an IVF embryo was or was not considered "conception" (*Laboratory Corp. of America v. Hood*, 2006). Assuming, as have a number of courts in the realm of posthumous reproduction (see chapter 7), that conception occurs upon implantation and not fertilization, North Carolina law would have recognized liability for a PGD error. From this author's perspective, it is virtually impossible to believe that, as these technologies become more widely used and better understood outside the medical realm, courts will rely on legal theories that depend on whether a prenatal test is performed on embryonic cells or amniotic fluid. If that prediction is sound, it is likely that we will see significant revisions and expansions to tort liability theories in the field of reprogenetics.

The *Hood* case raised other interesting defense theories, which the court also rejected. The court refused to apply a breach of contract analysis rather than a tort analysis or dismiss the husband's claims based on LabCorp's argument that it should have no duty to the husband, in part because he had no ability to force his wife to abort a pregnancy.

A set of interim decisions issued in a pending federal case have raised somewhat similar issues in the context of a Pennsylvania child born with Fragile X, purportedly due to poor screening of a sperm donor by a New York lab (*Donovan v. Idant Labs* (2009), discussed in chapter 4). The court initially ruled that the sale of sperm is subject to product liability law. It dismissed both the mother's claims as time-barred and the child's "wrongful life" claim as not recognized under New York law, but allowed the child's breach of contract claims to proceed as an intended third-party beneficiary of her mother's contract with the sperm bank under a strict liability theory. The product liability claim would have been barred under Pennsylvania's blood shield statute, which unlike New York's prevents claims against tissue as well as blood. The court reversed itself, however, and allowed the lab's motion for summary judgment on the strict liability claim, ruling that the child's damages was her medical condition, which essentially amounted to a "wrongful life" claim barred under New York law. The outcome of the case in terms of both legal theories and choice of law will be closely followed by legal observers.

Another unique case, brought in 2006, involved an unsuccessful malpractice claim against a teaching hospital's missed prenatal diagnosis of a novel genetic disorder. The defendants failed to diagnose partial Trisomy 9q through ultrasound and amniocentesis, a genetic disorder that had never been previously identified and that two subsequent hospitals also failed to identify pre-birth (*Hall v. DHMC*, 2006). The New Hampshire court ultimately ruled there was no wrongdoing on the hospital's part. Such cases are likely to continue to arise, with variable outcomes depending on the state of both the emerging law and the evolving genetic tests.

With PGD becoming more widely available, couples with known genetic risk factors have increasingly sought IVF with PGD to avoid the emotional and physical impact of achieving a pregnancy, undergoing prenatal testing, and having to decide whether or not to abort the pregnancy. Couples have begun to challenge their insurance companies with some success—in language reminiscent of the first case in this section, on the "medical necessity" of covering these procedures. In an ironic twist, insurers often initially reject such claims on the basis that the patients are not medically "infertile" (since they can achieve pregnancy) and thus the requested services are not a covered benefit under any required infertility coverage benefit. Such an analysis overlooks the question of whether the requested coverage is appropriate regardless of such categorization. A number of challenges, including some brought by this author, have ultimately resulted in insurance coverage. Such challenges have relied on two major arguments: that insurers will otherwise be required to cover substantial if not exorbitant costs of insuring any affected child; and that refusing such coverage is inconsistent with a policy that likely comprehensively covers family planning costs, including genetic counseling, diagnostic testing, prenatal care, delivery, and family coverage.

And finally, while there have been no reported appellate court cases to date, the growing use of PGD technology to select or deselect IVF embryos based on nongenetic qualities (known as preimplantation genetic selection or PGS) has, as Dr. Jones points out, been increasingly controversial and also reduces pregnancy rates by reducing the number of embryos for transfer. Current studies show conflicting results as to whether or not the technology successfully predicts embryo morphology. A 2007 ASRM Practice Committee Opinion on "preimplantation genetic testing" discusses both PGD and PGS. In addition to addressing counseling issues, the opinion contains specific recommendation relating to PGS, including a statement that "available evidence does not support the use of PGS as currently performed to improve live-birth rates" in patients with advanced maternal age, previous implantation failure, recurrent pregnancy loss, or to reduce miscarriage rates. To the extent that the efficacy of this technique remains unclear and may actually reduce pregnancy rates in older or other patients, promoting it as a clinical procedure will raise informed consent and potential liability issues. It is not difficult to imagine a patient of advanced maternal age advised to undergo PGS, at considerable additional cost, in an effort to select the healthiest-appearing embryos, subsequently to feel wronged if studies demonstrate that the procedure in fact reduced her chances of a pregnancy.

As all of these cases highlight, reproductive genetics is a rapidly evolving area of both medicine and law. On the legal side, the challenges are likely to illustrate continuing tensions in applying and expanding old legal theories to new alleged wrongs.

Litigation

9.1 Mother Sues M.D. over Erroneous Prenatal Diagnosis
June 1995
BY A. JAEGER

Ms. Sundi Greco gave birth to Joshua, who suffers from spina bifida. He is paralyzed from the hips down and suffers permanent fine and gross motor coordination problems and mental retardation. Ms. Greco sued her physician for medical malpractice, claiming he was negligent in failing to accurately conduct or interpret prenatal diagnostic tests and/or reveal she carried a severely deformed fetus. She claims she would have terminated the pregnancy and brought a wrongful birth case. The court (rejecting the label of "wrongful birth") found she was entitled to receive damages for medical malpractice, medical and custodial care expenses for Joshua, and for her emotional distress. The court recognized that there is no joy in watching a child suffer and the joys of parenthood would be overshadowed by the trauma of caring for the child. She was not entitled, however, to receive compensation for loss of companionship, since she would have terminated the pregnancy. The court rejected the child's cause of action for wrongful life, under which, essentially, Joshua claimed that it would have been better not to have been born than to endure his present life with severe disabilities. The Court followed other jurisdictions that do not recognize such claims, stating it was "very difficult, if not impossible" to make the judgment whether no life is better than a life of pain and deprivation.

The dissenting opinion agreed that the mother's claim should be recognized, but would have also allowed the child's wrongful life claim. The judge said he was not focusing on the philosophical or theological nature of life, but on the reality that the child was born and has extraordinary needs. His decision was "not premised on the concept that non-life is preferable to impaired life, but it is predicated on the needs of the living." That judge also noted individuals have the right to state their value toward life as evidenced by a statutory right to withdraw or refuse life-sustaining treatment.

Greco v. U.S., 1995 Nev. LEXIS 33

9.2 Genetic Predisposition to Cancer Is an Illness

Fall 1996

BY A. JAEGER

In the first case of its kind, the Nebraska Supreme Court considered whether a prophylactic hysterectomy and bilateral salpingo-oophorectomy were medically necessary for a woman with a family history of breast and ovarian cancer. The plaintiff and her physicians argued that Ms. Katskee suffered from a genetic condition known as "breast-ovarian carcinoma syndrome." She did not have cancer but due to her family history was at high risk for developing it and her physician prescribed surgery.

Ms. Katskee's physician explained that there was not a conclusive physical test to diagnose the condition, but that the syndrome was diagnosed by "tracing the occurrences of hereditary cancer throughout the patient's family." Despite the absence of a physical test, the court noted that Ms. Katskee, and women with a similar family history, had a 50 percent chance of developing breast cancer or ovarian cancer (compared to a 1.4 percent risk in the general population).

Her health insurer refused to pay for the surgery on the grounds that she did not have cancer, that a risk for developing cancer was not a "bodily illness or disease which was covered by the policy," and therefore, the surgery was not medically necessary. The Court held the insurer must pay for the surgery. It cited a Maryland case (*Cheney v. Bell Ntl. Life,* 1989), where a Maryland insurer argued that hemophilia was not a disease because it was a genetic or hereditary condition of the body that tended to make an individual more susceptible to certain diseases. The Maryland court rejected this argument and concluded that hemophilia is a disease because it is an abnormal condition that impairs or will impair the working of bodily functions.

This decision is significant because the court recognized that having a genetic predisposition to cancer is an illness. The court also recognized anxiety and stress due to the likelihood of developing cancer as important components of the illness.

Katskee v. Blue Cross/Blue Shield, 245 Neb. 808;
515 N.W. 2d 645 (Neb. 1994)

9.3 Duty to Warn Offspring of Genetic Disease
Fall 1996

BY A. JAEGER

Courts have begun to define the limits of a physician's duty to inform relatives of a genetic disorder that may affect them. A woman was being treated for medullary thyroid carcinoma. Three years later, her daughter learned she had the condition and sued the physician, claiming the physician knew the cancer was genetic and should have told the mother and her children it was heritable. The physician alleged that he only had a doctor-patient relationship with the mother, and did not have a duty to contact the children or inform them about their genetic risk for the cancer.

The Florida Supreme Court held that the physician had a duty to inform the mother the disease was genetic, since she was his patient. The court said even if the physician owed a duty to the children to warn them of a genetically transferable disease, he would satisfy that duty by warning the patient: "to require the physician to seek out and warn various members of the patient's family would often be difficult or impractical and would place too heavy a burden upon the physician." In sum, the physician had a duty to inform the mother that the condition was genetic and that her children were at risk, but not to contact the children and warn them.

Pate v. Threlkel, 661 So.2d 278 (Fla. 1995)

9.4 British Couple Travels to Italy for PGD Sex-Selection
Summer 2001

After an unsuccessful attempt to overturn a British ban on the use of preimplantation genetic diagnosis (PGD) to add a female child to their family of four, Louise and Alan Masterson traveled to Italy last summer as a last resort to secretly undergo treatment. The treatment, at a Rome clinic, resulted in the creation of one embryo. After PGD revealed a male embryo, the Mastersons chose to donate the embryo to an infertile couple rather than proceed with the transfer themselves. Without the money to go abroad for treatment again, the Mastersons have said they intend to use the British Human Rights Act to force the Human Fertilisation and Embryology Authority (HFEA) to allow them to get this treatment in England.

Sunday-Times, 3/4/01

9.5 Australian Authorities Grant Permission for Preimplantation Genetic Diagnosis and IVF

Summer 2002

In a case very similar to that involving Adam Nash in Colorado, a three-year-old Australian girl was born with Fanconi anemia, a rare genetic disease that is usually fatal before age thirty. Her parents, who were already planning to have more children, have been granted permission by Victoria's Infertility Treatment Authority to use IVF to create embryos and then select one with the same genetic tissue as the affected child, in the hope of ensuring a bone marrow match. The Authority's chief executive officer stated that the procedure would be allowed for use for a terminally ill sibling where all other avenues of treatment have been explored and where the child was not being produced solely as a means to an end.

Canadian Press, 4/16/02

9.6(a) Pro-Life British Group Blocks Embryo Testing for Genetically Compatible Sibling

Spring 2003

A British court has found no legal authority to support a couple's third IVF attempt to conceive a child who would be a potential cord blood donor for their seriously ill firstborn son. A High Court ruling in December found that HFEA had no right under current legislation to license clinics to perform the PGD technique. The successful legal challenge was brought by an interest group, CORE, which opposes the procedure as "ethically objectionable." HFEA issued a press release stating it was disappointed by the decision and would appeal. The court hearing the case expressed its great sympathy for the family and invited an appeal. One group suggested the challenge by a "pro-life" group was a sign that they had failed to win public or parliamentary support for their views and were thus turning to "legal technicalities." Others have termed the family's efforts an attempt to have a "designer baby."

Independent, 12/21/02; *Guardian,* 12/21/02;

BBC News Online, 12/20/02

9.6(b) British Court Allows IVF and PGD to Attempt Genetic Matching
Fall 2005

In a unanimous decision, a five-judge panel of the House of Lords, England's highest court, has affirmed a decision to allow the parents of a six-year-old boy born with a rare and potentially fatal blood disorder to attempt to have a genetically matched sibling through IVF and PGD. In doing so, the courts ruled that HFEA has the authority to issue such a license and rejected a challenge from a group that argued such "designer babies" violated their licensing authority. The boy suffers from beta thalassaemia major, requiring regular blood transfusions and daily drugs. The couple first tried to conceive a sibling on their own. Their first pregnancy was aborted after the fetus was found to have the same disorder. The second pregnancy would have resulted in a sibling who is not a genetic match. As one judge noted, in recognizing that IVF with PGD would have spared the mother undergoing an abortion and in now allowing the license and thus the procedure, "[t]here is a way to save the . . . family from having to play dice with conception. . . ."

http://www.dawn.com/2005/04/29/top14.htm;

Guardian (2/28/05)

9.7 Minnesota Supreme Court Allows Wrongful Conception Claim to Proceed
Spring 2005

Notwithstanding that state's statutes that bar both wrongful birth and wrongful life claims, the Minnesota Supreme Court has upheld the rights of a biological parent to sue three physicians whose negligence in diagnosing her first child with Fragile X Syndrome led to the mother's decision to have a second child. The mother had brought her first child to her pediatrician, concerned over developmental delays, noted her own brother's mental retardation, and requested genetic testing. Testing was discussed, including testing for Fragile X and testing was ordered and performed, but Fragile X testing was apparently inadvertently not included. The mother was then informed that all test results were normal, which she assumed included a negative test result for Fragile X. She claimed that had she known of her first child's condition, she would have had a tubal ligation and not conceived.

In allowing the claim, the court characterized it as one for "wrongful conception," not wrongful life or birth. When the second child was born to the mother and her new husband several years later, and also afflicted with Fragile X, the couple sued for failure to test the first child, failure to properly read test results, mistakenly reporting that testing had been completed, and failing to provide genetic counseling to the parents. Two of the three physicians had met face-to-face with the mother; the court found liability against all three.

The court held that a physician's duty regarding genetic testing and diagnosis extends beyond the patient to biological parents who foreseeably may be harmed by a breach of that duty. (The court did not extend the duty to a nonbiological parent, in this case the mother's new husband.) "Our decision today is informed by the practical reality of the field of genetic testing and counseling . . . [which] does not affect only the patient. Both the patient and her family can be harmed by negligent testing and diagnosis. . . ." Significantly, the court also found that the action was not time-barred even though the initial missed diagnosis occurred years earlier and Minnesota has a four-year statute of limitations for medical malpractice claims. The court found the claim was in the nature of "wrongful conception," i.e., that if the diagnosis of Fragile X had been properly made the mother would have avoided conception and that, although the wrongful act occurred much earlier, no injury or damage occurred until the point of conception, at which time the legal "cause of action" or right to sue accrued. The court recognized that usually malpractice actions based on failures to diagnose accrue at the time of the diagnosis but found that this is because some damage occurs then. The case is a significant one in terms of both the scope of physicians' duties with respect to genetic testing and counseling and to the applicable statutes of limitations involving genetic misdiagnoses.

Molloy v. Meier, 679 N.W.2d 711 (Minn. 2004)

9.8 No Malpractice in Unique Genetic Disorder Prenatal Screening Case
Summer 2006

A state appellate court has overturned a wrongful birth summary judgment verdict for parents of a child born with the first discovered case of "Partial Trisomy 9q." Multiple ultrasounds, genetic counseling, and amniocentesis involving at least three institutions repeatedly suggested the fetus had abnormalities, but ultimately ruled out multiple disorders including Trisomy 18 and Smith-Lemli Opitz (SLO), and the couple elected not to terminate. After the child was born in 2001 with severe congenital abnormalities, subsequent cord blood testing and FISH analysis revealed a longer "p" arm of chromosome 15, and the father was then found to have a balanced translocation of chromosomes 9 and 15, accounting for the infant's "unbalanced" translocation.

The couple's suit rested on claims that they were both insufficiently and untimely advised as to the likelihood and severity of the abnormalities, including being falsely reassured by specific negative test results. There were some delays in reporting certain test results, and the couple argued they did not have time to obtain an abortion following a meeting during the wife's twenty-third to twenty-fourth week. Although termination services at Dartmouth were not available after the twenty-second week, the couple transferred their care to Boston immediately following that meeting, where abortion services were still available.

The court analyzed the case under New Hampshire's existing "wrongful birth" standards and found against the couple. The court found the medical providers properly advised the couple that there was a very high likelihood of an abnormality, and the "possibility" of a serious birth defect, and provided such information in a timely manner. It found there was no legal duty to provide "whatever information a parent subjectively needs to make an 'informed decision' concerning the termination of a pregnancy." Moreover, it ruled the couple had not met their burden of proving untimeliness. The court took note that wrongful birth claims, unlike most medical malpractice cases, involve the uniquely personal choice of termination, and therefore courts should consider the "emotional and physical ability to digest and act upon the information . . . within the time period in issue . . . ," but found that the plaintiffs' expert had failed to offer testimony that might have supported this claim.

The decision highlights the application of existing legal theories to new technologies and suggests ways in which legal theories may expand in future scenarios. Given both the novelty and difficulty of diagnosing the precise abnormality, the information that was given, as well as the failure of the plaintiffs' expert to establish facts supporting their legal claims, the court's outcome was predictable and within established legal principles.

Hall v. Dartmouth Hitchcock Medical Center,
899 A.2d 240 (N.H. 2006)

9.9(a) Couple's Wrongful Birth Claims Turn on Conflict of Laws Question
Fall 2006

In a striking example of both the significance and variability of the law, a lab's liability for misreading an amniocentesis test will turn on what state law applies to its conceded failure to meet the standard of care. The case involves a Maryland couple who sought to avoid having a second child with cystic fibrosis (CF). After delivering their first, affected, child and learning they were both CF carriers, the couple had aborted their second pregnancy when pre-natal testing showed that child would be born with the disease. The parents, Karen and Scott Hood, conceived a third time and again underwent amniocentesis. The fluid was sent to Lab Corp., Inc., located in North Carolina. The lab was informed both parents were carriers. The lab admitted to misreading the chromatograph and mistakenly reporting that the fetus was not a carrier or affected. Based on the undiscovered misreading, the couple carried to term, and at three months their son was found positive for CF.

The couple sued in federal court under Maryland law, which recognizes "wrongful birth" actions and allows damages for extraordinary costs of child-rearing. In contrast, North Carolina does not allow recovery for "wrongful birth" claims, on the twin rationales that it does not want to hold health care professionals responsible for genetic abnormalities they did not cause and to discourage legal liability for actions that would result in an abortion. Lab Corp. has argued that North Carolina law should apply. As the federal court noted, "[d]eciding the choice of law is critical, because if this court were to apply the laws of North Carolina, the Hoods would not have a cause of action." Ironically, North Carolina does recognize "wrongful conception" claims, where a pregnancy would not have occurred absent a health care professional's negligence. The federal court has "certified" to the Maryland Court of Appeals the question of which state law should apply, which must render an opinion before the case can proceed.

The case presents a classic example, in an unusual setting, of what is known as a "conflict of laws" analysis, where two states have dramatically different approaches to the legal theories and recovery limits for the same wrongful actions. The defendant lab claims that it would be unfair to subject it to laws in any state where a family happens to reside and that it should be held only to the standards of the state where it is located. Additional arguments turn on intricate legal exceptions to "standard of care" principles [including whether to apply the law of the state where the injury occurred (Maryland) or where the last negligent act occurred (North Carolina)], as well as the lab's argument that any claim belonged solely to the wife, not the husband [since he was not the literal subject of the test]. The couple has argued that, especially for a national company doing business throughout the country (the lab reportedly operates in thirty-five testing locations with more than a thousand patient service centers, including eight in Maryland), it would be unfair to allow a company to "forum shop" for a favorable location and that any standard of care exception that might make North Carolina law applicable should be rejected as a matter of public policy since Maryland law so clearly protects "the rights of parents to make their own family planning decisions."

Ironically, since North Carolina recognizes "wrongful conception" claims prior to establishing a pregnancy, the family would have been able to recover under that state's laws had they been misdiagnosed through either carrier testing or PGD (preimplantation genetic diagnosis). As PGD becomes more widespread, that legal distinction may be difficult to maintain. Otherwise it will open a new venue for arguments as to when conception occurs or life begins.

With the increasing interstate nature of many ART and reproductive genetics scenarios, such legal intricacies and inconsistent laws may become significant in the event of subsequent complications or disputes.

9.9(b) Lab Must Comply with Law Where Family Lives, Not Where Located

Winter 2007

Refusing to force parents to play genetic roulette, the Maryland Court of Appeals has ruled that a North Carolina testing laboratory cannot use "conflict of laws" arguments to shield itself from liability.

The federal court hearing the dispute had sent ("certified") three questions of state law to the Maryland court for its interpretation. That court decided Maryland law should govern as the place where the final injury, the child's birth, occurred. It ruled inapplicable a legal "standard of care" exception, which would have made North Carolina law applicable. The court added that to apply North Carolina law would also violate important Maryland public policy, which allows parents to recover damages for the cost of raising a child resulting from a pregnancy they would otherwise have lawfully terminated. Finally, it found unpersuasive, under the facts of the case, Lab Corp's final argument that the duty and injury was only to the mother and that it did not owe the father a duty of care.

The ruling affirms, at least in Maryland, parents' right to bring wrongful birth claims under the laws of their home state and not be vulnerable to the state laws where a lab is physically located. Ironically, as prenatal testing expands rapidly into preimplantation genetic testing, the rationale for legal precedent such as North Carolina's law that permits only pre-conception claims, may find itself being tested.

Hood v. Lab. Corp. of Am., 2006 U.S. Dist. LEXIS
36464 (D. Md. 2006), and 911 A.2d 811 (Md. 2006)
(answering federal court's certified questions)

CHAPTER TEN

ART-Related Embryonic Stem Cell Legal Developments

✦ MEDICAL COMMENTARY, BY Howard W. Jones, Jr.

WITH EMBRYONIC STEM CELL research in the news on a daily basis, it is scarcely necessary to recount the disorders that can be potentially improved or cured by embryonic stem cell transplants. A dose of biological reality reveals that embryonic stem cells have shown two major biological problems to date.

First, contrary to the original hope, embryonic stem cells are rejected when transplanted into a genetically non-identical recipient. Thus, the recipient would have to be treated to suppress the immune system. This treatment is very severe and currently associated with significant complications.

Second, some of the animal data show that the differentiated embryonic stem cells are not entirely stable after transplantation. In particular, there have been some embryonic stem cells that develop into tumors. This problem surely will have to be understood and corrected before human use can be considered, and will not happen overnight.

However, in late 2007 some very significant steps were announced in the area of stem cell research.

At least three laboratories, at Kyoto, the University of Wisconsin, and Harvard, announced that they had reprogrammed animal and human somatic cells to exhibit the characteristics of stem cells. This is remarkable. If this can be replicated, the technology can be hailed as the solution to the ethical objection to the use of stem cells. With this technology, early embryos may not need to be involved and therefore destroyed.

While this could be a terrific development in the ethical area, most leaders in the field continue to believe that continued research is needed on both this and early embryos to understand and realize the full potential of stem cell research. To this observer, these developments may be far more important from a bioscience point of view.

From a bioscience perspective, these findings offer an avenue to overcoming the rejection problem. Somatic cells from the potential recipient can be reprogrammed to provide stem cells that differentiate into the desired tissue and can be transferred without the danger of rejection. This is absolutely an astonishing and significant development, one that solves one of the two major problems referred to above.

There have been further interesting developments in this area, including reports of animal studies that generated spermlike cells from embryonic stem cells and fertilization of eggs with those cells. Studies such as this will continue to raise the question of whether reproduction can take place without sperm and without eggs.

Are these developments going to be useful to humans in the immediate future? No. It seems unlikely because the procedures will have to be further developed, and it must be shown that they really will work in the animal, which has yet to be done. Will this happen sometime in the future? Yes. I don't think there is any doubt about it.

And what about ectogenesis, as described by Aldous Huxley in *Brave New World* and originally noted in a 1923 lecture by J. B. S. Haldane? There has been little or no laboratory research in this area in the recent past, but over the years there have been attempts to maintain fetuses in culture; for example, a decade ago the Japanese developed a lamb entirely in a jar to a certain point in its development. To date, however, scientists have not been able either to develop fully a conceptus of any kind outside the womb or to transfer a developing conceptus beyond a few days from outside the womb into the womb. Could there be a place for such a procedure in human reproduction? Probably, but if so, a very niche role. It would do away with the necessity for surrogacy. As mentioned in earlier chapters, surrogacy has caused much litigation, and in this specific situation, if scientists ever overcome the obstacles, ectogenesis may have a place.

If these procedures develop in the distant future, and I expect that they will, the legal ramifications of trying to determine parentage and other related issues will become even more complex than they are today. Stay tuned.

∽ LEGAL COMMENTARY, BY Susan L. Crockin

In recent years, embryonic stem cell research has emerged not only as a promising area of scientific research and potential medical advances but also as a virtual thicket of legal, ethical, and policy issues. It has generated an increasingly public debate that is inevitably intertwined with IVF embryos, gametes, abortion, and reproductive law and medicine.

Much as IVF development was stunted by restrictive federal policies throughout the 1980s and 1990s, until very recently advances in embryonic stem cell research on the federal level have been largely muted by executive orders and the enactment of laws and regulations that have prohibited federal funding for developing stem cell lines or creating research embryos. The results of such policies on ART were that IVF techniques developed largely in the private sector with little initial research on human subjects and mainly away from the restrictions of rules or regulations. In contrast, many recent embryonic stem cell research advances have been developing in a handful of states that have enacted pro–stem cell research laws and serve as incubators for more progressive, pro-research policies and laws. Those laws have both promoted the burgeoning science and been challenged by disgruntled citizens and entities. In some instances the state laws that have been enacted reflect compromises or even seeming ignorance of some of the competing and underlying issues impacted by these laws. With a new Democratic administration in 2009, many anticipate a sea change in how stem cell research will be regulated at the federal level. What remains less clear is the extent and timing of those changes, the form that opposition to the loosening of restrictions at the state or federal levels will take, and the effect on, and ideally coordination with, relevant ART practices and policies such as egg and embryo donation.

In March 2009, the Obama administration issued an Executive Order expanding federal funding for embryonic stem cell research to include funding for research using leftover IVF embryos. In April 2009, the

Department of Health and Human Services proposed regulations that would provide clear and detailed guidelines for patient consent to donation for that purpose and use. The Executive Order was largely acknowledged to be both a significant expansion of federal policy and a somewhat measured step to keep expanded funding within the bounds of what has largely garnered wide public support: leftover IVF embryos as opposed to embryos created for the research itself. Whether and how such federal support will expand in this field is a subject of intense interest, both by those who favor and by those who fear it.

The cases and laws reported in this section reflect both the legal developments and schisms that have arisen as they relate to the ARTs. Readers should also note the relevance of earlier constitutional challenges brought by IVF professionals to statutes that restricted IVF practices and earlier laboratory procedures involving embryos reviewed in chapter 1, including *Lifchez v. Hartigan* (1991), *Doe v. Shalala* (1995), and *Forbes v. Napolitano* (2001). Those cases were remarkably prescient as to the nature of the restrictions and challenges facing embryonic stem cell research today.

States have passed a variety of both pro- and anti-stem cell research laws. Passage of two pro-embryonic stem cell laws, in California (2002) and Massachusetts (2005), illustrate the difficulties such laws can encounter and, inadvertently, create. The California law, the Stem Cell Research and Cures Initiative, enacted to promote and fund stem cell research in that state, was met with multiple court challenges by citizens and anti-research groups, effectively delaying the law's implementation for a number of years.

The Massachusetts law illustrates a different type of difficulty in enacting such legislation. That statute, passed to much acclaim by stem cell proponents, nonetheless ultimately included a number of troublesome last-minute provisions. One provision mandates physicians to distribute descriptive pamphlets and detailed consent forms to all women undergoing in vitro fertilization (while a different section states that the law does not apply to reproductive IVF). Another provision authorizes the state to take custody of abandoned embryos for "medical care or treatment," which seemingly violates established legal principles involving the status of embryos and the constitutional procreative rights of those who created them. In addition, the law disallows payment to research egg donors, which has resulted in virtually no research donors being available to date. These compromises were made to assuage late opposition by anti-technology feminists and their arguments that the law would exploit poor and minority women by encouraging egg donation for compensation. Not only have the restrictions discouraged research egg donation but the provisions—if followed—would also layer restrictive provisions onto IVF procedures and run afoul of established legal characterizations of IVF embryos and constitutional protections for those who created them.

Even with more progressive laws in the future, embryonic stem cell research will still likely encounter legal challenges, including how to increase the availability for research of donated eggs and embryos formed through in vitro fertilization (IVF), whether and how to reconcile compensation disparities between reproductive and research egg donors, and how to resolve the ongoing semantic battles that have significant policy implications over the legal and moral status of the ex utero embryo.

Many of these challenges are familiar to those involved in the legal issues raised by the ARTs. Prior legal battles, legislation, and voluntary guidelines involving the ARTs have significantly advanced the elusive task of defining the legal status of the embryo and those with rights to it, while helping define and enhance legal protections for gamete donors and recipients.

Progress on embryonic stem cell research will not depend solely on medical and scientific advances. It will also be essential to develop laws and policies that support the science and regulate the business of stem cells and that at the same time recognize, reflect, and build upon the legal and policy developments that have already been established in related areas of the ARTs. Failure to recognize the intersections between these fields and to build on the legal lessons learned from each of them would serve only to impede and impair progress in both of these rapidly advancing and intertwined fields.

Litigation

10.1 California Enacts Anti-Cloning Legislation

Spring 1998

California has enacted a five-year ban on human cloning as well as a ban on the purchase or sale of a gamete, embryo, or fetus for the purpose of cloning a human being. The law imposes fines ranging from $250,000 for an individual to $1 million for a corporate or medical entity. In addition, the new law provides for a civil fine for anyone who profits from violating the law, or double the amount of such gain. The law is effective as of January 1, 1998.

[current: Cal. Health & Safety Code 24185]

10.2(a) Massachusetts Legislature Passes Stem Cell Law with IVF Consent Provisions

Summer 2005

Massachusetts joins California and New Jersey in enacting a law designed to promote stem cell research within a state. The bill is now headed to the governor's desk, where it is easily expected to override an anticipated veto. The law does not fund the research but approves it with certain caveats, including disallowing compensation to egg donors and prohibiting the creation of research embryos through fertilization. As currently drafted, the law will permit creation of embryos through somatic cell nuclear transfer and other nonfertilization methods. Excess IVF embryos are also permitted to be used, again with no compensation to the donors. Of particular interest to the ART community may be provisions that made their way into the final version of the compromise law after it came out of both houses. Notwithstanding a provision that "[n]othing in this chapter shall be deemed to prohibit or regulate the use of in vitro fertilization for reproductive purposes," an added section details specific requirements for taking IVF consents whenever eggs are retrieved from any patient. Those requirements include a standardized pamphlet that outlines the procedures, medical risks, drug-related known and unknown risks, and disposition options for any resulting embryos. In addition, a mandatory "notes" section must be completed referencing any issues specific to a particular patient and a copy provided to that patient. A different section added late in the process authorizes an investigation into the possibility of the state taking custody of abandoned embryos and deciding whether or not they can be used for "biomedical research or medical care or treatment."

[current: Mass. Gen. Laws ch. 111L, 1]

10.2(b) Massachusetts Stem Cell Legislation Hits Regulatory Snag
Fall 2006

Demonstrating how volatile the terrain can be for stem cell research at both state and federal levels, Massachusetts legislators are attempting to reverse recent restrictive regulations that threaten to limit stem cell research approved by the legislature in 2005. The regulations were adopted by a Public Health Council whose members are appointed by the governor. Lawmakers claim the regulations go beyond both the letter and intent of the law and are a deliberate and politicized attempt to restrict legally permitted research activities. The council has acknowledged working closely with the governor, who opposes research except on leftover embryos and is widely perceived as a contender for the Republican presidential nomination. Legislators and scientists expressed concern that the new regulations expanded the law's prohibition on creating embryos solely for the purpose of "donating" them (which would apply to donors) to a prohibition on creating embryos solely for the purpose of "using" them, a subtle but significant distinction that would preclude scientists from creating such embryos.

The Boston Globe, 8/30–31/06

10.2(c) Massachusetts Governor Moves to Loosen Stem Cell Restrictions
Spring 2007

The newly elected Democratic governor of Massachusetts has wasted little time in reversing anti–stem cell regulations put into place by his Republican predecessor and the state's appointed Public Health Council. The previous regulations interpreted the 2005 law as prohibiting scientists from using embryos created for research or stem cell lines derived from them and had been widely criticized for both limiting stem cell research and thwarting the intent of the legislation.

Governor Deval Patrick and his administration have made it known they want to support stem cell research and the scientific and economic advances it may bring to the state. The governor's actions, including the announced intent to reconstitute the state's Public Health Council, have been favorably received by the research and scientific community.

Boston Globe, 3/30/07; 105 CMR 960.00 et. seq.

10.3(a) California's Stem Cell Law on Hold Awaiting Court Ruling
Spring 2006

A trial recently concluded in Hayward, California, in a pair of lawsuits seeking to invalidate Proposition 71, the law approved last November by state voters that created the California Institute of Regenerative Medicine and authorized it to sell $3 billion in state bonds to fund stem cell research. The court's ruling is expected shortly. The People's Advocate and National Tax Limitation Foundation and the California Family Bioethics Council sued, claiming the committee overseeing the agency is beyond state control in violation of the California state constitution. The two plaintiff organizations are affiliated with various anti-abortion organizations, including James Dobson's Focus on the Family, and one of the suits is reportedly being handled and funded by the same group that paid for the legal efforts to keep Terri Schiavo on life support.

The defendant, the California Institute of Regenerative Medicine, has countered that there would be strict oversight by the state's treasurer and controller. Earlier, a judge refused to dismiss the lawsuit but indicated that since the ballot measures reflected the will of the voters, the plaintiffs had a high legal hurdle to prove the agency was "clearly, positively, and unmistakably unconstitutional." Although most commentators predict the Institute will win, the litigation has prevented the Institute from issuing bonds to fund research and resulted in at least a few sought-after researchers taking jobs elsewhere. While the Institute is exploring bridge funding, full funding will likely be delayed until all avenues of appeal are exhausted, a process that could take another year.

LATimes.com, 3/3/06; Boston Globe, 2/27/06

10.3(b) State Claims Victory in California Stem Cell Litigation
Summer 2006

On April 21, 2006, a state trial court upheld the constitutionality of Proposition 71, which created and funded the California Institute of Regenerative Medicine. The California court found the Institute was legally under the state's control, rejecting arguments that it was improperly constituted and run. The Institute has now awarded and funded its first sixteen stem cell grants for over 150 research fellows.

People's Adv. & Nat. Tax Limitation Fdtn. v. Ind. Citizens'
Oversight Comm. (Cal. Trial Ct., 4/21/06);
Cal. Family Bioethics Council, LLC v. Cal. Inst.
for Regenerative Medicine, 147 aff'd by 55 Cal. Rptr. 3d
272 (Cal. Ct. App. 2007)

10.4 Missouri Stem Cell Amendment Runs into Obstacles over Defining "Cloning"
Fall 2007

Proving that passing laws or constitutional amendments alone does not ensure changes on the ground, Missouri is finding that its stem cell amendment is meeting with continued resistance and resulting setbacks in embryonic stem cell research efforts there. The issue is turning on a debate over the meaning of "human cloning," which is banned under the provision that makes legal under state law any research or treatment allowed under federal law (but does not fund any such research). Opponents argue that the amendment's definition, which requires a resulting pregnancy, is too narrow, and that "geography"—whether the cells are placed in a uterus or not—should not be determinative. Opponents have introduced bills to ban some forms of the research, there is talk of another ballot initiative, and plans to expand prominent research facilities in the state are currently suspended, all suggesting that efforts to ensure support for embryonic stem cell research remains a challenging goal.

New York Times, 8/10/07

10.5 Colorado Puts "Personhood" on the Ballot
Summer 2008

Colorado voters this fall will be asked whether or not a fertilized egg is a person. Known as the "Human Life Amendment," the law would define person or persons in the state constitution to include "any human being from the moment of fertilization." The Colorado Supreme Court has approved allowing the measure to go on the ballet.

The initiative has been criticized as an anti-abortion measure intended to bring litigation and eventually place the issue before an increasingly conservative U.S. Supreme Court. It has also been criticized by anti-abortion groups as the wrong tactic at the wrong time. Critics and legal experts have suggested such a law would give embryos and fetuses equal rights with the women who created or are carrying them, including subjecting women who abort to murder charges. If passed, the measure would also have a substantial impact on Colorado's medical and scientific practices, likely placing extensive limits on patient and physician choices in IVF and embryo freezing protocols as well as likely precluding embryonic stem cell research.

Note: The measure failed by a three-to-one margin in the November 2008 elections. A similar bill in Nevada failed in April 2009.

Washington Post, 7/13/08

CHAPTER ELEVEN

ART-Related Adoption Litigation

∾ LEGAL COMMENTARY, BY Susan L. Crockin

A T THE OUTSET, "Legally Speaking" made a conscious decision to report only on adoption-related litigation or legislation that also related directly to ART practices. Despite multiple parallels in the two fields, in 1990 the risk was that adoption cases would far outnumber ART cases and be of limited interest to medical professionals. Thirty years later, the same decision—for very different reasons—holds true. Litigation in the field of ART has burgeoned, and the growing body of law surrounding reproductive technology and embryos now almost routinely raises and analyzes both the many parallels and the key distinctions between this developing law and that of adoption. Many of those issues arise in the context of new forms of family building. Thus, chapters 6 and 8, which address traditional and gestational surrogacy and same-sex parenting, reflect a number of adoption decisions and issues affecting those families. The remaining few cases reported in this general section are significant as both signposts and predictors of developing legal issues in the ARTs.

In 1999, several legal milestones occurred. Tennessee's highest court ruled that adult adoptees have a constitutionally protected unilateral right to access their original birth certificates and to learn the identities of their birth parents (*Doe v. Sundquist*, 1999). "Closed" adoptions had been the norm for many decades, and most states that allowed limited access to original birth records only did so with the mutual consent of both birth parents and adult adoptees or adoptive parents on behalf of their minor children. The notion that such children had a birthright to this information was accepted by the Tennessee court and, since that time, by a growing number of state legislatures. Also in 1999, this author was asked to give a plenary address to the Eleventh IVF World Congress to address the question of "Where is Anonymous Reproduction Taking Us?" a talk that drew what were then seldom noticed parallels between adoption and third-party ART families.[1] The response from adult DI offspring in the audience was surprisingly emotional, with many publicly and tearfully expressing gratitude for hearing their concerns acknowledged and validated in a public forum for the first time.

Fast-forward a decade later, and drawing parallels between adoption and ART families is increasingly common. "Yes" donors are now a standard option in sperm donation, enabling families to choose a donor who agrees to future contact from the outset. Legal agreements between even anonymous egg donors and recipients increasingly include provisions for future contact and potential identity disclosure. Privately run donor registries have sprung up to enable donors and the resulting families to deposit and later gain information about one another and, in many instances, to share identifying, as well as genetic, information. Practice guidelines for both sperm and egg donation promulgated by ASRM include directives to maintain permanent gamete donation records. In 2007 and 2008 an initial exploratory workshop (October 2007) followed by an inaugural public conference (March 2008) were convened to consider the establishment of a voluntary national donor gamete registry, partially in response to recent concerns over genetic conditions being transmitted by donors to offspring. Calls for, and efforts to establish, a national registry by various groups continue. A primary goal is to create a central repository of genetic and potentially identifying information for donors, parents, and offspring, something that does not currently exist despite professional guidelines that require permanent record keeping for both sperm and egg donation. The structure, scope, and limits of any such registry are not yet developed, and doing so will be challenging. With variable state laws (many states lack any law that clearly defines parentage for egg or embryo donation) as well as a lack of consensus in the field on a number of complex issues, many questions remain unan-

---

1. Later published within the proceedings of the Congress, "Towards Reproductive Certainty: Fertility and Genetics beyond 1999," 59:467, ed. R. Jansen and D. Mortimer.

swered. Interest in developing a voluntary or mandatory donor registry remains high among multiple constituent groups, and such efforts are ongoing.

Adoption issues came to the forefront within ART arrangements in the context of traditional surrogacy. The first surrogacy cases gave courts the opportunity to define "traditional" surrogates as birth mothers and to apply to them the same protections afforded by adoption laws regarding when and how these women could relinquish parental rights. As gestational surrogacy became more prevalent with the advent of IVF and the growing concern over disputed maternity for traditional surrogates, courts were forced to redefine motherhood—quite literally—recognizing the distinctions between traditional and gestational surrogate situations and the limitations on the applicability of adoption law to the latter situations.

Both traditional and gestational surrogacies have frequently raised the complicated question of whether and how to investigate an intended parent's "fitness" to parent and the appropriate role—if any—of medical and other professionals in evaluating them. While home studies, background checks, and other protections are accepted practices in the world of adoption, medical professionals are not used to or comfortable with evaluating patients' fitness to parent, nor are they protected from liability if and when they enter that arena. Some commentators distinguish these situations on the basis that adoption is about born children's needs, specifically the need to find a specific child a "good" home, a value that makes pre-adoptive screening appropriate as a way of trying to ensure that the best home has been identified for a particular child's needs. In contrast, ART medical treatment creates a child who, but for the treatment, would not exist and who, under many legal principles, is owed no duty of care prior to conception. Whether those distinctions are persuasive regarding parental fitness or parental evaluation is neither tested nor clear. Evaluating patients, in contrast to pre-adoptive parents, runs the very real risk of creating vulnerability for medical professionals to claims of discrimination or other illegal denials of access to treatment. An example of these tensions is evident in the case of Juanita Benitez (2008) discussed in chapter 2, in which two physicians' refusal to treat an unmarried lesbian woman on the alleged basis of their religious beliefs was ultimately ruled to be an illegal discriminatory denial of access.

As also noted in the medical commentaries, this tension between providing medical care versus screening in or screening out prospective parents has been a major and still-unresolved theme in the development of reproductive medicine and law.

Applying adoption laws and paradigms can also provide significant protections for some otherwise vulnerable ART families. Same-sex couples and single parents accessing ART treatment to create their families have at times availed themselves of adoption law protections. In the absence of same-sex marriage recognition or clear parentage laws that define such families in the context of ART treatments, confirming their legal status through adoption proceedings can provide a significant legal protection to both parent(s) and child. As one recent example, in late 2008 a same-sex male couple won a federal court ruling that Louisiana, where their adopted child was born, must give "full faith and credit" to the New York adoption decree and prepare an amended birth certificate listing both fathers on the child's new birth certificate (*Adar v. Smith*, 2008). And in a number of cases, single women who conceive with donor sperm may wish to undergo an adoption of their child to cut off any parental rights or parental obligations a sperm donor, as the child's biological father, might otherwise be deemed to have. Such a step could necessitate obtaining the man's agreement or consent as well as requiring a court's agreement to allow a parent to adopt his or her own child. Although unorthodox, at least in some jurisdictions (including Massachusetts, in cases brought by this author), these adoptions have been allowed. In a somewhat ironic twist, same-sex, legally married couples in Massachusetts, who are *not* required to adopt a child born to either of them to establish their legal parentage, are nonetheless routinely advised to undergo such an adoption to ensure their legal parentage status outside of the few states that currently recognize their marriage.

Until the laws surrounding ART families are more comprehensive, established adoption law remains an important element to securing legal parent and child status for many of these families.

As the parallels and distinctions between adoption and ART law develop, they continue to challenge and at times both protect and perplex those involved in modern family building efforts.

Litigation

11.1 Adoption Insurance
September 1991

Lloyds of London and Chubb and Sons are offering insurance to a limited number of potential adoptive parents pursuing independent adoptions. Currently offered through a select group of adoption attorneys, the policies are designed to protect pre-adoptive couples from most of the financial, if not emotional, risks of adoptive pursuits.

Since private adoption agreements cannot be enforced in courts, monies expended on behalf of a birth parent who changes her mind have historically been lost in their entirety. For those whose life's savings are involved, such a decision can mean the loss of the opportunity to adopt altogether.

Under the policies, legally recognized expenditures would be insurable at a premium cost ranging from $500 to $1,200 for $10,000 worth of insurance.

New York Times, 4/6/91

11.2 Birth Mother Settles for $1 Million over Child's Death
Winter 1999

Lisa Steinberg's biological mother, Michele Launders, has now settled her lawsuit against three New York City public agencies and the live-in companion of Joel Steinberg, the man who tortured her daughter to death after he adopted her as an infant. The lawsuit was brought against the agencies involved who had not performed a home study or assessment of Steinberg as a prospective adoptive parent, and against Hedda Nussbaum, Steinberg's live-in companion. Nussbaum claimed that she was forced to do Steinberg's bidding. Steinberg is serving a twenty-five-year sentence for manslaughter.

From a liability perspective, the case shows similarities to a lawsuit brought by traditional surrogate Phyllis Huddleston, who sued Noel Keane and affiliated professionals after the single man for whom she bore a child killed the infant [6.18]. Liability was charged in both cases based on professionals' failure to meet an obligation to properly screen or assess prospective parents despite the fact that the biological mother had not herself intended to raise the child. Lawyers for Ms. Launders reportedly will continue to seek additional damages from Steinberg himself.

Update: Launders was awarded a $985,000 settlement from New York City on September 30, 1999, and Lisa Steinberg's estate won a $15 million ($10 million for pain and suffering; $5 million in punitive damages) civil award against Joel Steinberg. After being released from prison in 2007, Joel Steinberg was granted reconsideration of the punitive damages award, including whether a percentage of his liability should be extended to Nussbaum and the city.

Launders v. Steinberg, 876 N.E.2d 901
(N.Y. 2007)

11.3 Tennessee High Court Upholds Law Allowing Access to Adoptees' Birth Records without Birth Parent Consent
Winter 1999

In a case with far-reaching implications for open adoption and open records advocates, Tennessee's highest court has upheld the constitutionality of a law there that allows the unilateral disclosure of previously sealed adoption records to adoptees over the age of twenty-one (or their legal representatives). The law, which now permits adoptees to obtain their original birth certificate without consent of the birth parent, does provide a "contact veto" whereby a biological parent, sibling, spouse, lineal ancestor, or lineal descendant may register to prevent contact by the adoptee.

In March 1997, a group of plaintiffs, including birth parents who had surrendered children for adoption many years ago, filed an action challenging the constitutionality of the law. The plaintiffs argued that disclosure of previously sealed, identifying adoption records invaded the right to familial privacy both by impeding a birth parent's freedom to determine whether to raise a family and by disrupting biological as well as adoptive families.

Tennessee's highest court disagreed, ruling that the legislation reflected the Tennessee legislature's determination that allowing limited access to adoption records is in the best interests of both adopted persons and the public. The court further held that the legislation did not impede traditional familial rights such as marrying or having or raising children. The court declined to extend constitutional protection to the nondisclosure of personal information.

Although relatively few states have such far-reaching laws, the growing trend is clearly toward allowing greater accessibility to such records by adoptees and birth parents alike. This, however, is one of the first times a state law has been drafted and upheld that permits adoptees to obtain what many have argued is their "birth right" without requiring consent of the birth parent being sought. Cases and laws such as this reinforce the thinking of many professionals that gamete or embryo donation may ultimately see many such record requests and fuel interdisciplinary debates over the creation, content of, and prospective access to potential donor registries.

Doe v. Sundquist, 2 S.W.3d 919 (Tenn. 1999)

11.4 Florida's "Scarlet Letter"

Summer 2003

In a victory for adoption advocates, attorneys, and birth mothers, Florida's recently enacted "Scarlet Letter" law has been declared unconstitutional. The law imposed more stringent notice requirements to possible birth fathers, including newspaper publication of the name of every possible birth father and every city in which a birth mother resided or traveled where conception may have occurred during the previous twelve months. The Attorney General had declined to defend the statute in the lawsuit. The law was intended to ensure due process to birth fathers and prevent heartbreaking and highly publicized cases where birth fathers who had no knowledge of or notice about the adoption come forward years after a child was adopted. The court recognized, however, that the law went too far. Given that the law impacts a fundamental right to privacy, it was incumbent on the state to bear the burden of proving that the law both served a compelling state interest and interfered in the least intrusive manner possible. The court found the requirements of newspaper notification failed to respect that principle and struck the law.

G.P. v. State, 842 So. 2d 1059 (Fla. 4th DCA 2003)

11.5 Two Dads Ordered onto Adoptive Son's New Birth Certificate under Full Faith and Credit Clause of U.S. Constitution

Spring 2009

A federal court has ordered the state of Louisiana to issue a new birth certificate to a boy adopted by his two fathers in New York State. Louisiana does not permit any two unmarried persons to adopt and the state's Office of Vital Records had refused to issue the amended birth certificate. Finding no factual issues and the law clear, the court granted summary judgment to the fathers. In unequivocal language, the court confirmed that the "full faith and credit" clause of the United States Constitution requires a state recognize a valid foreign court order regardless of whether or not that order is consistent with the state's public policy. Reviewing the history of the clause, the court noted it was enacted to ensure that no state could act as an independent foreign entity but rather all states must act as "integral parts of a single nation" and recognize one another's judicial pronouncements. The court explained that, in contrast to the "less demanding" adherence required of recognizing another state's statutes and the possibility there of an exception for public policy reasons, the Supreme Court has made clear that the constitutional full faith and credit obligation is "exacting" when it comes to court orders.

Adar v. Smith, 591 F.Supp. 2d 857
(E. D. La. 2008)

CHAPTER TWELVE

ART-Related Fetal Litigation and Abortion-Related Litigation

❖ MEDICAL COMMENTARY, BY Howard W. Jones, Jr.

ALTHOUGH THE CASES in this section have no direct relation to assisted reproductive technology, they certainly raise ART-related concerns. *Johnson v. State* (1992) raises an uncertainty that confronts anyone involved in ART: the age-old fundamental question of when during development the conceptus attains personhood. Personhood in this context is defined as that developmental status which acquires protection by society. The religious equivalent is ensoulment.

The controversy arises when there is a discrepancy in evaluating the moral status of the conceptus compared to the legal status. Note that I cited moral and not ethical status. Although ethics and morality are often used interchangeably, it can be helpful to distinguish between the two. I think of it like this: a moral judgment evaluates a status against an established standard or code that could also serve as a religious code. An ethical judgment evaluates a status using natural reason based on experience. Using these definitions, the conflict is between the moral—or "religious"—status of the developing conceptus compared to its legal status.

In *Johnson v. State,* the court refused to accept a prosecutor's attempt to make the conceptus a person in order to prosecute an addicted, pregnant woman under that state's law prohibiting delivering controlled substances to minors. Instead, the court ruled this was not the intent of the legislature.

This controversy over the status of the conceptus can involve legal, moral, and ethical perspectives. As mentioned several times throughout these commentaries all involved in ART will have greater peace of mind and perhaps a better chance of reaching a policy consensus if they know why they believe what they believe about the moral status of the developing conceptus.

∾ LEGAL COMMENTARY, BY Susan L. Crockin

Protecting women's procreative rights has always been a delicate legal balance where pregnancy is involved. On the one hand, in a long line of cases the U.S. Supreme Court has recognized a woman's constitutional right to control her own body, including the right to obtain contraception, refuse sterilization, and manage and control decision-making over any pregnancy and termination at least until fetal viability has been established. On the other hand, both legislators and courts have also wrestled in recent years with placing limits on abortion decision-making, including restrictions on pregnant minors and late-term abortions.

Some court cases result from the creative application of older laws to new scenarios, such as attempting to apply drug distribution crimes to pregnant women whose own drug use harms their fetus. New laws have also been enacted. Particularly in the wake of high-profile murders of pregnant women, both Congress and various state legislatures have enacted laws making it a crime to harm a viable fetus as well as a specific crime to kill or harm a pregnant woman.

Given the highly politicized nature of the abortion debate in the United States, any attempt to criminalize cases involving pregnant women and fetuses or to enact protective legislation for fetuses is inextricably part of a larger societal debate on what forms of nascent life are deserving of legal protection. These efforts also frequently trigger debates over how adult women's rights are to be balanced against the pregnancies they carry.

The ARTs provide a new arena in which these tensions may arise, as has been suggested in cases involving surrogacy as well as frozen embryos. Gestational carrier arrangements have provided an opportunity for some to suggest that the fetus or the intended genetic parents of the fetus have rights that must be balanced against those of the gestational carrier regarding any prenatal decision. There has yet to be a reported court case addressing such an argument, and it is difficult to see how one could be squared with existing constitutional protections involving

women's pregnancy and reproductive rights. As established legal principles do not permit even a husband to decide whether his wife continues
or aborts a pregnancy, there should be little question that intended parents could enforce such an act even in the context of a breach of contract.

Also, while primarily addressed in other sections, both fresh and cryopreserved IVF embryos available for procreation or various forms of
embryonic research trigger these questions. Embryos clearly do not meet
the legal definition of "viability" first announced in *Roe v. Wade*. On the
other hand, by being outside of a woman's body, IVF embryos provide an
opportunity—and a challenge—to rethink the legal analysis involved in
balancing rights. Louisiana stands alone in enacting legislation that recognizes an embryo as a separate legal entity, a law that would seemingly
be vulnerable to a constitutional challenge. A 2009 law enacted in Georgia entitled the "Option of Adoption Act" authorizes an expedited pre- or
post-birth "adoption," even though the law also makes clear that the
legal transfer of parental rights and responsibilities from embryo donors
to recipients occurs by contract prior to implantation. A 2008 ballot
initiative in Colorado and a 2009 proposal in Nevada to enact laws
recognizing the "personhood" of IVF embryos were defeated, but similar
efforts are reportedly under way in other states around the country. Any
such legal status accorded to an IVF embryo would transform the law in
a myriad of arenas and raise significant reproductive rights issues of
constitutional proportions.

The few cases in this section focus primarily on non-ART but relevant
court decisions that illustrate some of the approaches to and tensions
surrounding protecting fetuses without sacrificing the rights of the
women who carry them.

Litigation

12.1 Florida Refuses to Prosecute Mother for Cocaine Use
during Pregnancy
December 1992

Repudiating a growing sentiment in district attorneys' offices around
the country, the Florida Supreme Court has rejected a criminal prosecution of a woman whose children were born addicted to cocaine.

The state had attempted to prosecute her for breaking the law that prohibits delivering controlled substances to a minor. In rejecting the theory, the court noted the legislature never intended this law to apply to the birthing process.

Johnson v. State, 602 So. 2d 1288 (Fla. 1992)

12.2(a) Female Accident Victim Kept "Alive" to Bring Fetus to Term
March 1993

In Germany, hospital authorities are keeping a comatose woman alive as her pregnancy proceeds amid nationwide fury and as international criticism increases.

In October of last year, Marion Ploch, an eighteen-year-old unmarried German woman, ran off the road and suffered irreversible brain damage. After trying to save her for four days, doctors declared her legally dead. Since she was found to be fourteen weeks pregnant, a hastily assembled hospital ethics committee recommended leaving her on life-support systems in an effort to bring the pregnancy to term. Ploch's parents initially protested and sought to have her removed from them. However, they have since decided they are in favor of the hospital's efforts and plan to raise the child.

The decision to bring the fetus to term has caused an intense reaction far beyond Germany. Canadian feminists have argued that this is the logical, if grotesque, extension of surrogacy with a dead woman being used as a vessel for a fetus. Since public surveys show that over half of the German public disapproves of the hospital's actions, the debate is likely to intensify.

Calgary Herald, 11/15/92; *Newsweek*, 11/16/92

12.2(b) Comatose Woman Dies after Miscarriage and Removal from Life-Support Systems
June 1993

The German woman kept on life-support systems in an effort to gestate her fourteen-week-old fetus to term, miscarried five weeks later and died shortly thereafter. Her parents, who initially opposed the hospital's decision but later supported those efforts, have now charged their daughter's doctors with "moral blackmail."

The Plochs now claim that the doctors made it clear to them that medical efforts to bring the fetus to term would continue, even without their consent. They also claim they were afraid to speak out for fear of losing their rights to the child if it was born. This was reportedly the first attempt by a hospital to maintain such an early pregnancy in a brain-dead woman. Consequently, it triggered substantial controversy and criticism within and beyond Germany.

Facts on File, World News Digest, 12/2/92

12.3 New Jersey Court Appoints Lawyer for Fetus
Summer 1997

A thirty-three-year-old pregnant woman and mother of two, jailed for heroine distribution, has been granted a temporary release in order to have an abortion. While New Jersey law does not restrict a woman's right to abortion and the courts there have consistently held that a fetus is not a person, a judge has nevertheless appointed an attorney to represent the fetus. [The attorney] is planning an appeal to block the abortion, claiming he will "vigorously represent [his] client."

Associated Press, 3/31/97

12.4 Botched Abortion Results in Healthy Child and Lawsuit
Spring 2007

A forty-five-year-old woman from Massachusetts, whose abortion procedure failed to end her pregnancy, has sued Planned Parenthood and two doctors for the costs of rearing the healthy daughter she later gave birth to. Jennifer Raper's lawsuit is based on a Planned Parenthood physician's allegedly failed abortion procedure and another physician's subsequent failure to detect the continued pregnancy at twenty weeks. Raper alleges she had decided on an abortion for financial reasons, and only discovered she was still pregnant late in the pregnancy and then delivered a healthy child. While many states recognize the tort of "wrongful birth" following a failed abortion procedure or other medical steps that lead to an unanticipated birth, damages are frequently limited to the direct costs of the failed procedure and any extraordinary costs of rearing a child with medical problems. Only a few states, not including Massachusetts, have allowed damages for the costs of rearing a healthy child. A trial court in that state did order an IVF program to pay child support costs to a man whose ex-wife used their frozen embryos without his consent (*Gladu*, [1.11]) to have a child, but no appellate court in that state has endorsed the principle.

Raper v. Planned Parenthood League of Massachusetts et al.

(Suffolk Sup. Ct.); *Boston Globe,* 3/7/07

Conclusion

✥ BY Howard W. Jones, Jr.

THERE CAN BE little doubt that the myriad of professionals involved in ART would benefit from an awareness of the material in the twelve chapters of this book. The complete physician and his or her support staff will serve their patients better by knowing this information. Legal and other professionals involved in this technology will all benefit from a better understanding of this history and the developing issues, as will those interested in shaping policy through professional guidelines, ethics committees, or laws. From a medical perspective, the purpose of this work is not only to help the physician and staff avoid litigation but also, and more importantly, to minimize the uncertainty in novel or atypical patient reproductive combinations that seem predisposed to lead to litigation. To date, these situations primarily involve donor gametes, and traditional and gestational surrogacy. It is not paternalistic but simply excellent medicine in all such cases to insist on psychological screening and counseling, not only for the gamete donors and surrogate but for the recipient or contracting couple as well. In addition, of course, a review of the various physician or staff missteps that triggered litigation might uncover other areas where caution is warranted.

Generally speaking, technology precedes the law. How can it be otherwise? ART is in a changing field, and it will continue to advance. I have enough confidence in our legal system to believe that, if the innovative technology is designed to improve the human condition, innovative medicine will be supported by the law when the time comes for laws and policies to be developed and put in place.

~ BY Susan L. Crockin

As we turn to the future, this book takes a hard look at many of the overarching and specific issues and challenges facing today's and tomorrow's stakeholders and policy makers. What has gone right and, at times, terribly wrong with the families and professionals who have come before the courts is an unparalleled history lesson that is critical to shaping sound future policy and practice. It is vital that we examine and learn from this short, intense history of reproductive technology law. This conclusion recommends ways to help frame, address, and, we hope, resolve some of the most pressing challenges we will face as these remarkable technologies continue to propel society forward, whether we are ready for them or not.

Before 1978, IVF, cryopreserved embryos, and the assisted reproductive technologies were almost entirely unimaginable. Sperm and eggs met only inside a woman's body, prevailing medical definitions of *embryo* presumed it to be in utero, and reproductive law focused on a woman's right to privacy in areas of contraception, conception, and pregnancy termination. There were only two ways to become a mother: through biology or adoption. And there was only one place a human embryo could be created, exist, and grow into a fetus: in a mother's uterus following sexual intercourse or artificial insemination. Today, determining "motherhood" is often at the center of disputes involving every conceivable permutation of genetics, gestation, and intention. Meanwhile, IVF embryos continue to generate both legal disputes and policy debates involving divorce, cryopreservation, stem cell research, and disposition alternatives.

Many of the medical advances that now seem almost commonplace, including IVF and freezing embryos, continue to change the composition of ART families, including the addition of third parties, same-sex couples, and single men and women as parents. Posthumous reproduction continues to generate its own complex issues. Other medical advances are still novel, including advances in freezing technologies for eggs and ovarian tissues, embryo selection through preimplantation genetic diagnosis and selection, and reprogenetics.

These revolutionary advances in reproductive medicine have transformed the law—significantly impacting family, contract, constitutional, negligence, and malpractice law, as well as procedural rules such as jurisdiction and statutes of limitation. Future advances will undoubtedly continue to force a radical rethinking of traditional legal principles. Throughout these commentaries and cases percolates the theme that legal and medical naivete both hamper sound policy. The often-espoused arguments from the medical community that medicine is already overregulated will not provide the guidance needed for those involved in or affected by these still-evolving disciplines. Nor will general calls for or against "regulation" address these issues effectively. The medical and legal aspects of the ARTs have become undeniably intertwined and interdependent. What may once have been legitimately seen as an arena of private medical decision making is increasingly recognized to inextricably involve complex ethical and legal aspects. Courts resolving divorce disputes over cryopreserved embryos have shown an admirable willingness to analyze medical testimony over the nature of the IVF embryo and to expand legal paradigms in the effort to craft thoughtful and at times novel results. State legislatures have demonstrated a similar willingness and ability to delve into scientific evidence regarding embryonic stem cells.

From its inception, "Legally Speaking" sought to build a bridge between the legal and medical communities. By shedding light on what might seem to physicians to be mysterious and at times intrusive inner workings of the legal system, the column also sought to illuminate the vulnerabilities for the children of the ARTs and those who helped create them. Now, tracing the developing law through individual courts and legislatures provides a unique lens through which we can see how far we have come and brings into clearer focus how much work lies ahead. If we have any hope of achieving comprehensive policies that encompass a sophisticated understanding of the complex issues we face, it is critical for the medical, scientific, legal, and policy making communities both to educate and to work with one another.

Our goal in this book has been to document and examine critically the history of these myriad medical and legal developments and to make modest predictions and policy recommendations for the future. This effort has been a humbling experience. Our hope is that it will prove a useful one to current stakeholders and future law and policy makers.

IVF Embryos

The issues raised in the first chapter of this compendium will continue to challenge society on deeply fundamental levels. Law and policy makers need to reach a consensus definition of the IVF embryo from a legal, but not necessarily a moral or ethical, perspective.

IVF embryos, in large part, vex society for the same reasons that IVF and all its offshoots have captured our attention and imagination over these past three decades. What was previously unimaginable and literally impossible, the ability to create children and families outside the bedroom, has become almost commonplace. We need to recognize, and respect, that certain religious perspectives will likely never accept the concept that fertilization is not the beginning of human life, while others hold very different perspectives.[1] More constructively, we need to build on the *legal* consensus that is currently in place in reproductive law and policy. The law has always respected and protected the potential for life, including the long-recognized if politically charged constitutional rights of the individual to procreate or not, use contraception, or avail themselves of abortions within legally established parameters. In a pluralistic society, elevating an IVF embryo to the status of a legal human being belies all society has come to accept in terms of reproductive law and rights.

Consequently, as medical, religious, and political debates have raged throughout the history of IVF, multiple high state courts, beginning with the 1992 *Davis v. Davis* decision, have resolved divorcing couples' disputed claims to their cryopreserved preembryos. In a lengthy and thoughtful analysis, the *Davis* court ruled that "preembryos" were neither persons nor property but entitled to "special respect" due to their capacity to become a person, relying on professional guidelines. Although since that time courts have employed various terms, including *preembryo, zygote, pre-zygote,* and *embryo*, each court explicitly acknowledged that in vitro fertilized eggs prior to day fourteen (a category that encompasses all cryopreserved preembryos) constitute unique and distinctive entities. The courts heard and analyzed scientific evidence, and a notable consensus emerged on what can

---

1. Indeed, the Roman Catholic Church renewed its opposition to virtually all ART procedures in its most recent Instruction (December 2008), on the premise that "the human embryo has . . . from the very beginning, the dignity proper to a person."

and cannot be done with IVF embryos and by whom. Thus, the courts have tended to enforce couples' prior agreements that did not involve procreation (agreements to discard or donate for research, for example) but have refused to enforce what the Massachusetts high court first termed "forced procreation"—prior agreements to allow one spouse to use (or in two cases to donate to another couple) embryos to attempt a pregnancy over a contemporaneous change of mind and objection by the other. The New Jersey court relied on the 1995 Stedman's Medical Dictionary definitions of both "embryo" and "preimplantation embryo" and noted that "we use the term 'preimplantation embryo' rather than 'embryo' because preimplantation embryo is technically descriptive of the cells' stage of development."[2]

Furthermore, the few courts forced to confront whether or not "conception" occurs at fertilization seem unwilling to accept this as a legal construct. Indeed, courts have expressly rejected or shied away from characterizing IVF embryos as either "human life" or denoting "conception" in cases variously involving divorce disputes, widows seeking Social Security and workers' compensation benefits for posthumous born children, and "wrongful birth" and "wrongful conception" claims.

There is little doubt that patients who create embryos have a greater claim to them than any professionals who assisted in their creation. Only under Louisiana's Civil Code are IVF embryos defined as having independent legal status as a "biological human being" separate and apart from the adults who created them, making donation for research illegal in that state.[3] The Louisiana law goes even further, permitting "adoptive implantation" to a married couple (only) for such embryos with the physician acting as the embryo's "temporary guardian." By imbuing cryopreserved preembryos with personhood, in essence forcing infertility patients who complete treatment to "place" their remaining embryos with another family, the Louisiana statute would appear to deny adults decision-making control over their IVF embryos and to leave itself vulnerable to a constitutional challenge based on procreative liberty. From a strictly legal standpoint, it is difficult to see how patients who create IVF embryos

2. *J.B. v. M.B.*, 783 A.2d 707 (N.J. 2001). See ASRM Practice Committee Opinions: "2006 Guidelines for Gamete and Embryo Donation," *Fertility and Sterility* 2006 (Supp. 4), 90: 564–68; "Repetitive Oocyte Donation," *Fertility and Sterility* 2004 (Supp. 1), 82:S158–59.
3. La.R.S. 9:126M.

and have the legally recognized authority to discard them (or to abort a pregnancy resulting from their use) could be prohibited from controlling them for decisions such as donation for research. In recent years, a "personhood" movement has resulted in unsuccessful initiatives in states such as Colorado (2008) and North Dakota (2009) that would have deemed IVF embryos human beings.

If established reproductive law, including a woman's right to choose to be or remain pregnant, is to survive, then preimplantation IVF embryos simply cannot be elevated beyond the "special respect" noted by multiple courts to the level of a living human being. No appellate court to date has reached such a conclusion, nor should future laws and policies that strive to avoid religious bias do so. If as a community of stakeholders we can acknowledge *that* legal consensus, then many of the litigious conundrums raised in this book can be resolved.

Embryo Donation for Procreation

The experience of IVF programs and limited research studies teach us that relatively few patients ultimately opt to make their embryos available for others to create families. In contrast, as embryonic stem cell research has become more prevalent and more widely promoted, studies suggest that patients with leftover IVF embryos are more interested in pursuing that option than either donation for procreation or donation for previously unknown forms of research. Proponents of "embryo adoption" need to understand not only its largely legal nonstatus but the implications such language may carry.

"Embryo adoption" may seem endearing and may even be partially applicable in a psycho-social sense, but in virtually every state it is, and should remain, a legal misnomer, plain and simple. Legally recognized adoption occurs when born children are placed with previously approved families through established legal structures that carefully and clearly extinguish the rights of birth parents and affix those of adoptive parents to create a new family. In virtually every state, legally mandated post-birth "cooling off" periods apply to ensure birth parents make a thoughtful, deliberative decision to make an adoptive placement after the birth of their child. None of those legal requirements are applied in the context of embryo donation for procreation. The characterization has been widely promoted by religious groups (although the Catholic Church recently renounced the practice, which it labeled "pre-natal adoption," as part of its 2008 Instruction) as well by as the recent Bush administration (which created funding to "raise awareness" of "embryo adoption" options) and will likely continue to be advanced as part of a broad-based anti-abortion agenda to equate IVF embryos with live human beings. In 2009, the state of Georgia passed a compromise law, "the Option of Adoption Act," which provides recipients of donated embryos the "option" of undergoing a novel judicial "adoption" of embryos that the same law states are already theirs through a required contract with the donors. It remains to be seen if and how this law will be implemented or challenged. Unless the terminology is recognized and rejected as both legally inaccurate and intentionally value-laden, "embryo adoption" may find its way into both law and the common lexicon, perhaps more readily than the practice itself becomes a common family building option.

Leftover Embryos

Leftover and "abandoned" IVF embryos present unique challenges for those who store them in the absence of, or even despite, explicit patient choices. Notwithstanding professional guidelines and existing laws, concerns remain that patients may bring lawsuits to reclaim embryos long after they were initially created even in the absence of communication or payment of storage fees. In a litigious society, practical concerns and cost-benefit ratios may outweigh legal principles. Many medical programs choose to store indefinitely, despite recorded patient instructions, in an attempt to avoid the possibility of litigation. In my view, this should be one of the easiest areas of ART practice to address from a legal perspective. If patients' clearly stated, informed choices to discard within their original or any subsequent consent forms can be identified, following such directives—perhaps only after subsequent attempts to notify the patients—should be permissible and legally protected. This policy would clarify the distinction between "abandoned" embryos for which no disposition directions were given and those that patients authorized discarding after a certain period had passed or certain conditions (such as family completion, divorce, or death) had been met. Given the heightened sensitivities to procreative choices and the current and evolving research options that were unavailable at the time of any consents, re-consent for *any* form of donation is strongly recommended. Unless such disposition choices are clearly and accurately articulated and contemporaneously confirmed, using those IVF embryos for research or procreation should be strictly prohibited. Recent efforts to create model informed consents have included significantly clearer and more comprehensive disposition directives. Federal regulations on embryonic stem cell research using "leftover" IVF embryos proposed in 2009 include specific, detailed consent provisions for donating these embryos for embryonic stem cell research. More concerted efforts should be made to obtain comprehensive consents and directives from IVF patients regarding disposition of excess embryos at the outset of treatment, including a clear allocation of responsibility for maintaining contact information. These efforts should go a long way toward reducing future litigation concerns in this arena as well as reducing the cost, both monetary and psychological, of indefinite embryo storage.

Access to ART

Mandated insurance coverage for ARTs has been a state-by-state, largely grassroots effort thus far, with only a minority of states passing legislation to provide some form of required insurance coverage. Most of these efforts are over a decade old, and the current political and economic climate does not seem receptive to additional efforts. It is likely that current sensitivities to the growing need for basic health insurance for the millions of uninsured and the perceived high cost of ART treatment will hamper future efforts to expand comprehensive mandated infertility coverage. Thus, access to treatment will likely continue to be a major issue in ART policies.

To the extent that both infertility and genetic anomalies are increasingly recognized as medical conditions or diseases, however, it will be difficult to justify excluding diagnosis and treatment altogether from any comprehensive insurance coverage. Studies have demonstrated cost-effective ART treatment under mandates. Nonetheless, absent an explicit mandate to cover the costs or litigation establishing illegal discrimination based on a protective class status, discretionary coverage will remain legally permissible.

Although the infertility insurance successes of the past decades—both in legislatures and courtrooms—pioneered the exploration of coverage for the family building efforts of today, such broad approvals appear unlikely to be repeated in the foreseeable future. Even in states with mandated coverage, insurer requirements are frequently revisited and narrowed. In addition to narrowing medical eligibility criteria, coverage today is frequently denied for, among other scenarios, same-sex couples lacking a medical diagnosis of infertility, arguably perimenopausal women, and those requiring genetic testing or other treatment for a medical condition that does not meet an insurer's strict definition of "infertility." Yet, in numerous cases—at times encouraged by threats of litigation—insurers have agreed to cover IVF and PGD to diagnose serious genetic disorders. The future challenges for access to treatment may be to move beyond trying to fit newer developments into hard-fought and now accepted categories and shift the focus to similarly thoughtful arguments and policy proposals that address many of these newer family building efforts.

A second access issue will continue to be patients pressing their right to treatment in the form of discrimination litigation. The closely watched 2008 case brought in California by Juanita Benitez, a lesbian patient denied treatment based on the espoused religious beliefs of her infertility physicians, resulted in a ruling that California's antidiscrimination laws prohibit such actions. Similarly, the seminal Supreme Court decision in *Bragdon v. Abbott* established that reproduction is covered under federal disability protections. Unlike efforts to maintain or broaden coverage based on questionable medical criteria, challenges based on denial of care to an entire category of patients can raise distinct constitutional issues involving discrimination. More challenges of this sort are likely.

Same-Sex Marriage and Nontraditional Families

Same-sex unions and marriage are here to stay, and the parents, children, and those who helped make these long-awaited families possible will all need legal frameworks and protections. Despite setbacks such as the 2008 referendum in California blocking judicially recognized same-sex marriage in that state, both California and Massachusetts courts laid out the legal precedent and constitutional analysis for recognizing same-sex marriage. They have been followed in 2009 by Iowa, Vermont, and Maine, with other jurisdictions predicted to follow suit. In 2009, multiple lawsuits were filed challenging the constitutionality of DOMA's refusal to recognize same-sex marriages for purposes of federal benefits and law. There are also ongoing efforts to repeal the law legislatively. All of this leaves little question that same-sex families will be an increasingly visible, and legally recognized, part of the fabric of American family life.

Until more states have developed law in this area and the constitutionality of DOMA is resolved, state law variations will continue to impede legal recognition of these families, and adoption laws will continue to play an essential role in securing parent-child relationships. There is a rich history of states recognizing adoptions that were validly undertaken in another state. Thus, same-sex and other nontraditional couples (and those who assist them) will need to be cognizant of the legal vulnerabilities they face and the myriad of steps on both the medical and legal fronts that require careful consideration. A clear understanding of contracts and supplemental medical consents as well as of all potentially relevant jurisdictions and laws is an essential part of family-building preparations.

Third-Party Reproduction, Reproductive Tourism, and Adoption

Third-party reproduction, including multi-jurisdictional arrangements, is on the rise. For all such collaborative reproduction, parentage needs to be clarified so that would-be parents, gamete donors, and gestational carriers are not left vulnerable to inconsistent laws, jurisdictions, and legal interpretations. With increasing multi-jurisdictional and multi-party family building, these realities and families demand legal clarity, and efforts to establish model and consistent laws should be prioritized in the coming years. To date, most such efforts have been approached separately within either the legal or medical community. This author has been involved in both, and if we are to make real progress in protecting families and those who help make them possible, I strongly believe it is imperative for the medical and legal communities to come together to meet these challenges in the form of model or proposed legislation and policies. In overly simplistic terms, the ARTs may make babies, but only the law creates families and protects those who make them possible.

In a medical field that finds itself regularly targeted as unregulated, underregulated, and exploitive of women as patients, egg donors and gestational carriers (the more accurate term than *surrogate* for women who carry a nongenetically related fetus for another), professionals will need to be alert to the vulnerabilities that can accompany these advances in the ARTs. Until laws clearly define and protect these families and until we standardize the practices of those who assist them, patients and those who treat them will want to understand the role of the law and legal counseling and the best means of ensuring that the appropriate, available steps are taken to secure these much-wanted families.

Gestational surrogacy in ever more complex variations is increasingly common, but inconsistent laws fail to protect these families adequately. Both reproductive tourism and legal tensions have mounted as would-be parents look to legally receptive states or go abroad to locate gestational carriers, utilize donated gametes, and pursue creative arrangements without first securing legal assurances that they will be recognized as parents of the resulting child. Clearly, the legal protections have simply not caught up with the growing medical possibilities of the last thirty years. In the absence of needed legislation, parties and professionals rely on contracts and informed consents and local practices to the extent they exist. The limits of such contracts and consents are still being explored, at times with disastrous results.

For intended parents seeking to create a child with no genetic *or* gestational link, through donated gametes or embryos and gestational surrogacy, the vulnerabilities of this "parentage by contract" are predictable. In my view, intent-based parentage through contracts alone is an insufficient and inappropriate basis to establish legal parentage. Real-life examples abound. In one ongoing dispute, two unmarried women from different states—one the originally intended mother and the other the gestational carrier—are locked in a parentage and custody dispute over a child they agreed to conceive using both donor egg and sperm, under a likely unenforceable contract based on no established law in either state. When such an intended parent changes his or her mind, contract principles become a flimsy basis on which to determine parentage. ART arrangements with no genetic connections and no parentage guidelines fly in the face of centuries of parentage and adoption law and leave no clear path to a determination of parentage. At a minimum, advance judicial approval of such arrangements may be necessary to safeguard the resulting children.

Some have made a simple, but not necessarily simplistic, suggestion that before such an arrangement should be allowed to proceed, intended parents (or a single intended parent) must have at least two of the following three parentage-related factors: genetics, gestation, and intention. Such a formula would avoid parentage attempts by contract alone and would temper intent-based parentage with at least one additional, and legally recognizable, means of recognizing parentage. At the very least, until and unless laws recognize legal parentage via contract, such would-be families will be legally vulnerable and the professionals who create them open to malpractice claims if intentions go awry.

Looking to the future of adoption law, even a murky crystal ball leaves little question that the legal distinctions between adoption and third-party reproduction will continue to blur and that policy makers will need to evaluate both the differences and similarities of these family building approaches to establish comprehensive policies for families created through the growing variety of third-party reproductive arrangements.

Gamete donation for procreation has become a permanent part of the family-building landscape, and without question, egg donation will continue to expand and be utilized by all sorts of potential families. Although egg donation may be the second most secure form of third-party parentage, given its analogous status to sperm donation (clearly the longest, most traditional, and most legally protected form of third-party arrangements), legal uncertainties remain. A few courts have rejected the analogy to sperm donation due to the different medical procedures involved, and only a very few states have explicit statutes governing egg donation. Even donor insemination, not technically an ART procedure, continues to generate legal controversy, especially for same-sex couples and single parents. Two test cases in Kansas (2007) and Pennsylvania (2008) approved single motherhood through donor insemination as an acceptable form of family building that does not violate public policy. Those developments will need to be squared with existing laws in most states that hold men financially, if not legally, responsible for children they help create. Looking to the future of egg donation, there needs to be not only clarity around the definition of a parent but also greater health protections for donors, intended parents, and offspring; more uniform rules for compensation; and a reliable mechanism for obtaining and storing donor information for future retrieval by offspring. Current practices are woefully inadequate. Donor recruiting entities can (and do) open and close without any form of regulation or uniform requirements for data collection and storage. Frequently, vital information is irretrievably lost in the process. Physicians' offices follow variable state laws on record keeping. Professional guidelines that require permanent record keeping do not instruct how to maintain such information, much less provide the means to do so.

Compensation practices need to be more structured, transparent, and consistent, both across the spectrum of reproductive donors and in at least rough parity with research donors (discussed below). We need more effective and enforceable methods to cap donor fees that sometimes exceed $25,000 for procreative egg donors. While there may always be outliers, current voluntary guidelines and practice have simply proved insufficient. Recruitment and compensation practices for egg donors today are inconsistent at best. Reproductive donors are currently recruited by patients, ART medical programs, stand-alone recruiting entities (often self-described as "agencies"), and over the Internet and elsewhere. Compensation for reproductive egg donors is accepted practice, with fees over and above out-of-pocket expenses ranging from a few thousand dollars per cycle donation to many thousands of dollars. Voluntary professional guidelines and ethics statements issued by the American Society for Reproductive Medicine (ASRM) recommend per cycle payments for donors at approximately $5,000 ("sums of $5,000 or more require justification and sums above $10,000 are not appropriate") and have recently required any recruiting program listing on its website to agree to adhere to those principles.[4] At last count, over fifty recruiting programs were listed on ASRM's website, with no external mechanism to ensure compliance and much evidence of noncompliance. ASRM guidelines also recommend egg donors donate not more than six times (for reasons of both consanguinity and possible unknown health risks) and state that compensation is for a woman's "time, inconvenience and dis-

4. ASRM Practice Committee Opinions: "2006 Guidelines for Gamete and Embryo Donation," *Fertility and Sterility* 2006 (Supp. 4), 90:564–68; "Repetitive Oocyte Donation," *Fertility and Sterility* 2004 (Supp. 1), 82:S158–59; ASRM Ethics Committee Report, "Financial Compensation of Oocyte Donors," *Fertility and Sterility* 2007, 88:305–9.

comfort" in undergoing the rigors of being an egg donor and is not payment for the eggs themselves or any specific qualities of the donor. Despite these guidelines, some reproductive donors receive tens of thousands of dollars from both individuals and recruiting programs and additional fees for a desired ethnicity or proven fertility. More globally, as freezing inevitably becomes accepted practice in egg donation (as it is in sperm donation), intended parents will be able to access eggs without necessarily having to recruit a donor themselves or to rely on a recruitment program to do so. Instead, frozen eggs will be stored and disseminated either from the medical programs where they were retrieved or from tissue bank facilities such as those that currently maintain sperm and embryos. Patients will pay these intermediaries rather than today's recruiting programs for contemporaneous donors. Those who maintain and dispense frozen eggs will have potential liability for lost genetic material or genetic abnormalities, much as sperm banks have faced. Multiple clusters of eggs, much like sperm samples, will be available from a single donation to multiple intended parents. With expanded egg freezing a near certainty in the near future, the policy challenges will go far beyond curtailing current compensation and recruitment excesses and require a willingness to face the challenges this new paradigm presents.

The technologies are here to stay. The legal and policy challenges are to make using them a smooth path to parenthood, not an unpredictably rocky one to the courthouse door.

ART and Embryonic Stem Cell Research

As developments in embryonic stem cell research have unfolded, the passions and heated debates surrounding it have resulted in a number of seemingly compromise measures, including compensation restrictions for egg donors placed into both state laws and voluntary guidelines of various professional research groups. Those restrictions have done little either to placate opponents or to further stem cell researchers' need for donations of genetic material. In the absence of compensation, research egg donors have been sparse. From a legal perspective, these restrictions are both at odds with compensation to reproductive donors (current ASRM guidelines recommend compensation for both reproductive and research donors) and deviate significantly from established principles governing human research subjects. They also seem driven by ideology rather than objective evidence of undue influence from either the scientific or the reproductive communities.

Despite a century-old tradition of paying human research subjects (within IRB frameworks designed to minimize influence on informed consent) and routine compensation for reproductive donors, paying research egg donors has become a virtual "third rail" in the shaping of ESCR policy. Whether through well-meaning but problem-riddled legislation or well-intended but politically compromised voluntary guidelines, it seems foolhardy to deny ESC researchers and the women who want to serve as human subjects the opportunity to move this promising science forward under the same ethical, legal, and policy paradigms that are applied to every other area of scientific inquiry. Moreover, a rigorous, thoughtful IRB process addressing appropriate payment amounts could ideally help shape, or at least model, compensation limits for the reproductive community.

Even with the 2009 change in federal administrations and positions, the Executive Order and proposed regulations authorizing expanded federal funding for ESCR have stopped short of allowing women to donate eggs for research, and they authorize funding only for research using leftover IVF embryos donated by patients. The current administration has taken an acknowledged pragmatic stance, guided (or constrained) by what it perceives has wide public support rather than moving forward more boldly and consistently with scientific practice. Time, science, and politics will tell how these various policies and positions will unfold.

Reprogenetics

"Reproductive wrongs" will take their place beside "reproductive rights," as courts are called upon to resolve genetic testing disputes and define legal duties owed to donors, carriers, would-be parents, and, potentially, offspring. The explosion in reprogenetic technologies has already begun to test established concepts of "wrongful birth," "wrongful life," and "wrongful conception" as well as their applicable statutes of limitations. The "genetics revolution" and its application to reproduction ("reprogenetics") through PGD, PGS, and other advances are also raising new questions of when "conception" legally occurs and will almost certainly require a rethinking of the law on prenatal testing liability.

From a legal perspective, "reproductive wrongs" will likely expand on four specific fronts. First, tort liability for genetic errors will need to be analyzed in a more expansive manner, forcing distinctions between wrongful birth and wrongful conception to diminish and ultimately disappear. Second, tort litigation for a professional's failure to properly screen or properly report screening results of sperm or egg donors will continue to test applicable theories of liability. To date, two courts have rejected wrongful birth theories against medical professionals on the grounds that the donor (in one instance, sperm; in the other, egg), not the physician, caused the genetic anomalies. A third lawsuit pending as of publication is wrestling with the availability of a products liability theory against a sperm bank that allegedly disseminated affected sperm. As physicians and other professionals select a donor or gametes and as frozen genetic material becomes more standardized for egg as well as sperm donors, arguments will continue to be made that the selection itself did in fact "cause" the anomaly. And as the field of genetics grows, courts will be faced with more cases challenging missed diagnosis, misreported health histories of donors, and potentially available genetic information that was never tested for, all of which will likely result in expanded theories of liability. A third prediction is that both genetic susceptibility and genetic privacy will increasingly raise legal issues. To the extent that genetic testing or medical histories disclose genetic susceptibility, and to the extent that DNA databases continue to expand in other arenas, patients and insureds will need and seek privacy protection to avoid discrimination, and there will likely be more laws enacted to address these types of concerns, such as the federal Genetic Information Nondiscrimination Act of 2008 ("GINA," enacted to prohibit discrimination in health insurance and employment). Fourth, it is also all but certain that both the statutes of limitations and the theories for late filing of such cases will be vastly extended as many genetic anomalies are not discovered until the births of subsequent offspring and generations.

Looking Back and Moving Forward

By tracing together the extraordinary developments in reproductive medicine and law, our goal has been twofold: First, to capture a sense of the history of these evolving struggles, including the multiple layers of courts often involved in a single case and the often conflicting rulings by different courts on similar issues; and second, to glean from those struggles the unique wisdom and lessons they offer to guide future laws, policies, guidelines, and practices. The jurists, juries, and lawmakers who wrestled with the issues and disputes placed before them each shed another beam of light on the IVF labs and medical programs and individuals that together have helped to make previously inconceivable families real, here and now.

The future will undoubtedly bring even greater medical opportunities and challenges. More widely available frozen human eggs and ovarian tissue and enhanced embryo selection are clearly on the near horizon. Third-party reproduction will continue to be used by an ever-widening number of would-be parents and those who want to assist them. There is also little doubt that the future holds dramatic improvements in embryo analysis and the very real possibility that germ cells will be successfully developed from IPS cells and used to make embryos, thereby enabling a person of any age to have a biological child. There is talk of artificial gametes, artificial wombs, and cloned babies, as well as an accompanying need to wrestle with the efficacy, ethics, access, cost, and insurance coverage associated with these approaches. The field of reprogenetics is just in its infancy, and the issues arising from the developing technology and uses will be explosive. Ultimately, policies, laws, and regulatory frameworks will all need to be developed to address this growing list of family building possibilities.

Medically and legally speaking, the next thirty years will likely propel society forward in ever more challenging and presently inconceivable ways. As two poignant examples illustrate, in 1976 defining the word *embryo* was as simple and straightforward as defining the word *mother*. Today, both require a sensitive, nuanced, and multi-dimensional analysis if we hope to reflect and shape these newly possible families. The extraordinary medical advances of the past three decades that have redefined the very concept of family demand an ongoing transformation of reproductive law and policy. *Legal Conceptions* bears witness to and reflects upon these remarkable developments, and through that effort attempts to both predict the future challenges ahead and recommend paths to meet them. We hope that our efforts will help shape the law and related policies in this field as it continues to advance and thereby provide both guidance and security to future participants and society as a whole.

TABLE OF CASES

Boldface Page References indicate main case summaries. Bracketed entries refer to case numbers in this book.

Case Name and Citation	Page References
A.H.W. v. G.H.B., 772 A.2d 948 (N.J. Super. Ct. Ch. Div. 2000)	**252–53 [6.25]**
A.Z. v. B.Z., 725 N.E.2d 1051 (Mass. 2000)	17, **41–44 [1.8]**, 48, 63
Adar v. Smith, 591 F. Supp. 2d 857 (E.D. La. 2008)	**367 [11.5]**
Adoption of Matthew B., 284 Cal. Rptr. 18 (Cal. Ct. App. 1991) (*petitions for reh'g and review denied*)	**227–28 [6.4]**
Adoption of Tammy, 619 N.E.2d 315 (Mass. 1993)	17, **308–9 [8.2]**
Adoptions of B.L.V.B. and E.L.V.B., 628 A.2d 1271 (Vt. 1993)	17, **308–9 [8.2]**
Alexandria S. v. Pac. Fertility Med. Ctr., 64 Cal. Rptr. 2d 23 (Cal. Ct. App. 1997), *review denied*, No. S062452, 1997 Cal. LEXIS 4831 (Cal. July 30, 1997)	**149–50 [4.14]**
Anderson v. Vasquez, 827. F. Supp. 617 (N.D. Ca. 1992) (dismissing claims as no right to conjugal visits), *aff'd*, No. C-91-4540-VRW, 1995 U.S. Dist. LEXIS 1985 (N.D. Ca. Feb. 13, 1995)	**167–68 [4.30]**
Andrews v. Keltz, 838 N.Y.S.2d 363 (N.Y. Sup. Ct. 2007)	**186 [4.49]**
Anonymous v. Anonymous, N.Y. Sup. Ct. N.Y. (1/18/91)	**141 [4.3]**
Anonymous v. Mt. Sinai Hospital, N.Y. Sup. Ct. (Manhattan) filed 12/3/96	**180–81 [4.45]**
Arredondo v. Nodelman, 622 N.Y.S.2d 181 (N.Y. Sup. Ct. 1994)	**234–35 [6.13]**
Baby Doe v. Doe, 421 S.E.2d 913 (Va. Ct. App. 1992) (litigating a guardian's suit); Va. Code Ann. 20-49.1 (2009)	**230–32 [6.9]**
Baird v. Eisenstadt, 405 U.S. 438 (1972)	25
Berner-Kadish v. Minister of Interior, HCJ 1779/99 [2000] IsrSC 54 P.D. 368	**312 [8.7]**

Case Name and Citation	Page References
Bohn v. Ann Arbor Reprod. Med. Assocs., P.C., No. 213550, 1999 Mich. App. LEXIS 2210 (Mich. Ct. App. Dec. 17, 1999)	**45–46 [1.10]**
Bragdon v. Abbott, 524 U.S. 624 (1998)	17, 78, **91–94 [2.8]**, 382
Briody v. St. Helen's and Knowsley Health Authority (2000) 2 FCR 13	**251–52 [6.24]**
Carparts v. Auto. Wholesalers Ass'n. of N.E., 37 F.3d 12 (1st Cir. 1994)	85
Casas v. Fertility Center of CXA, Orange Cty., Sup. Ct., Cal. 1/12/93	**177 [4.41]**
Chambers v. Chambers, No. cn99-09493, 2005 Del. Fam. Ct. LEXIS 1 (2005)	**315 [8.11]**
Cheney v. Bell Ntl. Life, 556 A.2d 1135 (Md. 1989)	341
Clapp v. Northern Cumberland Mem'l Hosp., 964 F. Supp. 503 (D. Me. 1997)	**95 [2.10]**
Colorado Dept. of Public Health & Env. v. E.C.V. et al., Colo. S. Ct. No. 00SA-272 (unpublished opinion)	**313 [8.9]**
Commonwealth v. Edelin, 359 N.E.2d 4 (Mass. 1976)	25
Culliton v. Beth Israel Deaconess Medical Center, 756 N.E.2d 1133 (Mass. 2001)	213, **254–56 [6.27]**
Davis v. Davis, 842 S.W.2d 588 (Tenn. 1992)	ix, x, 16, 20, 27–28, **31–34 [1.2]**, 42, 44, 48, 63, 377
Del Zio v. Presbyterian Hospital, No. 74-3588(CES), 1978 U.S. Dist. LEXIS 14450 (S.D.N.Y. 1978)	15, 27, 29
Doe v. Attorney General, 487 N.W.2d 484 (Mich. Ct. App. 1992)	**229 [6.7]**
Doe v. Doe, 710 A.2d 1297 (Conn. 1998)	**249–50 [6.22]**
Doe v. Shalala, 516 U.S. 1145 (1995)	**35–36 [1.5]**, 353
Doe v. Sundquist, 522 U.S. 810 (1997)	**365–66 [11.3]**, 360
Donovan v. Idant Laboratories, No. 08-4075, 2009 U.S. Dist. LEXIS 48899 and 625 F.Supp.2d 256 (E.D. Pa. 2009)(6/10/09)	138, **186–87 [4.50]**, 338
Eckard v. Lamitina, OrlandoSentinel.com, *Florida Times-Union*, 10/11/07	**273 [6.44]**
Egert v. Connecticut General Life Ins. Co., 900 F.2d 1032 (7th Cir. 1990)	**81–82 [2.1]**

Case Name and Citation	Page References
Erickson v. Board of Governors, 911 F. Supp. 316 (N.D. Ill. 1995), *rev'd*, 207 F.3d 945 (7th Cir. 2000) (reversing denial of university's motion to dismiss, finding private federal litigation to enforce ADA claim cannot proceed, but employee can bring ADA claim in state court)	87, **88–89 [2.6]**
Estes v. Albers, 504 N.W.2d 607 (S.D. 1993)	**145 [4.8]**
Eubanks v. Legacy Emanuel Hospital, AP Wire, 10/12/97	**181 [4.46]**
Ezzone v. Ezzone, Lake City Dom. Rels. Ct. (Ohio Oct. 24, 1997)	194, **200–201 [5.6]**
Fasano v. Nash, 723 N.Y.S.2d 181 (N.Y. App. Div. 2001)	**52–55 [1.14]**
Ferguson v. McKiernan, 940 A.2d 1236 (Pa. 2007) (reversing and remanding lower court decision)	135, **161–64 [4.25]**
Fertility Ctr. of New England v. Tufts Associated HMO, No. 99-2597, 2002 Mass. Super. LEXIS 242 (Mass. Supp., July 18, 2002)	**127–28 [3.9]**
Finger v. Omni Publications Int'l, 566 N.E.2d 141 (N.Y. 1990)	**115 [3.2]**
Finley v. Astrue, 270 S.W.3d 849 (Ark. 2008)	281, **296–97 [7.12(a)]**
Finley v. Farm Cat, Inc., 103 Ark. App. 292 (Ark. Ct. App. 2008)	**298 [7.12(b)]**
Finstuen v. Crutcher, 496 F.3d 1139 (10th Cir. 2007)	**324–25 [8.18]**
Forbes v. Napolitano, No. 99-17372, 2000 U.S. App. LEXIS 38596 (9th Cir., 12/29/00)	**60–62 [1.19]**, 353
Frisina v. Women and Infants Hosp. of R.I., No. 95-4037, 2002 R.I. Super. LEXIS 73 (R.I. Super. 2002)	**39–40 [1.7]**
G.P. v. State of Florida, 842 So.2d 1059 (Fla. Dist. Ct. App. 2003)	**366 [11.4]**
Gill v. Office of Personnel Management, No.1:09 cv-10309 (D. Mass. 2009) (motion to dismiss filed 9/18/09)	**331 [8.22]**
Gillett-Netting v. Barnhart, 231 F. Supp. 2d 961 (D. Ariz. 2002)	**294–95 [7.10]**
Ginestra v. Hale, Cook Cty., Ill. (temp. ruling 9/29/99); *Chicago Tribune*, 9/30/99	**56–57 [1.15(b–c)]**
Gladu v. Boston IVF, MA Lawyers Weekly, 32 M.L.W. 1195, Feb. 9, 2004 (Middlesex Probate & Fam. Ct. 1/30/04)	**46 [1.11]**, 373
Goodridge v. Dept. of Public Health, 798 N.E.2d 941 (Mass. 2003)	18, 306, **319–20 [8.15]**, 321
Greco v. United States, 893 P.2d 345 (Nev. 1995)	**340–41 [9.1]**

Case Name and Citation	Page References
People's Adv. and Nat. Tax Limitation Fdtn. v. Ind. Citizens' Oversight Comm. (Cal. Trial Ct., 4/21/06); *Cal. Family Bioethics Council, LLC v. Cal. Inst. for Regenerative Medicine*, 55 Cal. Rptr. 3d 272 (Cal. Ct. App. 2007)	**357–58 [10.3]**
Perdue v. Miss. State Bd. of Health (Miss. Chancery Ct. Civ. No. G-2001-1891) (3/5/03)	**315–16 [8.12]**
Perry-Rogers v. Fasano, 715 N.Y.S.2d 19 (N.Y. App. Div. 2000); *Perry-Rogers v. Obasaju*, 723 N.Y.S.2d 28 (N.Y. App. Div. 2001); *Fasano v. Nash*, 723 N.Y.S.2d 181 (N.Y. App. Div. 2001)	**52–56 [1.14]**
Prato-Morrison v. Doe, 126 Cal. Rptr. 2d 509 (Cal. Ct. App. 2002)	**122–23 [3.6(f)]**
R. v. Human Fertilisation and Embryology Act ex parte Diane Blood [1997], 2 All ER 687	279, **287–90 [7.4]**, 291
R.R. v. M.H., 689 N.E.2d 790 (Mass. 1998)	213, **247–49 [6.21]**
Raper v. Planned Parenthood League of Massachusetts (Suffolk Sup. Ct.).; *Boston Globe*, 3/7/07	**372–73 [12.4]**
Robert B. v. Susan B., 135 Cal. Rptr. 2d 785 (Cal. Ct. App. 2003), *review denied*, No. S117664, 2003 Cal. LEXIS 6671 (Cal. 2003)	**64–66 [1.23]**, 194
Roe v. Wade, 410 U.S.113 (1973)	20, 25, 60, 71
Roman v. Roman, 193 S.W.3d 40 (Tex. Ct. App. 2006), *cert. denied*, No. 07-926, 2008 U.S. LEXIS 2480 (U.S. 3/17/08)	**70–72 [1.30]**
Runnebaum v. Nations-Bank of Maryland	92
Sharon S. v. Superior Court of San Diego, 73 P.3d 554 (Cal. Aug. 4, 2003), *cert. denied*, 540 U.S. 1220 (2004)	**316–17 [8.13]**
Soodman v. Wildman, Harrold, Allen & Dixon, No. 95-C-3834, 1997 U.S. Dist. LEXIS 1495 (N.D. Ill. Feb. 10, 1997) (granting employer's motion for summary judgment re: employee's claim for intentional infliction of emotional distress on reconsideration)	**94–95 [2.9]**
Soos v. Superior Court of Arizona, 897 P.2d 1356 (Ariz. Ct. App. 1994), *reh'g denied*	**237 [6.16]**
State Dep't of Human Services v. T.D.G., 861 P.2d 990 (Okla. 1993)	**146–47 [4.10]**
Stiver v. Parker, 975 F.2d 261 (6th Cir. 1992), *reh'g denied*	16, 113, 215, 232, 240, 242
Stone v. Regents of Univ. of Cal., 92 Cal. Rptr. 2d 94 (Cal. Ct. App. 1999)	**117–21 [3.6]**
Strauss v. Horton, 93 Cal. Rptr. 3d 591 (2009), as modified by 2009 Cal. LEXIS 5416 (2009), *reh'g denied*	**330–31 [8.21(b)]**

Where appropriate, key page numbers within an entry are *italicized*. **Boldface italic** entries direct the reader to the Table of Cases.

Insurance coverage and infertility (*cont.*) nancies and, 259; infertility counseling and, 82; in vitro fertilization and, 82; legislation and, 2, 76–78; mandates and, 77, 381; marital status and, 81, 105; multiple miscarriages and, 81; same-sex couples and, 80; surrogacy and, 259–61

Intracytoplasmic sperm injection (ICSI), 15, 99, 159, 184

Iowa, 18, 28, 66–67, 89–91, 168, 303

Israel, 45, 228, 236, 270, 312

Italy, 202, 215, 342–43

Jacobson, Cecil, M.D. See *United States v. Jacobson*

Jaeger, Ami, 239, 340–42

Johnson, Anna. See *Johnson v. Calvert*

Jones, Georgeanna, M.D., xi, 3, 14

Jones, Howard W., Jr., M.D., xi, 14, 16, 26, 339

Jones Institute, xi, 4, 133, 189

Kansas, 134–35, 164–66, 385

Kentucky, 267–68

Libel, 5, 127–28, 131

Louisiana, 63, 89, 278–79, 285–86, 290, 363, 367, 370, 378

Maine, 95, 303, 383

Malpractice. *See* Claims: legal malpractice; Claims: medical malpractice

Maryland, 16, 77, 92, 112, 123, 235, 269–70, 337, 341–42, 347–49

Massachusetts, 13, 18; abortion, ART-related and, 372; adoption, ART-related and, 363; embryo litigation and, 17, 27, 41, 43–44, 46, 48–49, 63, 67, 378; gamete (egg and sperm) donation and, 148, 204; insurance and, 76–79, 96, 102–3; posthumous reproduction and, 279–80, 289–90, 293, 295, 299; professional liability, general, 127–28; same-sex parentage and, 12, 17, 303, 304, 306, 308–11, 313, 319–21, 382–83; stem cell research and, 353, 355–56; surrogacy and, 213, 247–49, 252, 254–55, 257, 267–68

Media coverage of fertility, 111, 114, 119

Michigan, 45, 97–98, 229–31, 236, 240, 314

Minnesota, 176–77, 314, 337, 344–45

Mississippi, 315–16

Missouri, 135, 166, 358

Montana, 76–77

Mt. Sinai Medical Center, 116, 176, 180–81, 197, 199–200

Multiple pregnancies and births, 18, 22, 58–59, 62, 106–8, 131, 258

Nebraska, 336, 341

Nevada, 359, 370

New Hampshire, 249, 279–80, 299, 303, 310, 338, 346

New Jersey, 378; abortion, ART-related and, 372; embryo litigation and, 27, 47–48, 50, 52–53, 63, 67; insurance and, 77–78, 104; posthumous reproduction and, 279, 290, 292, 295; same-sex parentage and, 310; stem cell research and, 355; surrogacy and, 233, 236, 252–53

New York: adoption, ART-related and, 363–65, 367; egg donation and, 194, 197, 199, 201, 206; embryo litigation and, 35–38, 52, 54–55, 63; genetics and, 338; insurance and, 77, 104; posthumous reproduction and, 278, 292, 296, 299–300; professional liability, general, and, 115–16, 124, 128; same-sex parentage and, 304, 311–12, 319, 327; sperm donation and, 141, 143–45, 170, 176, 180, 181, 186–87; stem cell research and, 358; surrogacy and, 226, 228–29, 234–36, 265–67, 270

New Zealand, 208

NIH Human Embryo Research Panel, 35–36

North Carolina, 112–13, 137–38, 347–49

North Dakota, 379

Octuplet birth, 2009, 18, 106. *See also* Multiple pregnancies and births

Ohio, 15, 77, 178–79, 194, 201, 208, 261–64

Option of Adoption Act (Georgia), 19, 370, 380

Oregon, 139–40, 142, 147, 181, 326

Ovarian stimulation/ovulation induction, 4, 14, 106–7, 189, 192, 197

Parmet, Wendy, 91, 93, 94, 95

Pennsylvania, 83, 116, 135, 161–64, 167, 186–87, 240–41, 261–64, 338, 385

Pontifical Academy of Sciences, 21–22

Posthumous reproduction, 17, *275–300;* artificial insemination statute(s) and, 281, 295, 297; conception, defining with, 338; consent and, 277, 280, 282–83, 285, 287–89, 291–94, 299–300; eggs and, 277, 283; embryos and, 275, 277, 281, 283, 297, 298; FDA regulations and, 278; HFEA and, 279, 285, 287–89, 291; inheritance and Social Security, 17, 277–78, 280, 283–84, 285–87, 289–90, 292–97, 299; military personnel and, 281–82; parental or donor status and, 279–80, 282, 288–91, 293–97; sperm, posthumous extraction for, 275, 277–78, 285, 287, 290–92, 299–300; sperm storage and, 282, 288, 291, 294, 298; workmen's compensation benefits and, 279, 281, 298. *See also* Human Fertilisation and Embryology Authority

Preembyo. *See under* Embryos, characterizations of

Pregnancy Discrimination Act (PDA), 78–79, 82–84, 87–90, 95, 97–98

Preimplantation genetic diagnosis (PGD) and selection (PGS), 2, 8, 112–13, 207, 332–40, 347, 388; abortion and, 335, 337–40, 344–49; chromosomes and, 333; "designer baby" and, 332, 344; genetic disorders and, 15, 80–81, 337–38, 344–45, 347, 382; insurance issues and, 9, 80, 338, 339, 375, 382; "savior siblings" and, 334, 336; sex-selection and, 332–33, 336, 339, 342–43. *See also* Genetic screening and testing

Privacy claims, 110–11, 114–15, 375, 389; adoption and, 365–66; gamete (egg

and sperm) donation and, 169, 173, 182–83; IVF and, 31, 33, 70; posthumous reproduction and, 284, 286; same-sex couples and, 317; surrogacy and, 229, 317, 375

Professional guidelines, 106, 113, 127, 193; General Medical Council (GMC), 107. *See also* American Society for Reproductive Medicine (ASRM)

Proposition 8, California, 18, 330–31

Psychological screening and counseling, 109, 132–33, 239, 268, 362–63, 374

Reed, Candice, 1

Reproductive genetics ("reprogenetics"). *See under* Genetic screening and testing

RESOLVE, 79, 83, 85, 87, 102–3, 198, 247–48, 255–56

Rhode Island, 39, 40, 77, 80, 96, 105, 247

Rose, Jo and Adam, 169

Same-sex couples, *301–31;* adoption by, 12, 17, 142–43, 148, 150, 303–4, 306–7, *308–26;* agreements between, 203–6, 306, 307, 323; artificial insemination and (*see* Sperm donation, same-sex couples); consent forms and, 304, 305–6; custody disputes and, 203–7, 314–15, 316, 323, 324, 326–27; discrimination and, 99, 312, 317–19, 331, 382; egg donation and, 203–6; marriage and, 10, 18, 303–4, 307, 319–21, 328–31, 382–83; parentage issues of, 142–43, 150, 203–4, 304, 305, 307, 309, 311–13, 316, 320–23, 325–27; parentage orders (pre-birth) and, 306, 321–23; and Proposition 8, 18, 330–31; shared pregnancy and, 304, 313. *See also under* Constitutional issues and claims; Sperm donation; Surrogacy

Social Security benefits. *See* Posthumous reproduction: inheritance and Social Security

Society of Assisted Reproductive Technology (SART), 1

South Carolina, 177

South Dakota, 145, 229

Sperm banks, 17; liability of, 17, 133–34, 138, 181–83, 186–87, 190, 207, 338, 387, 389; records of, 181; and scams/fraud, 172–76. *See also* Cryopreserved sperm; Sperm donation

Sperm donation, *132–87*; adoption and, 134, 139, 141–43, 145–46, 148–49, 150, 159–60, 314, 320–21; agreements for, 147, 149, 160, 162, 164–66; anonymity and identification issues of, 109, 159, 163, 169, 171, 182–83; consent and consent forms for, 139, 140–41, 145–46, 149–50, 154, 176–77, 178, 301; "fresh" donation and, 301; genetic abnormalities and, 17, 181–84, 187, 301; HIV and, 178, 301; husband, paternity presumption and, 139–40, 141, 148, 161; husband, lack of consent from, 149, 176, 179; known donors for, 134–36, 139, 140, 146, 152, 158–59, 165, 166, 305, 321; natural conception versus, 145, 146; paternity and child support, donor, claims by or against, 142, 144, 145, 147, 151–53, 160–66, 314–15, 321–22; physician role affecting, 142, 149, 155, 179, product (strict) liability and, 137–38, 186–87, 338; psychological screening (*see* Psychological screening and counseling); registry for, 169, 171, 386; same-sex couples and, 138, 140–41, 142–45, 148, 150, 158, 164, 301–3, 308, 310, 311, 313, 320–23; single, unmarried women and, 139, 145, 148, 154, 158, 302; sperm mixing and/or mix-ups, 137, 159, 184–86; statutes (*see under* Artificial insemination); surrogacy (gestational carrier) and, 153, 210, 211, 214, 216, 242–43, 245, 273

Sperm mix-ups, 137, 159, 179–80, 184–86

Sperm storage. *See under* Cryopreserved sperm

Standardized practices, 113; standards of care, 128, 348; uniform consent forms, 113; voluntary professional guidelines, 113

Statutes of limitation, 335, 337, 345, 346, 389

Stem cell (embryonic and adult) research, 10, 193, *350–59*, 387–88; abortion and, 35; and California Stem Cell Research and Cures Initiative, 353, 357; and Colorado "Human Life Amendment," 358–59; donors (and compensation) for, 28, 193, 379–81, 387–88; induced pluripotent (iPS), 350–51, 390; lawsuits challenging, 35, 68, 357; Massachusetts, 353–54; Missouri, 358; parentage and reproduction with, 351–52; regulation and funding, federal, 352–54, 381, 388; regulation and funding, state, 60, 370; somatic cells, reprogrammed and, 350–51. *See also* Fetal research/experimentation laws

Steptoe, Patrick, M.D., 4, 13

Sterilization, 1, 25, 31, 369

Stone, Sergio, M.D., 117–21

Surrogacy, traditional and gestational, *209–74*, 374, 384; adoption and, 213–14, 216, 220–21, 222–23, 225–27, 232–38, 243–45, 248–50, 255, 257, 260–62, 265–66, 272, 384; agreements for, 212, 215, 217–18, 220, 222, 225–28, 232, 235–36, 242–49, 256, 257, 260, 266, 267, 270; "brokers" (recruiters) for, 16, 112, 225, 230–32, 240–41, 262; custody claims (traditional) and, 221–26, 228–29, 229, 233, 238–39, 247–49, 249–50, 273; custody claims (gestational) and, 210, 216–17, 233, 237, 258, 261–64, 267–69, 384; distinctions between, 209–12, 213–15, 225, 233, 247–48, 256; donor gametes (egg and sperm) and, 212, 214, 216, 242, 253–54, 256, 261, 262, 265, 269, 270–74, 384; duty of care and, 16, 112–13, 210–12, 214–15, 230–31, 240–42; FDA and, 189–90; international developments and, 215–16, 226, 228, 247, 251–54, 258–59, 264–65, 268–69, 270–74; parentage claims and disputes (gestational), 16, 153–54, 195, 208, 216–21, 234–35, 237, 242–46, 258, 262–63, 384; parentage claims and disputes (traditional), 213, 221–26, 227–28, 237,